About the Book

The development of organ substitution technology has been among the most dramatic and publicized advances in modern medicine. Organ transplantation and artificial organ implantation have created exciting possibilities for health care; previously untreatable conditions are being significantly ameliorated, and lives are being saved. At the same time, the technology raises daunting social problems: How are patients to be selected? How are organs to be made available? What problems may be created by prolonging the lives of recipients? Who will pay for the technology? And who really will benefit from it?

These questions cannot be answered solely by medical criteria or by appeals to standards of efficiency or "the market." Policymakers must deal with ethical concerns as well as medical and economic ones. In particular, satisfactory policy must recognize the values of fairness and patient autonomy.

Although the focus of this book is organ substitution technology, many of the issues discussed are quite general and directly relevant to other health care technologies. Of special interest is a section of papers devoted to problems raised by the development of the artificial heart.

These and other issues are treated dispassionately but sensitively and in depth by leading scholars from medicine, law, economics, philosophy, and political science. Recognized as authorities in their respective fields, they take definite and often provocative stands on concrete issues of social policy. Professor Mathieu's lucid introductions provide an accurate scientific and historical background, as well as a systematic conceptual and normative framework of the policy issues.

The essays, most of which appear here for the first time, will prove essential reading for scholars, students, and interested citizens concerned with health care, medical ethics, or public policy studies.

Organ Substitution Technology

Ethical, Legal, and Public Policy Issues

EDITED BY

Deborah Mathieu

Westview Press
BOULDER & LONDON

Copyright © 1988 by Westview Press, Inc.

Published in 1988 in the United States of America by Westview Press, Inc.; Frederick A. Praeger, Publisher; 5500 Central Avenue, Boulder, Colorado 80301

Library of Congress Cataloging-in-Publication Data
Organ substitution technology : ethical, legal, and public policy
  issues/edited by Deborah Mathieu.
    p. cm.
  Bibliography: p.
  ISBN 0-8133-0544-6
  1. Transplantation of organs, tissues, etc.—Moral and ethical
aspects. 2. Transplantation of organs, tissues, etc.—Government
policy—United States. 3. Transplantation of organs, tissues, etc.—
Law and legislation—United States. I. Mathieu, Deborah.
RD120.7.069 1988
174'.25—dc19   87-29448
                                                                        CIP

Printed and bound in the United States of America

The paper used in this publication meets the requirements of the American National
Standard for Permanence of Paper for Printed Library Materials Z39.48-1984.

10   9   8   7   6   5   4   3   2   1

Contents

**Part 4
Decisions at the Experimental Stage:
The Case of the Artificial Heart**

**Part 5
Appendixes**

About the Contributors

George J. Annas, J.D., M.P.H., is Edward Utley Professor of Health Law, Boston University School of Medicine, and chief of the Health Law Section, Boston University School of Public Health, Boston, Massachusetts.

Mary Ann Baily, Ph.D., is adjunct associate professor of economics, George Washington University, Washington, D.C.

Christopher R. Blagg, M.D., F.R.C.P., is executive director of the Northwest Kidney Center and professor of medicine, University of Washington, Seattle, Washington.

Dan W. Brock, Ph.D., is professor of philosophy and professor of human values in medicine, Brown University, Providence, Rhode Island.

Arthur L. Caplan, Ph.D., is director of the Biomedical Ethics Center, University of Minnesota, Minneapolis, Minnesota.

Norman Daniels, Ph.D., is professor of philosophy, Tufts University, Medford, Massachusetts.

H. Tristram Engelhardt, Jr., Ph.D., M.D., is professor of medicine and community medicine, Baylor College of Medicine, and a member of the Center for Ethics, Medicine and Public Issues, Baylor College of Medicine. He is also professor of philosophy (part-time), Rice University, Houston, Texas.

Roger W. Evans, Ph.D., is senior research scientist, Battelle Human Affairs Research Centers, Seattle, Washington, and principal author of the National Heart Transplantation Study.

Norman Fost, M.D., M.P.H., is professor of pediatrics and director of the Program in Medical Ethics, University of Wisconsin Medical School, Madison, Wisconsin.

Leslie P. Francis, Ph.D., J.D., is associate professor of philosophy and professor of law, University of Utah, Salt Lake City, Utah.

Kenneth V. Iserson, M.D., M.B.A., F.A.C.E.P., is associate professor, Section of Emergency Medicine, Department of Surgery, University of Arizona Medical School, Tucson, Arizona.

Dale Jamieson, Ph.D., is associate professor of philosophy and associate of the Center for Values and Social Policy, University of Colorado, Boulder, Colorado.

Deborah Mathieu, Ph.D., is assistant professor in the political science and philosophy departments at the University of Arizona, Tucson, Arizona.

Paul T. Menzel, Ph.D., is professor of philosophy, Pacific Lutheran University, Tacoma, Washington.

Karen Merrikin, J.D., serves as counsel to the Group Health Cooperative of Puget Sound and is a former member of the staff of the Battelle Human Affairs Research Centers, Seattle, Washington.

Thomas D. Overcast, J.D., Ph.D., is an independent consultant and former research scientist with the Battelle Human Affairs Research Centers, Seattle, Washington.

Mark V. Pauly, Ph.D., is Robert D. Eilers Professor of health care management and economics and executive director of the Leonard Davis Institute of Health Economics. He also holds academic appointments at the University of Pennsylvania's Wharton School and School of Arts and Sciences as professor of health care systems, public management, and economics.

John A. Robertson, J.D., is Baker and Botts Professor, School of Law, University of Texas, Austin, Texas.

Daniel Wikler, Ph.D., is professor in the Department of Philosophy and professor in the Program in Medical Ethics, Medical School, University of Wisconsin, Madison, Wisconsin.

PART ONE

Introduction

1

Organ Substitution Technology: Identifying and Framing the Key Issues

Deborah Mathieu

The United States has seen a dramatic increase in the use of organ substitution technology—the transplantation of human donor organs and utilization of artificial organs—within the past few years. Between 1981 and 1983, for instance, the number of kidney transplantations increased over 40 percent, the number of heart transplantations increased almost sevenfold, and the number of liver transplantations increased over elevenfold.[1] In 1984, approximately 7,722 solid organs were transplanted in this country,[2] and in 1986 the number of transplants had risen to over 11,297: 8,960 kidneys, 1,368 hearts, 924 livers, and 45 heart-lung combinations.[3]

The media have taken note of this activity and have responded with enthusiasm. The plights of children needing organs (usually livers) and of adults needing money to pay for organ transplants are televised regularly: The camera moves in for close-ups of the tearful family and the sickly but hopeful patient, then turns to a sports star or a political figure (sometimes it is the Chief Executive himself) who encourages the public to donate the organs of their recently deceased relatives and/or send money to help defray the costs of the transplant. A person who receives medical treatment for cancer or severe burns is not news; but a person who receives an organ transplant—now there's a story. And what is the story? Often it is merely a description of some small action of the patient: a man with an artificial heart who drinks a beer, a woman with a new donor heart who smiles at her physician. A recent article in the *Los Angeles Times*, for instance, was about a young liver recipient who "squeezed his mother's fingers in a recovery room decorated with stuffed animals and an autographed photo of President Reagan." The article was headlined, "Boy With a New Liver Reaches Out for Mother."[4] Of course, more serious note is also taken of the use of organ substitution technology. Articles and editorials appear regularly decrying injustices and inefficiencies in the use of the technology or applauding heroic attempts to save a life—often in response to the same incident. One result of this attention is that certain recipients of artificial and human donor organs, such as Barney Clark and Jamie Fiske, evolve into media events, almost becoming household names.[5]

But the media are not alone in examining the workings of the new technology. The federal government has devoted considerable time and expense to the subject. In 1983, for instance, the House Science and Technology Subcommittee on Investigations and Oversights as well as the Senate Energy and Commerce Subcommittee on Health and Environment invited experts in a wide variety of fields to offer testimony regarding the transplantation of cadaver organs, and in that same year the surgeon general convened a workshop to discuss similar concerns. The Department of Health and Human Services in 1980 commissioned a five-year study to examine the financial, social, legal, and ethical issues involved in covering heart transplants under Medicare.[6] And in 1984, Congress passed legislation establishing a multidisciplinary task force to assess an even broader range of issues (the main conclusions of which appear in Appendix A).

In addition, state governments have recently been making serious attempts to gain more control over the dissemination of organ transplantation technology. The state of Ohio, for instance, formed a committee to oversee organ transplants throughout the state (including selection of the recipients) and created a special fund to be used to pay for the transplants of those patients who are not covered by private insurance, Medicaid, or Medicare.[7] And Massachusetts created an interdisciplinary task force to make recommendations regarding the proper use of the technology within the commonwealth.

Even private insurance companies, which are usually fairly quick to add a new medical technology to the list of covered benefits, have devoted extra care to the consideration of organ transplants. As one insurance executive noted, "Our traditional method of technology assessment has been severely strained" by the special circumstances of organ transplantation technology.[8]

Yet despite the considerable attention paid to organ substitution technology within the past few years, most questions regarding its proper utilization remain unanswered—questions that involve a complicated set of value issues and social problems. Indeed, every aspect of the technology seems to carry its own ethical dilemmas: from research on human subjects to use of the technology as therapy, from procurement of the organs to choice of the recipients, from control of the resources to responsibility for payment.

It is important to understand, however, that organ substitution technology is not an anomaly within the U.S. health care system and that other expensive technologies generate similar ethical dilemmas and pressures on resources. Nor should organ substitution technology be scapegoated for creating problems, such as obstacles to fair distribution, that it really only exacerbates. Instead, an analysis of organ substitution technology is important precisely because the issues it raises are fundamental to the health care system in general and because many of the problems it faces are problems inherent in the system.

Thus although the particular ethical, legal, and public policy dilemmas raised by the rapidly evolving technology are important in their own right, these issues have a much wider significance as well. The debate over the uses and abuses of organ substitution reflects in microcosm society's attempts to understand and to control a wide range of new technologies that may dramatically affect our lives as private individuals as well as our legal and political institutions. A close examination of the myriad social issues raised by organ substitution technology, then, is valuable not only because it helps us to understand the issues at stake concerning this particular technology and thus to formulate suitable policies to deal with them, but also because it helps us to understand better and hence to respond more adequately to the wider social issues involved in the U.S. health care system in general.

Costs and Benefits

Physicians have been successfully transplanting skin, bone, and corneas for many years and, of course, have been performing blood transfusions for even longer. But they have been replacing the solid organs of one person with those of another only since the mid-fifties, when the first kidney transplantations were performed. Major advancements in the technology have been made since then, but it is only very recently that organ substitution technology in general has begun to be perceived as leaving the domain of the experimental. And it is only within the past few years that the success rates for the transplantation of most of the major organs has been decidedly encouraging. The one-year patient survival rate for patients with transplanted kidneys is now approximately 92–95 percent; for patients with heart transplants, 75–85 percent; for patients with pancreas transplants, 75–80 percent; for patients with liver transplants, 60–70 percent; for patients with heart-lung transplants, approximately 50 percent.[9]

But an organ transplant is not a panacea. In addition to the very real and constant possibility of organ failure or rejection, an organ recipient must contend with recurrent infections as well as a lifetime of compliance with treatment regimens (adherence to a strict diet and the administration of medications several times a day). Although some of these medications—specifically the immuno-suppressants—are largely responsible for the improvement in patient survival rates, they are far from wonder drugs. A variety of serious side effects are associated with them, including tremors, seizures, kidney and/or liver failure, hypertension, lymphomas, diabetes, vision disorders, and anemia.[10] The pros and cons of one of the most important of the immunosuppressants, cyclosporine, are described in Appendix B of this volume.

Artificial organs also have their disadvantages. The drawbacks of renal dialysis are well documented: weakness, lethargy, depression, loss of appetite, and sleep disturbance, as well as the constant restriction of fluid intake and adherence to a restrictive diet.[11] In addition, a dialysis patient has a constant battle with end-stage renal disease itself and the toll it takes on other body systems. As one physician remarked:

> End-stage renal disease leaves no organ spared. It is a systemic illness that challenges the therapist to the utmost. Each attempt by physicians to intervene creates a new series of problems. Drug toxicity is rampant. While methods of dialysis ameliorate certain complications and afford symptomatic relief in some areas, the patient often becomes subjected to progressive bone disease, access-related infections, and insidious encephalopathies.[12]

The only other artificial organ available today, the artificial heart, has even more serious shortcomings: Patients have suffered debilitating strokes, life-threatening episodes of bleeding, renal failure, and severe infections.[13] In addition, if the well-known Jarvik-7 is used, the patient spends his or her life tethered to a vibrating 400-pound machine.

There are also significant monetary costs involved. The federal government has estimated that it would cost another $130 million (on top of the $200 million it has already spent) to develop a totally implantable artificial heart, for instance. And estimates of the costs of transplanting just one type of organ, the heart, run to the millions of dollars annually. One analyst calculates the cost to be between $2 and $3.5 million;[14] another calculates the range to be between $150 million and $4.5 billion;[15] while a third suggests that $2.5 billion might be more accurate.[16] Medicare, which is already spending $2 billion a year to provide kidney dialysis and kidney transplants, has estimated that it will spend an additional $5 million during its first year of covering heart transplants (for approximately sixty-five heart transplants).

Thus although organ substitution technology can prolong thousands of lives each year, it can do so only at an enormous cost to the patients *and* to society. Clearly we need to reflect carefully—especially about issues of efficiency and fairness—before proceeding with the widespread dissemination of this extremely costly technology. Important and difficult decisions must be made. We need, for example, to assess the value of this technology relative to other goods and services; we need to decide whether we wish to offer organ substitution technology on a widespread basis and if so, what role the patient's ability to pay for the procedure should play.

Old Problems, New Problems

There are several themes running throughout this book. The first is that although considerable progress has been made over the years in the utilization of organ substitution technology, in some ways we have merely substituted one set of problems for another. Before the federal government agreed to cover the cost of medical care for end-stage renal disease patients, for instance, few sufferers of that condition had access to the very expensive treatments available, and therefore most died fairly quickly. Choosing which patients among many would receive the scarce life-prolonging technology was a tremendous challenge to health care professionals, a challenge that was met in a variety of ways.

Perhaps the best-known process of patient selection was that employed by the Admissions and Policy Committee of the Seattle Artificial Kidney Center. An early article describing the workings of the committee, which was formed in 1961, provided an interesting list of some of the criteria used: "sex of patient; marital status and number of dependents; income; net worth; emotional stability, with particular regard to the patient's capacity to accept the treatment; educational background; nature of occupation, past performance and future potential."[17]

The Seattle committee was not alone in using nonmedical criteria in selecting patients, and many other centers excluded patients for reasons that now seem suspect: mental deficiency, poor family environment, criminal record, poverty, poor employment record, lack of transportation, and lack of state residency.[18] But the Seattle committee seems to have been singled out for the harshest criticism. Because of its overt reliance on "social worth" criteria, the committee was accused of prejudice and bias in its selection of patients. Perhaps the best-known diatribe was launched by David Sanders and Jesse Dukeminier in 1968:

> The ethical muddle of selection committees comparing human worth is well illustrated by the operations of the selection committee at the Seattle Artificial Kidney Center. The description of how this committee makes its decisions . . . are numbing accounts of how close to the surface lie the prejudices and mindless cliches that pollute the committee's deliberations. . . . The magazines paint a disturbing picture of the bourgeois sparing the bourgeois, of the Seattle committee measuring persons in accordance with its own middle-class suburban value system: scouts, Sunday school, Red Cross. This rules out creative nonconformists, who rub the bourgeoisie the wrong way but who historically have contributed so much to the making of America. The Pacific Northwest is no place for a Henry David Thoreau with bad kidneys.[19]

In the committee's defense, it should be noted that it was doing its best, according to its own lights, to make difficult and emotionally wrenching choices. But the decision to recognize some end-stage renal disease sufferers as more "worthy" of treatment than others is a decision that many people feel should never be made. How can, as a matter of social policy, one person (assuming that he or she has not betrayed the country or committed murder) be judged less worthy of life than another?

Since that time, patient selection criteria have shifted from notions of patient worth to notions of patient benefit, and lay selection committees have given way to decisions by physicians. Patients who are evaluated as likely to benefit from a medical intervention—those who are deemed medically suitable according to objective standards—are treated on a first-come-first-served basis. The two components of this method express the conviction that both efficiency (or maximizing benefit with the resources available) and fairness are important values: Medical suitability focuses on benefit, and treating on a first-come-first-served basis from the pool of the most medically suitable is supposed to approximate the fairness of a random lottery.

A strictly utilitarian approach to the distribution of human donor organs, that is, relying only on calculations of patient benefit, would not be appropriate, because it would fail to show proper regard for issues of fairness and the equal worth of persons. But a distribution that concentrated on considerations of fairness alone, without regard for efficiency, would not be an improvement. Although instituting a purely first-come-first-served system to approximate the randomness of a lottery would show equal respect for persons, it goes too far in eschewing all considerations of how much benefit an allocation will produce. Unless some initial threshold of expected benefit to the patient is used as an eligibility requirement for joining the queue (or for participation in the lottery), use of this randomizing method will mean that lives of extremely poor quality will be prolonged for a short time at the expense of much longer lives of higher quality.

Although many people may agree that this method of choosing transplantation recipients is superior to the Seattle committee's method, they may disagree quite radically on how it should be implemented. The problem stems from the fact that in order to apply this method consistently, we must balance the two values of efficiency and fairness, and there is widespread disagreement on how this should be done.

There is another difficulty with utilizing this method of patient selection: The medical suitability criteria used today are as value laden as were the social worth criteria utilized twenty years ago. It could not be otherwise: It is impossible to develop objective, value-free medical criteria with which to select patients. As Dan Brock notes in Part Two, "It is important to emphasize that there are *no* value-neutral selection criteria that could permit bypassing the need to make ethical judgments in the recipient selection process." This point is well illustrated by the procedures used to select treatments for victims of end-stage renal disease and end-stage heart disease.

When the federal government first decided to pay for the medical care of victims of end-stage renal disease, the likelihood that a patient would benefit from life-prolonging therapy was determined according to a fairly strict set of criteria: The very elderly were generally not offered dialysis, for example, nor were patients suffering from other major diseases (such as diabetes). Now the very elderly and the very ill—patients who would have been allowed to die twenty years ago—are frequently dialyzed. The treatment has not really changed, nor has the prognosis for these patients; what have changed are the view of medical suitability and the corresponding view of patient benefit that are appropriately applied. This is the result of a change of values, not a change of facts.

The history of the dialysis program shows an interesting interplay between political institutional changes and social values. The political change (federal entitlement to renal dialysis) was perhaps chiefly motivated by a desire to save lives and avoid controversial ethical choices (such as those confronting the Seattle committee). The resulting change in reimbursement structure radically altered health care providers' incentives in a way that enabled them to escape certain painful value choices and that also enabled them to espouse certain socially important values (such as nondiscrimination, equal worth of patients, infinite value of human life). In addition, it provided an incentive to extend coverage to those who formerly had been denied the treatment—a change that in turn was defended with the rhetoric of equal worth and nondiscrimination. Thus we now pat ourselves on the back for implementing a system that is "superior" to the old system and to the one utilized by the seemingly harsh British, who continue to ration dialysis treatments fairly tightly (most prominently according to age criteria).[20]

But extending this extremely expensive treatment to patients whose benefit was likely to be low did not totally eliminate the moral dilemmas and social problems created by the need to ration scarce resources; it merely shifted the burden of restraint elsewhere (especially to other expensive medical technologies such as treatment of hemophiliacs and newer forms of organ substitution technology). In addition, the political decision to pay for almost all dialysis procedures created new problems of patient care: Now, for instance, we must contend with the enormous social and personal costs of prolonging lives of dubious quality. As Roger Evans and Christopher Blagg point out in Chapter 14, the cost of dialysis is only one component in the total cost of caring for end-stage renal disease (ESRD) patients. Many are chronically ill and require frequent hospitalizations, and nearly two-thirds of the ESRD population are receiving federal income support.

Patients needing heart and liver transplants are now facing some of the same problems that confronted ESRD patients before federal funding became available to them, but these problems are presented in a different guise: that of "medical suitability." Although there are no other artificial organs that work as successfully as the artificial kidney, not all victims of end-stage heart disease or end-stage liver disease are offered transplants, because not all of them are considered to be medically suitable candidates for organ transplants.

There are variations among the criteria utilized for determining medical suitability for heart transplantation, but a basic set usually consists of the following:

1. The patient is able to manage only a bed-to-chair existence and/or is expected to live no more than six months;
2. There are no alternative treatments available that offer better prospects for the patient;
3. The patient suffers from no other medical conditions (such as another unhealthy major organ) that would preclude successful transplantation;

4. The patient is able to endure the pain and stress of the operation and the recovery;
5. The patient shows a will to live;
6. The patient enjoys a stable family situation (broadly construed) or work environment to which he or she can return;
7. The patient has exhibited the likelihood of complying with a life-long medical regimen;
8. The patient is not over age fifty or fifty-five.[21]

(See Appendix C for the counterindications to heart transplantation recommended by the National Heart, Lung and Blood Institute.)

A considerable degree of concern has been voiced about these so-called medical criteria. The former secretary of the Department of Health and Human Services, for instance, worried that at least some of them might be unfairly discriminatory and suggested that they be analyzed for their usefulness and impact. Especially troubling items are the more obviously social criteria: the requirement of a stable family situation, for instance, and the age cutoff. The concern is that these particular criteria are too open to bias; they need to be scrutinized carefully to ascertain that unfair prejudices are not being masked as medical criteria. We also must be careful to recognize the concerns for efficiency (and the weight accorded to efficiency relative to fairness) that underlie *all* criteria of medical suitability. Unless the various and potentially conflicting value factors that go into patient selection are clearly distinguished, critical assessment of the process will be hindered.

There are other troubling influences on the selection of patients. Although there continues to be a serious shortage of transplantable organs, it could be argued that the relatively few organs procured are not allocated either fairly or efficiently. Luck seems to be the primary distributive force: The city in which a patient (or his or her transplant surgeon) lives can play an important role in determining whether or not that person will receive an organ, as can his or her ability to pull the heart (and purse) strings of the right people. Clearly, there is a very serious need for a more coherent system of allocating these scarce resources. Although the recently established national organ procurement network will no doubt go far in helping to alleviate some of the problems, the more serious difficulties cannot be expected to disappear entirely or soon.

Experimentation with human beings also suffers from serious flaws. Although there are numerous standards governing the conduct of research on human subjects—for example, the Nuremberg Code, the American Medical Association Ethical Guidelines for Clinical Investigation, the National Institutes of Health Guidelines, and the Regulations of the Department of Health and Human Services—patient autonomy and well-being too often are ignored (as the chapters in Part Four attest). In addition, the actual experimental use of organ substitution technology has been open to serious criticisms on scientific grounds.

One major goal of the book, then, is to describe and assess some of the more important difficulties and defects in the current utilization of organ substitution technology. The chapters that follow make it clear that we can no longer comfort ourselves with the illusion that the most fundamental questions regarding the allocation of scarce medical resources, including organ transplants and implants, will go away or will be resolved somehow by scientific expertise or through totally unregulated market forces.

Responsible Decision-Making

Another recurrent theme of the book is the issue of responsible decision-making. The most visible and publicized kind of decision involves a particular procedure and an individual patient (e.g., a baboon heart for Baby Fae, an artificial heart for Barney Clark, a human liver for Jamie Fiske). But of course this type of decision is only the end point of a series of choices made at different levels by different agents, both individual and collective: the decision to support the research, to use the technology on human patients, to pay for its use, and so on.

The issue of responsible decision-making raises two important questions: What principles and procedures ought to guide decisions, and who ought to apply these principles in making decisions? But there is an even more fundamental question to be addressed here: Who is to make the higher-level determinations of the decision-making framework? That is, who is to judge which principles and procedures are to be used and who is to identify the appropriate agents for applying those principles and procedures in the making of substantive decisions?

It is important to see that doing nothing to create a formal public policy is a policy decision nonetheless. The decision *not* to have government control and to leave the dissemination of the technology entirely to the market, for instance, is itself a policy decision. To what extent should this or opposing policy decisions concerning organ substitution technology be left to medical and scientific experts and their entrepreneurial backers? To what extent are such decisions properly within the sphere of political decisions? If they are, to what extent should they be democratized? If certain problems in the dissemination of the technology are to be dealt with by government, what level of government should be involved? Are our current legal and political institutions equipped to respond effectively to these problems?

The struggle to resolve the more fundamental issue of the decision-making framework is perhaps best characterized as a competition among a number of groups, both within and outside government, for the greatest share of authority. But analysis of interest-group competition, no matter how valuable, is not a substitute for ethical analysis. What is needed, instead, is an integrated approach that spans disciplinary fissures. After all, a group competing for control of the decision-making framework is unlikely to succeed unless it can convincingly present itself and its agenda as being supported by a widely held and reasonably coherent set of ethical values or principles. The competition for control of the decision-making framework is a struggle for legitimacy, and legitimacy in this area is to a large extent a matter of perceived conformity to ethical standards, which themselves have been identified as successful competitors in the wider public and scholarly debate over values.

Consider for a moment a fairly straightforward issue: reducing the costs of using the various organ substitution technologies. This seems at first to be a noncontroversial improvement. But once it becomes clear that the issue is not simply how to cut costs—but rather how to cut costs in a manner that is both ethically appropriate and politically feasible—it becomes clear that the decision rests on disputed social values, not on economic expertise alone. And thus the decision is not one entirely for the so-called experts. As Richard Rettig and Ellen Marks pointed out with regard to Medicare's End-stage Renal Disease Program:

In fact, we know how to control costs: simply shift an increasing proportion of patients from higher cost to lower cost treatment settings. This probably involves a double movement from hospital-based to free-standing units, and from institutions to the home setting. What we do not know how to do, however, is to control costs without sacrificing other values: patient autonomy, freedom of physicians to prescribe the treatment setting, and the refusal to ration access. All cost control policies, therefore, require moral justification that commands political consensus and supports authoritative public policy.[22]

The issues raised by the concern for responsible decision-making are enormously difficult and complex. But there does seem to be at least one issue that is clear: Physicians, scientists, and their financial backers cannot legitimately claim exclusive authority over the use of these scarce resources on the basis of their special expertise. Instead, the public has a right to participate in the process of forming social policy concerning these technologies, a right that is strengthened by the fact that public tax money largely supported the development and application of the technology. And because so many of the fundamental issues regarding organ transplantations are ethical—not scientific nor even economic— it makes sense for the public to be involved in the process.

The most reasonable conclusion to draw from all of this is that the proper use of this technology is a social issue that stands as a challenge to all of us. Despite the problems and the high costs, the U.S. health care system will no doubt continue to include at least some types of organ substitution technology. The overarching goal of this book, then, is to contribute to a reasoned and informed debate on the subject by providing a critical analysis of the issues as well as some concrete proposals to improve the situation.

Ethical Values and the Assessment of Policy

One last issue deserves to be addressed at length, and that is the interplay of ethical values (especially the values of fairness, equity, justice) and public policy analysis. The issue is significant because policymakers and policy analysts often neglect questions of fairness by focusing exclusively on efficiency criteria, an approach that is not appropriate, as efficient systems of allocation may be patently unjust. This will become clear as we consider the two most popular economic standards for assessing allocational issues: utility maximization and Pareto optimality.

The Principle of Utility

According to the principle of utility, allocational states are to be ranked according to how much net, overall utility they produce (utility may be defined as happiness, satisfaction, well-being, and so on). This is calculated by adding up the net utility (the benefits minus the costs) for each individual affected. Since the object is to *maximize* utility, the allocation that offers greater net utility than its alternatives is to be chosen.

The principle of utility is only one among several competing standards for evaluating the distribution of scarce resources, and hence it is inappropriate simply to assume the correctness or relevance of that principle to a particular allocational system. To hold that utility is the appropriate standard for evaluating allocations involves the ethically controversial assumption that the proper goal of society is to maximize utility. The problem is that a strictly utilitarian society may use people as means to achieve social ends. To those who hold that individual autonomy is of paramount importance and that persons should not be used as mere means, utilitarianism fails to show proper respect for persons as such.[23] In addition, a particular allocation might maximize overall utility and yet be grossly unjust. John Rawls, for instance, pointed out that a system in which some persons were slaves could in fact maximize overall utility as long as the gain to the masters exceeded the losses to the slaves.[24] That the criterion of utility maximization would not only permit but would actually require such a system—if it did in fact produce the greatest utility—is a significant objection to the principle. This extreme example illustrates a more general objection to utility maximization: Evaluating the distribution of benefits and burdens solely according to their tendency to maximize overall utility neglects fairness as a fundamental value.

But even if this hurdle were somehow overcome and the principle of utility maximization were judged to be the appropriate standard for evaluating a particular distribution of scarce resources, another, more formidable hurdle still remains: the problem of making interpersonal utility comparisons. Recall that in order to determine whether a particular allocation maximizes utility for people in a society, it is necessary to sum up the costs and benefits for different individuals, that is, to make interpersonal utility comparisons. This involves measuring each individual's state of well-being according to the same criterion and locating each individual's net utility along the same scale. However, a very serious difficulty arises here: There is no rational method for selecting a common baseline from which different individuals' utilities could all be measured, nor is there a nonarbitrary method for determining a common unit for measurement. In other words, it appears that there is no nonarbitrary basis for relating different individuals' utility scales to one another in a way that achieves the needed aggregation. Hence the calculation of overall net utility—needed to determine whether an allocation maximizes utility—simply cannot be performed reliably.

Paretian Conception of Efficiency

Many policy analysts turn to the Paretian conception of efficiency in order to avoid the obstacles of interpersonal utility comparisons to which the principle of utility maximization is liable. There are two Pareto principles: A state of a system is Pareto *superior* to another if and only if at least one individual is better off in it and no one is worse off; a state of a system is Pareto *optimal* if and only if there is no feasible alternative state in which at least one person would be better off and no one would be worse off (in other words, a state is Pareto optimal if and only if there is no feasible state that is Pareto superior to it).

In determining whether one state is Pareto superior to another, interpersonal comparisons are not required. Rather than comparing one individual with another, we simply compare the status of an individual in one state with his or her own status in the alternative states. Hence it does not matter how individuals fare relative to each other; what matters, instead, is assuring that no individual's status is worsened. The object is to move from one Pareto superior state to another until a Pareto optimal state is reached. Although this may not maximize utility, because it is conceivable that a state may be Pareto optimal to all others and still not maximize utility, each step still involves an increase in utility, because at least one person is better off and no one is worse off.

However, as Pareto optimality focuses only upon well-being or the satisfaction of preferences, a state may be Pareto optimal and still not be morally acceptable.[25]

The Paretian conception of efficiency ignores other features of an allocation that usually are considered to be relevant: the moral status of the preferences themselves, for instance, and the moral status of the process by which the Pareto state arises. In addition, it ignores issues of personal desert. All that matters according to the Paretian conception is that improvements in the condition of some are made without worsening the condition of others; it is irrelevant that those whose condition is improved did not deserve it and that those whose condition does not change deserved to receive the benefits. Further, the Paretian principles say nothing about whether there are moral limits concerning the proportionality of gains among different individuals or groups.

Thus to assume that a social arrangement is appropriate if it is efficient (in the Paretian sense) is to ignore questions of justice or fairness entirely. Attempts to evaluate allocations using the Paretian criteria of efficiency are also subject to the same serious ethical criticisms as utility maximization: An allocation may be Pareto optimal yet still be grossly unjust. If it were impossible to improve the condition of some of the slaves mentioned above, for instance, without worsening the condition of some of the slaveholders, then it would be illegitimate—if the Paretian conception of efficiency were our dominant tool for policy assessment—to better the condition of the slaves.

The Paretian conception of efficiency suffers from another shortcoming: There are few serious real-world policy issues in which any of the feasible alternatives will be a Pareto improvement. In most if not all actual policy issues, there will be some winners and some losers, no matter which alternative is chosen; that is what makes them serious issues of policy.

Some analysts do not make the mistake of assuming the Paretian conception of efficiency to be the fundamental criterion for policy evaluation and instead view this conception as a sort of second-best alternative to utility maximization (conceding that interpersonal utility comparisons cannot be made). As pointed out above, a Paretian improvement (a movement to a Pareto superior state) will at least increase utility, even if it may not maximize utility. These same proponents of the Paretian principles often assume or assert that one of their advantages is that they are value neutral and nonnormative. But this is mistaken, because to use the Paretian principles as a second-best stand-in for the criterion of utility maximization is to assume the truth of one particular ethical theory: utilitarianism.

It follows that an ethically neutral policy analysis (if it could be achieved) would be incomplete: It would not even address, much less answer, some of the most fundamental questions for which legislators and other government officials, health care professionals, and citizens are urgently seeking answers. So those policy analysts who evaluate allocations solely by the standard economic, that is, Paretian, criterion of efficiency are either mistakenly assuming that they have avoided controversial ethical issues or are offering a fundamentally incomplete evaluation that must be supplemented by ethical criteria, including considerations of justice.

Reducing Fairness to Efficiency

Some analysts insist, however, that fairness and efficiency need not be considered independently. They claim instead that considerations of fairness can be reduced to considerations of efficiency by incorporating concern for fairness into an analytical technique for comparing the positive and negative consequences of alternative ways to allocate resources. As Mark V. Pauly has explained:

If people place positive values on additional consumption of primary education by others, or negative values on the consumption of cigarettes, these valuations ought in principle to be incorporated into any cost-benefit analysis. In this sense, if "citizens" value additional consumption by an individual as a way of improving "fairness" in the distribution of a service, these valuations ought to be added to the individual's valuations as a consumer of that service.[26]

There are two analytical techniques with which we are concerned: cost-benefit analysis and cost-effectiveness analysis.[27] In a cost-benefit analysis, all costs and benefits are stated in dollar terms, and the bottom line is a net monetary value. Opponents of cost-benefit analysis object that it is impossible to give some things such as the value of a human life a monetary value. This objection has led many to prefer cost-effectiveness analysis, which does not attempt to state all costs and benefits according to one measure. Instead, it allows certain intangibles (such as the value of a human life) to be expressed in nonmonetary terms (such as quality-adjusted life years).

In a cost-effectiveness analysis, first the goal is specified (without attaching a monetary value to it), then the cost and degree of effectiveness of each alternative policy proposal for achieving that goal are estimated. The policy that best accomplishes the goal at the least cost is considered to be the best. One advantage of cost-effectiveness analysis is that it is flexible enough to include ethical components, including considerations of fairness or justice. Such values can be addressed by including them as part of the overall goal of the project (a particular conception of fairness can be given an operational definition and specified as an appropriately weighted component of the goal). In the case at hand, for instance, one goal might be to reduce the mortality rate due to end-stage heart disease. But the goal could be more complex, taking fairness into account as well: Thus the goal might be to reduce the mortality rate due to end-stage heart disease in a manner that is nondiscriminatory (i.e., so that reduction of mortality rates occurs not just for whites but also for nonwhites). Alternatively, the goal might be to reduce the mortality rate due to end-stage heart disease in a manner that is equitable (with equity understood as narrowing the gap between access to the health care system of the poor and the rich to within certain limits).

Some advocates of this type of policy analysis mistakenly suggest that a sophisticated utilization of it, in which ethical components are part of the goal, can avoid moral argumentation. Moral considerations of fairness, they claim, can be reduced to considerations of cost-effectiveness, so that fairness need not be an independent factor for policy analysis. This is accomplished first by conducting empirical research regarding people's external preferences: that is, people's preferences about other people's well-being or utility or about inequalities among various groups. Once we know how much inequality is in fact acceptable to the majority of people, we simply include these data about the majority's actual external preferences in the cost-effectiveness analysis of the policy (by including the majority's conception of acceptable inequality—or of morally required equality—in the goal to be achieved). The point of the analysis, then, would be to determine which of the alternative policy options satisfied these preferences in the least costly manner. In this way, it is argued, we avoid having to consider fairness as a separate issue as we replace ethics with empirical research plus means/ends rationality.

Thus it is concluded that there is no need for ethics as a normative enterprise in policy analysis. We no longer require argumentation about what is fair; all we need are data about what most people consider to be fair. In this way, the distinction (made above) between efficiency and fairness is obliterated: The latter is reduced to the former. This reductionist approach, if sound, would afford us a convenient alternative to ethical theory: We simply state moral values in terms of preferences that people happen to have, without critically assessing those preferences.

However, this approach is not sound. There are two important and related reasons why attempts to reduce considerations of fairness (or justice or equity) to considerations of efficiency must fail. The first is that reducing considerations of fairness to choosing the policy that best satisfies the majority's preferences (including those about other people's welfare or about inequalities between groups) is to beg the question against those who hold that fairness is an independent factor in policy analysis. The reductionist method simply assumes the correctness of one or the other of two particular and quite controversial moral theories, utilitarianism or majoritarianism (i.e., unrestrained democracy). But this is to ignore a long and important tradition in moral theory that argues that the whole point about justice as a moral principle is that it is *not* reducible to utility maximization and that justice imposes important limitations on majority rule. According to this tradition, justice (or fairness) involves individual rights, which are justified claims that trump appeals to what would maximize utility and appeals to the majority's preferences.[28]

The issue of rights is an enormously complex and controversial one, and a host of fundamental questions remain open: Whether there are rights that outweigh considerations of utility, and if so what these rights are, as well as how we should argue for them. This is properly the subject matter of ethical theory. These issues cannot be avoided by describing preferences people happen to have, and by assuming, without argument and without responding to the objections raised by competing ethical theories, the suitableness of a particular moral theory, whether it be utilitarianism or majoritarianism.

In sum, then, the attempt to use cost-effectiveness analysis without taking fairness into account as an independent value seems to rest on an undefended assumption that utilitarianism or unconstrained democracy is the correct moral theory, and thus the whole enterprise is open to the charge of begging the question.

Ethical Relativism

There is, however, another source of attempts to eliminate appeals to fairness or justice in policy assessment: ethical relativism. According to this view, groups have different ethical values, including beliefs about fairness and justice, and there is no way of critically assessing them. Ethical beliefs are like tastes: One simply has them or does not, and there is no room for argument. Hence, at least in a democratic society, all that is necessary is that the policy analyst build into the goal specified in the cost-effectiveness analysis the majority's beliefs about fairness, whatever they happen to be.

This ethical relativist version of the reductionist move commits two errors. First, it assumes that an identifiable majority view exists for every policy choice, and of course this is overly optimistic. Especially in the area of new technology, consensus is something that must be won through policy debate; it is not available at the outset of the process. Second, it fails to distinguish between the majority's beliefs about fairness and what is fair. The majority may be mistaken about what is fair, and it may, in response to argument, even come to see that it was mistaken. Indeed, theorizing about fairness and justice is an argumentative process in which we revise our moral conceptions in response to critical scrutiny and the demands imposed by public standards of argumentation.

Ronald Dworkin has pointed out that we recognize distinctions between what a group happens to think is fair at any particular time and what is fair because we recognize that people's moral beliefs are open to criticism on the grounds that those beliefs do not meet the minimal standards for rational argumentation.[29] Dworkin argued that an analysis of our ordinary ways of using moral concepts reveals that we implicitly endorse certain minimal standards of rational argumentation about ethical matters. These standards are built into the complex set of normative beliefs that structure commonsense moral consciousness and are the rules that govern our ordinary usage of the term *morality*.

Dworkin recognized two fundamental rules of rational argumentation. The first is the minimal requirement that the set of moral beliefs be internally consistent. The second is the more demanding requirement that the moral beliefs be supported by reasons of a certain sort. We accept certain considerations as good reasons and reject other considerations as not counting at all. For instance, a prejudice, such as the claim that a person is of less moral value due to some irrelevant difference like color of skin or place of birth, cannot support a moral position. Nor can a mere emotional reaction, such as disgust at the thought of interracial marriage, support a moral position. Instead, if a view is put forward as a moral position, we demand that it be supported by reasons, by considerations that are publicly acceptable. Among these are certain substantive considerations that are believed to ground moral views, such as concern for human well-being, respect for individual autonomy, and regard for justice. It follows that we cannot settle the question of what is fair simply by poll-taking or head-counting techniques designed to record what most people believe is fair at any particular time, because the beliefs people happen to have are relevant to determining what is fair only if they measure up to those minimal standards of rationality in moral discourse.

It should be noted, however, that to uphold the distinction between fairness and the majority's (or society's) beliefs about or perceptions of fairness, one need not be an ethical absolutist (that is, someone who claims that there is one universally valid set of objective moral values). John Rawls, for instance, demonstrated that it is consistent to eschew moral absolutism and still uphold the conviction that considerations of fairness are not reducible to descriptions of people's actual external preferences (for instance, their beliefs about what is fair at a given time).

Rawls's view of ethical theory, at least in his later writings, demonstrated that it is consistent to maintain both that relativism is true *and* that ethical principles are subject to rational argumentation.[30] According to Rawls, the task of the ethical theorist is to articulate, clarify, and refine the fundamental moral principles and ideals of a society: those moral principles and ideals that are expressed in a given society's most basic and enduring political institutions and that provide the deep structure of the moral consciousness of its members. Thus the ethical theorist always works within the limits of the moral principles and ideals of a particular society at a particular point in history. Nevertheless, the process of articulating, clarifying, and refining these ideals and principles is one of rational argumentation, as long as the moral consciousness that is dominant in the society in question includes minimal standards for critically assessing moral positions.

Consequently, even if ethical relativism is true—even if there are no substantive ethical principles that are valid across all societies—it is still possible to engage in rational argumentation about conceptions of fairness. And it is still possible, therefore, to distinguish between what the majority in a particular society happens at a particular time to believe is fair and what is fair.

Conclusion

The policy analyst has only three choices:

1. Ignore issues of fairness or justice entirely—with the result that the evaluation of policies will not answer (or even address) vital social questions.
2. Vainly attempt to reduce issues of fairness to actual external preferences, thereby either simply assuming the correctness of one very controversial ethical theory (utilitarianism or unrestrained majoritarianism), thus begging the question against all competing ethical theories, including those theories that take individual rights seriously, or failing to see that there are standards of moral argumentation that allow us to criticize the majority's beliefs about fairness.
3. Acknowledge that cost-effectiveness analysis requires ethical analysis, the only tenable alternative.

It follows that ethical analysis is *not* an optional adjunct to adequate policy evaluation through cost-effectiveness analysis, but rather is an integral component of it. Because the same conclusion was established (in the preceding section) regarding the other efficiency analyses (including Paretian efficiency and utility maximization), the conclusion can now be generalized: Policy analysis through the use of efficiency criteria requires ethical analysis. Indeed, there is no way of getting around the need for ethical theorizing in policy evaluation.

Scope of the Book

The volume is divided into five major sections. The first is the shortest and consists of this chapter and an introduction, by Dan Wikler, to what may be called the conceptual dynamics of the policy debate. Wikler examines some of the fundamental social norms and moral concepts that underlie the current application of organ substitution technology: the distinction between an "experimental" and a "therapeutic" medical intervention, the designation of a patient as "medically suitable" for an organ transplantation, the concept of "voluntary" organ donation, and the definition of "brain death." He argues that all of these normative and conceptual elements are "soft spots" in the theoretical framework surrounding organ substitution technology, and upon close scrutiny they can be seen to be too weak to support current practices. Hence he concludes that they may be expected to give way to other norms and concepts as pressures for changes in the utilization of organ substitution technology increase.

The proper role of these social norms and moral concepts—and their deficiencies—are addressed at greater length in the following three sections. These sections deal with the most fundamental and important aspects of organ substitution technology: the procurement of organs and the selection of recipients; costs, funding, and diffusion of technology; experimentation with human subjects. Among the specific issues addressed in the individual chapters are the place of the market in the dissemination of the technology and the procurement of the organs, the role of the patient's ability to pay in gaining access to the technology, the value of a technology that is enormously expensive and is needed only by a relatively few in relation to the value of other medical treatments, the importance of informed consent procedures, the value-laden aspects of all medical criteria for recipient selection, the difficulties of obtaining enough organs for transplantation and proposals to mitigate those problems, and the role of the state in disseminating the technology.

These sections are not designed to stand on their own: Each section is preceded by an analytical introduction by the editor, and a set of factual appendixes is included at the end of the volume. The introductions are substantive, providing the historical context, offering critical analyses of the issues at stake, identifying the value conflicts, articulating the relevant ethical principles, and discussing alternative frameworks for policy assessment. The appendixes, which comprise the fifth and final section, are designed as concrete supplements to the more theoretical chapters. An extensive bibliography is also provided.

There is one significant limitation on the scope of this volume that should be noted: The book examines in detail issues involving solid organs but only glances at tissue transplantation. There are two reasons for this. The first is that most of the major concerns—such as informed consent, responsibility for payment, access to treatment, patient selection criteria, and so on—arise regardless of the material in question. Thus the considerations raised and the conclusions drawn vis-à-vis organ transplantation are applicable in large part also to tissue transplantation (including blood transfusion). To discuss them separately, then, would be redundant.

The second reason, however, pertains to the *differences* between solid organ transplantation and tissue transplantation. The use of tissues raises many complex, controversial issues that do not play so important a role in the use of solid organs. For instance, although all human body parts are carefully screened for contagious diseases, most of the problems associated with screening blood for AIDS, such as donor confidentiality, reporting requirements, public distrust of the product, discriminatory effects on homosexuals and intravenous drug users, do not occur in the screening of solid organs. Likewise, many of the problems that plague organ substitution technology simply are not relevant to tissue use. The fact that solid organs can be kept outside the body for only a relatively short time, for instance, creates extraordinary difficulties for the development of a fair and efficient distributional system—problems that do not arise with tissues, which can be stored successfully for relatively long periods. Any responsible attempt to deal with the major ethical, legal, and public policy issues of *all* body parts would have made this book considerably longer, so the decision was made to concentrate on issues raised by solid organs and their artificial replacements. This conclusion was a difficult one to reach, however, in part because one of the most exciting and revolutionary medical procedures on the horizon today involves tissue transplantations.

Recent experiments with primates have demonstrated that fetal tissues may be transplanted successfully into adults, leading to the possibility that human fetal tissues could be transplanted into adult humans.[31] Should this prove feasible, researchers anticipate that many devastating and now incurable conditions, such as Parkinson's disease, Alzheimer's disease, spina bifeda, and spinal cord injury, will be able to be treated successfully. Thus the effects of fetal tissue transplants on improved human health could be dramatic, and these transplants might become one of the most frequently performed procedures in medicine. Needless to say, the possibility of using fetal tissues to treat a variety of deleterious conditions raises a host of ethical, legal, and public policy issues. As the procedure is still in the experimental stages, the first order of questions to be resolved concerns proper research protocols, but it is not too early to address other issues that are certain to arise when the technology has advanced enough to be considered therapeutic. The subject is important enough to warrant immediate and widespread attention.

Although the major ethical, legal, and public policy issues of organ substitution are examined in this volume, it also should be noted that not every single question raised by the advent of the technology is addressed. Some readers may be disappointed that a topic of particular interest to them has been omitted: the causes and implications of Medicare's failure to maintain complete and accurate records of its end-stage renal disease program, or the relatively high rate of suicide among chronic dialysis patients, or the status of organ substitution technology in other nations. These and other issues were excluded not because they are unimportant or uninteresting, but because choices had to be made, and the topics included seemed (perhaps idiosyncratically) to be more vital and more generally relevant than the topics excluded.

Notes

1. Office of Organ Transplantation, "Organ Transplantation Background Information," 1985, Reprinted in Jane K. White, "Update," *Health Affairs* 4: 109–114, p. 109.

2. Task Force on Organ Transplantation, *Organ Transplantation: Issues and Recommendations* (Washington, D.C.: Government Printing Office, 1986), p. 17.

3. Robert Pear, "New Law May Spur Organ Donations," *New York Times*, September 6, 1987, p. 1.

4. "Boy With a New Liver Reaches Out for Mother," *Los Angeles Times*, February 26, 1987, p. 4.

5. In December 1982, Barney Clark became the first human to receive an artificial heart (the Jarvik-7) as a permanent implant; he survived with it for 112 days. Jamie Fiske was a small Massachusetts girl who needed a liver transplant. She came to national attention when her father appeared on the major television networks to plead for an organ for his daughter and for help in defraying the costs of the transplant. A family in another part of the country whose son was killed in an automobile accident heard Mr. Fiske's appeal and donated their son's liver to Jamie Fiske.

6. The multivolume report was prepared by Roger W. Evans, D. L. Manninen, T. D. Overcast, et al., *The National Heart Transplantation Study: Final Report* (Seattle, WA: Battelle Human Affairs Research Centers, 1984).

7. The fund is composed of 25 percent of the transplant teams' professional fees and institutional gifts related to transplant technology. David L. Jackson, "Letter to the Editor: Ohio's Plan for Organ Transplantation." *New England Journal of Medicine* 312: 995–996, 1986.

8. Lawrence Morris, senior vice president of Blue Cross/Blue Shield Association, Testimony Before the Committee on Labor and Human Resources, U.S. Senate, October 20, 1983.

9. Task Force, *Organ Transplantation*, p. 17.

10. See, for instance, B. D. Kahan et al. "Complications of Cyclosporine-Prednisone Immunosuppression in 402 Renal Allograft Recipients Exclusively Followed at a Single Center for from One to Five Years." *Transplantation* 43: 197–204, 1987. See also T. E. Starzl, "Clinical Aspects of Cyclosporine Therapy: A Summation," *Transplantation Proceedings* 15 (supp. 1): 3103–3107, 1983.

11. William J. Stone, "Medical Complications of End-Stage Renal Disease," in *End-Stage Renal Disease*, William J. Stone and Pauline L. Rabin, eds. (New York: Academic Press, 1983), pp. 57–58.

12. Stone, "Complications," pp. 57–58.

13. The shortcomings of the artificial heart are discussed at length in Part Four of this volume.

14. Roger W. Evans, "Coverage and Reimbursement for Heart Transplantation," *International Journal of Technology Assessment in Health Care* 2: 425–448, 1986, p. 431.

15. John B. Reiss et al. "Costs and Regulation of New Medical Technologies," in *Critical Issues in Medical Technology*, B. J. McNeil and E. G. Cravalho, eds. (Boston: Auburn House Publishing Company, 1982), pp. 399–417.

16. Ward Casscells, "Heart Transplantation: Recent Policy Developments," *New England Journal of Medicine* 315: 1365–1368, November 20, 1986. These widely disparate estimates of the total annual costs of heart transplants will be discussed at greater length in Part Three.

17. Shana Alexander, "They Decide Who Lives, Who Dies," *Life* 53: 106, 1962.

18. A. H. Katz and D. M. Proctor, "Social-psychological Characteristics of Patients Receiving Hemodialysis Treatment for Chronic Renal Failure," Public Health Service, Kidney Disease Control Program, 1969, in Renee C. Fox and Judith P. Swazey, *The Courage to Fail: A Social View of Organ Transplants and Dialysis*, 2d ed. (Chicago: University of Chicago Press, 1978), p. 230.

19. David Sanders and Jesse Dukeminier, "Medical Advance and Legal Lag: Hemodialysis and Kidney Transplantation," *UCLA Law Review* 15: 377–378, 1968.

20. For a comparison of the British and U.S. systems, see H. J. Aaron and W. B. Schwartz, *The Painful Prescription: Rationing and Hospital Care* (Washington, D.C.: The Brookings Institution, 1984). For responses to their study, see Norman Daniels, "Why Saying No to Patients in the United States Is So Hard," and F. H. Miller and G.A.H. Miller, "The Painful Prescription: A Procrustean Prospective?" *New England Journal of Medicine* 314: 1381–1385, 1986.

21. This list was taken from Chapter 9 by Karen Merrikin and Thomas Overcast in Part Two of this volume. These standards are being relaxed somewhat, as techniques of transplantation and patient care improve. See Jack Copeland et al., "Selection of Patients for Cardiac Transplantation," *Circulation* 75: 2–9, 1987.

22. Richard A. Rettig and Ellen Marks, *The Federal Government and Social Planning for End-Stage Renal Disease: Past, Present, and Future* (Santa Monica, CA: The Rand Corporation, 1983), p. 42.

23. Immanuel Kant, *Foundations of the Metaphysics of Morals*, Translated and Edited by Louis White Beck (Indianapolis: The Bobbs-Merrill Company, 1959); Robert Nozick, *Anarchy, State and Utopia* (New York: Basic Books, 1974).

24. John Rawls, *A Theory of Justice* (Cambridge, MA: Harvard University Press, 1971).

25. For a more detailed analysis of relations between ethical evaluations and efficiency evaluations see Buchanan, *Ethics, Efficiency, and the Market*.

26. Mark V. Pauly, "Equity and Costs," *Law, Medicine and Health Care* 13: 28–31, 1985, p. 30. Reprinted here in Part Three.

27. For a discussion of the value of these analytical techniques, see Edith Stokey and Richard Zeckhauser, *A Primer for Policy Analysis* (New York: W. W. Norton, 1978). For criticisms of them, see Charles W. Anderson, "The Place of Principles in Policy Analysis," *American Political Science Review* 73: 711–723, 1979; Charles Wolf, Jr., "Ethics and Policy Analysis," in *Public Duties*, Joel Fleishman et al., eds. (Cambridge, MA: Harvard University Press, 1981), pp. 131–141; Tom L. Beauchamp and Norman Bowie, eds., *Ethical Theory and Business* (Englewood Cliffs, N.J.: Prentice-Hall, 1979).

28. For contemporary positions, see Ronald Dworkin, *Taking Rights Seriously* (Cambridge, MA: Harvard University Press, 1977); Joel Feinberg, *Social Philosophy* (Englewood Cliffs, N.J.: Prentice-Hall, 1973); Rawls, *A Theory of Justice*.

29. Ronald Dworkin, "Lord Devlin and the Enforcement of Morals," in *Morality and the Law*, Richard A. Wasserstrom, ed. (Belmont, CA: Wadsworth Publishing Company, 1971), pp. 55–72.

30. John Rawls, "Kantian Construction in Moral Theory," *The Journal of Philosophy* 77: 515–571, 1980; Rawls, "Justice as Fairness: Political not Metaphysical," *Philosophy and Public Affairs* 14: 223–251, 1985.

31. D. E. Redmond et al., "Fetal Neuronal Grafts in Monkeys Given Methylphenyl-tetrahydropyridine," *Lancet*, May 17, 1986, pp. 1125–1127, 1986; Walter Sullivan, "Cell Implants Curb Parkinson's in Two Monkeys," *New York Times*, May 17, 1986, p. 8; Mary B. Mahowald, Jerry Silver, and Robert A. Ratcheson, "The Ethical Options in Fetal Transplants," *Hastings Center Report* 17: 9–15, 1987.

2

Ethical and Ideological Assumptions of Organ Substitution Policy

Daniel Wikler

Stresses in the Normative Structure of Organ Transplantation

Just as coursing fluids are contained and channeled by the ducts through which they flow, social practices are bounded and directed by a fabric of norms, values, and moral concepts. In both cases, acceleration of the flow increases pressure on the conduit, reshaping the container, exposing soft spots, and pushing open new pathways.

The social enterprise of organ transplantation, which comprises the technique itself, its funding, the selection and care of donors and recipients, and much else besides, is similarly shaped by a set of ethical and social norms. Understanding the place of transplantation in U.S. society requires an understanding of these norms and of the conditions under which they might give way or change as the pace of transplantation increases.

As a philosopher, I am not in a position to make credible speculations on transplantation's place and future in the social fabric. My only hope is to attempt to determine the validity (i.e., coherence, consistency, and truth) of the norms at issue. This exercise does have some relation to prediction, however, because an idea that is valid is more likely, everything else being equal, to be *believed*, and belief affects behavior. Thus, an effort to assess the logic of the moral concepts that undergird and direct the transplantation exercise can promise some basis for understanding transplantation's future.

The Growth of the Transplantation Enterprise

Transplantation has grown hugely in scope and ambition. What began as an experiment with laboratory animals has now mushroomed into an industry. The now-routine inclusion of human beings as donors and donees and the ever-increasing number of operations are striking enough in themselves; but just as impressive has been the development of a full-fledged infrastructure. Operating rooms are built specifically to house transplantations. Helicopters are purchased, crews trained, transplant coordinators hired, and suppliers of dry ice engaged. Medical residencies with the primary goal of training physicians whose bread-and-butter will be the practice of transplanting organs are established. New professions and paraprofessions are created, such as "scavengers" (experts in removing and transporting human organs), whose skills may be useful only in the transplantation enterprise.

All of this creates expectations on the part of professionals, patients, and the public that transplantation will occur when needed. Patients and their families come to assume that deaths avoidable by organ transplantation will be avoided. They, and the professionals serving them, change their view of such deaths from tragedies to injustices. And people generally come to feel obliged to do what is necessary to foster organ transplantation. They offer their own organs and those of stricken loved ones, and they might approve of financial support by government or insurors of transplantations for others.

It comes as no surprise, then, that the Task Force on Organ Transplantation, impaneled to advise the secretary of the Department of Health and Human Services, has called on the government to provide financial support for organ transplantation for those unable to pay.[1] This appeal is indicative of a movement toward universal entitlement to organ transplantation. This in turn would spur further development of the infrastructure. And, needless to say, these developments would increase pressures to increase the supply of human organs needed for transplantation.

Our interest in forecasting the future of transplantation, then, should lead us to look for conceptual and ideological soft spots in the normative structure of the organ transplantation enterprise. My impression is that there are many. In what follows, I examine four: the notion of "experimental" treatment; the concept of the "medically unsuitable" potential recipient; the standard of voluntarism in donation; and the definition of death. The first two are used to limit the provision of the therapy and to resolve financing dilemmas; the last two affect the supply side, helping to determine how many organs will be available for transplantation. None of these, I argue, is sufficiently fortified on the conceptual level to stand up to the pressures induced by the increased volume and importance attached to organ transplantation. If, due to conceptual weaknesses, these norms are likely to give way, we have a place to look for new directions in transplantation policy.

The Demand Side: Norms Affecting Access to Organ Transplantation

Lester Thurow has remarked[2] that the tendency toward irrational overexpenditure in the U.S. health care system is fueled by the simultaneous acceptance of two simple rules: (1) never stop anyone from obtaining the finest medical care that he or she can, and (2) everyone should receive a health care benefit if anyone does. These jointly imply that everyone should get the best. Even if this were achievable, it would often be undesirable because the money needed for this might be better spent elsewhere.

These two propositions also figure in the organ transplantation enterprise. Of course, limits to the supply of organs may make it impossible to meet all needs. But the two premises require doing all transplantations that are technologically feasible (and paid for) as long as there is benefit, and they may imply that everyone should get some kind of fair chance to be among the lucky recipients.

These norms present problems to policymakers. The latter may realize that the funds have better uses. They may be caught in a political crosscurrent: The public, although wanting the medical services, may be unwilling to support the expenditures. And ensuring "fairness" (that is to say, equality) in access to the organs may be administratively and politically difficult.

Resolving the policymakers' dilemma requires some strategy for resisting the push toward universal access to the therapy. Two of these involve concepts whose logical integrity may prove insufficient in the face of pressure: the notions of "experimental" treatment and "medically unsuitable" candidates for organ transplantation.

Experimental Treatment

It is no secret that the category of experimental treatment is used strategically. Governments and insurors find it easier to refuse reimbursement for "experimental" than "proven" treatments. Thus, some treatments have been classified as experimental for long periods of time. The decision whether to accept a type of organ transplantation as proven seems transparently to be a decision whether to offer access to that treatment for those with general entitlements to health care.

What is less clear is whether, in addition to this strategic definition of experimental, there could be an objective definition. To complain that the bureaucracy is misusing the term is to suggest that there is an objective definition; that is, that experimental could be defined by certain criteria independently of the use to which we wanted to put the term. But there is reason to suspect otherwise.

What, precisely, does experimental treatment mean? The bureaucratic definition might be, "new medical treatment that we do not want to fund." We can overlook that definition. The objective definition, in contrast, would seem to be "new medical treatment that is not yet appropriate for general use." Our question here is whether there is enough real content to this notion to allow authorities to wield it in any future attempt to limit or direct the demand for organ transplantation.

Why would a treatment be unsuitable for general use? Someone might respond: if it is under development and is still not effective enough, or if it is too unsafe, or expensive, or impractical. But clearly these dimensions admit of degrees. Precisely where on these dimensions the treatment crosses over from "undesirable" to "desirable" depends on who is asking the question. Though those paying for the technique and for development of the infrastructure—training, facility construction, and the like—may want to wait for high effectiveness, low risk, and low cost, the patient may not feel the same way. A long shot is better than a certain prospect of death. Great expense becomes tolerable to an individual who "can't take it with him," and in any case the patient may not be paying the bill. The patient may be ready to embrace the developing therapy long before the government, representing the rest of society.

To be sure, there is a bedrock meaning for experimental that does not require this kind of weighing and judging. If the treatment is, all things considered, unlikely to benefit the patient, it can objectively be said to be unproven. This will be the case with procedures that are more likely to kill the patient than to prolong the patient's life, but may also be true of procedures that trade off extension of life for quality of life. Barney Clark's artificial heart may be an example of the latter, so that in retrospect, we would call his experience with the device purely experimental and not therapeutic. But this stringent criterion is not at work in the controversial cases. If it were, patients would not be so likely to clamor for access to the treatment.

Translating the label *experimental* to a complex judgment of effectiveness, safety, and cost, however, tends to undermine its utility. A therapy still under development and insufficiently effective, safe, or cheap may still be better in each of these respects than some therapies whose development has long been completed. Medical care does not restrict itself to those therapies that are highly effective, safe, and cheap. Sometimes physicians must make do with the best possible therapy, even if far from ideal; and some therapies are retained even though there are better therapies at hand. If these nonideal therapies are financed by the government and by insurors, why not finance developing techniques of organ transplantation that are similarly nonideal?

The experimental category, then, is ill suited to be a holding station for transplantation techniques in development, except in their earliest phases. Once they begin to offer, on balance, any sort of hope at all, many patients will want them. Unless the funding agency has a standard of effectiveness and safety that is consistently applied to procedures long established in standard medical practice, the experimental tag provides little support for policies that seek to limit demand for organ transplantation.

Medically Unsuitable

If an organ transplantation technique is pried loose from the experimental category, then Thurow's dilemma threatens—unless some other nonfinancial strategem can be found for limiting access to the therapy. One that has been used in Britain consists of finding that patients who might very well benefit from the therapy are "medically unsuited" for it ("a bit crumbly," in vivid words of one of Aaron and Schwartz's respondents).[3]

When the supply of the resource is expandable (given sufficient funding), medical pseudo-disqualification is a relatively transparent dodge. This would be the case now in the United States with kidney dialysis, as we can always build more dialysis machines if we are willing to pay for them. In the case of human organs, however, the subterfuge is less apparent. If only a portion of the needy patients can be saved through transplantation because there are simply not enough organs to go around, then medical suitability will often have to be taken into account. In these cases, the question will indeed be *how much* benefit would accrue to the potential recipient rather than whether the transplant would, on balance, be in that patient's interest.

If the supply of organs were increased, however, the principal reason for making this comparative judgment would be financial. Perhaps it will remain true, for example, that patients over sixty tend to have lower survival rates in heart transplantation; still, the oldest patients may find the risks worth taking. As with dialysis, our notion of which patients are appropriate and medically suited for the therapy will be less medical in character than financial and moral. In the process, these notions lose their perceived objectivity and definiteness and could not play their accustomed role in limiting and channeling demand for access to organ transplantation.

The Supply Side: Norms Governing the Procurement and Donation of Organs

If demand for organ transplantation increases markedly, and if interested parties invest so much in the infrastructure that a high volume of operations is expected and required, pressure will build up on all limiting factors. The supply of human organs, along with money and expertise, has been among the most important factors holding back the growth of the transplantation enterprise. To the extent that moral norms inhibit the procurement of organs, we can expect these norms to come under increasing scrutiny. Those that prove logically and structurally unsound may give way. Two of these—that donations should be voluntary and that donors of hearts and other vital nonreplaceable body parts should be dead—involve conceptual problems that may prove to be crucial factors in controlling organ supply.

Voluntarism

It has been generally accepted that organ donations should be voluntary, and it is hard to imagine that this norm would be renounced. The government is not about to begin requisitioning human body parts. Nevertheless what "voluntary" means in this context could well change as demand for organs builds.

The purest form of voluntarism involves spontaneity: donors, seeing an opportunity to do good, initiating discussions with their physicians. As freedom preserving as this process might be, it is bound to be frustrating to those impatient to obtain organs and save lives. They are unlikely to be satisfied with the idea of patients dying of organ failure while physicians wait around for the idea of donation to occur to potential donors or their families.

The debate over the ethics of organ procurement, therefore, has been concerned with how much pressure can legitimately be placed on the potential donor. The progress of that debate has shown how concerned those involved with trans-plantation are to avoid any hint of coercion. Even the "required request" rule, which simply involves raising the possibility of the donation of a deceased person's organs with his or her family, is a matter of controversy. Each step that leads further from the ideal of complete spontaneity will be similarly suspect.

Why the insistence on complete voluntarism? For some, this requirement may stem from deeply felt moral principles. Others may believe it legitimate to trade voluntarism for lifesaving, especially when the needed organs are of no benefit to the donor and make all the difference to the recipient. But some of those so inclined may be concerned to avoid the slightest suggestion of pressure, fearing that it may only provoke resistance in some potential donors and their families.

Moral concern over the trend away from complete voluntarism in organ donation is sometimes voiced as a concern that transplantation policy is heading down a slippery slope: We begin with required request, continue with required briefings, go further with presumed consent unless otherwise indicated, and finally attach penalties to refusal to donate.[4] The concern here is that as a matter of social reality, one of these will lead to another. I propose that there is also a logical slippery slope to be concerned with, in which we begin the first step and then are compelled, on pain of inconsistency, to proceed to the finish.[5] This slope is formed by the structural contours of the notion of voluntarism and has already had some small role in the debate over organ transplantation policy.

Briefly stated, the logical slippery slope that could undermine the norm of complete voluntarism in transplantation policy has to do with social expectations of donors. As an illustration, consider the well-publicized Iowa case of Mrs. X and the Bone Marrow Transplant.[6] William Head, a leukemia patient, learned that the University of Iowa hospital had both a bone marrow transplantation program and, in its computer files, the name of an individual whose tissue typing indicated she might be a suitable donor. The university twice asked the individual if she would consider donating marrow if the need should arise and was told that she would not consider it except for a relative. Mr. Head went to court to attempt to compel the university to tell this woman that a specific patient (himself) might be helped by a donation. The university prevailed in the suit and no such request was made.

Though the case was argued in large part in reference to the donor's right of confidentiality, which need not concern us here, many observers also felt that a specific request to her would have been unfairly coercive. The conceptual issue, then, is whether this was actually the case. David Zimmerman, a philosopher who has written on the concept of coercion and voluntarism, argued the negative case, and his analysis is of general interest.

According to Zimmerman, it is wrong headed to view a specific request ("If you do not donate your bone marrow, a specific individual will lose his only hope of continued life") as coercive:

> In the paradigm case of coercion the gunman says, "Your money or your life," thereby forcing his victim to choose between two disagreeable alternatives. The [specific request] to Mrs. X is superficially similar in that she too would face two disagreeable alternatives: to offer herself as a donor with all the attendant inconvenience and discomfort, or to refuse and perhaps suffer some degree of psychological discomfort and pangs of conscience.
>
> But there is a significant difference: [the specific request] would neither be altering the structure of Mrs. X's choices nor attaching a negative sanction to one of them (refusing to cooperate) that was not there before, as they would be, for example, if they threatened to make public her refusal. The sanction is indeed real (we do, after all, speak about the "sanctions of conscience"), but it is not something that the [request] attaches to the choice; it is, rather, a feature of Mrs. X herself.[7]

The rightness of asking, then, is congruent with the rightness of consenting. If Mrs. X should say yes, then, according to this line of argument, she has no right not to be asked. Those who ask will not be creating the moral predicament, but merely pointing it out. Even if her choice is not entirely free, everything considered, it is voluntary vis-à-vis those who request the donation. This kind of relational voluntarism is a common feature of everyday life.

Now suppose that with the transplantation enterprise growing in scale and visibility, the public experiences a change of opinion about the moral obligations of potential donors. Imagine, in particular, that we come to think that though organ donation should remain wholly voluntary, people really ought to donate if the opportunity arises. Then, according to the line of reasoning we are following here, it will follow that moral pressure of the sort that Zimmerman would want visited on Mrs. X could be placed on potential donors generally without undue loss of voluntarism.

The conclusion of this kind of argument is that what counts as voluntary depends on what we think donors should do. If, as the transplantation enterprise expands, we come to expect donors to contribute their organs, we could reclassify some techniques of persuasion that we now may view as coercive or manipulative. Though the norm of voluntary donation may be nominally retained, its substance is open to revision.

Organ Donation and Brain Death

Norms governing contemporary transplantation policy dictate that cadavers be the source of major nonrenewable organs. What counts as a cadaver is, of course, determined by the definition of death. How death is defined, that is, what death *is*, stands to be rethought as pressure builds for an expanded supply of transplantable tissue.

Indeed, this has already happened. Though the definitive history of the definition of death has yet to be written, it is likely that the definition we have now was devised in part to facilitate organ transplantation. Surgeons who for medical reasons had to remove organs from bodies in which respiration was being artificially maintained were uncomfortable with the idea that their work caused the death of the donors. The whole-brain definition of death (that is, the complete cessation of all brain functions) permitted death to be pronounced before the organs were removed, thereby shielding the surgeons from the charge that they ended one life in the course of saving another.

It has never been acknowledged that the definition of death was changed simply in order to protect transplant surgeons and encourage transplantation. Even if this is true (and I do not know that it is), there are good reasons for denying it, at least in public. Most of us prefer to think of the question of whether one is dead or alive as an objective matter, a question of fact, not a strategic issue. Whether we should permit organ transplantation is one question, whether a patient is alive or dead quite another, and we would not expect the answer to the second to follow from the answer to the first.

Thus, if the definition of death were changed for strategic reasons, it would hardly do to admit this. And the most authoritative explanation of the redefinition, the report *Defining Death* of the President's Commission for the Study of Ethical Problems in Medicine strains mightily to portray it as a scientific determination of fact.[8] Nevertheless, perusal of the literature on the definition (most of it less careful and self-conscious than the commission's report) suggests that strategy was, if not the only reason, then at least an important motivation for adopting the new definition. To be sure, facilitation of organ transplantation was not the only goal; an interest in legal permission to discontinue care for the brain dead was present as well. But in respect to all of these, the redefinition of death was seen as a strategy for licensing certain kinds of behavior that were believed to be otherwise proscribed.

Indeed, the multiplicity of goals, together with the uncertainty over whether the redefinition was a recognition of fact or a strategy for action, has resulted in widespread uncertainty over the justification for settling on whole-brain death. This lack of clarity is, in my experience, just as prevalent among lawyers and physicians as among lay patients. A poll of professionals asking the question, "Why are whole-brain-dead patients considered dead," elicits a wide variety of answers, ranging from "because they will be dead in a matter of weeks," to "because their lives are not worth living," to "because definition is just a semantic issue."[9] None of these square with the explanation given in the President's Commission report.

If professionals are this uncertain over the basis for the new definition of death, it is understandable that many families of dying patients fail to grasp the subtleties involved. A brain-dead individual on a ventilator may not appear appreciably different from a permanently comatose individual on a ventilator. There may be a doctor in the house who could explain to the families why the former is considered to be dead while the latter is considered to be alive; but then again there may not. And unless these subtleties are grasped (assuming that they are valid to begin with),[10] they lack the basis on which to resist further revision. The recent proposals to increase the supply of organs for infants by extending the definition to include anencephalic infants—who seem very much alive—is symptomatic of this intellectual uncertainty.

Under pressure for more organs, then, the norm limiting donating of major body parts to cadavers may prove to change in its substance. It is conceivable that the norm would be dropped, so that patients regarded as death bound, but not yet dead, would be deemed suitable for donation. Or the norm may be nominally upheld, but the definition revised to include some of those who are now judged alive. This could include not only those fated to be whole-brain-dead, but even the "cortically" dead, who in other respects remain healthy and stable. Thus an individual such as Karen Quinlan, who remained in a persistent vegetative state for over a decade, would be classified as dead—and hence as a legitimate source for organs, assuming permission were granted. Once again, the structural flaws in the concepts making up the norm itself lay the rule open to revision or abandonment once pressure builds.

Conclusion

Our behavior, individual and collective, is shaped in part by moral norms and assumptions. How we think about their constituent moral concepts helps to determine what effect they will have. Under stable social conditions, these norms may exert their influence without much reciprocal effect, remaining in force without revision. As conditions change, and as obedience to the norms comes to have increasingly significant costs, pressure may build to rethink the norms or to abandon them entirely. Some of these norms and concepts will prove to be particularly exposed to challenge due to inherent structural and logical flaws.

The transplantation of organs from one human body to another is not just another medical operation. The resource is literally vital. The technique is justly regarded as a sensitive issue by those involved in the enterprise. Any hint that surgeons, "procurement managers," and other players are not playing by the rules could lead to public reaction that could inhibit the development and provision of the technique.

At the same time, the growing success of transplantation creates both demand for its benefits and the means for its delivery. As the process continues, building on itself, a social movement gets underway. The delicate norms that have governed transplantation practice, norms regulating its financing, its scientific refinement, the choice of recipients, the protection of donors, the restriction (for nonrenewable organs) to cadavers, are bound to be challenged.

It behooves us, then, to attempt to assess the soundness of these norms. Some will stand the test of time. Some may bend to the pressure of the demand for organs, for financing, or for the means of a professional's livelihood. Some will give way. Some deserve to. Orderly and appropriate growth in the transplantation enterprise will be enhanced by the development of a defensible and reasonable normative foundation.

Notes

The author wishes to extend thanks to Norman Fost, Alan Weisbard, and Deborah Mathieu for helpful comments.

1. Task Force on Organ Transplantation, *Organ Transplantation: Issues and Recommendations* (Washington, D.C.: Government Printing Office, 1986).

2. Lester Thurow, "Learning to Say 'No,'" *New England Journal of Medicine* 311: 1569–1572, 1984.

3. Henry J. Aaron and William B. Schwartz, *The Painful Prescription: Rationing Hospital Care* (Washington, D.C.: Brookings Institution, 1984).

4. I am not convinced that this process is inevitable once the first steps are taken, nor even that the final policies would necessarily be wrong. But I will not argue these positions here.

5. In other words, the "social" slope involves one event, the first step, causing another, which eventually causes the last. This kind of moral argument states that although the first step may seem right, it should not be taken because of the bad consequences (i.e., that the last steps probably will be taken). The "logical" slope does not posit any causal process. It states that if one takes the first step, one is thereby (or in conjunction with certain other facts, some of them changing social realities) logically committed to taking the later steps. Whether the later steps will be taken depends in part on whether people are consistent.

6. See the discussion of this case by Charles W. Lidz, Alan Meisel, Loren H. Roth, and David Zimmerman, "Mrs. X and the Bone Marrow Transplant," *Hastings Center Report* 13: 17–19, 1983.

7. Lidz et al., "Mrs. X," pp. 18–19.

8. President's Commission for the Study of Ethical Problems in Medicine and Biomedical and Behavioral Research, *Defining Death: Medical, Legal and Ethical Issues in the Determination of Death* (Washington, D.C.: Government Printing Office, 1981).

9. These and others are evaluated in Michael Green and Daniel Wikler, "Brain Death and Personal Identity," *Philosophy and Public Affairs* 9: 389–394, 1980; and in Karen Gervais, *Redefining Death* (New Haven: Yale University Press, 1987).

10. I do not think these subtleties are valid. See Green and Wikler, "Brain Death."

PART TWO

Organ Procurement and Recipient Selection

3

Introduction

Deborah Mathieu

In 1973, there were approximately 11,000 end-stage renal disease (ESRD) patients, 3,000 of whom received kidney transplants. Ten years later, there were more than 72,000 patients with ESRD, and there were more than 6,000 kidney transplants performed that year.[1] Transplants are encouraged for many reasons: They are less expensive than long-term dialysis treatments;[2] they afford a higher quality of life for many patients than does long-term dialysis;[3] and the success rate of the procedure is now very high (over 95 percent survive the first year).[4] Yet although the number of kidney transplants has doubled in ten years, it has not kept pace with the number of ESRD patients. Whereas approximately 27 percent of ESRD patients in 1973 received kidney transplants, for instance, only about 8 percent received transplants in 1983, even though the success rate for renal transplantation has increased significantly (the one-year patient survival rate rose from about 72 to 95 percent).[5]

The decline in the percentage of ESRD patients receiving kidney transplants is due in large part to the changing nature of the patient population. Because the federal government pays for the medical care of almost every patient with end-stage renal disease, cost of the treatment is not an issue, so more and more very elderly and very ill people are being put on dialysis. These patients would not have been given the treatment in the early years of the program (and hence would not have been part of the ESRD program). But because of the belief that many of these patients probably could not survive a kidney transplant, that therapy is rarely offered to them. Thus although there are a great many people in the ESRD program today, many of them are not considered to be suitable candidates for kidney transplants. The patient selection criteria, then, determine to a large extent which sufferers of the disease will receive which types of treatment (if any).

There is another reason why the majority of ESRD patients do not receive transplants, a reason that is external to the patient population: There simply are not enough donor kidneys in good condition to go around. This is the case for all organs, not just kidneys. It has been estimated that at any one time, between 8,000 and 10,000 people are waiting for a donor organ to become available.[6] A large proportion of these people will never receive the organs upon which their lives depend.

The chapters in this section address both patient selection criteria and organ procurement procedures. The two are interrelated in important ways: The dearth of transplantable organs puts pressure on health care professionals to tighten patient selection criteria so that only those patients expected to benefit sufficiently from a transplant will be chosen, while the difficulty of eliminating patients from consideration for lifesaving treatment creates pressure to obtain more organs. But because the issues raised by patient selection and organ procurement are so wide ranging and complex, we will deal with them separately here, while noting their interrelation where appropriate.

Organ Donation and Procurement

There are many reasons for the scarcity of transplantable organs in the United States today. The first is that organs are donated in this country on a voluntary basis, and only a small percentage of people have agreed to be organ donors. The law governing the voluntary donation of organs, that is, the law that allows people to determine beforehand what will happen to their organs after death, is the Uniform Anatomical Gift Act. It is valid in all states and the District of Columbia and is very simple to apply: One need only sign a donor card or check a box on a driver's license. Yet comparatively few people have done so.

A 1985 Gallup Poll indicated some interesting public attitudes toward organ donation. Although 93 percent of those polled knew about organ transplantation and 75 percent of these approved of the *concept* of organ donation, only 27 percent said that they would be willing to donate an organ, and only 17 percent had completed donor cards. The majority—66 percent—did not want to donate their organs after death. These people were questioned further about their refusal, and they indicated a variety of concerns, such as: (1) fear that physicians would hasten their death in order to obtain their organs, (2) reluctance to think about their own mortality, and (3) unwillingness to be cut up after death (e.g., because of a general aversion to the thought of it or because of a belief that an intact body is needed in the afterlife).[7]

So the first obstacle is that most people do *not* volunteer to donate their organs after death. This difficulty is compounded by the fact that even those who agree to be donors may not end up providing organs after their deaths. There are several reasons for this: Perhaps disease processes have rendered their organs unusable, or the people die under suspicious circumstances and are autopsied instead (as required by law in most states). Or perhaps their relatives object. Although physicians may legally remove organs even over the objections of the deceased's relatives, they rarely do so; nor do they usually take the organs of an accident victim who has signed an organ donor card but whose relatives cannot be located to give their approval of the donation. Three reasons are usually cited for medical professionals' requiring the consent of relatives even with documentation of the deceased's wishes to donate: (1) fear of legal liability, (2) respect for the wishes of grieving families, and (3) fear of bad publicity.[8]

Another very important reason for the dearth of transplantable organs is the unwillingness of physicians to begin the process of obtaining them. Their reluctance is understandable. Physicians who work in hospitals that do not have transplant programs rarely are given any institutional support to get involved in the process, as the hospitals have no vested interest in it. And the process itself can be very time consuming because each organ usually is handled by a separate agency. A conscientious physician might have to call as many as a half-dozen different places so that the vital organs and tissues can be used.

And each time the physician calls, he or she will have to provide detailed information about the status of the deceased. This may take hours.

Fortunately, the situation is improving somewhat: A few hospitals employ transplant coordinators to make these calls, and Congress now requires that organ procurement agencies seeking grants for expansion must first develop effective working relationships with tissue banks. But for many physicians, getting involved in organ procurement remains very inconvenient indeed.

There is another problem, and this is perhaps the most obvious: The health care staff often finds it psychologically difficult to bring up the issue in the first place, to ask the grieving family to donate the organs of their recently deceased relative. Although some health care institutions have developed training programs to teach the appropriate staff members to approach the families of recently deceased patients—and this training does seem to help—reluctance of the health care team to approach the grieving family still remains a major obstacle to organ procurement.

In Chapter 4, Kenneth Iserson describes in greater detail the obstacles to obtaining organs encountered by the health care team, both in the acute care setting and in the chronic care unit. Iserson, who is an emergency department physician, gives us a firsthand look at the practical, emotional, and legal barriers to efficient organ procurement, and in doing so he addresses a wide range of important concerns: conflicts of duty, reasons the best candidates for organ donations are not used, the emotional repercussions that harvesting organs have on people who are trained to save lives, and the difficulty of determining death. Most of the obstacles to obtaining sufficient organs in good condition for transplantation can be overcome, he concludes, but only if people outside the medical community get involved.

One especially sensitive issue that Iserson correctly claims requires the involvement of those outside the medical community concerns the determination of death. The problem is not, as some people believe, the need to provide protection against a premature declaration of death by a physician who is overeager to procure an organ. The Uniform Anatomical Gift Act offers a considerable safeguard against that by prohibiting the physician who makes a declaration of death from participating in harvesting the organ. The problem is, instead, that many people do not understand what death *is*.

There currently are two standards for determining death. Ascertaining the irreversible cessation of circulation and respiration is the traditional, time-honored method of determining death with which we are all familiar. The second method—ascertaining the irreversible cessation of all brain functions—is a more recent development.[9] The President's Commission for the Study of Ethics explained the reasons for the addition of this second criterion of death:

> With the advent of transplant surgery employing cadaver donors—first with kidney transplantation in the 1950's and later, and still more dramatically, with heart transplantation in the 1960's—interest in "brain death" took on a new urgency. For such transplants to be successful, a viable, intact organ is needed. The suitability of organs for transplantation diminishes rapidly once the donor's respiration and circulation stop. The most desirable organ donors are otherwise healthy individuals who have died following traumatic head injuries and whose breathing and blood flow are being artificially maintained. Yet even with proper care, the organs of these potential donors will deteriorate. Thus, it became important for physicians to be able to determine when the brains of mechanically supported patients irretrievably ceased functioning.

Yet the need for viable organs to transplant does not account fully for the interest in diagnosing irreversible loss of brain functions. . . . Medical concern over the determination of death rests much less with any wish to facilitate organ transplantation than with the need both to render appropriate care to patients and to replace artificial support with more fitting and respectful behavior when a patient has become a dead body. Another incentive to update the criteria for determining death stems from the increasing realization that the dedication of scarce and expensive intensive care facilities to bodies without brain functions may not only prolong the uncertainty and suffering of grieving families but also preclude access to the facilities for patients with reversible conditions.[10]

The cardiopulmonary criterion of death and the whole-brain criterion of death do not reflect different conceptions of death, nor are they different definitions of death.[11] Rather, they simply are two different *methods* of determining the same thing: death as the irreversible cessation of all bodily functions. In the first, cardiopulmonary activity is measured; if there is no activity, the patient is dead. When the patient is being artificially ventilated, however, the existence of cardiopulmonary activity cannot be ascertained, so the second method of determining death must be employed. If there is no brain activity (including no activity of the brain stem), then the patient is dead. (For a view of the painstaking care that goes into making a determination of brain death, see Appendix E).

Many people still do not understand the relationship of "brain death" to death: They do not understand, that is, that brain death simply is death. One often hears television news commentators mistakenly report, "The brain-dead patient was removed from the respirator and allowed to die." This is not what happened. If a patient is determined to be brain dead, then that patient is as dead as possible, and removing the body from artificial ventilation does just that and only that: The machine ceases to breathe for the patient. It is clear that more extensive educational efforts are needed to acquaint people with the two methods for determining death. An understanding of that may help to alleviate some anxiety regarding the donation of organs.

There is another difficulty with the determination of death, which Daniel Wikler mentioned in Chapter 2: Demands to increase the supply of transplantable human organs put pressure on the way we determine death—and indeed on the way we view death itself. According to our current view of death, an individual in a permanently comatose state (whose higher-brain functions have failed and who retains only brain stem use) and an anencephalic infant (a newborn with no capacity for higher-brain functions) are considered to be alive. But it has been suggested that the definition of death be altered from the failure of the whole brain to the failure of the higher brain; and this would mean that the persistently comatose and the anencephalic would be regarded as dead and that their organs could be harvested.

There are strong, principled arguments for the higher-brain concept of death that are independent of the need for transplantable human organs.[12] One major argument is that it is not the lower brain's ability to coordinate and regulate bodily functions that matters; what matters, instead, is the higher brain's ability to think, feel, reason, plan, and so on. The foundation of this position is the belief that we characteristically think of persons (in the moral sense) as having the following capacities: (1) they are capable of consciousness and self-consciousness; (2) they have the capacity to choose and to act on reasons; (3) they have the capacity to think of themselves as existing through time, as having a past, a present, and a future. There are other suggestions for the descriptive content of personhood, of course.[13] But although these suggestions for the descriptive content of the concept of personhood differ in detail, they are unanimous in relying on cognitive abilities as the relevant criteria. These qualities are given moral weight because they are essential for the life of the individual as a social and moral being.

According to this view, once a person loses higher-brain functions, he or she no longer exists. That the body continues to function does not matter in the determination of death because the relevant aspects of the person, the cognitive abilities, are gone. And a human who is born without these higher-brain functions cannot be said to exist as a person in any morally relevant sense. Hence, it is concluded, the whole-brain concept of death, which places value on the brain's ability to maintain the body's homeostasis, should be replaced with a higher-brain concept of death, which places value on the brain's cognitive capacities.

Although this higher-brain-function concept of death has not yet received widespread political support, Wikler pointed out that the desire to increase the supply of human donor organs may make it more acceptable. Settling on the proper definition(s) of death and methods for determining death clearly are social issues, not exclusively scientific or medical ones. And they are issues with which we all should be concerned. After all, as the opening sentence of the president's commission's report on the definition of death noted, "Death is the one great certainty,"[14] even if uncertainty exists about precisely when it occurs and how we are to measure its occurrence.

Increasing the Supply of Transplantable Cadaver Organs

In Chapter 5, Arthur Caplan examines several proposals for increasing the supply of donor organs. One is that we should adopt the method of "presumed consent" utilized by many European countries, such as Austria, Greece, Spain, Sweden, and France. In these countries, hospitals are *required* to utilize cadaver organs for transplantation unless the individual had previously explicitly refused to participate in the program or unless a relative comes forward to object to the procedure.

Although twelve states now have presumed consent laws for corneas, it is unlikely that this method will be widely adopted in the United States. In a recent survey, over 86 percent of those polled declared that physicians should not have the power to remove organs from those deceased who had not signed organ donor cards, without consulting the next of kin.[15] Many people see this power as too coercive. Their argument (and it is one that has found strong political support) is that our society respects its plurality of values too highly to want to presume of anyone something as intimate as organ donation. Caplan once championed this method of increasing the supply of transplantable organs,[16] but he now argues that it may be both unethical and unworkable.

A more likely alternative is the "required request" method. States could pass laws requiring medical professionals to ask the family of the deceased for permission to remove his or her organs for transplantation into another person. This method has been seen by many, including a majority of the members of Congress, to be an acceptable compromise between respecting the autonomy and privacy of the donors' families and providing organs to those who need them. In the fall of 1986, Congress ruled that Medicaid and Medicare payments would be withheld from those hospitals that do not establish written protocols

for identifying potential organ donors. But this method too has its critics. Some
people complain that asking family members for the organs of their recently
deceased relative is too painful—for the family member as well as for the health
care professional who broaches the subject—and thus a required request law
would be inhumane.

Financial Incentives to Donate

A third alternative to the problem of a shortage of organs is to create some
financial incentives for people to donate organs. The payment could either be
in the form of cash or in-kind aid (such as a reduction of health care expenses
or funeral expenses); it could be direct (through an organ market) or indirect
(by issuing tax credits for transplantable organs). There already have been several
proposals to amend the Internal Revenue Code to provide income and estate
tax deductions for those who donate their organs after death. Congressman
Philip Crane, for instance, has proposed a $25,000 deduction per qualified organ
donation in the last taxable year of the donor's life. The bill was not passed.

There are two sources of human organs available for marketing—the living
and the dead. Advocates of financial incentives to part with an organ while
one is still alive point out, for instance, that one advantage of selling body
parts is that it may offer the poor an opportunity to break out of the poverty
cycle that they otherwise would not have. Someone who has little money and
two kidneys could sell one kidney to someone with plenty of money and end-
stage renal disease. The human body can function well with only one kidney,
which simply enlarges to do the work of two.

The most frequently voiced argument in favor of an organ market is based
on the values of individual liberty and privacy. Proponents argue that there are
no good reasons to forbid this practice, that it is none of society's business if
someone freely and knowingly contracts to have an eye removed in return for
a house or a college education or a trip to Hawaii. Such an agreement, they
contend, should be treated like any other contract that involves harm only to
the competent, autonomous adult bargaining party and should be left in the
sacred domain of private decision-making.

Marketing cadaver organs also has its proponents. One advantage of such
a market is that it is likely to increase substantially the number of organs
available for transplantation—people might be more willing to give up their
organs if their estates were to receive some remuneration. But it also may have
the added advantage of redistributing burdens more fairly. Under the current
system, the only person involved in the transplant process who does not benefit
from it is the donor. The recipient gains a healthier organ, and the health care
team receives financial remuneration for its work. Because the donor contributes
a necessary element, there seems to be no reason to exclude him or her from
the list of those who benefit.

Of course, as Caplan points out, there may be some unappealing side effects
of such a market. If the price is right, the unscrupulous might murder someone
in order to sell his or her organs. It is not clear, though, how forceful an
objection this really is. After all, the sale of organs probably would not offer
any greater temptation to murder than does a large insurance policy. And
perhaps the advantage of a greater store of organs would be worth the risk.

However, this country's lawmakers have not been persuaded by the advantages
of cadaver organ markets. The Senate Committee on Labor and Human Resources,
for instance, concluded that individuals should not profit by the sale of human

organs for transplantation and that human body parts should not be viewed as commodities. The House Committee on Energy and Commerce concurred with that general conclusion, but for a more utilitarian reason: The committee worried that permitting the sale of human organs might result in the collapse of the nation's system of voluntary organ donation. Hence marketing organs in the United States is now a federal crime (insofar as the marketing relates to interstate commerce) punishable by a $50,000 fine and/or five years in prison. (See Appendix D for a copy of the federal statute pertaining to the sale of organs for transplantation.) Legislators from some states (such as New York, Maryland, Virginia, California, and Michigan) have agreed with this assessment of the organ market and have passed laws prohibiting it in their states. The issue is not a closed one, however, so Caplan discusses at some length the pros and cons of an organ market.

Despite our efforts to the contrary, it seems reasonable to predict that the supply of transplantable organs will continue to fall short of the need and that pressures to increase the supply of organs will grow. One outcome of this, Caplan argues, is that we will begin to seek other sources of organs: fetuses, abortuses, the permanently comatose, primates, anencephalic infants. Currently, organs for transplantation are being taken from a few of these beings. Primates, for instance, have been used in the recent past—with unhappy results.

Primates as Donors

Experimental transplantations of primate organs into human patients were performed in the early 1960s, but met with such a lack of success that the endeavor was generally abandoned. Thus in the fall of 1984, surgeons at the University Medical Center at Loma Linda, California, gained immediate notoriety when it was announced that they had implanted a baboon heart into a human infant who had been born with hypoplastic left heart syndrome.[17] The child, who was called Baby Fae by the media, survived for twenty days before her body rejected the new heart.

This case raised a host of ethical concerns, several of which were based on the dubious scientific status of the procedure. Critics argued that it was still too experimental to be used on a human infant, that at least one other procedure existed that offered a greater chance of benefit to the child, and that the best interests of the child had not been pursued. Indeed, the prestigious journal *Nature* complained in an editorial that the operation "may have catered to the researchers' needs first and to the patient's only second."[18]

Other criticisms of the procedure were based on the use of primates as organ donors. Opponents of such use saw this as an example of speciesism, a form of discrimination analogous to agism, sexism, and racism. As Peter Singer argued, the basis of speciesism is simply a "selfish desire to preserve the privileges of the exploiting group," and it should not be permitted.[19]

In addition to the ethical issues, there are practical issues that militate against using primates as organ donors.[20] There is a severe shortage of primates, for instance, and using them for their organs would directly conflict with other research needs, many of which can be expected to benefit more people. And raising chimpanzees is very expensive, so resorting to xenografts from them would increase the cost of transplantation significantly. In addition, the chances for survival of a xenograft are slim. Indeed, "No evidence exists now to support an expectation that a xenograft would continue to function for 2–6 months even with maximum blockade of immune response."[21] For all of these reasons, there is little enthusiasm for using primates as organ donors.

Anencephalic Infants as Donors

Anencephalic infants form another controversial group of potential organ donors. Anencephaly, a neural tube defect in which most or all of the cerebral hemispheres are missing, occurs approximately once in every 2,000 births. The condition is incompatible with life: Most anencephalic infants are either stillborn or die within a few days after birth. The unique situation of the anencephalic infant—it will die soon despite the most aggressive medical intervention, the infant has no cognitive capabilities, and its organs usually are in good condition— leads some commentators to argue that its organs should be harvested. But the infant often has a functioning brain stem, and this creates the dilemma: Because the brain stem is operating, the infant is not considered to be dead, and taking its organs would be tantamount to homicide under the current law; but if one waits until the infant is legally dead, the organs will not be usable, and children whose lives could have been saved by using its organs will instead die.

There have been three proposals for dealing with this situation: (1) alter the definition of death so that anencephalic infants are considered to be dead; (2) maintain the current definition of death and refrain from using the organs of anencephalic infants; (3) maintain the current definition of death, but change the rule that organs can be taken only from the dead.

An article in the *New England Journal of Medicine* recently reported the successful transplantation of kidneys from anencephalic infants, the authors having subscribed to the first alternative: They considered the infants to be dead.[22] As noted above, there are good reasons for altering the concept of death to include anencephalic infants, reasons that are independent of the desire to obtain their organs. There also are strong reasons for resisting this move. Alexander Capron has argued that the concept of death should not be altered in this way, nor should the anatomical gift act be amended to allow an exception for anencephalic infants. He offered a variety of reasons for his position, for instance: A breathing body simply is not what we have in mind when we think of a dead body; changing the definition of death could result in legalizing some unintended and unacceptable practices; it would cloud the distinction between those who are dying and those who are dead; an anencephalic infant is worthy of our concern and respect and should not be used as a mere means; allowing organs to be taken from these infants may undermine the public's support for organ transplantation.[23]

In Chapter 6, John Robertson argues against both of these positions and offers reasons for choosing the third alternative: Maintain the current definition of death, but allow organs to be taken from anencephalic infants. Robertson does not believe that we are ready now for this change (too many facts are still in doubt, for instance), but he does anticipate that there may come a time when such a change is appropriate.

Living, Related Donors

One other group of potential donors are living human beings—especially relatives of the patient. Perhaps it goes without saying that the issue of obtaining organ donations from living human beings is not appropriately applied to single, nonregenerative organs such as the heart and the liver, but rather refers to renewable tissues (such as blood and bone marrow) and kidneys (since the human body can function adequately with only one kidney).

Even with the introduction of new and more effective antirejection drug therapy, transplantations using organs donated by living, related donors are still much more likely to be successful than are transplantations using cadaver organs. In 1977, for instance, the one-year graft survival rate (in contrast to the patient survival rate) for kidneys from living, related donors was 70 percent, while the one-year graft survival rate for kidneys from cadavers was 51 percent. By 1980, the one-year graft survival rate for kidneys from living, related donors had increased to 82 percent, and the one-year graft survival rate for cadaver kidneys had increased to 61 percent.[24] And by 1984, the one-year graft survival rate for kidneys from living, related donors had risen to 88 percent, while the one-year graft survival rate for cadaver kidneys had risen to 71 percent.[25] As these figures indicate, the chances of success of a particular transplant were significantly increased if the organ was taken from a living, related donor, and the difference in relative success rates had not changed much over time (in 1977, an organ from a living, related donor had a 19 percent greater chance of succeeding; by 1984, the chance of its succeeding was still 17 percent greater).

Thus despite improvements in surgical techniques and in postoperative care, the survival rate for organs from living, related donors continues to exceed the survival rate for organs from cadavers.[26] Because of this fact and because there remains a shortage of cadaver organs, organs from living, related donors continue to be an important factor in the transplantation enterprise.

One major ethical problem in obtaining renewable body parts from a living donor arises from the importance and notable difficulty of determining whether his or her willingness to donate the organ is substantially autonomous. The problem, in other words, lies in securing the voluntary and informed consent of the donor. Reports have indicated that some donors decide to give an organ even before they are apprised of the risks of the procedure; therefore, they do not really assess the information given, and hence their decision is not truly informed. And some potential donors are under such enormous family pressure to aid a relative in distress that their decisions are not truly voluntary.[27]

Of course, the difficulty of obtaining voluntary and informed consent is not unique to organ donation. Some critics even scoff at the possibility of ever obtaining it even for common medical problems.[28] Nonetheless, the principle of voluntary, informed consent remains of fundamental importance to the practice of medicine, and the inadequacies of some cases do not reduce its significance as a legitimate goal.[29] Hence health care professionals do what they can to mitigate the difficulties inherent in the situation: They may offer to provide a "medical" excuse for a potential donor's not giving a body part in order to alleviate family pressure on him or her, for example, and they strive to educate the donor about the risks of the procedures involved.

One important question raised by the issue of informed consent is *Who* is appropriately considered to be a potential donor? Is it permissible, for instance, to take organs from donors such as young children and the mentally impaired who cannot truly give their consent?

Some mentally incompetent persons have been used as organ donors, even though in some instances they were able to understand only very little of what was being asked of them. One especially interesting case involved Jerry Strunk and his brother Tommy.

Tommy Strunk, aged twenty-eight, needed a kidney transplant, and his physicians discovered that the most compatible donor was his brother Jerry, aged twenty-seven. Jerry, however, had an I.Q. of 35 (a mental age of six) and was institutionalized. Their parents agreed that Jerry should donate one of his kidneys to his brother, and the case was taken to court as a precautionary measure. The county court ruled that Jerry should donate a kidney because "his well-being would be jeopardized more severely by the loss of his brother than by the removal of a kidney." The circuit court—to which the case was appealed—agreed, and the operations were performed.[30]

It is clear that in this case the best interests of the donor were not really the primary concern of the court. As the dissenting opinion in *Strunk v. Strunk* noted, "The majority opinion is predicated upon the finding of the circuit court that there will be psychological benefits to the ward but points out that the incompetent has the mentality of a six-year-old child. It is common knowledge beyond dispute that the loss of a close relative or a friend to a six-year-old child is not of major impact."[31] Although the judge's psychological generalization may be somewhat overdrawn, it does point out that there is a very strong burden of proof to be born by those who say that a six-year-old child (or someone with the mental capacity of a six-year-old) would suffer enough to warrant the pains and risks of major surgery as well as the permanent loss of a kidney.

Just as importantly, the risks to the donor were not given much weight: The court found them to be equal to commuting sixteen miles a day by car. But these are only the risks of living with one kidney. The court failed to take seriously the other costs involved, such as the risks of undergoing major surgery and general anesthesia and the pains involved in recovery. There was also another significant risk to this donor: If Jerry had lost normal functioning of his remaining kidney, dialysis probably would not have been made available to him. This case occurred before the cost of dialysis was covered by Medicare, and the state of Kentucky did not at that time offer dialysis treatments to the mentally retarded.[32]

In reaching its decision, the court in the Strunk case applied the "substituted judgment" doctrine. In other words, the court said that it was choosing as Jerry Strunk would have chosen, had he been competent to do so. As John Robertson explained:

> For over 150 years, the substituted judgment doctrine has regulated the judicial response to claims of needy relatives upon incompetents, and has permitted depletion of incompetent estates with no direct benefit to them solely to help others. The rationale for this practice—that respect for persons requires courts to follow the putative wishes of the incompetent were he otherwise, even if such a course provides no direct benefit to the incompetent—is prima facie relevant in determining whether tissue and organs may be taken from incompetents to benefit close relatives in need. If property can be invaded because of minimal risk to the incompetent's interest, then presumably the body could also be invaded if the risks are commensurate.[33]

One could argue that this presumption is too hasty. Instead, a very strong argument must be made for treating someone's body as alienable property. It is not at all clear that one's body may be invaded by others to the same degree as one's property may be. It is not even clear to what degree one's property may justifiably be invaded by another. Further, even if we believe that it is sometimes legitimate to invade someone's property for the sake of a family member, it does *not* follow that it is sometimes legitimate to invade a person's *body* in order to help another.

In addition, the use of the substituted judgment doctrine as the basis for deciding this case was problematic. Because Jerry Strunk had never been competent, he had never expressed his preferences. Indeed, we cannot even legitimately ask what his preferences might have been because he never had the conceptual ability to frame any such preferences. As one commentator noted, "The question of whether an individual, if competent, would choose a particular treatment can only be sensibly asked of one who at some times in the past had certain complex beliefs, values, and preferences and the conceptual framework that these presuppose."[34] Hence it may well have been impossible to apply the substituted judgment principle reliably in this case and to determine what Jerry Strunk's preferences actually were (or would have been).

It does not follow, however, that organs may never be taken from individuals who are unable to consent to the donation. It simply means that different tests should be employed in determining the proper course to follow. Other courts have stood on firmer ground than the Strunk court in permitting a kidney to be taken from an incompetent. In 1973, for instance, a court ruled that a retarded girl could donate a kidney to her mother—her sole parent—on the grounds that the loss of her mother would be worse for the child than the loss of her kidney.[35] The interests of the potential donor played a major role in this decision, not simply the interests of the recipient.

It seems reasonable to argue that a test based on the interests of the donor is appropriately applied also to young children, in considering them as potential kidney donors. This has not usually been the case: As Norman Fost notes in Chapter 7, except for instances in which identical twins were involved, pre-adolescent children have largely been excluded as organ donors.[36] The argument usually is that, because children are especially vulnerable and deserve extra protection, their inability to give their voluntary and informed consent rules them out as potential organ donors. But Fost argues that, rather than following an informal policy of excluding minors from being renal donors, we should allow a child to donate a kidney if, and only if, doing so provides significant potential benefits to him or her.

Recipient Selection

No matter what we do to increase organ supply, it seems clear that, at least in the foreseeable future, there will be more people who need organs than there are organs available. Until there are enough organs in good condition accessible to those who need them, someone will have to decide that this particular organ will go to this particular person. Usually the transplant surgeons themselves decide who among their patients are candidates for transplants, and they are relied upon to judge according to "objective medical criteria." But there are serious weaknesses in this system.

Troubling Cases

Take the case of Thomas Creighton, whose diseased heart was removed in the spring of 1985 at the University Medical Center in Tucson, Arizona. He was provided with three other hearts, two human and one artificial, in an extraordinary but ultimately futile attempt to keep him alive. The first heart transplanted into Mr. Creighton was not in optimal condition, and it failed.

The second heart was an artificial device—the controversial and experimental Phoenix heart—and was never intended to be permanent. The third and final heart given to Mr. Creighton was a human heart in excellent condition, but by then Mr. Creighton was beyond saving.

This case received an extraordinary amount of media attention. Comments in the media were both laudatory, concerning the transplant surgeon's remarkable efforts to save his patient's life, and defamatory. Although each of the hearts given to Mr. Creighton raised serious ethical questions, the heart that received the most media attention and raised the loudest criticisms was the artificial device, the so-called Phoenix heart (these issues are addressed in Part Four of this volume). But it was not just the use of the Phoenix heart that was problematic in this case, despite the impression created by the media. The use of the two *human* hearts for Mr. Creighton also raises important ethical concerns.

The first heart transplanted into him had been taken from an accident victim who had been hospitalized for several days with fevers and fluctuating blood pressure and who, the transplant surgeon confessed, "wasn't what we would call an excellent donor candidate." But Mr. Creighton was failing fast, and no other human hearts were available. The third heart transplanted into Mr. Creighton (and the second human heart) was in significantly better condition. But by the time Mr. Creighton received this heart, his condition had deteriorated drastically, and he was no longer a plausible candidate for a heart transplant. Part of the problem was the length of time during which Mr. Creighton was attached to a heart-lung machine. Medical experts claim that an adult who has been on a heart-lung machine for even half the length of Mr. Creighton's attachment to the machine has virtually no chance of survival.

In other words, when Thomas Creighton was healthy enough to be a good candidate for a heart transplant, he was given a less than healthy heart because of the unfortunate shortage of human donor hearts. And after he had been on the heart-lung machine for many hours and almost certainly would not survive— no matter what was done for him—he was given a healthy human heart.

That Mr. Creighton received a healthy human heart even though he could not be expected to benefit from it is troubling because of the extreme scarcity of this resource. Although it is difficult to piece together exactly what happened, it appears that the transplant surgeon called the organ allocation hotline and described Mr. Creighton as a top priority patient, meaning that he would surely die if he did not receive a human heart immediately. The problem, however, was that although this was true, it *also* was true that he would almost certainly die if he *did* receive a heart. There is evidence, then, that the allocation of the second human heart to Thomas Creighton was an inefficient and unfair use of this precious resource.

This is not an isolated incident. The case of Bernadette Chayrez, who underwent eight major operations, including two heart transplants and two artificial heart implants, raises similar concerns.

Ms. Chayrez entered University Medical Center in Tucson in January 1986 with a severe case of viral myocarditis. The virus had destroyed about 40 percent of her heart muscle, and her heart could no longer support her other organs. After her liver, kidneys, and lungs began to fail, she was given a mini-Jarvik-7, a smaller version of the well-known and FDA-approved artificial heart. But Ms. Chayrez experienced a considerable amount of internal bleeding, which physicians traced to the artificial heart. Four days after the implantation of the artificial device, it was removed and a human donor heart was transplanted in its place, even though tests indicated that Ms. Chayrez's body still harbored the virus that had killed her own heart. Two days later, Ms. Chayrez's new heart failed, and she was once again put on an artificial device.

The artificial heart never worked well—she continued to suffer severe internal bleeding—but it did keep her alive. She remained tethered to the mini-Jarvik-7 for 240 consecutive days, undergoing in the meantime a series of operations to counteract multiple system failure. At one point, she was on dialysis and a respirator, her spleen ruptured, and she contracted pneumonia. Although she eventually recovered from most of these life-threatening conditions, she was still faced with the awesome combination of a hyperactive immune system (precluding transplantation of a human donor heart) and serious viral infections (precluding her remaining on the artificial device). Ms. Chayrez eventually developed a life-threatening infection around the mechanical heart that physicians were powerless to treat. The decision was made to transplant a human heart into Ms. Chayrez, even though by now the chances of her body's accepting a donor heart were almost zero. Thus no one was very surprised when the donor heart, which was considered to be in excellent condition, failed. Ms. Chayrez was finally allowed to die.

The choice of who is to receive the life-giving scarce resource will always be morally troubling. But some allocation decisions are especially hard to justify and should raise fundamental questions about the present system of allocation. It is almost certain that there was someone in need of a heart transplant who was more likely to benefit from it than Bernadette Chayrez: Approximately one thousand people die each year while awaiting heart transplants. It is very likely that there was someone whose heart had failed who could have benefited from the two hearts that were sacrificed to Ms. Chayrez's virus. Perhaps a young man or woman died because Mr. Creighton, who was no longer a good candidate for transplant, was given a second human heart.

Rationing Available Organs

What transpired in these cases raises a fundamental challenge to the way in which the system of patient classification has worked. In theory, potential recipients were selected according to a standard of medical suitability. Only if the expected benefit (in terms of quality-adjusted life years) exceeded a certain threshold would a patient have been placed on the list of potential recipients. But as we have seen, this did not always work in practice.

One reason was that the system sometimes recognized urgency alone as an appropriate criterion. Those patients who were the sickest, including those who had rejected a transplant and those who had received an artificial heart as a temporary bridge to transplant, were the first in line to get a heart. This criterion of allocation expressed a concern for critically ill patients and an unwillingness to abandon those in greatest need. But it did so at the expense of efficiency because the most urgent cases were less likely to do so well as healthier candidates.

If we assume that human donor organs are a scarce social resource (because of the enormous public support for transplant technology), then inefficient use of these organs as evidenced by these two cases is grounds for an ethical criticism. An allocation system that allows urgency alone to determine priority, without consideration of relative expected benefit, can be expected to waste precious social resources.

It is important to understand, however, that the opposite sort of classification system, one that assigned priority to potential recipients solely on the basis of expected benefit, would be objectionable from the standpoint of fairness, as are strictly utilitarian allocations in general. A system which gives some weight to each individual's medical need, independently of whether satisfying that need will maximize expected benefit, can be seen as an expression of equal respect for persons as such. We have already seen, however, that allocating on this basis alone, without a proper regard for expected benefit, may squander precious resources.

What is required, then, is a set of criteria that takes into account both of these important values: urgency and expected benefit. Reasonable people may disagree, of course, about what the proper trade-off between them is. Indeed, as Dan Brock points out in Chapter 8, "There is no philosophical consensus on any principled account of how this trade-off between fairness and maximizing the good should be made, either in general or in this context in particular." At the very least, however, we need to develop appropriate guidelines that would distinguish urgent cases that are virtually hopeless from those that are not and assign lowest priority to the former. Until more donor organs are made available, it is irresponsible to expend organs on cases where expected benefit is extremely low.

Public Goods Problems

The Creighton and Chayrez cases highlight another problem with the allocation of donor organs: In many centers, the surgeon who sought an organ assigned the priority status to his or her patient, and there was no independent check on the accuracy of this classification. It is not difficult to see that there was a fundamental problem of incentive compatibility built in to the system. The surgeon who took pride in being a single-minded advocate for his or her patient was in effect asked to judge whether that patient should get a scarce resource for which others were in competition. It is undoubtedly socially beneficial to encourage this kind of patient advocacy in physicians, but only if there are institutional constraints to keep it within the bounds of efficiency and equity.

Everyone may agree that no one should take advantage of the organ allocation hot line by inflating one's own patient's case for an organ. Yet without some effective system of sanctions or positive incentives, voluntary compliance with such an "honor system" is likely to founder on the familiar free-rider problem. Further, even the physicians who have no desire to take advantage of the self-restraint of others may be unwilling to put themselves and their patients at a competitive disadvantage if they have no assurance that others will exercise similar self-restraint. In other words, the attainment of a fair and efficient allocation system is a public good in the technical sense. Recognizing this simple point helps direct our attention to a very crucial question: How do we structure the allocation system so that all the participants have the appropriate incentives?

There are a variety of possibilities, of course. A system of checks and balances, in which a transplant surgeon's priority classification of a particular patient would have to be confirmed by a health care professional not personally involved in the patient's care, could be instituted. Or a post hoc review with sanctions might be worthwhile: Organ transplants would be reviewed after the fact, and physicians who repeatedly waste organs would be removed at least temporarily from the list of surgeons to whom human donor organs are distributed.

There was another weakness of the patient selection system that deserves comment: the "territoriality" of the transplant centers. As the past director of organ procurement at the University of Pittsburgh Medical School explained, "In Pittsburgh, we want to use our kidneys for local recipients. That's our basic value judgment."[37] It was very common for transplantable organs to have been considered for local use first and to have been offered to other transplant centers only if there were no suitable local recipients. This meant that a heart that became available in Pittsburgh would have been given to a patient in Pittsburgh who still had a good amount of time to go before a transplant was really necessary, instead of having been sent to Houston or Tucson to save a patient whose time had run out. Thus location, the place of residence of a patient awaiting transplantation or the place of work of the transplant surgeon, may have meant the difference between life and death.

This method might make sense where hearts are involved, as they can be kept viable outside the body for only about four hours. But it is perhaps less justifiable in the case of livers (which can be kept for up to twelve hours) and kidneys (which can be kept for two days). In any case, a patient's place of residence played perhaps too important a role determining his chances of receiving one of these scarce lifesaving resources. This criticism is strengthened by the fact that millions of federal tax dollars—*not* state funds—were spent to develop the technology.

There is one more issue that deserves comment: There has been some indication of unequal and suspect treatment in the selection of patients for transplantation. In Washington, D.C., for instance, approximately 22 percent of the transplants performed using cadaver kidneys in 1985 involved foreign national patients. This rate was considerably higher than the national rate for kidney transplantation into foreign nationals, which was about 5 percent. But it is especially noteworthy for two reasons: (1) a major military hospital located in the District of Columbia refused to accept additions to its waiting list for organ transplants because of the shortage of organs; and (2) the incidence of patients on dialysis in Washington is more than double the national average.[38] One concern here, of course, is that foreign nationals are getting organs that could have gone to U.S. citizens. But another concern is that the majority of people who lost out are those of a particular minority group: black Americans. About 70 percent of the Washington, D.C., population is black, and the rate of end-stage renal disease among blacks is four times that among whites in the United States.

In general, blacks tend to receive proportionately fewer organ transplants than whites. The reasons for this are enormously complex and may have little to do with overt discrimination. Blacks, for instance, are less likely to want a transplant than are whites, and blacks do not do as well as whites after transplantation.[39] Nonetheless, the relatively lower rate of transplantation in blacks is a cause for concern, and much of the answer may lie with the patient selection criteria in general.

A National Organ-Sharing Network

In the fall of 1986, Congress passed important legislation designed to produce a more fair and efficient allocation of transplantable human organs. The new law, which took effect in October 1987, required all hospitals with organ transplantation programs to participate in a national organ-sharing network funded by the federal government. A private, nonprofit organization, the United Network for Organ Sharing (UNOS) is responsible for overseeing the network.

UNOS began by matching patients and donor kidneys according to a computerized point system and intends to widen the system to include other organs as well. Points are given for such things as the amount of time a patient has been on the waiting list for an organ, the closeness of the tissue match, and the distance between the organ and the patient. A patient anywhere in the country who is a perfect match for a particular kidney is considered first for transplantation, and the point system is used to help determine who will get the organ should no perfect match exist.

Because this is a nationwide system in which all transplantation centers must participate, certain failings of the prior rather ad hoc system of matching patients with organs will be mitigated: In theory, all patients will be judged according to the same criteria, organs will not be wasted, and the territoriality of transplant centers will be undermined. The new system cannot guarantee an equitable or efficient allocation of transplantable organs, however, for many of the old pressures and deficiencies still remain. A physician will still be tempted to overstate his or her own patient's case, for instance, and because physicians may override the computer's recommendation, the possibility for unfair discrimination still exists. In addition, it is unclear whether under the new system, a patient who happens to be a perfect match for a particular organ will get that organ regardless of his or her capacity to benefit from it; without proper accord for patient benefit, organs will continue to be wasted. The crux of this last matter lies in the difficulty of determining and applying appropriate criteria that would distinguish between those patients who are indeed medically suitable for a transplant and those who are not.

Medical Suitability

It was mentioned above that organs are (or at least should be) distributed to patients according to strict criteria of medical suitability: that is, according to standards designating who among the large set of patients with organ failure truly needs a transplant (as opposed to some other form of treatment, including palliative care). The need for the transplant is usually based on the ability of the patient to benefit from a transplant. But "need" and "benefit" are often subjective concepts, and as Roger Evans and Christopher Blagg point out in Part Three of this volume, the concepts change as other factors (such as payment mechanisms and availability of the technology) change. Currently, the elderly are often excluded from consideration for transplantation for so-called medical reasons: Either they are not expected to survive the transplant itself, or it is judged that they will not benefit sufficiently from it. Many transplant centers will not accept patients who are over sixty years old, and some refuse patients who are fifty or older.[40] This rule is not inflexible, nor is it universal, and elderly patients have on occasion received transplants. But an age cutoff is used frequently enough to raise concerns regarding fair access to the technology. Even the secretary of the Department of Health and Human Services requested specifically that this issue be examined.[41]

It is important to note, though, that because all of the criteria for medical suitability are based on a concern for patient benefit, none of them are objective. As Daniel Brock explains in Chapter 8, "There are *no* value-neutral selection criteria that could permit bypassing the need to make ethical judgments in the recipient selection process. Notions of 'medical criteria,' 'medical eligibility,' or 'medical need' for treatment, so common in medical practice generally, implicitly embody value judgments when used for determining how a scarce resource like organ transplantation will be distributed." In other words, each criterion employed in the patient selection process requires ethical justification as well as scientific support and should be examined for discriminatory effect.

This is the task of Thomas Overcast and Karen Merrikin, who in Chapter 9 review patient selection criteria in the light of major federal statutes: the Rehabilitation Act of 1973 (which prohibits violations of the rights of the handicapped), Title VI of the Civil Rights Act of 1964 (which prohibits discrimination of the basis of race, color, and national origin in federally assisted programs), and the Age Discrimination Act of 1975.

Their chapter is preceded by Dan Brock's contribution. He explores, analyzes, explains, and evaluates the major ethical issues raised by the necessity of choosing some patients among many to receive this scarce lifesaving technology. In addition to the subject of medical suitability criteria mentioned above, he also addresses the enormously complex issues of the patient's quality of life, the proper trade-off in selection criteria between urgency of need and expected benefit, and fair access to treatment (of both U.S. and foreign nationals).

Notes

1. Roger W. Evans et al., *The National Heart Transplantation Study: Final Report* (Seattle, WA: Battelle Human Affairs Research Centers, 1984), p. 44-10.

2. The Health Care Financing Administration has concluded that "A group of transplant patients will cost the Medicare program less than a group of dialysis patients after four years when considering aggregate costs across the four-year period for the respective groups." Statement of Carolyne Davis, administrator of the Health Care Financing Administration, Hearing Before the Subcommittee on Investigations and Oversight of the Committee on Science and Technology, U.S. House of Representatives, April 13, 14, 17, 1983. See also Jerome Aroesty and Richard A. Rettig, *The Cost Effects of Improved Kidney Transplantation* (Santa Monica, CA: The Rand Corporation, February 1984).

3. R. W. Evans, D. L. Manninen, L. P. Garrison, L. G. Hart, C. R. Blagg, R. A. Gutman, A. R. Hull, and E. G. Lowrie, "The Quality of Life of Patients With End-Stage Renal Disease." *The New England Journal of Medicine* 312: 553–559, 1985.

4. The one-year survival rate for patients who received a kidney from a living, related donor is approximately 97 percent; it is 95 percent for patients who receive a kidney from a cadaver. Task Force on Organ Transplantation, *Organ Transplantation: Issues and Recommendations* (Washington, D.C.: Government Printing Office, 1986), p. 17.

5. Aroesty and Rettig, *Cost Effects*, p. 6.

6. Task Force, *Transplantation*, p. 16.

7. Gallup Organization, Inc. "The U.S. Public's Attitudes Toward Organ Transplant/ Organ Donation," Gallup Survey 1985. Cited in Task Force, *Transplantation*, p. 38. These figures correspond closely with a Gallup poll conducted in 1983 for the National Heart Transplantation Study. This earlier poll indicated that almost 94 percent of the respondents had heard about organ transplantation, but that only 14 percent carried donor cards, and only about 28 percent of those who did not carry a donor card said that they would be willing to do so in the future. Evans et al., *Heart Study*, pp. 17-3–17-17.

8. In 92 percent of states, surgeons require the permission of the family. Thomas D. Overcast, Roger W. Evans, Lisa E. Bowen, Marilyn M. Hoe, Cynthia L. Livak, "Problems in the Identification of Potential Organ Donors," *Journal of the American Medical Association* 251: 1559–1562, 1984.

9. All states subscribe to the cardiopulmonary criterion of death and the majority to the whole-brain criterion of death. Twenty-six states have passed legislation adopting the neurological standard of determining death, and it has been recognized in important court

decisions in six other states. Most (but not all) of these states base their laws on the Uniform Determination of Death Act, which states, "An individual who has sustained either (1) irreversible cessation of circulatory and respiratory functions, or (2) irreversible cessation of all functions of the entire brain, including the brain stem, is dead. A determination of death must be made in accordance with accepted medical standards." Uniform Determination of Death Act, 12 U.L.A. 270 (Supp. 1985). For more on this subject, see Alexander M. Capron, "Anencephalic Donors: Separate the Dead From the Dying." *Hastings Center Report* 17: 5–9, 1987.

10. President's Commission for the Study of Ethical Problems in Medicine and Biomedical and Behavioral Research, *Defining Death: Medical, Legal and Ethical Issues in the Determination of Death* (Washington, D.C.: Government Printing Office, 1981), pp. 23–24.

11. This point has been made by Capron, "Anencephalic Donors."

12. For arguments in favor of a higher-brain concept of death, see Michael Green and Daniel Wikler, "Brain Death and Personal Identity," *Philosophy and Public Affairs* 9: 389–394, 1980; Robert Veatch, "The Whole-Brain Oriented Concept of Death: An Out-moded Philosophical Formulation, *Journal of Thanatology* 3: 13–30, 1975.

13. Joel Feinberg, for instance, has suggested that "In the commonsense way of thinking, persons are those beings who, among other things, are conscious, have a concept and awareness of themselves, are capable of experiencing emotions, can reason and acquire understanding, can plan ahead, can act on their plans, and can feel pleasure and pain." Joel Feinberg, "Abortion," in *Matters of Life and Death*, 2d ed., Tom Regan, ed. (New York: Random House, 1986), p. 262. And Mary Anne Warren proposed the following criteria for personhood: "(1). Consciousness (of objects and events external and/or internal to the being), and in particular the capacity to feel pain; (2) reasoning (the developed capacity to solve new and relatively complex problems); (3) self-motivated activity (activity which is relatively independent of either genetic or direct external control); (4) the capacity to communicate by whatever means, messages of an indefinite variety of types, that is, not just with an indefinite number of possible contents, but on indefinitely many topics; (5) the presence of self-concepts, and self-awareness, either individual or social, or both." Mary Anne Warren, "On the Moral and Legal Status of the Fetus," *The Monist*, January 1973.

14. President's Commission, *Death*, p. 3.

15. Evans et al., *Heart Study*, p. ES-33.

16. Arthur L. Caplan, "Organ Transplants: The Costs of Success." *Hastings Center Report* 13: 23–32, 1983. A similar method was proposed by Arthur J. Matas, John Arras, James Muyskens, Bibian Tellis, Frank Veith, "A Proposal for Cadaver Organ Procurement: Routine Removal With Right of Informed Refusal," *Journal of Health Politics, Policy and Law* 10: 231–244, 1985.

17. Hypoplastic left heart syndrome is a rare defect in which the left side of the heart is unable to pump enough blood to support life for more than a few weeks.

18. "Grandstand Medicine," *Nature* 312: 88, 1984.

19. Peter Singer, *Animal Liberation: A New Ethics for our Treatment of Animals* (New York: Random House, 1975), p. xi.

20. See John C. Fletcher, John A. Robertson, Michael R. Harrison, "Primates and Anencephalics as Sources for Pediatric Organ Transplants," *Fetal Therapy* 1: 150–164, 1986.

21. Fletcher et al., *Sources*, p. 152.

22. W. Holzgreve et al., "Kidney Transplantation From Anencephalic Donors, *New England Journal of Medicine* 316: 1069–1070, 1987.

23. Capron, "Anencephalic Donors," pp. 5–9.

24. Aroesty and Rettig, *Cost Effects*, pp. 6–7.

25. Task Force, *Transplantation*, p. 17.

26. See also S. J. Najarian, M. Strand, D. S. Fryd, R. M. Ferguson, R. L. Simmons, N. L. Ascher, D.E.R. Sutherland, "Comparison of Cyclosporine Versus Azathioprine-antilymphocyte Globulin in Renal Transplantation," *Transplantation Proceedings* 15 (supp. 1): 2463–2468, 1983: "We included kidneys from related and cadaver donors in our trial, and, in the CsA [cyclosporine] group, related donor kidneys had a better survival rate

than cadaveric grafts (94% vs. 83% functioning at 1 year), the same relative difference that occurred in the Aza (azathioprine) group (87% vs. 76%)."

27. For difficulties in obtaining the informed consent of organ donors, see C. H. Fellner and J. R. Marshall, "Kidney Donors—The Myth of Informed Consent," *American Journal of Psychiatry* 126: 1245–1251, 1970; F. J. Ingelfinger, "Informed (But Uneducated) Consent," *New England Journal of Medicine* 287: 465–466, 1972.

28. Jay Katz, "Informed Consent: A Fairy Tale?" *University of Pittsburgh Law Review* 39: 137–174, 1977. The bibliography in this book contains references to an array of works on this subject.

29. As Caplan made clear, the issue of individual autonomy and the importance of informed consent have been central to organ procurement efforts from the very beginning. For other discussions of the importance of informed consent to the medical enterprise, see President's Commission for the Study of Ethical Problems in Medicine and Biomedical and Behavioral Research, *Making Health Care Decisions* (Washington, D.C.: Government Printing Office, 1982); Angela R. Holder, "Informed Consent: Its Evolution," *Journal of the American Medical Association* 214: 1181–1182, 1970; John C. Fletcher, "The Evolution of the Ethics of Informed Consent," in *Research Ethics*, Kare Berg and K. E. Tranoy, eds. (New York: Alan R. Liss, 1983).

30. *Strunk v. Strunk*, 445 SW 2d 145 (1969). Tommy was being dialyzed, but the court found that this procedure could not be continued much longer. A consulting psychiatrist, a representative of the Department of Mental Health, and Jerry's parents all testified in favor of the kidney donation from Jerry. See also *Little v. Little*, 576 SW 2d 493 (1979)— a fourteen-year-old girl with Down's Syndrome was allowed to donate a kidney to her younger brother.

31. *Strunk*, p. 150.

32. William Cook, "Incompetent Donors: Was the First Step or the Last Taken in Strunk v. Strunk?" *California Law Review* 58: 754–774, 1970.

33. Robertson reported this position, did not endorse it; he disagreed with the court's decision in this case. John Robertson, "Organ Donations by Incompetents and the Substituted Judgment Doctrine," *Columbia Law Review* 76: 62, 1976.

34. Allen Buchanan, "Our Treatment of Incompetents," in *Health Care Ethics: An Introduction*, Donald VanDeVeer and Tom Regan, eds. (Philadelphia: Temple University Press, 1987), p. 217.

35. *Howard v. Fulton-DeKalb Hospital Authorities*, 42 USLW 2322 (1973).

36. In one case, a seven-year-old child was judged by a court to be a suitable kidney donor to her twin. In this instance, the court found that the enormous benefit to the recipient of the organ and the consent of the parents, plus the combined approval of the guardian ad litem and the psychiatrist, justified taking the organ from one child in order to benefit another. *Hart v. Brown*, 29 Conn Supp 368, 289 A2d 386 (Super Ct 1972).

37. Donald Denny, "How Organs Are Distributed," *Hastings Center Report* 13: 26, 1983.

38. Office of the Inspector General, DHHS, *The Access of Foreign Nationals to U.S. Cadaver Organs* (Boston, MA, August 1986).

39. See Appendix F of this book for some general statistics regarding blacks with end-stage renal disease. See also Clive O. Callender, ed., "Renal Failure and Transplantation in Blacks" (entire issue), *Transplantation Proceedings* 19(supp. 2): 1986.

40. See, for instance, the contraindications to heart transplantation recommended by the Special Advisory Group of the National Heart, Lung and Blood Institute (Federal Register, 46[14]: 7072–74, Jan. 22, 1981); reprinted here as Appendix C.

41. R. A. Knox, "Heart Transplants: To Pay or Not to Pay," *Science* 209: 570–575, 1980.

4

Organ Procurement in
the Acute Setting

Kenneth V. Iserson

The ambulance speeds through the darkening drizzle, its siren straining to be heard above the rainfall and traffic noises. Blinding flashes of red and white barely pierce the night, while inside desperation impels the frantic paramedics trying to save the dying embers of what had been, all too recently, a dynamic, healthy college student driving to a party.

Strapped down tightly to a rigid board to protect against damaging his spine, with his neck immobilized in hard plastic, the patient lies inert. The medics struggle to place the breathing tube and intravenous fluid lines needed to buy the few minutes it will take to get to the emergency department.

Notified through hurried and breathless radioed messages of the disaster that has befallen the ambulance crew's young patient, the emergency department stands ready. The physicians, nurses, and technicians have all broken away from ministering to the dozens of other patients who have sought help this night. They stand ready to work as a team to restore a life. Their adrenaline flowing, their reasoning clear, their purpose sure—this is why they have dedicated their lives to work in medicine.

The patient, bloodied and disfigured from the terrible injuries to his head, is hurriedly wheeled in to the waiting team. Directed by the physician, each team member acts out his or her well-learned part of the drama. Initial evaluation suggests that there is some hope for life. Physicians and nurses work desperately at each of the patient's arms and legs, attempting to place intravenous lines, used to replace the blood and fluid that he has lost. Endotracheal tubes are placed in the patient's trachea to protect his airway and allow the team to do his breathing for him with a ventilation-assist device. Catheters are placed in his bladder to monitor urinary outflow, in an artery to monitor blood pressure, in his abdomen to check for the presence of bleeding, into his chest cavities to drain blood compressing the lungs, and down his esophagus to drain his stomach. Blood and fluids are instilled as rapidly as possible. Designed to restore the patient's life-giving circulatory volume, the fluid-filled bags are often squeezed by hand to provide the extra pressure needed to get the fluids in just that much faster. Into the mass of activity marked by the beeping of monitors and bustle of the resuscitation team, lab personnel scurry to draw their blood samples, X-ray technicians struggle to get their cumbersome portable machine close enough to the patient to take radiographs of the neck, chest, and pelvis. The struggle to fan the remaining spark of life into a flame, the constant evaluation for signs of improvement, go on for over an hour. But in the end there is no hope.

The severe head injury has, despite treatment, progressed. The heart has stopped. The patient has died. The medical team that had invested its spirit, its energy, its strength to save a life is drained—it has failed.

Relatives and friends of the boy crowd the waiting room. They had sent him off, their pride and joy, just hours ago to a party at a friend's house. Now they await word that these life-givers, these healers, have saved his life and will eventually heal him.

The physician goes out to meet the family. He will tell them that their child is dead. And he was the one who could not save the child's life.

Staff Reaction

The stress, the depression, and the sense of failure evoked by such a scene is a common occurrence in all emergency departments. This, rather than the sterile conference room or lecture hall, is the setting in which organ donation must often be requested. In other situations, death may be expected and in some cases welcomed as a relief from chronic disease and suffering. But traumatic deaths usually occur in young, otherwise healthy, individuals. They come unexpectedly and are disasters to friends and family. To emergency medical personnel, steeled to the constant barrage of pain, blood, and death, it still comes as a shock—death so sudden in the midst of life and death that even their modern miracles of science can not thwart.

The stress the situation places upon both the medical staff and the family colors the entire situation. It acts as a psychological barrier to conveying information not only about organ donation, but also often about the death itself. The latter task is, in some cases, passed on to chaplains, morticians, and others not directly involved with the patient's care. But in most instances, being professionals, the medical staff personally convey to the family the notification of death. They also usually are the ones who broach the subject of organ donation with the family. The question of organ donation, no matter how simplified in the lay literature, and often in the law, is complicated by a heavy emotional overlay on the part of the medical personnel involved.

This case illustrates the most straightforward situation amenable to organ retrieval in the emergency setting. The patient's heart has permanently ceased functioning, and he is clearly dead. However, because the heart is no longer beating, no blood (and therefore no oxygen) is being supplied to the vital organs. Needing a constant supply of oxygen to remain viable (and transplantable), organs such as the kidneys, liver, heart, and pancreas quickly die, and thus cannot be used for transplantation. One of the sad ironies of this situation is that the best organ donor candidates, young, otherwise healthy individuals whose deaths are due to sudden traumas, often cannot donate most of their organs. Instead, only those parts that require minimal oxygen to survive, such as the cornea, skin, bone, and the valves of the heart, can be successfully retrieved for future transplantation.

Yet the greatest need is for donation of the "vital" organs: hearts, lungs, kidneys, and livers. Because these organs cannot be transplanted after they have ceased functioning, they must be harvested from humans who are considered to be dead even though their hearts have not stopped. Such an individual is called "brain dead": His or her brain has permanently ceased functioning even though the heart continues to beat and respirations (oxygenation) are supported by artificial means.

When Is the Patient Dead?

The popular conception of Caesar gasping out his last words before collapsing in death rarely occurs. The uncertain and unknowable chasm of death is normally much more indistinct. Hearts beat on and lungs continue to breath even when only the most basic of the body's reflexes remain active in the hulks of what once were thinking human beings. And with cardiopulmonary resuscitation techniques, many people have been restored to normal lives who were, in fact, clinically dead.[1] These, though, are more than just interesting facts for an intellectual discussion or a new twist for the daily soap operas (they have already been used there). They complicate the entire area of organ retrieval in the emergency setting. And though the lay press, and often the law, denies it, medical realities make the declaration of death very difficult in the acute setting, especially in traumatic deaths.

If death is defined as the absence of cerebral activity, then there is a variety of cases where a patient can be alive and yet appear clinically dead. The most common of these cases involves the presence of drugs in the patient. The drugs, either self-administered or given in the course of resuscitation at the emergency department or in the prehospital care (ambulance) system, can make the determination of death (or life) difficult. Many drugs given in the course of medical therapy can depress the reflexes, such as the pupils' reaction to light, which are used to test activity in the central nervous system. Some medications, including some prescription medications that have been used in suicide attempts, can even "silence" the electroencephalograph (EEG).[2] If any drugs are present that could affect the central nervous system, including alcohol, which is found in most adolescent and adult trauma patients, then a determination of brain death must usually be delayed.

Other factors that can confuse the determination of brain death include hypothermia (a low body temperature) or the presence of hypotension (low blood pressure) during the resuscitation. Patients presenting in hypothermia, seen often in cases of near drowning, may not be breathing (and may, in fact, have been under water more than thirty minutes), have no palpable pulse or blood pressure, and may have no demonstrable activity normally associated with a functioning brain. Yet many of these individuals have survived and gone back to normal activities—including practicing medicine.

Hypotension, another confusing factor, is present during the resuscitation of most trauma patients. (Patients with isolated head injuries may not be hypotensive until either life-support measures are withdrawn or the heart stops.) Following a period of hypotension (or a period of diminished oxygen) the brain may also show markedly diminished activity. This may be clinically indistinguishable from brain death.

The question naturally arises: Aren't there some irreversible injuries? Certainly there are. Decapitation is one, 100 percent third-degree burn is another. Yet individuals who have suffered these injuries seldom are brought to the hospital. Instead, they generally are taken directly to the morgue. Most patients arriving at the emergency department do so to receive treatment. And they receive the best care available. Only when resuscitation attempts have proven to be unsuccessful should organ donation be considered. Even then the utmost care must be taken.

There have been cases, though, in which a patient with severe injuries (that appeared to the clinician to be consistent with brain death) has been designated for potential organ donation, only to be resuscitated by another set of physicians. But this is rare indeed. In the case of the potential organ donor, so much extra care and expertise is brought into play by the requirements of all organ donor protocols that the patient, once entered into a protocol, will always have the benefit of the maximum assessment and resuscitation before being declared brain dead.

The answer then for the clinician working in the emergency department is to defer a decision on brain death until the patient has been observed over a period of time, the vital signs stabilized, and blood toxicology levels determined, with any active substances acting on the central nervous system (brain and spinal cord) given time to metabolize or to be excreted. However, this often means waiting while the heart stops beating adequately, the blood pressure falls, and the irreplaceable organs are rendered useless.

Because the emergency department is usually not equipped or staffed to monitor these patients over extended periods of time, they usually are transferred to the intensive care unit (ICU) of the hospital.

Intensive Care Unit

Very often the patient's heart does not die in the emergency department. Connected to machines to support respirations and monitor vital functions, the prospective organ donor, already suspected of being brain dead (due to the nature of the injury), is transported to the ICU. Nearly 95 percent of the pronouncements of brain death occur in this setting.

Here, the potential donors receive the same care as the other patients in the ICU, even while studies are being conducted to evaluate whether brain death has occurred. Nurses in this setting have the consistent mission of preserving remaining life. The physicians, however, often have the dual and conflicting roles both of preserving life functions and of arranging for tests and consultations designed to determine whether brain death has occurred.

If the patient is being considered as a potential donor or has been determined to be dead, it is the physician's duty, often in concert with the organ bank personnel (but not the transplant team), to request permission from the family for organ donation. In teaching hospitals, this responsibility is often relegated to a junior resident who may not be emotionally prepared to accept this role. In the private hospital, the physician who approaches the family is often the on-duty surgeon or an internist called in to take care of the acute patient.

Although physicians may feel a societal and professional duty to request organ donation from the family, it is an emotionally wrenching experience with little or no reward. Rarely do the transplant surgeons, who forever bemoan the lack of transplantable organs, deign either to thank or to give patient follow-up to the physicians who had requested the organs. In most cases, there is no transplant program at the hospital at which the patient dies. It then is not usually a high priority of either the institution or the medical staff to support the often arduous and time-consuming process of getting the potential organ donor ready for transport to the appropriate transplantation facility or to prepare for the arrival of the transplant team to "harvest" the organs. The latter often takes massive coordination of efforts: Appropriate tests of the compatibility of the various organs with potential recipients must be conducted; appropriate teams connected with these recipients must be contacted; and the necessarily precise timing of the organ retrieval effort must be coordinated. For example, the heart may be removed by a team from another state, the kidneys may go across town, and the corneas may go to a patient at the same institution. Each of these teams must retrieve the organs in a precise order and in a time-efficient manner.

In many areas of the country, with the added publicity given to successful organ transplants, areawide, and in some cases, national networks have been set up to facilitate this process. In the best of cases, a single phone call from the initial attending physician will alert the organ transplant coordinator that a potential donor is present. This individual then is responsible for assuring that the entire protocol involved with the donation, including meeting the criteria for brain death, contacting the appropriate transplant teams, and contacting the family to get permission for the donation, is accomplished. More than seventy organ transplant centers are currently linked through a national computer network to expedite this process.[3] The physician can then continue to direct his or her attention solely to the patient. This type of service exists in most states. But in some cases, especially in smaller locales, the individual who arranges the organ donation may be an employee of one of the transplant teams. In these situations, there is no question that a possible conflict of loyalties exists between working for the best interests of the potential organ donor and those of the potential recipients. Health care workers placed in this situation are acutely aware of the ethical conflicts involved. The direction nationally is to separate the procurement (coordinating) agencies from the transplant teams to reduce these potential conflicts.

But even before the family can agree to donate the organs of a recently deceased relative and before the complex coordinating efforts can begin, another hurdle must be overcome before the organs can reach the patients who so desperately need them. This is a hurdle that only the state legislators can overcome successfully.

Medical Examiner Laws

Of the 20,000 individuals each year in the United States who are potential cadaver donors of perfusable organs (brain dead and meeting transplant criteria), nearly 80 percent have died from a traumatic cause. Many states have enacted laws that give the medical examiner custody of the body of anyone who dies unexpectedly, traumatically, under unusual circumstances, during surgery, or who has not seen a physician within the previous twenty-four hours (i.e., virtually everyone not dying of a chronic disease in a hospital or nursing home). The rationale for such laws is that it is in society's interest to ascertain instances of wrongful death and to determine causes of death. Not only is it for the public good to do so (seatbelts and motorcycle helmets are two results), but it also is important for insurance purposes and legal settlements. However, these laws also have a disadvantage in that they interfere in many jurisdictions with the procurement of organs for transplantation. The problem is that the organs of many deceased patients (those who died after long illnesses, for instance, and those who suffered from most cancers) are in less than optimal condition and cannot be used for transplantation, so the prime organ donors are those who have died from traumatic injuries. Yet their bodies usually are taken by the medical examiners. Although this is not a problem in every state—interpretations of the law can vary, with some medical examiners being quicker to allow organ donation than others—it still acts as a major hindrance to many transplant programs.

The medical examiners (or coroners in some areas) have a defined responsibility to the public to investigate any death not clearly resulting from natural causes (including victims of crimes long past, who die after repeated hospitalizations). Medical examiners are therefore unwilling to release a body under their jurisdiction to be dismembered, as the process may destroy vital information which might be needed in a criminal case. And even when taking organs from the body does not remove evidence, it still may cast doubt on the validity of the evidence obtained subsequent to the organ retrieval.

Better relations between those who desire to harvest organs and medical examiners is not the answer. The medical examiners have a well-defined and important responsibility to the public, and it is reasonable to expect them to fulfill it. Perhaps the answer lies with a specific refinement of the laws. The laws could be designed so that organs may be taken from victims of motor vehicle fatalities, as long as toxicologic specimens, pre-organ-retrieval photographs, and the remainder of the corpse are available for later examination. Hence, the solution lies with state legislators.

Operating Room

If the patient has died from a nontraumatic cause or the medical examiner has given permission for organ donation, the request to the family can proceed.

If the family denies the request, the life-support systems are turned off and the patient is transported to the morgue. If the family agrees to allow the organs to be taken, the donor is wheeled to the operating room (OR), where a whole new set of problems confront the medical personnel involved.

In the OR, the donor appears to be similar to any other patient undergoing general anesthesia: For instance, an anesthesiologist maintains oxygenation while the organs needing perfusion are removed. However, there is an important difference in the way this body is treated from the way other bodies in the operating room are treated. The ventilator is turned off as soon as the vital organs are gone, the anesthesiologist leaves the room, and monitoring is discontinued. Additional organs and tissues are then taken, often with disfiguring of the body (e.g., removal of long bones and skin for tissue banks). In most instances, however, considerable effort is taken to reconstruct the body, to the extent that donation usually does not interfere with even an open casket funeral service. The OR nurses are then left to prepare the body for the morgue.

These are all deviations from the rituals and procedures accepted as norm during major surgery. Death is not accepted graciously when it occurs (rarely) in the OR; it is vigorously battled. Not so in organ donation. Both nurses and physicians often feel shock, discomfort, and guilt when initially participating in these procedures. And yet it has been suggested that they cannot show their "emotional distress, because they worry about its being interpreted as weakness, incompetence, disloyalty, or interference with medical progress."[4]

The Future

It has been understood, at least since 1979, that participation by the entire emergency medical system is necessary to increase the number of cadaver organs available for transplant.[5] And it is becoming clear of late that patients needing transplantation of organs requiring perfusion, especially hearts, do much better with those obtained locally.[6] So it appears that rather than relying on donations from areas of the country that are active in retrieval, all acute care facilities will need to be more actively involved in the organ donation effort. As seen, however, considerable emotional barriers lie in the way of increasing participation.

At the same time, the relatively small amount of preventative medicine that is carried out by acute care specialists (primarily emergency physicians and trauma surgeons) is geared toward legislating public safety measures designed to further reduce the supply of cadaver organs. Such measures include a push for mandatory seat belts and child restraints, installation of air bags in cars, requiring bicycle and motorcycle and All-Terrain Vehicle (ATV) helmet use, banning ATVs altogether, increasing the legal drinking age, tightening up the drunk driving laws, and lowering speed limits.[7]

The problems of personnel stress and dislike for requesting organ donation in patients whom they have failed to resuscitate, the difficulties in declaring death in the acutely ill or injured patient, the societal conflicts inherent in the medical examiner statutes, and the conflicts of duty for the primary care provider can all be resolved. Some can be legislated; others can be lessened through changes in hospital or organ retrieval systems. Yet nothing will happen without a concerted societal interest and effort that will have to transcend the medical community.

Notes

1. Cardiopulmonary resuscitation is a procedure designed to restore life after the heart has stopped. In its most basic form, it involves a combination of chest compression and ventilation of the patient's lungs. Advanced techniques used by trained prehospital (ambulance) and medical personnel include the use of medications and electricity to restore a heartbeat.

2. An electroencephalograph (EEG) is a recording of the electrical activity coming from different areas of the brain. Brain activity is accompanied by specific forms of electrical activity, and these forms will change with injury or disease of the brain. A flat (isoelectric) EEG is often used synonymously with brain death, but this is inappropriate if certain drugs or disease states (e.g., low body temperature) are present.

3. B. Ryon, "Voice Technology: A New Tool in Healthcare," Hospital Topics 64: 33–35, 1986.

4. S. J. Younger, M. Allen, E. T. Bartlett, et al., "Psychosocial and Ethical Implications of Organ Retrieval," New England Journal of Medicine 313: 321–324, 1985.

5. F. C. Whittier, D. R. Boyd, J. Warren, "The Role of the Emergency Medical Services in Organ Donation," Proceedings of the Dialysis Transplant Forum 1980, 155–159.

6. R. W. Emery, R. C. Cork, M. M. Levinson, et al., "The Cardiac Donor: A Six Year Experience," Annals of Thoracic Surgery 41: 356–362, 1986.

7. G. P. Lenehan, "The Gift of Life: Organ Donation and the Emergency Nurse," Journal of Emergency Nursing 12: 189–191, 1986. See also A. S. Levey, S. Hou, H. L. Bush, "Kidney Transplantation from Unrelated Donors: Time to Reclaim a Discarded Opportunity," New England Journal of Medicine 314: 914–916, 1986.

5

Beg, Borrow, or Steal: The Ethics of Solid Organ Procurement

Arthur L. Caplan

The Rapid Evolution of the Field of Solid Organ Transplantation

The first successful solid organ transplant was carried out at the Peter Bent Brigham Hospital in Boston, Massachusetts, in 1954. A kidney was taken from the body of a young patient and implanted into his twin. Throughout the 1950s and well into the 1960s, the majority of kidneys used in transplantation were obtained from living, cosanguinous donors.[1]

Even with the bulk of kidneys coming from related donors, the success rates of the procedure during this period were so poor that some commentators refer to this era as the "black years" of kidney transplantation.[2] Solid organ transplants were, for the most part, restricted to kidneys because in the event of failure, it was possible that the recipient could be placed on the newly developed hemodialysis machine in order to maintain his or her renal function.[3]

By the mid-1980s matters had become very different in the field of solid organ transplantation. More than two-thirds of all kidneys transplanted in the United States are obtained from cadaver sources. Cadaver sources are utilized even more extensively in the many other nations where kidney transplants are performed.[4]

Donors and recipients no longer must be biologically related. Instead they are now matched for tissue type and blood type. Nor must donors and recipients be physically adjacent to one another at the time of transplantation. Kidneys can be shipped vast distances, crossing over state and national boundaries when necessary.

The success rates associated with renal transplantation are quite impressive. The average percentage of patients surviving five years or more with a cadaver kidney exceeds 60 percent. At many transplant centers the survival statistics for those who have received a kidney from a live, related donor exceed 80 percent.[5]

The success of kidney transplantation has been paralleled in many other areas of organ transplantation. The survival rate for those receiving heart transplants exceeds 50 percent at five years postsurgery. Impressive achievements have also been made in transplantation of the liver, heart/lung, and pancreas.

Surgeons are optimistic about the prospect of extending the techniques of solid organ transplantation to the lung and the large intestine.

Major breakthroughs in scientific, technical, and medical areas of transplantation are responsible for the advances of the past three decades. Improvements in the surgical techniques of transplantation, the ability to preserve organs outside the body for brief periods of time, the capacity for maintaining bodily functions by means of artificial life-support technologies, the ability to determine antibody and blood types from small tissue samples, the growing confidence with which physicians can diagnose brain death, and the emergence of powerful immunosuppressive drugs such as azathioprine and cyclosporine have been responsible for the rapid expansion in both the number and kind of transplants that are now being performed.

The ability of transplantation teams at many medical centers in the United States and, indeed, around the world, to succeed at extending life beyond the onset of organ failure has commanded a great deal of attention from those outside the field of transplantation. Difficult questions concerning the need to advance further the art of transplantation relative to other pressing health care problems, the importance of providing equitable access to existing transplant centers, the criteria that ought to be invoked in determining who should receive a transplant, and the most efficient means for providing transplantation services to those who require them have occupied a prominent place in both legislatures and the media.

Perhaps the most pressing policy issue facing both those within and outside of the field concerns the shortage of organs available for transplantation to those with end-stage organ failure. A great deal of debate, discussion, legislation, and regulation among many different elements within U.S. society has been directed at the question of whether and how to increase the supply of organs for transplantation. Because the number of organs available is, in large measure, now determined by the number of cadaver donors and because the need for organs has grown and continues to grow at a staggering pace, with thousands awaiting a kidney, heart, or liver, ethical and policy issues related to organ procurement currently command a high profile among the many issues raised by organ transplantation today.

The Centrality of Autonomy and Voluntarism in Organ Procurement in the United States

The relatively rapid increase in the success with which solid organs can be transplanted between human beings somewhat obscures the ethical and legal controversies that characterized the field when it first emerged in the late 1950s. Those involved in the development of kidney transplantation were confronted with a series of moral objections that bear an uncanny resemblance to many of the moral controversies that currently swirl about the development of the artificial heart, xenografting, and pharmaceutical agents and vaccines intended to combat the epidemic of Acquired Immune Deficiency Syndrome today.[6]

The earliest days of kidney transplantation involving human subjects were characterized by the inability of transplant surgeons to overcome the problem of organ rejection. Many approaches to the problem were tried, including various drugs and massive exposure to total body irradiation, but none proved effective. Many physicians, knowing that little could be done should rejection take place, felt that it was unethical to offer kidney transplants to patients.[7] Others within and outside medicine worried about the advisability of developing transplantation as the intervention of choice for kidney failure. Some favored putting social resources into the development of artificial kidneys. Still others argued for prevention or for the use of public moneys for other purposes for which established therapies already existed.[8]

Courts and legislative bodies were confronted with the need to address themselves to protecting the interests of both donors and recipients who might become involved with this evolving technique. As surgeons were almost entirely dependent upon live donations in order to attempt kidney transplants, one of the major concerns of courts and government was to assure that the interests and welfare of prospective donors were adequately considered by those involved in or seeking transplants.

During this early period, U.S. courts indicated that it was permissible for a competent adult to decide to give a kidney to a family member. The possibility of providing a lifesaving organ to a family member seemed to outweigh the risks to personal health that were involved in the donation of a kidney. Even though the chances of the operation's succeeding were small, the courts were of the view that a decision to help a family member ought be respected as long as that decision was based upon an informed, voluntary choice on the part of the donor.

The courts of this era were particularly concerned about the voluntary nature of decisions to donate. This was a result of three factors. First, there were serious if small risks associated with the surgery to remove a kidney. Second, those making donations seemed particularly vulnerable to coercion in that the people who needed the organs were biological relatives. Third, in some cases children or adults or children afflicted with certain physical or mental impairments that might adversely limit their decision-making capacities were asked to consider donation.

It is not surprising that the legal system during this era based solid organ donation on autonomous choice. The courts believed that the welfare of those confronted with the option of donating a kidney could best be protected by insisting that decisions be made in an informed, uncoerced manner by those competent to do so. Autonomy and voluntarism became the ethical linchpins of organ procurement and have remained so.

The Uniform Anatomical Gift Act and Donor Cards

In the 1960s a number of technological and pharmaceutical advances occurred that allowed transplant surgeons to alter the composition of sources for solid organs. Respirators and heart/lung bypass machines allowed physicians to maintain physiological functions in cadavers when all brain activity had ceased. New immunosuppressive agents permitted the transplantation of solid organs between non–biologically related donors and recipients. And methods that allowed for the retrieval and storage of kidneys for short periods of time evolved.

These developments led to pressures to reexamine traditional definitions of death based upon the cessation of cardiac and respiratory functions. The concept of brain death was advanced in part in response to the urgings of members of the transplantation community who sought ways of making viable organs available from cadaver sources. At the same time, a number of proposals were advanced concerning the nature of public policies that ought to govern the procurement of organs from cadaver sources.

By the late 1960s many of the limitations that had characterized solid organ transplantation in the 1950s no longer existed. Solid organs could be obtained from both the living and the dead. It was no longer necessary that donors and recipients be in the same hospital or medical center in order for transplantation to occur. Congenital biological differences were no longer an absolute prohibition to successful solid organ transplantation. The success rates associated with transplantation of the kidney had undergone marked improvement. Transplant surgeons were beginning to experiment with the transplantation of other solid organs, such as the heart and the liver.

These relatively rapid developments required a new public policy capable of guiding health care professionals, prospective donors, families, and prospective recipients in the procurement of organs. A variety of possible policy approaches were advanced.

One option, favored by such persons as Paul Ramsey, Jay Katz, Alfred and Blair Sadler, and many others, was to increase voluntary, autonomous donation by not only procuring organs from the living but also harvesting organs from the dead. The method for assuring that organ procurement was sensitive and respectful of the autonomous choices of individuals was the donor card.

If people could be encouraged to consider, while alive, organ donation upon their demise, they could indicate their interest by means of a donor card. The donor card would serve as a version of what we have now come to recognize as a "living will." Although no one would be obligated either to be a donor or to carry a donor card, those who wished to serve as a cadaver donor could so indicate by means of a card that would, in turn, constitute a legally binding directive upon family members and health care professionals.

A second option that was advanced at the time was adopting a policy of presumed consent.[9] It was argued that organs could routinely be harvested from cadavers as long as an opportunity was presented to family members to refuse donation if they believed the deceased would have had objections to serving as an organ source. As long as adequate protections were offered for allowing persons to "opt out" of donation, a presumed consent policy would yield more organs than a public policy that required individuals to "opt in" through the use of a donor card.

Critics of presumed consent argued that allowing the state to grant authority to the medical teams simply to take organs from cadavers raised such danger of violating individual preferences that the adoption of this policy could not be justified. Moreover, some commentators argued that it was ethically preferable to ground organ procurement on the norm of altruism rather than utility.[10] Giving was morally preferable to taking where human beings and their bodies were concerned.

Presumed consent ultimately foundered as a result of the pragmatic claim that a policy encouraging the use of donor cards ought to be tried before a more drastic policy was instituted. If respecting autonomy and encouraging altruistic behavior were worthwhile values for public policy to articulate, then an approach to cadaver organ procurement that reflected these values was deserving of at least a trial run.

Why did autonomous choice retain its centrality for guiding the procurement of organs? In part, autonomy was viewed as an important protection against abuse or coercion either of potential donors while alive or of family members once a death had occurred. By requiring prior consent, those who favored a public policy of voluntarism hoped to ensure that the individuality and dignity of the donor would be protected against professional or community interests in obtaining organs. Distrust of the medical profession's motives, combined with a desire to balance the utilitarian benefits of efficient organ procurement against the need to affirm the rights and dignity of the individual produced a special emphasis on voluntarism and altruism as key values that had to be nurtured if individual autonomy was to be given adequate weight in public policy.

Concerns about abuse were also based on the discovery that some medical examiners had, during the 1960s, surreptitiously removed tissues from cadavers without obtaining either the prior written consent of the donor or the consent of family members. Some advocates of the importance of autonomy maintained that a public policy that failed to emphasize this value risked sacrificing the rights of those members of society who, on religious grounds, opposed organ donation.

Contrary to popular belief, efforts to enact a Uniform Anatomical Gift Act and to legitimize the use of donor cards as a means of permitting organ donation from cadaver sources were not based upon a desire to increase or enhance the efficiency of solid organ procurement. Those who favored voluntaristic policies rather than a policy of presumed consent acknowledged that the latter was more likely to increase the supply of organs available for transplantation. The movement that resulted in the adoption of the Uniform Anatomical Gift Act in all states during the late 1960s and early 1970s was fueled by a distrust of those involved in organ procurement and a desire to ensure that individual autonomy would be respected in the process of obtaining organs. As was the case with respect to the norms governing human experimentation, which were evolving about the same time as the debate on cadaver organ procurement, the dignity of the individual was held to be of more moral worth than the needs or interests of the community.

The Maturation of Solid Organ Transplantation and the Inadequacy of Simple Voluntarism in Organ Procurement

As solid organ transplantation continued to evolve throughout the 1970s, it became increasingly clear that the laws and regulations enacted under the aegis of the Uniform Anatomical Gift Act were not providing a sufficient number of solid organs for those in need of transplants. Waiting lists at transplant centers of people requiring kidneys, hearts, livers, and other organs and organ combinations grew at a rapid pace. Both heart and liver transplantation achieved rates of success sufficient to persuade both health care providers and third party payers that they were legitimate therapeutic options for the treatment of end-stage cardiac and liver disease in many patients.

By the early 1980s the shortage of organs for transplantation had grown to crisis proportions. The desperate plight of patients and families begging for organs in the media and before state and federal legislatures made plain the level of suffering caused by the inability of a public policy based upon voluntary donation through donor cards to provide an adequate supply of solid organs. Although obvious limits existed as to how many donors would be available at any given time, the consistent failure of the donor-card-based system to obtain organs from more than 10 percent of possible cadaver donors led to a renewed and oftentimes heated discussion of policy options regarding organ procurement.

During the 1980s presumed consent enjoyed something of a revival among those interested in the ethics and politics of organ procurement.[11] Proponents renewed their claims that a policy of presumed consent was compatible with the moral obligation society has to respect the religious and personal beliefs of those opposed to serving as the source of organs and with the overall social goal of maximizing the number of organs for transplantation.

A second approach to organ procurement that gained both adherents and notoriety was the creation of a market in cadaver organs. A number of individuals and companies announced their intention to create brokerage firms that would, for a fee, match donors with recipients. The proposed arrangements were relatively straightforward. Donors would be recruited both in the United States and in foreign countries. Only donations involving replenishable tissues or paired organs were to be accepted from living donors. Potential sellers of nonrenewable organs would be free to negotiate contractual arrangements while still alive, and firms would do business with the families of those who had died under circumstances that permitted the harvesting of organs.

Somewhat less dramatic were proposals involving the creation of various tax incentives aimed at encouraging donation. Such proposals would circumvent the need to involve the services of brokers or intermediaries, while retaining the advantages imputed to the incentives of the market.

Neither of these approaches generated a great deal of enthusiasm on the part of policymakers. The case for instituting an open market in organs foundered in part on the fact that the character of some of those who announced their intentions of entering into such arrangements was, at best, highly dubious. Arguments to the effect that a market in organs would result in the exploitation of the poor by the rich or provide incentives to conceal health problems among sellers that might threaten the well-being of transplant recipients also were effective in discouraging a policy based on a market approach.

The case for presumed consent encountered a very different sort of problem— one based on empirical facts rather than moral niceties. Although common sense would suggest that a policy allowing routine harvesting of organs would produce more organs than one depending on autonomous decisions to opt for organ donation, the experience of countries that had adopted policies of presumed consent did not conform to expectations. Rates of donation in European countries with policies of presumed consent, such as France, were not significantly higher than those that prevailed in the United States.[12] Physicians and hospital personnel were reluctant, despite the enactment of laws granting them authority to remove organs and tissues unless an objection was made, to do so without explicit permission from family members. In practice, organ procurement in nations with presumed consent policies followed voluntaristic, altruistic models along U.S. lines.

A third policy option was devised that aimed at preserving the long-standing commitment to autonomous choice in the United States while at the same time ensuring that individuals and families were presented with the option of cadaver organ donation. Referred to as required request or routine inquiry, this policy urged the enactment of state laws requiring that the families of prospective donors be approached at the time death was pronounced about the possibility of organ donation.[13] Those making requests were to receive appropriate training in order to act in a sensitive and informed manner.

Required request was the policy approach seized upon by both the health professions and policymakers as the most attractive organ-procurement reform.

As of June 1987 thirty-eight states had adopted versions of required request. A federal regulation, which took effect in October 1987, made required request a condition for Medicare eligibility.

Required request was enthusiastically endorsed by the transplant community and politicians for a variety of reasons. As was true in an earlier decade with the enactment of versions of the Uniform Anatomical Gift Act, required request appeared to be an incrementalist policy option that was far less radical than either the creation of a market in body parts or the enactment of presumed consent. Required request placed the burden of offering the option of donation on health care providers while retaining the traditional value emphasis on altruism and voluntarism where individual donors and families of donors were concerned. The policy seemed to be respectful of autonomous choice while at the same time likely to elicit and encourage altruistic behavior on the part of potential donors and their families.

It is too soon to tell whether required request policies will prove effective both in respecting the autonomy of prospective donors and in securing increases in needed organs. Early information concerning increases in organ and tissue donation is hopeful, but insufficient time has passed to assess the degree to which the medical professions, schools, and government are willing to comply with the required request laws.

However, it can reasonably be predicted that if required request policies fail to increase considerably donations from cadaver sources, the debate begun in the late 1960s about the ethics of organ procurement will quickly reopen.[14] Although there is no reason to expect that the need for such a debate will again arise, it might be prudent to consider a few ethical arguments concerning policy alternatives on the chance that further public discussion and legislation may eventually be called for.

Good and Bad Moral Arguments Concerning Policy Options for Organ Procurement

Markets in Cadaver Organs: Pros and Cons

Many commentators believe that the creation of a market in organs would provide the requisite incentives for assuring that an adequate supply of organs would be available for transplantation. Proponents of such a view note that U.S. society already tolerates the commercial sale of human materials with respect to sperm, blood plasma, and some cell lines. They also note that whereas surgeons, hospitals, procurement agencies, and other third parties are reimbursed for the costs associated with transplantation, those who provide organs are the only group prohibited by federal and in some cases state laws from being reimbursed for their services. Because prospective donors and their families would be free to make voluntary donations even if a market were created, proponents of a market in cadaver organs argue that it is both inequitable and coercive to restrict the freedom individuals have to contract for commercial consideration where their bodies are concerned.

A number of arguments have been raised against the desirability of creating a market in organs. Some critics note that if a market were to be created it would have the unsavory consequence of encouraging the less affluent to sell their organs to those who could afford to pay for them. If markets were extended to include sellers from any nation, then those in underdeveloped nations would in all likelihood become the source of many of the organs used in transplantation in the United States.

A somewhat related objection to the creation of a market in organs from cadaver sources is based upon the experience with the sale of whole blood during the 1950s and 1960s. Critics note that the creation of a market in whole blood encouraged those with health problems not to disclose them in order to remain eligible for reimbursement for their blood. The incentives of the market not only encouraged blood donation but also resulted in a lowering of the quality of blood that was collected.[15]

The final ethical reservation that seems to characterize objections to the creation of a public policy that would tolerate the existence of a market in cadaver organs is that it seems morally wrong to allow individuals to sell portions of their bodies in advance of their deaths or for their families or guardians to do so after a death has occurred.

It is important to note in considering the ethics of the market where organs are concerned that little data exist to support the claim that markets are incompatible with safety in the procurement of organs. Recent studies have not found significant correlations between disease and the absence or presence of a market in blood banking.[16] Hepatitis appears to have more to do with racial and ethnic identities of donors than whether or not they were paid for their blood.

Arguments about the moral inequities that would arise from a situation in which the poor were exploited by the rich ring a bit hollow in a world in which huge economic differences are a constant fact of life. Although there may be reasons of safety to discourage the sale of organs from living donors, allowing a market in organs from cadavers would only be exploitative if the poor did not feel that the rich were willing to compensate them for what they felt their organs were worth. Arguments about exploitation of the poor smack a bit of a kind of class snobbery in which the poor are only entitled to engage in the kind of commercial activity that the rich find aesthetically or morally acceptable. It is hard to see why the dignity of the poor would necessarily be jeopardized by creating public policies that allowed for the sale of body parts from the dead, either rich or poor.

What is more problematic is whether adequate policing could ensure that those who serve as cadaver donors enter into such a state as a result of natural processes. It currently costs less than five hundred dollars to arrange a murder for hire in many large urban areas of the United States. A cadaver with marketable kidneys and other organs could be worth far more.

A somewhat neglected ethical reason for concern about market solutions to the problem of increasing organ procurement from living or cadaver sources is the adverse impact a market might have on the public's perception of and trust in the medical profession. Healers depend on trust to secure information and even access to patients. If medical personnel were to acquire a public reputation as a profession willing to profit from body parts, this image might damage the willingness of the public to trust in their health care providers. It is hard enough to get the public to trust physicians who drive expensive cars. It would be worse if the public believed those cars were paid for by parts obtained at death from their patients and sold for profit on the open market.

Presumed Consent Policies

The primary moral argument against an opt-out or presumed consent policy is that it will not adequately protect the rights of minorities who are opposed to donation. But such an objection ought not be taken seriously. It would be simple enough to construct a policy wherein prospective cadaver donors would only be utilized when consent had been obtained from a family member or guardian. The burden of objecting would be put on the family member or guardian, but the rights of all citizens could be protected simply by refusing to utilize as donors any cadavers for which no relatives could be located.

Ironically, some states have adopted policies that are precisely the opposite of that described above. Organs and tissues can be removed from unclaimed bodies in some cities and states after a reasonable effort has been made to locate next of kin. It should be noted, however, that in every case in which such procurement is legal, procurement must follow a mandatory autopsy. Nonetheless, it does seem strange that the only arena in which public policy has evolved toward presumed consent in the United States is for unclaimed cadavers.

To some extent the answer to the shortage of organs may not lie simply in modifying public policy to allow for a free market in organs or presumed consent. Neither of these policies is guaranteed to increase the supply of organs available and both have significant problems both ethical and practical.

Expanding the Definition of Donor

It may be that public policy could still respect the values of free choice, autonomy, and altruism if efforts were made to revise the definition of donor that presently prevails within the transplant field. Currently, only those declared dead by competent medical experts can serve as the source of vital organs. In most states this means that a declaration of brain death must precede organ procurement.

But there are human beings who could be used as donors who do not meet this standard of donorship. Anencephalic infants, who suffer from a terminal, massive neurological defect, are one such group. Abortuses, either from elective or spontaneous abortions, are another. Yet a third group are those persons who are dead on arrival at hospitals. It may not be possible to save them, but resuscitation may restore sufficient vital function to allow organs to be harvested. And a fourth group are those who are in a permanent vegetative state—not dead but irreversibly unconscious and insensate.

Little debate has focused on the moral merits of expanding the definition of donorship. So much effort has gone into the effort to link brain death with the definition of cadaver organ donor that it may be difficult to rouse the transplant community or the public to embrace enthusiastically the emotionally disturbing issue of who ought be allowed to serve as a donor. But this may be the most important direction for public policy debate in light of the problems that loom for those who favor further modifications in the overall organ-procurement policies.

Notes

1. Renee C. Fox and Judith P. Swazey, *The Courage to Fail*, 2d ed. (Chicago: University of Chicago Press, 1978).

2. Fox and Swazey, *Courage*, p. 71.

3. F. Moore, "Medical Responsibility for the Prolongation of Life," *Journal of the American Medical Association* 206: 384–386, 1968.

4. Arthur L. Caplan, "Organ Procurement: It's Not in the Cards," *Hastings Center Report* 13: 23–32, 1983.

5. American Council on Transplantation, Personal Communication, January 8, 1987.

6. Arthur L. Caplan, "Ethical Issues Raised by Research Involving Xenografts," *Journal of the American Medical Association* 254: 3339–3343, 1985.

7. Moore, "Responsibility."

8. Fox and Swazey, *Courage*.

9. Jesse Dukeminier and David Sanders, "Organ Transplantation: A Proposal for Routine Salvaging of Cadaver Organs," *New England Journal of Medicine* 279: 413–419, 1968.

10. William F. May, "Attitudes Toward the Newly Dead," *Hastings Center Studies* 1: 3–13, 1973; Paul Ramsey, *The Patient as Person* (New Haven: Yale University Press, 1970).

11. Arthur L. Caplan, "Organ Transplants: The Costs of Success," *Hastings Center Report* 13: 23–32, 1983; C. Dougherty, "Body Futures: The Case Against Marketing Human Organs," *Health Progress* 68: 51–56, 1987; James Muyskens, "An Alternative Policy for Obtaining Cadaver Organs for Transplantation," *Philosophy and Public Affairs* 8: 88–99, 1978.

12. Caplan, "Organ Procurement."

13. Caplan, "Organ Procurement."

14. Dougherty, "Body Futures."

15. Alvin W. Drake, S. N. Finkelstein, and H. M. Sapolsky, *The American Blood Supply* (Cambridge, MA: MIT Press, 1982).

16. Drake et al., *Blood*.

6

Relaxing the Death Standard
for Organ Donation
in Pediatric Situations

John A. Robertson

A major ethical and legal constraint in organ procurement is the requirement that organs be removed only from dead patients. Although kidneys and bone marrow are obtained from living donors, the dead donor rule controls procurement of hearts, livers, and most kidneys. Brain-death tests of death, which permit removal of organs from heart-beating but brain-dead sources, allow efficient organ retrieval to occur in a manner consistent with the dead donor rule.

The shortage of pediatric organs for transplant now forces us to consider whether the dead donor rule should be strictly adhered to in all circumstances. Several pediatric situations arise in which viable organs can be obtained only from persons who are irreversibly comatose and near death but who do not yet satisfy brain criteria of death. One such situation obtains with pediatric patients who appear to be brain dead, but because of the uncertainty of brain-death diagnosis in infants and children, have not been used as cadaveric organ sources. Similarly, anencephalic newborns cannot now be sources of organs for transplant, as they still have brain-stem function.

Because public confidence that organ donation does not harm or slight the interests of donors is crucial for our voluntary system of organ procurement, it is with much trepidation that I raise the question of altering the dead donor rule in order to facilitate organ procurement. The taboo against using nondead donors is so strong that any discussion of altering the rule could stimulate fears (reflected in novels and films such as *Coma*) that organs will be taken from vulnerable living patients and thus discourage organ donation.

Yet the needs of children with end-stage organ disease and of parents faced with near-brain-dead infants present a strong case for assessing the merits of continued adherence to the dead donor rule. The potential use of anencephalic newborns as organ sources illustrates the need for such a reassessment.

The 2,000–3,000 anencephalic infants born each year could be an important source of organs for a variety of perinatal and pediatric conditions, possibly

A similar version of this chapter will appear in Howard H. Kaufman, ed., *Pediatric Brain Death* (New York: Plenum Press, forthcoming).

saving the lives of infants who would otherwise die. Parents of anencephalics are increasingly requesting that their organs be used for transplant. If anencephalic infants are to be a source of viable organs, it may be necessary to remove organs before brain-stem function ceases. Yet since brain-stem function remains, anencephalics are not yet legally brain dead and cannot be used under existing law. The dead donor rule would have to be changed to permit use of anencephalic organs.[1]

Given the great utility of anencephalic organs to recipients and their families and the meaning that the parents of anencephalic newborns would derive from donation, it is appropriate to examine more closely the reasons for adherence to this rule in the case of anencephaly and other situations of near death.

Limiting Conditions for Relaxing the Dead Donor Rule

To highlight the significant value issues, let us consider a situation that meets the following restrictive conditions. First, the family has freely and knowingly consented to the donation and has on its own requested that the anencephalic child's organs be donated to other needy children so that some good may emerge from the family's own personal tragedy. The attending physician has had no part in the family's discussion of donation with organ procurement and transplant personnel.

Second, organ removal before total brain death is the only way to assure a viable heart, liver, or kidney for transplant. If waiting for the cessation of brain-stem function were to enable the organs to be used, then there would be no need to violate or change the dead donor rule. In the situation envisaged, however, this alternative does not exist.

Third, the use of the anencephalic organ is essential to save the life of the prospective pediatric recipient. Sufficient research has occurred to establish that transplant of the anencephalic heart, liver, or kidney is a safe and effective therapy for the recipient and will enable him or her to have an otherwise normal life. No other organs are available and temporary therapies are no longer efficacious.

Fourth, the diagnosis of anencephaly is accurate to a high degree of medical certainty. The diagnosis has been made according to a consensus protocol agreed on by leading medical experts in the field. Three physicians have confirmed that the potential donor clearly fits the diagnostic category.

If these four conditions are met, should removal of the anencephalic organs before brain-stem function ceases be permitted? That is, should the dead donor rule—a legal requirement that would bar use of anencephalic organs before brain-stem function ceases—be relaxed in this situation to permit the desired organ donation and transplant to occur?

A change in the law to permit the use of anencephalic organs in this situation could occur in one of two ways. The law could be changed by redefining brain death to mean cortical or upper-brain death rather than the total absence of brain activity, including brain-stem activity, as the law now states. For example, Veatch and others have argued for brain death to be redefined as cortical death, which would thus preserve the rule that only dead persons may be an organ source.[2]

An alternative approach would keep brain death as total brain death and address directly the legality of relaxing or altering the dead donor rule in the situation described above. If the dead donor rule is to be altered, this approach would seem to be preferable. As Alexander Capron has pointed out, "Adding anencephalics to the category of dead persons would be a radical change, both in the social and medical understanding of what it means to be dead and in the social practices surrounding death."[3] Relaxing the dead donor rule will also have complications, but they will be fewer than would occur through reaching the same result by redefining death.

What then are the arguments against relaxing the rule in these cases? Two concerns—the interests of the donor and the interests of others and society—need analysis.

The Dead Donor Rule
and Harm to the Organ Source

A major reason for the requirement that the organ donor be dead is to protect the donor from being harmed by organ removal. If the donor is dead, taking his organs will not harm him. In contrast, if he or she is alive, it is assumed that removing organs will kill or otherwise injure the donor.

This view of the dead donor rule, however, assumes that the live donor has interests in continued living and in not being physically injured. Whereas this assumption is true in most instances and thus should be strictly followed, it may not apply to situations of irreversible coma, near-dead pediatric patients and anencephalics.

Such patients, though legally still alive, may no longer have interests in living or in avoiding physical harm that should be respected. Consider first the situation in which an organ or tissue is removed without causing brain death, as would occur with removal of bone marrow or a kidney for transplant from an anencephalic newborn. Such infants are not sentient and thus would not be harmed by the surgical intrusion. Indeed, even removing a kidney would not harm the source. Such patients lack interests that can be harmed by nonlethal organ or tissue removal.

A similar conclusion should follow even if organ retrieval directly caused death, as would occur if the heart or liver were taken from an anencephalic newborn to transplant to another infant. It is widely accepted that all sustaining medical treatments, including nutrition and hydration, can be withheld from anencephalic patients.[4] Because they will not recover and while still alive have none of the experiences that make living a good for them, it may reasonably be said that they have no further interest in living. Therefore they may be allowed to die by having treatment withheld. Indeed, some people would recognize a societal duty or moral obligation to withhold treatment in order that they might die.

If anencephalic infants have no interest in living and thus no right to be treated, it is unclear how actively causing their death by organ removal injures them any more than passive killing by withholding treatment would. Active killing by organ removal does not harm the anencephalic infant or violate its right to life because it has no further interest in living and thus would no longer have a right to life. Thus concern for the rights and welfare of the organ source cannot justify the dead donor rule with anencephalic organ sources. (In arguing against use of anencephalic donors because they are "the most vulnerable patients," Professor Capron has assumed without analysis that they have interests to protect, when that is the very issue that needs to be addressed.)[5]

Some people, however, might argue that anencephalic infants still have an interest in being treated with dignity and with respect and that removing their organs or tissue before death violates the dignity or respect owed all living human subjects. Indeed, the law would still treat them as legal subjects and at the present time might treat organ removal causing brain death as homicide. Yet if anencephalics lack all cognitive capacity, have no interest in further living, and are insensate, it is difficult to see how they retain an interest in being treated with dignity or retain other interests that the law should protect. Cortical death with some remaining brain-stem function deprives them of all interests, including the interest in being treated with dignity.

In sum, viewing the matter from the perspective of anencephalic patients, it is difficult to see how their interests can be harmed by tissue or organ removal before total brain death. It may be that they are still legally alive, but a requirement that they be dead before organ removal cannot be justified as necessary to protect their interests. They fall into the class of living, human entities who lack interests that must be protected. Protecting their interests thus does not justify foreclosing this source of organ donations in the situations described.

Of course, the need to treat vulnerable, incompetent patients with dignity and respect is an important societal or community concern. But it is a concern of society—of other persons—and not of the irreversibly comatose or near-dead patient himself. Societal interests, rather than the interests of the cortically dead but living patient, must then be examined to understand the dead donor rule.

Harm to Others and the Dead Donor Rule

Surely society has an interest in how we treat near-dead but living persons, even if they no longer have interests that require protection. Two kinds of societal interests exist in such situations.

Slippery Slopes and Loose Categories

A major societal concern in such near-death situations is restricting the proposed practice to organ sources that clearly lack interests at the time of removal, thus preventing the practice from spilling over to incompetent patients who retain interests in avoiding pain, death, and undignified treatment.

Although often presented as a slippery slope problem, this concern is more accurately viewed as a problem of loose categorization. The danger in accepting a category of living human subjects who lack interests and thus may be used as an organ source is that this category will not be defined carefully and strictly enough to confine the practice to those for whom it is justified.

The danger here is not that we will become so inured to removing organs from live persons that anyone in the hospital will become fair game for the organ procurement team. Rather, the danger is that the category will defy strict specification and spill over to less clear cases. These cases might include persons who have real interests in avoiding pain and in staying alive, even though they have severely diminished capacities and are not competent to make choices concerning their treatment. If taking organs before death from some clear cases will inevitably lead to removal in nonjustifiable cases, then the interest of those persons who are erroneously included in the category argues against it.

Although the risk of loose and inaccurate categories cannot be ignored, the power of this concern depends on how likely the risk is. No program of removing organs from near-dead persons should begin until this danger has been thoroughly examined and negated, as the restrictive conditions set out above attempt to do. It may be that the categories can be defined strictly enough to dispose of this risk. For example, better tests of pediatric brain death will greatly reduce the risk that near-dead infants with valid interests will be used as organ sources. Similarly, criteria for defining anencephaly can also be tightened, and diagnostic safeguards built in to assure that it is a true case of anencephaly rather than a case of microcephaly, hydraencephaly or other conditions that do not justify treatment similar to that of anencephaly. The mere risk of error and mistake should not prevent such schemes if reasonably tight safeguards and procedures for applying the criteria have been adopted, any more than the risk of misdiagnosis prevents taking organs from brain-dead adults.

Use as a Mere Means: Taking Organs Without Causing Death

A second major societal concern arises from the symbolic or cultural meaning of using people in this way. This concern has two components. One is the mere use of the incompetent as means to the utility of others, which arises whether or not organ removal causes the organ source's death. The second component of concern arises when procurement itself actively causes the death of the organ source.

The first aspect of this symbolic concern is the violation of human dignity that some persons perceive in any use of a living human subject to advance the good or interest of others. Although the organ source has no interests being harmed, it appears that he or she is being used as a means to the good of others. In this instance the good advanced is that of the recipient and his or her family, as well as that of the family who request that the organs be used.

Some persons would object to use of anencephalic or other near-dead subjects in this way, since it apears to denigrate their worth and to exhibit a crass willingness to use others as a mere means. Treating near-dead subjects as organ sources, even with consent of family, might be perceived as a violation of community norms of respect for persons.

Such objections arise frequently in medical ethical discussions. They reflect a principle of Kantian ethics that makes some sense when applied to rational, autonomous beings, if the consent of those beings to the use is missing.[6] However, it is not a compelling objection (other than in some symbolic sense) when the subject used is not harmed by the intervention in question. Indeed, established practices in a wide variety of circumstances show societal willingness to use both competent and incompetent subjects to advance the interests of others. The key ethical question in such cases is whether a competent subject has consented to such use or if incompetent to decide, whether the use harms or benefits him or her.

The debate over use in research of children who are incompetent to consent illustrates the issue. The policy position that emerged from the famous McCormick-Ramsey debate was that children could with parental consent be used in research that might benefit them or if no therapeutic benefit was likely, research that posed minimal risk.[7] The mere fact of use to aid others was deemed ethically acceptable if no harm to the subject would occur and a benefit to others could be shown. Similarly, bone marrow and kidneys may be taken from children and incompetent patients if they derive a net benefit from the donation, for example, are not harmed.[8]

The important question is not the use of one patient for the good of others, but the circumstances of the use. Even if we recognize some constraints on such use, we cannot and should not forbid all such uses. The question is whether the use is respectful and justified. When parents find meaning in donating organs at a time of tragedy from an infant who is not harmed by the donation and another person and family gain immeasurably, one may reasonably view the entire transaction as respectful of human needs and dignity, even though a nonconsenting subject is used as a means to the good of others. A contrary view may motivate persons not to donate or accept such organs, but it does not suffice to ban the practice in the restrictive conditions described above.

Symbolic Concerns in Actively Causing Death

The symbolic concern with actively causing death to obtain organs from near-dead persons who lack interests poses a more difficult problem than merely using the near-dead subject as a means for the good of others. Although the near dead persons lack interests in further living and thus are not harmed by organ removal, the prohibition against active killing is violated.

The importance of this threshold is evident in developing norms and practices for withholding life-sustaining treatment. Although withholding this treatment is now medically, ethically, and legally accepted when the patient consents or if incompetent, ceases to have further interest in living, a firm line in favor of passive and against active euthanasia exists.[9] Active killing is legally proscribed, even when a fully informed, competent patient requests it to avoid severe pain.

The concerns behind maintaining the firm line against active euthanasia involve slippery slope and category spillover of the kind discussed above. But even if those concerns could be assuaged, the symbolic costs of permitting active killing in a medical setting would remain. Legalization of active killing might symbolize a weakening of the societal commitment to respecting all human life and the prohibition against taking life. The ferocity of the abortion debate illustrates the strength of such a commitment and the need to hold the line even more firmly in other settings.

Yet once we see that the prohibition against taking life is a symbolic or constitutive commitment, and not a matter of rights or obligations of justice when the patient lacks interests, we can ask whether the symbolic gains are always so great that the loss of benefits to persons as a result of deviating from the prohibition is justified. Despite the firmness of the norm against active killing, some breaches have been accepted in certain exceptional circumstances. For example, certain practices with dying patients that hasten death are widely accepted. Giving opiates that repress respiration in terminally ill patients is justified by the specific intent to relieve pain, even though such drugs may actively hasten death.

Consider also the common practice in organ procurement of shifting management of a patient at a certain point from saving the donor's life to preserving his or her organs for transplant. The therapy designed to save life by withholding fluids to minimize brain swelling and herniation suddenly shifts when further treatment is considered hopeless and fluids are aggressively pushed to assure perfusion of the organs to preserve their viability for use in transplantation.[10] Such shift in management actively hastens brain death. Yet it occurs in a patient who no longer has any meaningful interests. Although not yet widely known or debated, it is likely that such a practice would be accepted. The symbolic loss is small, and the benefits to recipients and society are great.

The line against active killing should be staunchly maintained, but it is not clear that it need be absolute. Situations testing this line will increasingly occur, as the present case shows. Once we protect the interests of persons at risk, however, the symbolic costs and benefits of maintaining or deviating from the line must be addressed. In the restrictive circumstances that I have assumed, a reasonable argument for recognizing an exception to the rule against active killing (and hence the dead donor rule) can be made.

Whether other pediatric and adult situations would also qualify requires further study. Each situation has to be examined on its own terms, once the symbolic barrier ceases to be absolute. The question for policymakers in each case should be whether the benefits of maintaining this symbolic line outweigh the benefits to others of breaching it. When carefully addressed in these terms, few cases may qualify for the exception, though an occasional situation, such as relaxing the dead donor rule for anencephalic organ sources, might be identified. Good ethical analysis thus may enable us to keep the rule without losing the benefits that accrue from a few narrow deviations from it.

Conclusion

We have seen that the arguments against tissue and organ retrieval from patients who are not yet brain dead cannot easily be sustained on grounds of preventing harm to the organ source. The central concern is that others will be hurt by loose categories and slippery slopes or, more likely, by the discomfort at openly recognizing that near-dead persons are actively being killed to obtain organs. In the final analysis, the concern is a symbolic rather than a patient's rights concern.

But symbols are sources of meaning and constitute the moral nature of the community. They have a substantive weight of their own, even if the organ source's rights or welfare are not implicated and thus cannot easily be ignored.

A crucial difference between symbolic concerns and rights concerns is that the former may be more easily traded off than the latter. The community may not override the rights of persons, but it may, if persuaded of the wisdom of doing so, alter its investment in key symbols. Without violating rules of justice or obligations to persons, the community may choose to give meaning to grieving families and life to needy transplant recipients at the price of loosening the barrier against active killing.

In the case of organ removal from near-dead pediatric patients and anencephalics, the issue between utility and symbolic concerns is squarely posed. If the very restrictive conditions described above are satisfied, a good argument for relaxing the dead donor rule exists.

At the present time, however, those restrictive conditions probably cannot be satisfied. Too much is still experimental and unknown in pediatric transplantation to make the case for giving up the symbolic benefits of the dead donor rule. (Experimental use of anencephalic organs may also be premature.) Furthermore, it has not yet been clearly established that anencephalic organs would be nonviable when brain-stem function ceases or that preservation options such as cooling of the dying anencephalic would not preserve organs. As with many medical ethical dilemmas, it appears that the factual array that would make otherwise unethical actions ethical often cannot be met.

But the current difficulty in satisfying these conditions should not blind us to the nature of the conflict and the possibility of meeting the conditions in the future. Indeed, a separate issue is whether the same restrictions should be met to justify nonlethal donations of bone marrow and kidneys from anencephalics. If organ removal does not itself cause death, the symbolic costs of using anencephalic organs is lessened and may be justified in circumstances that would not justify lethal organ removal. Symbolic costs, however, will remain and will still require compelling justification, such as a last resort for the needy patient, even if the standard of efficacy that might justify active killing could not be met. Thus it may be ethical to begin experimental use of anencephalic kidneys, which can be obtained without actively causing the source's death, even if removal of hearts and livers cannot now be justified.

Until more certain benefit from relaxation of the dead donor rule can be established, this important threshold—though rooted in symbolic rather than rights concerns—should be staunchly maintained. The problem of pediatric organ supply, however, will continue to focus attention on these issues and require us to compare the symbolic costs and the gains to recipients and families of a change in the dead donor rule in certain narrow circumstances. There may be a time when such a change is desirable.

Notes

1. John C. Fletcher, John A. Robertson, Michael R. Harrison, "Primates and Anencephalics as Sources for Pediatric Organ Transplants," *Fetal Therapy* 1: 150–164, 1986.

2. Robert M. Veatch, "The Whole-Brain Oriented Concept of Death: An Outmoded Philosophical Formulation," *Journal of Thanatology* 3: 13–30, 1975; Michael Green and Daniel Wikler, "Brain Death and Personal Identity," *Philosophy and Public Affairs* 9: 389–394, 1980.

3. Alexander M. Capron, "Anencephalic Donors: Separate the Dead From the Dying," *Hastings Center Report* 17: 5–9, 1987.

4. Even the restrictive "Baby Doe" rules allow medical treatment to be withheld from anencephalics. Public Law 98-457 (1984); Child Abuse Amendments, 45 C.F.R. Part 1340 as amended by 50 Federal Register 14887–92 (1985).

5. Capron, "Donors," p. 8.

6. Peter Singer and Helga Kuhse, "The Ethics of Embryo Research," *Law Medicine and Health Care* 14: 133–138, 1986.

7. See, for instance, Richard A. McCormick, "Proxy Consent in the Experimental Situation," *Perspectives in Biology and Medicine* 18: 2–20, 1974; and Paul Ramsey, "The Enforcement of Morals: Nontherapeutic Research on Children," *Hastings Center Report* 6(4): 21–30, 1976. See also Michael Harrison, "The Anencephalic as Organ Donor," *Hastings Center Report* 16: 21–23, 1986.

8. John A. Robertson, "Organ Donations by Incompetents and the Substituted Judgment Doctrine," *Colorado Law Review* 76: 48–78, 1976.

9. John A. Robertson, *The Rights of the Critically Ill* (Cambridge, MA: Ballinger, 1983), pp. 92–94.

10. Pittsburgh Transplant Foundation, "Post Mortem Organ Procurement Protocol," Pittsburgh, PA, 1984; see also Appendix E.

7

Children as Renal Donors

Norman Fost

The suggestion of forced altruism is abhorrent to most Americans. In contrast to some European countries, our laws do not require us to come to the aid of a person in peril.[1] Similarly, in the field of kidney transplantation, the idea of removing a kidney from a person, without his consent, for the benefit of another has generally been unacceptable. The objection is greater when the potential donor is a child, lacking the verbal, physical or political power to resist or protest. Opposition to the use of minor donors is not absolute, however, for identical-twin minors have been used for nearly 20 years, since the earliest days of transplantation.[2,3] Recently, adolescents who were technically minors in the legal sense have been used,[4] but all were close to adulthood and could be assumed to be as capable of consenting as adults. There are no published cases using non-twin minors younger than the teen years, although attempts have been made to remove a kidney from non-twin adults who could not consent because of mental retardation[5-7] or mental illness.[8]

Good ethical decision making starts with good facts. The facts of renal transplantation—technics of tissue typing, survival rates, costs of dialysis and increased psychosocial knowledge about renal donors—have changed dramatically over the decades. It is possible that the resistance to using minor donors derives from considerations that were appropriate 20 years ago but may not be valid today. This paper examines the justifications for using children as kidney donors, and those given for excluding them. "Children," in this discussion, means those in their preteen years, since there is less controversy about procedures on adolescents who approximate adults in their ability to provide meaningful consent.[9,10] To guide the reader, the conclusion is stated at the outset: a systematic exclusion of such children is not ethically required and may, in fact, be difficult to defend.

The Legal Background

The law is not always right, in the moral sense, but it does provide some insight into community mores. There is a consistent principle running through all the legal opinions regarding renal transplantation from an incompetent donor: the requirement that a benefit be found for the donor if the transplantation is to be allowed. Although most of these cases involved adolescents, often with nearly adult competence to consent, there was a general assumption that the donors were not legally competent. For this reason, the cases have relevance to general considerations involving non-consenting donors, including younger children.

The first legal tests came in 1957 in three unpublished decisions from the Supreme Judicial Court of Massachusetts.[2,11-13] Doctors at the Peter Bent Brigham Hospital, with the consent of the parents, wished to perform three renal transplantations: in one case between 19-year-old identical twins, and in two other cases between 14-year-old twins. They asked the Court to state whether there would be legal liability for the hospital or its employees. The hospital attorney thought there would be liability for the infliction of "a serious and permanent physical injury without benefit to [the well twin] and without his intelligent consent."[13] But the Court, on hearing testimony that the donor would probably suffer "serious emotional impact" if his brother died, concluded that the operation was "necessary to [the donor's] future welfare and happiness." Having found the procedure to be beneficial to the donor, the parental consent was considered valid, and therefore the hospital was protected against future liability. There was also direct testimony from the donor, demonstrating his understanding of the relevant facts, his close relation with his brother and his desire to have the operation done. His only question, in fact, was why it was any of the Court's business.[13]

After this experience, more than a dozen requests for the use of minor donors in Massachusetts were granted by the Court. In 1969, a Connecticut court granted such a request in the case of Hart vs. Brown,[14] involving identical twins seven years of age. The judge again relied on testimony from persons other than the parents or the physicians caring for the potential recipient. A guardian ad litem for the donor consented, and a psychiatrist, after examining the donor and noting a strong identification with the twin, testified that the operation, if successful, would be of "immense benefit to the donor in that the donor would be better off in a family that was happy than in a family that was distressed and in that it would be a very great loss to the donor if the donee were to die from her illness."[14,15]

In 1969 a Kentucky court granted permission for the use of a kidney from a 27-year-old retarded donor to his 28-year-old brother.[5] The court found that the donor's "well-being would be jeopardized more severely by the loss of his brother than by the removal of a kidney."

In 1973 a Louisiana court denied a request to use a severely retarded child as a donor to his sister, finding it "highly unlikely" that the sister's continued survival would be of any advantage to the donor.[6]

In 1975 the Supreme Court of Wisconsin turned down a request to take a kidney from an institutionalized catatonic schizophrenic man for donation to his sister, noting that the sister's previous lack of interest in her brother suggested that her survival would not be likely to benefit the donor.[8] Although these last two cases appear to run counter to the previous examples in that the request to use an incompetent donor was denied, they were consistent with the principle stated above: an incompetent donor may be used only if there is a likelihood of benefit to the donor. Stated more generally, the best interest of the donor has been the standard for deciding.

The underlying principle in these cases is that a physical intrusion must be for the benefit of the subject. The law, as well as our moral tradition, does allow for non-beneficial intrusions, provided there is uncoerced, informed consent, but such consent has been assumed to be invalid with children. This interpretation does not mean, however, that non-beneficial intrusions may never be done on children, for such a rule would preclude all non-therapeutic research on non-consenting subjects, a policy that even strong child advocates oppose as being against the interests of children as a class.[16,17]

There are two possible justifications, therefore, for using a child as a renal donor. In the first place, one could argue that the procedure is beneficial and can therefore be justified, provided the concern about the absence of consent can be overcome. Secondly, one could acknowledge that the procedure is not beneficial for the donor, but meets the generally accepted criteria for non-beneficial interventions on unconsenting subjects.

Justifications for Non-Beneficial Procedures on Children

Non-beneficial research on children has been advocated in England and the United States when four conditions are met:[9,16-19] the use of children is a "last resort" (i.e., legally competent subjects are either not appropriate or unavailable); there is no more than a trivial risk; there is a firm medical basis for expecting definite benefit for others; and consent is provided by a legally authorized representative of the subject.

The use of a minor as a renal donor is rarely the "last resort." At the least, dialysis is available, which is roughly comparable to transplantation as a life-saving intervention over two years, even though dialysis is associated with many nonfatal disadvantages, such as lack of normal growth, increased cost and serious psychologic problems.[20] There is also the possibility of finding a cadaver kidney. It is conceivable, in some circumstances, that cadaver transplantation would not be possible (owing to preformed antibodies, for example) and that prolonged dialysis would be unacceptable (because of neuropathy or lack of vascular access). In such circumstances, the argument for using a minor donor, as a last resort, to save a life would be more compelling. This was essentially the situation when the first minor-twin cases went to court, with chronic dialysis unavailable and cadaver transplantation yet to be developed.

The second justification for non-beneficial intrusion on a minor would be an assertion that the risk is trivial. The definition of "trivial" may be subjective: some might consider a venepuncture of minimal risk, whereas others believe there is a risk of serious psychosocial injury from such a procedure, if it is performed in a particularly coercive way on a fearful child. "Trivial" might also apply to the statistical probability of harm, rather than to the severity of the harm. In this sense, the operative risk of harm from donating a kidney is small (less than 0.1 percent),[21-24] and the long-term survival is essentially no different from that of the normal population.[25] There may be psychosocial risks that are more common, such as a change in one's life-style to avoid injury to a solitary kidney. The donor may also come to think of himself as especially vulnerable, on an irrational basis, and avoid marriage or romance because of a fear of premature death. Simmons showed that a minority of adult donors do experience negative psychologic consequences of renal donation.[26] In summary, the combined organic and psychosocial risks of renal donation could not be fairly called minimal or trivial.

The third justification for a non-beneficial intrusion would be the expectation of an immediate and profound benefit to others. With the exception of transplantation between twins, the marginal advantages of receiving a kidney from a living, related donor, as compared to a cadaver organ or dialysis, do not seem to be of this proportion. Three years after receiving a kidney from a sibling, 80 per cent of the recipients were alive, as compared with 62 per cent after a cadaver graft.[27]

In summary, then, if the use of a minor donor is seen as being of no benefit to the donor, there does not seem to be a compelling argument for the intrusion. Justification for the procedure will therefore have to depend on a finding of benefit, or on the doctrine of "substituted judgment," which would base the decision on what a rational person would do in the child's situation, even if there were no benefit.[28]

The Benefits Argument and Substituted Judgment

Benefits from renal donation have not been difficult to find, in theory or empirically. The expected feeling of increased self-esteem from performing an altruistic act has been documented in adults by Simmons,[26] and by Lewis[29] in a meticulously detailed case report involving seven-year-old twins. Other benefits used in argument in court have included the continued companionship of the surviving sibling, the prevention of an adverse reaction to the death of the sibling and the avoidance of possible guilt on discovering later in life that one could have saved his sibling's life. There has been some dispute about the minimum age necessary to experience these psychologic reactions,[3,30,31] but appreciable psychopathology has been reported in children who lost a sibling when they were as young as two and a half years old.[32,33] It is conceivable that if a transplanted kidney should fail and the recipient died, a child would be more susceptible than an adult to fantasies of having been responsible for the recipient's death. This has been a particular concern in graft-versus-host reactions after bone-marrow transplantation, in which such concerns have a solid basis in biologic fact.

When a non-consenting donor is involved, there is the obvious danger that a decision maker, such as the parent, with an overt conflict of interest, will overestimate the possible benefits for the donor. The courts have therefore generally stipulated that the probability of benefit be determined by a guardian ad litem, and in some cases have required a triumvirate of lawyer, psychiatrist and clergyman to give assent on behalf of the minor donor.[14] This situation creates, for the guardian, the problem of how to decide for another. Three general guidelines have been used.

First of all, some have suggested that the decision should center on what the person ought to do.[34] One difficulty with such a notion of moral responsibility is that it forces a duty on the child that one would not be willing to force on an adult. Few would suggest that adults should be compelled to perform altruistic acts, without their consent, simply because they ought to.[35,36]

Secondly, a decision could be based on what the child wants, as expressed by his overt statements, just as one allows adults' statements to be accepted at face value. One problem with such a standard for children is that it would argue against obviously beneficial intrusions that were opposed by the child because of his inability to make a rational decision, such as a refusal to be immunized because of the pain of the injection.

The third and, in my view, only valid basis for making a substituted judgment for the child is an assessment of what is in the child's best interest, which can be best approximated by the question of what a competent adult would do if placed in the child's position. Since the great majority of adults placed in this position agree to donate their kidneys,[37] for benefits and risks that are not substantially changed by the situation of being a child, one could reasonably conclude that the child, if presented with the same information, and if endowed with the same faculties as the adult, would be likely to consent.

Consent as a False Issue

For some, informed consent has such profound importance in the protection of human subjects as to be a quasi-religious principle. An absolute adherence to a requirement for informed consent from human subjects would, of course, preclude any interventions on a child, beneficial or not, if the child were deemed incompetent.

There is a more fundamental reason for questioning the traditional allegiance to consent. A growing body of literature suggests that consent, as traditionally practiced, is "an elaborate ritual," in which messages sent often do not correspond to messages received, resulting in the passage of words, but not in what could be called a comprehending, understanding, informed state.[38-41] Particularly in the field of renal donation, it has been shown that the great majority of adults make their decisions before even being presented with the relevant facts,[37] and therefore by definition make their decisions in an uninformed state. This is not to say that such decisions are therefore irresponsible or unethical. On the contrary, adult donors make decisions that would probably be the same even after an assimilation of the relevant facts. On follow-up questioning, adult donors are virtually unanimous in saying that they would give the organ again.[37,42] The implications of the ritual nature of this consent for children are that it makes it possible to face up to the reality that socially acceptable renal donation can occur even though the donor may not fulfill the generally accepted criteria for informed consent.[43,44]

Whether renal donation by adults who make decisions before being presented with the relevant facts can be ethically defended is a more complicated issue.

If the absence of informed consent is a reason to exclude persons as renal donors, many adults would have to be excluded. A consistent position would be to say that only informed and consenting donors could be used, and then to administer a test to determine whether or not the prospective donor is actually capable of achieving a state of being informed.[45] If the person passed the test, age should not be a barrier to donation.

Another consistent position would be to acknowledge that renal donation can occur, and can be ethically defensible, even though the donor may not be informed, in the sense of understanding the relevant medical facts. If one concludes that the present system of obtaining adult donors is ethically defensible, there is no reason to suspect that transgressions would occur if minors were to be used. If one can acknowledge that decisions to use adults are ultimately as "coerced" as decisions to use children, and if one concludes that the present system is justified for adults, there is no reason to exclude children from the same benefits. Theoretically, adults can say no, and their consent might have some meaning, even if uninformed. In practice, few adult donors even contemplate saying no. In Fellner's study of 30 donors, "not one . . . weighed alternatives. . . . They never considered refusing." In Eisendrath's study of 57 donors, and 25 prospective donors, most believed they were "unable to refuse," or said, "I had no choice."[37,42]

One could show homage to the principle of autonomy by respecting the right of refusal, as is customarily done with adults. Children who are not even old enough to participate in the decision to this degree would be excluded. The traditional "age of reason"—seven years—might be a reasonable lower limit. This is not meant to suggest that children over this age can give truly informed consent, but rather that their decision, pro or con, is not qualitatively different from an adult's in its dependence primarily on non-cognitive factors.

Not All Children Should Be Eligible

Even if one acknowledged the benefits available to children who donate a kidney, and accepted the validity of substituted judgment for such an intrusion, it would not follow that all children should be used. There might be medical contraindications, such as the risk of renal disease in the donor's remaining kidney, or an abnormal operative risk, owing to non-renal disease. There might be unusual psychologic risks, such as a morbid fear of hospitalization, or an estranged relation with the recipient, that would mitigate the hypothesized benefits. There might also be familial factors, such as disagreement between the parents, with the risk of continued acrimony and grief for the child after the transplantation. The advantages of using the child as a donor might be so marginal as not to justify the risks, such as a poor histocompatibility-locus-A or mixed-leukocyte-culture match, or a high risk of recurrence of disease in the transplanted kidney. In summary, there would have to be a net benefit to the donor.

Assuming that all the above factors support using a child, he should still not be considered a candidate unless he falls into a class similar to adults who experience psychologic benefits from donating. Since the major benefits reported primarily concern feelings that are generally experienced only by first-degree relatives (children, parents and siblings), distant relatives would be less clearly eligible. (This caveat is cautionary rather than conclusive, since some have questioned the exclusion of unrelated donors.[46])

It should be emphasized that the arguments proposed here for using a child are predicated on the notion that most adults donate because of an obligation to themselves, rather than an altruistic feeling toward the donee.[47] Whether or not any so-called altruistic acts are really free of self-interest is beyond the scope of this paper.[48]

Residual Issues

One might ask why children, with the rare exceptions noted above, have come to be excluded as possible renal donors. It may be, as Lewis has suggested,[29] that there is an excessive concern about the preservation of physical integrity as compared to psychologic integrity. The present policy may also reflect a generally heightened sensitivity resulting from a small number of widely publicized cases of alleged abuses involving nonconsenting subjects.[8,49,50]

In the present system, the decision to use or exclude a person as a donor is generally made by the medical team. This "gatekeeping" role has been questioned as being beyond the expertise of the physician when it is applied to selection of recipients.[51] Since these decisions are ultimately ethical or value questions, for which the physician may not be any more expert than the layman, the authority of the medical team to include or exclude systematically any class of donors, whether children or adults, may be questioned. The problem has not aroused the general concern that surrounds the selection of recipients, because life and death are not so starkly on the line.

Conclusions

These comments are not intended to encourage a widespread use of minor donors, but only to question the systematic exclusion of such donors. Indeed, the circumstances in which there would be a strong argument for using such donors would constitute a small percentage of renal transplants. With continued improvements in procuring and matching of cadaver organs, one could look forward to a reduction in the use of live, related donors of all ages.

In summary, I propose the following thesis: renal donation cannot be justified unless there is likely benefit to the donor, or the donor is capable of giving informed consent; age is not a meaningful index of the capacity to give informed consent in this area; children have the same potential benefits from renal donation as adults, and should not be systematically excluded; decisions about adults, in this field, are as paternalistic as decisions about children (if one group is excluded, the other should also be); since the use of adult donors, despite the apparent absence of informed consent, is not apparently resulting in abuse, there is some basis for believing that children would not be abused, and they should be included in the pool of possible donors; and to neutralize the overt conflict of interest faced by the parents, the traditional use of guardians ad litem and court proceedings should be continued, until a less unwieldy procedure can be devised.

Notes

I am indebted for the thoughtful comments of the following people, who obviously assume no responsibility for content or style: Dr. Folkert Belzer, Dr. Russell Chesney, Dr. Robert E. Cooke, Prof. John Robertson, Dr. David Uehling and Prof. Daniel Wikler.

1. Prosser W: Law of Torts. Minneapolis, West Publishing Co., 1972
2. Masden v Harrison, Mass Supreme Judicial Court, Equity No. 68651, June 12, 1957
3. Baron CH, Botsford M, Cole GF: Live organ and tissue transplants from minor donors in Massachusetts. Bost Univ Law Rev 55:159–193, 1975
4. Simmons RL, Thompson EJ, Kjellstrand CM, et al: Parent-to-child and child-to-parent kidney transplants: experience with 101 transplants at one center. Lancet 1:321–324, 1976
5. Strunk v Strunk 445 SW2d 145 (Ky Ct App 1969)
6. In re Richardson 284 So2d 185 (La App 1973)
7. Howard v Fulton DeKalb Memorial Hosp Auth Civil No. B90430 (Super Ct Fulton County, Ga, Nov 29, 1973)
8. Lausier v Pescinski 67 Wis2d 4, 226 NW2d 180 (1975)
9. Curran WJ, Beecher HK: Experimentation in children: a reexamination of legal ethical principles. JAMA 210:77–83, 1969
10. Pilpel HF: Minors' rights to medical care. Albany Law Rev 36:462–487, 1972
11. Huskey v Harrison, Equity No. 68666 (Mass Aug 30, 1957)
12. Foster v Harrison, Equity No. 68674 (Mass Nov 20, 1957)

13. Katz J: Experimentation with Human Beings. New York, Russell Sage Foundation, 1972, pp. 964–972

14. Hart v Brown, 29 Conn Supp 368, 289 A2d 386 (Super Ct 1972)

15. Curran WJ: Kidney transplantation in identical twin minors—justice is done in Connecticut. N Engl J Med 287:26–27, 1972

16. Lowe CU, Alexander D, Mishkin B: Nontherapeutic research on children: an ethical dilemma. J Pediatr 84:468–472, 1974

17. Capron AM: Legal considerations affecting clinical pharmacological studies in children. Clin Res 21:141–151, 1973

18. Campbell AGM: Infants, children, and informed consent, Br Med J 3:334–338, 1974

19. Protection of human subjects: policies and procedure. Fed Reg 38:31738–31749 (November 16), 1973

20. Rubin MI: Pediatric Nephrology. Baltimore, Williams and Wilkins, 1975

21. Bergan JJ: Current risks to the kidney transplant donor. Transplant Proc 5:1131–1134, 1973

22. Leary FJ, Deweerd JH: Living donor nephrectomy. J Urol 109:947–948, 1973

23. Uehling D, Malek GH, Wear JB: Complications of donor nephrectomy. J Urol 111:745–746, 1974

24. Smith MJV: Living kidney donors. J Urol 110:158–161, 1973

25. Santiago EA, Simmons RL, Kjellstrand CM, et al: Life insurance perspectives for the living kidney donor. Transplantation 14:131–133, 1972

26. Simmons RG, Klein S, Simmons R: The Social Impact of Transplantation. New York, Wiley-Interscience (in press) [published, 1977]

27. Advisory Committee to the Renal Transplant Registry: The 12th Report of the Human Renal Transplant Registry. JAMA 233:787–796, 1975

28. Robertson JA: Organ donations by incompetents and the substituted judgment doctrine. Columbia Law Rev 76:48–78, 1976

29. Lewis M: Kidney donation by a 7-year-old identical twin child: psychological, legal, and ethical considerations. J Am Acad Child Psychiatry 13:221–245, 1974

30. Cook WF: Transplantation—incompetent donors: was the first step or the last taken in Strunk v Strunk? Calif Law Rev 58:754–775, 1970

31. Curran WJ: A problem of consent: kidney transplants in minors. NY Univ Law Rev 34:891, 1959

32. Cain AC, Fast I, Erickson ME: Children's disturbed reactions to the death of a sibling. Am J Orthopsychiatry 34:741–752, 1964

33. Pollock GH: Childhood parent and sibling loss in adult patients. Arch Gen Psychiatry 7:295–305, 1962

34. McCormick RA Jr: Proxy consent in the experimentation situation. Perspect Biol Med 18:2–20, 1974

35. Fost NC: Ethical issues in pediatrics, Curr Probl Pediatr 6(12):1–31, 1976

36. Ramsey P: The enforcement of morals: nontherapeutic research in children. Hastings Cent Rep 6(4):21–30, 1976

37. Fellner CH, Marshall JR: Kidney donors—the myth of informed consent. Am J Psychiatry 126:1245–1251, 1970

38. Ingelfinger FJ: Informed (but uneducated) consent. N Engl J Med 287:465–466, 1972

39. Fletcher J: Realities of patient consent to medical research. Hastings Cent Stud 1:39–49, 1973

40. Gray B: Human Subjects in Medical Experimentation. New York, Wiley-Interscience, 1975

41. Leonard CO, Chase G, Childs B: Genetic counselling: a consumers' view. N Engl J Med 287:433–439, 1972

42. Eisendrath RM, Guttmann RD, Murray JE: Psychologic considerations in the selection of kidney transplant donors. Surg Gynecol Obstet 129:243–248, 1969

43. Leichter D, Strauss H, Mandel E: The Nuremberg code. Experimentation with Human Beings. Edited by J Katz. New York, Russell Sage Foundation, 1972, pp 13–25

44. United States Department of Health, Education, and Welfare: The Institutional Guide to DHEW Policy on Protection of Human Subjects (DHEW Publication No. [NIH] 72–102). Washington, DC, Government Printing Office, 1971

45. Miller R, Willner HS: The two-part consent form: a suggestion for promoting free and informed consent. N Engl J Med 290:964–966, 1974

46. Fellner CH, Schwartz SH: Altruism in disrepute: medical versus public attitudes toward the living organ donor. N Engl J Med 284:582–585, 1971

47. Fellner CH: Organ donation: for whose sake? Ann Intern Med 79:589–592, 1973

48. Nagel T: The Possibility of Altruism. Oxford, Oxford University Press, 1970

49. Goldby S, Krugman S, Giles J: Experiments at the Willowbrook State School, Experimentation with Human Beings. Edited by J Katz, New York, Russell Sage Foundation, 1972

50. Sterilized: why? Time Magazine, July 23, 1973, p 50

51. Fox R, Swazey J: The Courage to Fail: A Social View of Organ Transplants and Dialysis. Chicago, University of Chicago Press, 1974

8

Ethical Issues in Recipient Selection for Organ Transplantation

Dan W. Brock

For all major forms of organ transplantation now possible and currently part of either accepted or experimental medical practice, there is some scarcity of available organs. There are more patients who both desire and would likely be benefited by organ transplantation than can receive transplants with the current supply of organs. As a result, it is not possible simply to respond to all in medical need of transplantation; instead, criteria and procedures are necessary for selecting, from among all in need, those whose needs for transplantation will be met and those whose needs will remain unmet or who must remain longer on waiting lists until their needs will be met. The distribution of a scarce good of this sort that promises substantial benefits to those who receive it, in some cases the stark difference between a return to normal function and a premature death, obviously poses extremely difficult choices. This chapter addresses some of the ethical issues and choices involved in developing and employing a recipient selection process.

It is worth underlining at the outset, however, that the existing organ scarcity is a function of both the number of patients whose medical condition is such that it could be significantly improved with transplantation and the available supply of organs for transplant. The size of the pool of potential recipients who could be benefited by transplantation is largely beyond the control of medical practice and health policy. The supply of organs for transplantation, however, could probably be significantly affected by changes that might be instituted in procurement policies and procedures. For example, a number of states have recently adopted so-called required request laws that place positive responsibilities on health care institutions and personnel to ask all potential donors or their families about their willingness to donate. It is not yet clear how much this particular step will increase supply, but such programs do illustrate that new more aggressive measures are possible that hold significant prospect of increasing the supply of organs for transplantation and thereby reducing scarcity. Given the very great ethical and political difficulties of selecting recipients under conditions of scarcity, perhaps the most important policy response to the problems of recipient selection may be to increase organ supply so as to reduce scarcity and in turn the necessity of choosing among candidates for transplantation. At least for the present time, however, we cannot avoid the fact of scarcity.

Many goods that are scarce and whose supply cannot easily be expanded are distributed in our society by economic rationing, that is, by various mechanisms that essentially auction them off to the highest bidder. Although that would be possible with scarce organs, virtually no one seriously advocates such measures. It is widely agreed that ability to pay should not be the criterion for distributing a scarce medical resource that can be the difference between life and death. The adoption of the special federal program under Social Security for funding treatment of end-stage renal disease illustrates the broad reluctance in our society to let ability to pay determine access to life-sustaining treatment, especially when it is needed by identified individuals. Ability to pay, however, at present does influence recipient selection for extrarenal transplants such as hearts, but I am aware of few arguments that this is ethically justified. Whether and/or when particular forms of organ transplantation should be available to all citizens is a serious issue for a just distribution of health care. I shall not explore that complex and controversial matter here, but I will assume that, in general, ability to pay should not be used as the means to ration access to transplantation of scarce organs.[1]

Selection of Recipients by Medical Criteria

At the present time, organs for transplantation are generally obtained through regional procurement networks. Both current practice and the major proposed alternatives to it involve a two-stage selection process: formation of a waiting list and selection of recipients from the list. Teams at various transplant centers maintain waiting lists of patients desirous of and in need of transplantation. The teams generally determine the criteria for both the first stage of selection, inclusion on the waiting lists, and for the second stage, selection from the lists. Organ procurement agencies use these criteria in decisions about the distribution of organs. Perhaps the most important proposed change in current recipient selection procedures is the recommendation in the Report of the Task Force on Organ Transplantation of the U.S. Department of Health and Human Services (hereafter, HHS report)[2] to shift from these local and regionalized procedures, which inevitably result in geographical differences in selection criteria or even differences from one transplant center to another, to a single national network of organ sharing.

The proposed national network would continue to use a two-stage selection process: There would be a single national waiting list for renal transplants, for which there is usually time to permit nationwide sharing, and a single procedure employing uniform criteria for selection of recipients from that list. In the case of other organs, such as hearts and livers, where problems of organ preservation limit both the area for sharing and the sophistication of matching procedures that can be used, sharing would be over as wide a geographic area as feasible. The report "recommends that selection of patients both for waiting lists and for allocation of organs be based on medical criteria that are publicly stated and fairly applied."[3] This appeal to "medical criteria" for recipient selection is extremely common but, I believe, misleading about the nature of the ethical choices involved.

The fundamental ethical conflict in the distribution of scarce organs is between doing the most good with a scarce resource and ensuring that it is distributed fairly. How these values should be traded off, particularly when the good in question is needed for life itself, is controversial among not only moral philosophers but also the general public. As a result, there is a strong temptation to seek to avoid or obscure the ethical or value judgments in selection of recipients, and the principal means of doing so is by appeals like that noted above in the HHS report to medical criteria for selecting recipients.[4] Even in discussions of the issue of recipient selection that are sensitive to the ethical nature of the problem, such as the HHS report and the Report of the Massachusetts Task Force on Organ Transplantation (hereafter, Massachusetts report),[5] it is common to find appeals to processes that are said to employ only objective medical criteria to establish a pool or waiting list of eligible recipients and to select recipients from such waiting lists.

It is important to emphasize that there are *no* value-neutral selection criteria that could permit bypassing the need to make ethical judgments in the recipient selection process. Notions of medical criteria, medical eligibility, or medical need for treatment, so common in medical practice generally, implicitly embody value judgments when used for determining how a scarce resource like organ transplantation will be distributed. When a medical service is not scarce (in the sense that it can be distributed to all who might benefit from it), the appeal to medical need is not ethically controversial, at least in its function of simply directing the resource to all and only those who might be benefited by it. To give it to others would be uncontroversially wasteful and pointless. (Of course, it is ethically controversial whether social resources should be used to fund transplantation for all who might receive any benefit from it, no matter how limited, instead of using those resources for other medical or nonmedical purposes that might promise greater benefits for comparable costs.)

When the medical resource is scarce, however, so that all who might be benefited by it inevitably will not receive it, the appeal to medical criteria is not ethically uncontroversial. When medical need is interpreted broadly and used only to establish the initial pool or waiting list of potential recipients from among whom actual recipients are selected, this use of medical criteria remains uncontroversial; as before, to provide transplantation to persons with no need for it and no prospect of being benefited by it would simply be wasteful. It is when medical factors, such as organ size, blood type, tissue typing, and donor-recipient cross-matching, are used to narrow down who will in fact receive the resource from among all those with some need for transplantation that these and other medical criteria are no longer ethically neutral or uncontroversial. Thus they are misleadingly referred to as objective medical criteria.

These factors clearly are medical criteria in the sense that they are ascertained by medical personnel employing medical techniques and procedures and they are causally relevant to the likelihood of success of the medical procedure in question—organ transplantation. But it is in the goal, what is to count as success in the transplantation procedure, that the value judgments implicitly lie. People may be in need of transplant surgery either because their medical condition is life threatening and they need the transplant for life itself or because, as is often the case with kidney transplants where dialysis is an alternative treatment, an organ transplant is expected to improve substantially their level of function and quality of life. But although this may show that we cannot entirely avoid value judgments in the transplantation process, perhaps these goods or values (implicit in transplantation) of preserving life and improving the quality of life are sufficiently uncontroversial that it is harmless just to assume them as given; factors like HLA tissue typing can then be treated as value-neutral medical criteria promoting those goods.

Consider the prolongation of life, seemingly the most uncontroversial value assumed. On closer inspection, it is neither as simple nor as uncontroversial as it might seem. For the moment, let me indicate two respects in which this is the case. First, it is not merely prolonging life that is the goal of transplantation; how long a person's life is prolonged is also important and, other things being equal, the longer it is prolonged, the better. If a medical procedure can be performed that will prolong a patient's life for five years instead of an alternative procedure that will prolong it for only one year, then the first procedure produces a substantially greater benefit for the patient. Transplant centers commonly require some minimum life expectancy with the transplant, for example two years, for potential recipients even to be placed on waiting lists. Second, for virtually all patients it is not simply how long their life will be prolonged by a transplant that determines the transplant's value but also what the quality of the life prolonged will be. If a patient's life can be prolonged with a restoration of normal functioning, then the patient receives a substantially greater benefit or good than if he or she is left severely disabled. My point is that to what extent and precisely how both life expectancy and the quality of life after transplantation should affect recipient selection is not completely uncontroversial, as the value of simply prolonging the lives of patients who want their lives prolonged may be. Yet it is this more complex goal that is in fact pursued. As the HHS report notes about the current system, "the prevailing ethos and practice are to allocate organs to the recipient who will live the longest with the highest quality of life."[6]

Medical criteria for recipient selection are then implicitly in the service of doing the most good with scarce organs and must implicitly contain value judgments about what are "good" outcomes. Why then is it so common for studies like the HHS report and the Massachusetts report, as well as for persons involved in transplantation such as directors of transplant facilities, to seek to limit recipient selection criteria to "objective medical criteria" and to exclude value judgments, in particular value judgments about candidates for transplantation? The confusion here arises in part from the mistaken belief that in order to avoid the use of certain kinds of value judgments that seem ethically unjustified, one must avoid *all* value judgments. But this is not necessary—nor is it even possible.

To see this, suppose the goal is simply expected survival of the patient with a successful graft for at least two years beyond the time of transplant. Factors like organ size, blood type, and tissue typing then are all relevant to the probability of achieving the desired goal. But now compare other factors like the presence of a family support system and the psychological stability of the patient. Both of these are also believed to affect two-year graft survival by affecting the likelihood, degree, and quality of the patient's compliance with treatment. These factors are medical and medically relevant in the same sense as factors like blood type—they affect the probability of achieving the desired medical outcome of patient and graft survival. Thus, whether a potential recipient is a member of a well-functioning family unit or instead a homeless "loner" may be medically relevant and need reflect no judgments of the value or social worth of the individuals in question.

Nevertheless, these are factors that commonly enter into many judgments about the social worth or value of individuals and are often the basis for unjustified discrimination. In medicine in particular, there is a strong tradition that no judgments about the value or worth of the patient should enter into treatment decisions. This means that the crucial task for evaluating the legitimacy of the use of factors like whether the patient has a strong social support network is to determine why the factor is used. Used because it positively affects the probability of successful patient and graft survival, and if there is adequate evidence that it in fact does so, it is ethically unproblematic. Used because the transplant team selecting candidates considers upstanding family members more socially valuable than homeless loners or just feels more comfortable with the family member, it is an ethically unjustified, or at the least ethically problematic, influence on the selection process. Factors like having a strong social support network are similar to race or gender, which are treated as "suspect classifications" in some areas of the law. Because having a strong social support network can easily be used as the basis of unjustified discrimination, there should be a high burden of proof that it positively affects the legitimate goal of patient and graft survival to warrant employing it as a medical criterion. If that burden is satisfied, this factor does not reflect unacceptable judgments of the social worth or value of the patient. Thus, I would conclude that any factor that can be shown to have a positive effect on the likelihood of graft survival, whether it be like blood type, organ size, and tissue typing, or like having a strong social support system, is medically relevant to the assessment of how to do the most good with these scarce resources.

Doing the Most Good with Scarce Resources: Some Additional Selection Criteria

Let us now consider some other ethically controversial selection factors to see whether they may also reasonably be taken to contribute to the amount of good done with these scarce resources. For the moment, I do not differentiate whether they are used at the first stage of selection, formation of the waiting list, or the second stage, selection of actual recipients from the waiting list. Would these factors, if used at either stage, contribute to doing the most good with scarce organs for transplantation?

First, consider the age of the recipient. We have already noted that it seems all would agree, other things being equal, that a greater benefit is done for a patient by prolonging his or her life, for example, by five years rather than one year, and that in general the longer life is prolonged, the better. This means that age is relevant in selecting patients so as to do the most good with the scarce organ, at least in cases in which the increased age of the patient correlates negatively with life expectancy with the transplant. Because chronological age is not always a reliable guide to the physiological age of the patient or to the presence of other factors that may affect life expectancy with the transplant, however, age is at most usable as a rough rule of thumb. Expected length of patient survival with the transplant, in contrast, is directly relevant to doing the most good with scarce organs.

It might be argued that when the transplant is needed for life itself and the patient will soon die without it, whatever the differences in life expectancy with a transplant, all who do not receive one will die and so will equally lose "everything." Whether one would have lived one year or five years with a transplant, if one doesn't receive it, one loses all one's future. Although this is true enough it does not imply that more good is not done when a life-prolonging transplant *is* provided for a patient who will likely live five years with it instead of for a patient who will likely live only one year with it.

A second factor is the quality of the life extended. I have already indicated why this too is relevant to assessing how much good is done for any particular transplant recipient. The important point will be to assess the quality of life prolonged from the standpoint of the person whose life it is. There is thus no single objective set of criteria for making quality-of-life assessments of potential recipients. In the case of kidney transplants, patients can usually survive on dialysis without receiving a transplant and then the comparison should be of the degree of improvement in quality of life different patients would likely experience as a result of receiving a transplant and moving off dialysis. This restricted use of quality-of-life assessments does not sanction ethically problematic assessments of the value of an individual's life to others or assessments of the quality of one individual's life by anyone's standards but his or her own. If factors such as the likelihood of returning to work after receiving a transplant are relevant to this quality-of-life assessment, it will be because the patient values being able to return to work and not, for example, because he or she will then be less of an economic burden on the rest of society.

A third factor affecting how much good is done by selecting one as opposed to another potential recipient for transplantation is far more ethically controversial than either the length or the quality of the life that will be prolonged. This factor is the beneficial and harmful effects for others of the selection of a particular person for transplantation. In this case, whether there is a family that cares deeply about and depends on the patient, or the patient instead is a "loner" with few social ties, is relevant because of the value of the patient to others and not only because having a social support network contributes to the probability of a successful graft. There seems no plausible reason why the effects on others besides the potential recipients should be excluded from an assessment of the overall benefits and harms done as a result of who is selected for transplantation. Some other ethical consideration is needed to restrict concern only to the effects on the patient.

The effects on third parties seem in no plausible sense medical criteria or criteria of medical need, but we have already seen that this restriction to the "medical" begs the question and is misleading. The traditional patient-centered ethic in medicine holds that the physician's recommendations and decisions should be guided only by a concern for the well-being of the patient and not by effects on third parties or society generally, but it is not clear how it applies to the choice of recipients for transplants. The issue here is not the choice of treatment for a single patient but the social choice of which patients will receive a scarce resource when not all can.

A fourth factor often used as one medical criterion for selecting patients for transplantation is the urgency of the potential recipient's need for a transplant. Both the HHS report and the Massachusetts report endorse giving at least some weight to urgency of need for transplantation in selection of recipients. This factor is especially important with potential recipients of most extrarenal transplants, for whom no alternative to transplantation like maintaining the patient on dialysis exists: These patients are expected to die soon without transplantation. It is also consistent with broader medical practice to consider urgency as a component of medical need. The intuitive idea underlying the use of urgency as one consideration relevant to attempting to do the most good with a scarce resource may be that unless this patient is selected for transplantation now, he or she will die and the opportunity of benefiting him or her will be lost forever. But if this is the reasoning, then it is important to distinguish between two forms of scarcity.

Persistent scarcity exists when the scarcity of a particular organ is sufficiently great and persistent that any selection procedure that might be adopted cannot prevent the death of some patients on the waiting list. Temporary or periodic scarcity exists when at times it is not possible to provide organs, or well-matched organs, to all persons on a waiting list, but over the longer term the overall supply is adequate so that all, or virtually all, patients on the waiting list can receive transplants; none need die from want of a transplant. Under conditions of temporary or periodic scarcity, moving patients to the beginning of the waiting list on grounds of their medical urgency will use these temporarily scarce resources best. If a patient's need is urgent and transplantation must be performed very soon or the patient will die, then unless he or she is moved to the top of the waiting list, there will be one less patient in the long run who receives a transplant than who could have received one. In order to do the maximum number of transplants over time when scarcity is temporary, it is necessary to move urgent cases to the front of the line.

In conditions of persistent scarcity, however, some on the waiting list must inevitably die for want of available organs for transplant. Moving patients to the top of the waiting list when their need for a transplant becomes urgent has the effect not of increasing the total number of patients over time that can receive transplants, as that is limited by the persistent scarcity, but of determining *which* patients will receive transplants and which will die for want of them. In conditions of persistent scarcity, consequently, moving patients ahead in line on grounds of urgency cannot be justified in order to do the most good with these scarce resources. At least for extrarenal forms of transplantation like liver and heart transplants the current scarcity of organs is persistent, not temporary. In the case of renal transplants, the alternative to receiving a transplant is usually dialysis rather than death, so the response to urgency will not determine who lives and who dies. The scarcity of kidneys for transplant at the present time is persistent, however; thus, responding to urgency does in some cases determine who receives a renal transplant and who does not.

There is a further reason why urgency generally should *not* be used as a criterion for recipient selection, whether scarcity is temporary or persistent, if the goal is to do the most good with these scarce resources. Patients whose need for transplantation becomes extremely urgent are commonly much sicker than other patients; therefore, rates of patient and graft survival for a reasonable period of time are significantly lower in urgent compared to nonurgent cases. This results in the extremely difficult conflict between using scarce organs to produce the most good and turning away an identifiable patient for transplantation when an organ is available. That very sick patient will die without it, but it will be given to another patient for whom the likelihood of graft survival is higher.

A fifth factor often included among criteria of medical need, or of urgency of need, is patient sensitization. From a variety of causes, some patients develop antibodies to a large number of different antigens so that these people are bad matches for most of the available organ pool. It is thus much more difficult to find a well-matched organ for such patients. As a result, some have argued that sensitized patients should be given a high priority for receiving organs for which they are well-matched, even over patients who would otherwise be better candidates for the organ. This raises the same issue as giving priority to urgent but sicker candidates: Should the sensitized patients be given preference in conditions of persistent scarcity when doing so can be expected to do less good than giving the organ to a nonurgent or unsensitized patient with a higher probability of a successful graft? If the sensitized are to be given priority, it seems clear that it must be on the basis of ethical considerations other than attempting to do the most good possible with a scarce resource.

Finally, it should be noted that one important reason for establishing a single national organ-sharing network (or pools covering the largest possible geographical areas in cases of organs for which national pools are not feasible), as proposed in the HHS report, is that this would increase the efficiency with which these scarce resources are used. One single larger pool of donated organs, together with one single larger pool of potential recipients, will improve the quality of the matches that are possible between donor organs and recipients, thus reducing both the number of unsuccessful grafts (which are a major cause of patient sensitization) and the number of organs that are never transplanted and thus are wasted for want of an adequate match.

Distributing Scarce Organs Fairly

The other principal ethical concern in the distribution of these scarce resources, besides using them efficiently to do the most good, is to insure that they are distributed equitably or fairly. When organs are not donated to a specific recipient, as they commonly are in the case of living, related donors, then it is plausible to argue as the HHS report does that they "are donated on behalf of all potential recipients."[7] Among all those in need of an organ for transplantation, there seems no reason to hold that any have a substantially greater moral claim than do others to *deserve* an organ. One can consider that either none is responsible for his or her need for an organ or where the need is associated with the patient's behavior (such as with alcoholism and liver failure), that there is sufficient question about the causal relation between the behavior and the medical need, as well as about the voluntariness of the behavior, to make it ethically problematic to deny an organ on the basis of that patient's moral responsibility for needing it.[8]

If this pool of donated organs is a public resource of the society on which none in need have a substantially greater claim than others, then it can be argued that each person in need should have an *equal* chance of being selected to receive it when because of scarcity all who need it cannot have it. A lottery selection system from among all those who desire and might be benefited by transplantation is one method for giving each an equal chance to be selected for transplantation. Procedures of first come, first served, such as taking those who have been on a waiting list the longest, may also be reasonable approximations of giving each the equal chance of being selected that a lottery provides. (It would be useful to have studies and data on how closely first come, first served approximates random selection of transplant recipients.)

It is widely agreed that it is morally important that procedures for selecting recipients for transplantation be fair or equitable. There is less agreement, however, about just what equity or fairness requires, as well as what weight it should be given if it conflicts with efficiency in doing the most good with these scarce resources. Some forms of discrimination are widely agreed to be unfair and ethically unacceptable, for example, allowing racial or gender prejudice to affect the selection process. More generally, if a public, democratic decision process arrives at agreement about the criteria to be used to select transplantation recipients, then equity requires that these criteria be consistently applied to all.

I believe the crux of the fairness issue is whether it requires some form of random selection among all those in need, as the argument sketched above suggests, or whether it merely requires that irrelevant grounds such as racial or other prejudices not be allowed to influence the selection process. These two interpretations of what fairness requires—the equal chance or lottery interpretation and the no-irrelevant-distinctions interpretation—have dramatically different implications. If fairness requires that all in need have equal chances of being selected, then that interpretation will be in strong conflict with the various factors we have considered above that are relevant to doing the most good possible with these scarce resources. The equal chance/lottery interpretation yields the familiar conflict between utility maximization, or doing the most good, and fairness. If this is the proper interpretation of the ethical conflict between maximizing the good and fairness in organ transplantation, then few persons would be prepared to give absolute weight to either value; instead, they must be traded off against each other.

To see the implausibility of giving absolute weight to either value interpreted in this way, consider the implications of doing so. A simple lottery selection process among all who want and might receive any benefit from transplantation would require random selection between these two patients, each of whom will die very soon without an organ transplant: an otherwise healthy twenty-five-year-old who is expected to have a normal life span without any significant disability if she receives a transplant; a seventy-year-old patient who is expected to die from unrelated medical conditions within one to two years whatever is done, who has a low probability of a successful transplant, and who will have a severely compromised quality of life for her remaining one to two years even if the graft succeeds. Even the hardiest of egalitarians and the strongest proponents of fairness are very unlikely to be willing to support a random selection process between those two patients.

However, it also seems unacceptable to let very small differences in the expected good to be produced determine whether one gives the transplant to one rather than another patient, at least if doing so means ignoring a requirement of fairness that all in need be given an equal chance to be selected: For example, when two relatively young patients appear otherwise identically good prospects for transplant, except that one has a life expectancy with transplant only slightly greater than the other, say forty years instead of thirty-seven years. If being fair to both requires giving each an equal chance to be selected for transplant, then there is not a large enough difference in the expected good that would be produced by preferring the one with the slightly greater life expectancy to outweigh fairness and thereby to justify not treating them fairly. This interpretation of the conflict between treating all fairly as opposed to maximizing the good requires that these values be balanced in a manner that gives significant independent weight to each. There is no philosophical consensus on any principled account of how this trade-off between fairness and maximizing the good should be made, either in general or in this context in particular.

What is the alternative interpretation of the requirement of equity or fairness in the selection of recipients? I have already indicated one aspect of this interpretation, that no irrelevant bases such as race or gender influence the selection process; fairness will thus exclude some factors from influencing the selection process. With this alternative interpretation, how do we respond to the idea that none morally deserves the benefit more than another and so each should be given an equal chance to be selected? There are at least two possible lines of argument in this case that are not themselves incompatible.

The first holds that what fairness requires is that all members of society must have a roughly equal input into the decision process that will determine what criteria are to be employed for selection of recipients. Moreover, that decision process should be one that imposes some condition of impartiality on those taking part in it, so that participants do not simply tailor their proposals to suit their own known interests at the expense of others. One way that this might be realized in practice is if the vast majority of those taking part in the decision process know that they, and/or others about whom they care such as family members and friends, are not then in need of an organ for transplantation, but at some future time might be. And this seems to be a condition that would generally be satisfied in any broadly based, public debate and subsequent federal-level decision process to determine the criteria to be used for selection of recipients in a national organ-sharing system. If the legitimacy of the recipient selection criteria is to derive from their having been selected in a broadly based, democratic decision process, then one must carry out that process and not instead substitute assertions, predictions, or arguments about what its results would or should be. One of the important issues that would have to be addressed and decided in that public debate and decision process is just what selection criteria and processes would be fair to all in need of scarce organs for transplantation.

The second line of argument, within the no-irrelevant-distinctions interpretation of fairness, offers an alternative substantive interpretation that might be considered by the parties to the democratic choice process suggested above. According to this argument, which persons happen to become diseased and in need of an organ for transplant, which properties particular patients happen to have that influence their relative desirability or undesirability for transplant within a system that attempts to do the most good with scarce organs, as well as which properties the organs that become available for transplant have that affect which recipients they best match, are all essentially random matters. They are all outcomes of a biological and social lottery. In this argument, the randomization that fairness requires is not to be imposed by a deliberate lottery after all the facts are known about how each particular individual will fare under the system. Instead, fairness is achieved by randomization at an earlier stage, in the interplay of forces that determine who will and who will not be favored by a system that distributes organs according to the criterion that benefit is to be maximized. In this view it is compatible with fairness to use scarce organs in the manner and for the patients for whom they turn out to do the most good, as long as these criteria are consistently applied.

Proponents of the equal chance/lottery interpretation of a fair selection system would likely respond that it is fairer to actual, historically placed individuals now suffering from the need for a scarce organ for transplantation to randomize now among those patients actually in need. For example, a recipient selection system designed to do the most good with scarce organs would likely result in sensitized patients receiving transplants much less frequently than unsensitized patients. Pointing out that whether or not one is sensitized is simply a matter of luck, a random result of the "natural lottery," would not be sufficient to show that this system is fair to actual sensitized patients.

There is not space here to explore further these alternative interpretations of a fair distribution process for scarce organs. Much more could be said about them, but I do not know which interpretation would ultimately turn out to be more persuasive, much less which might in fact persuade more in actual democratic debate. Perhaps some altogether different interpretation of a fair selection process would win the day. I am at least sure that in a debate over what would be an ethical selection process for distributing scarce organs for transplantation among those in need, one central issue would be what is fair or equitable.

Two-Stage Selection Procedures

All the recipient selection methods either now in use or proposed as better alternatives are two-stage procedures that involve some combination of an initial pool or waiting list together with some means for selecting actual recipients from the waiting list. Precisely what form the two stages ethically ought to take will depend in substantial part on the positions taken on the ethical issues discussed above. Many of those issues are controversial and unsettled and as a result, so are the issues about appropriate, detailed decision-making procedures. What I shall do in this section is to illustrate in broad terms how the structures of the selection procedures one ought to favor depend on one's positions on the underlying ethical issues that have been discussed above and in particular on the conflict between maximizing the good and fairness.

One broad alternative two-stage selection procedure is that favored in the HHS report. Its recommendation is for a national organ-sharing system using a single unified waiting list (at least for renal transplants), with inclusion on the list determined primarily by medical criteria or need. The report states that there is "debate about whether these medical criteria should be broad or narrow. Many believe that the fairest procedure is to use broad medical criteria to establish the waiting list and then to use narrower medical criteria to determine who actually receives an available organ."[9] The HHS report does not explicitly endorse this position, but it is at least a reasonable interpretation of its recommendation that medical criteria be used both for inclusion on, as well as for selection from, a waiting list. Broad medical criteria presumably will result in a widely inclusive waiting list that places on it all who want and might reasonably be expected to receive at least some minimal benefit from transplantation. Narrow medical criteria for selection from the list then will identify those patients who are expected to receive the greatest benefits from the particular organs available. Setting aside the issue of benefits to others besides the patients, this is a system designed to maximize the good done with these scarce resources while treating all potential recipients fairly or equitably in the specific sense of using no irrelevant bases for selection.

A quite different two-stage selection process is recommended in the Massachusetts report. It supports establishment of an initial pool or waiting list on "objective medical grounds" together with selection from the pool to receive an organ on a first come, first served basis from among all adequately well-matched candidates. (In the case of heart and liver transplants, where recipient-donor matching is much less sophisticated than with kidney transplants, there will presumably be fewer distinctions made by the quality of the match and more use of first come, first served criteria.) The recommendation of first come, first served selection seems grounded in an appeal to fairness or equity, interpreted as requiring that each person who might reasonably benefit by receiving the scarce resource be given an equal chance of being selected to get it.

Precisely what trade-off this proposal represents between doing the most good with a scarce resource and distributing it fairly (in what I have called the equal chance/lottery interpretation of fairness) depends upon the following factors: (1) how broadly or narrowly the medical criteria are drawn for inclusion on the waiting list, and (2) how closely the potential recipients must match the donor organ when they are being considered on a first come, first served basis. Suppose that patients whose expected benefit from getting an organ is increasingly small are included on the waiting list, and the first come, first served rule is applied to far-from-optimal matches of patients with organs. Such an arrangement implicitly accords greater weight to fairness and less to using the scarce resources efficiently. Conversely, the narrower the standards—restricting inclusion on the waiting list to patients likely to receive very high benefits from transplantation and requiring a close match of potential recipients to donor organs during the first come, first served stage—the less weight is implicitly accorded to fairness and the more, to using the resources most efficiently.

The Massachusetts report's proposal has an undesirable feature no matter how broadly or narrowly the standards for inclusion on the initial waiting list and for consideration on a first come, first served basis are drawn. The difficulty is that the degree of expected benefit for different potential recipients varies continuously across a broad range, and this fact cannot be reflected adequately by the on-off standards of the proposal. Thus the trade-off between doing the most good and fairness is at best a crude one.

A third broad alternative form of two-stage selection process could provide a more sensitive trade-off between doing the most good with these scarce resources and treating all candidates fairly, where fairness is understood in the equal chance/lottery interpretation. The idea is to use some form of lottery selection method weighted for differences among potential recipients in the expected benefits of providing them with scarce organs. For example, a waiting list of potential recipients might be grouped into three broad classes—high, medium, and low expected benefiters. Then, a weighted random selection method is used to select a recipient from all those on the waiting list who are adequately matched with the donor organ. For example, a random selection method might give each medium benefiter twice the probability of being selected as each low benefiter, and each high benefiter three times the probability of being selected as each low benefiter. This would have the advantage over the Massachusetts report's proposal, which gives all patients who are above some single waiting list cutoff and adequately matched with the donor organ the same chance of being selected to receive the organ and gives all patients below that waiting list cutoff no chance of being selected. The weighted lottery alternative provides a better trade-off between doing the most good with these scarce resources and treating all fairly because it reflects at least to some degree the continuous and broad variability in the expected benefits different patients would receive from transplantation in a way that a single, uniform waiting list with a cutoff does not. Because of the additional and controversial distinctions among potential recipients that someone would have to make with the weighted lottery alternative, however, there would be formidable practical and political difficulties in implementing it, as well as reasonable worries about possible abuses of it in practice. In that respect, the Massachusetts report proposal has the advantage of requiring fewer highly controversial differentiations among patients.

The three alternative selection procedures that I have sketched above are, of course, not intended to be detailed policy proposals. I have employed them only to illustrate in very broad terms how alternative selection procedures reflect different ethical values and, in particular, different interpretations of what fairness requires as well as what weight fairness is to be given when it conflicts with using scarce resources efficiently to do the most good.

Two Residual Issues

I shall conclude with brief comments on two additional ethical issues in selection of recipients. The first concerns performing transplants on nonimmigrant aliens with organs procured in the United States. The HHS report notes reports of some transplant centers jumping foreign recipients ahead on waiting lists on the basis of their willingness to pay higher prices for transplantation. This employs the widely rejected means for distributing these scarce resources of essentially auctioning them off to the highest bidder. Even when nonimmigrant aliens are not wrongly given priority in this way, it remains ethically controversial whether they should have access to organs procured in the United States at all, and if so, on what terms. This was the only issue of recipient selection that divided the HHS task force.

The HHS report recommended that nonimmigrant aliens represent no more than 10 percent of the total number of kidney transplant recipients at any transplant center and that extrarenal organs should be offered to a nonimmigrant alien only when no other suitable recipient can be found.[10] Eight members of the task force dissented from the recommendation about kidney transplants, holding that, as with extrarenal organs, kidneys should be offered to nonimmigrant aliens only when no other suitable donor can be found.[11] As the HHS report noted, it is not ethically controversial to make organs, whether renal or extrarenal, available to nonimmigrant aliens when no other suitable recipient exists and the organs would otherwise be wasted. The HHS report favored the 10 percent limit as a morally and politically reasonable limit on either a duty or ideal of charity to neighbors, as well as a means to avoid what it saw as the inequities of an essentially two-class system that would always put nonimmigrant aliens at the bottom of the waiting lists. The dissenting members favored the systematic priority for U.S. citizens and residents on the grounds that "the national community that donates the organs and operates the organ procurement and transplantation system can reasonably expect to be offered the opportunity to receive a donated organ whenever a suitable one is available."[12]

The unusual division on the task force on this issue, in my view, reflects the fact that both of these positions have considerable plausibility (though of course the precise figure of 10 percent is to some extent arbitrary) and either reasonably might be adopted as a matter of public policy. Even the dissenters who believe that priority should go to members of the national community that cooperates to produce the benefit would presumably grant that it would at least be ethically permissible, even though not required, for the members of that community to decide together to make some portion of the organs, like 10 percent, available to persons outside of the community. If I am correct that it would be ethically permissible for the community to adopt this alternative but that it is not clearly and uncontroversially ethically required, it seems appropriate that such a decision be left to the discretion of democratic, public policymaking processes. For example, the decision might be left to whatever representative public body might be used to establish and oversee the national organ-sharing network.

The other residual issue concerns the ethical acceptability of giving one or more additional organs to a single recipient after the failure of a previous graft. This issue is especially pressing in transplantation of organs such as hearts and livers for which scarcity is often severe, no alternative therapy besides transplantation is available (unlike dialysis for most potential renal transplant recipients), and patients are dying because no organ is available for them. These cases sometimes capture a great deal of media attention that can create strong pressure on the transplant team to try to find an additional organ to replace the failed graft. The emotional response by the public and by health care professionals to the widely publicized plight of an identified and sympathetic patient with a failed graft who will lose his or her life if not given a transplant again soon can be very powerful indeed. Moreover, this may be pressure that the transplant team, either consciously or unconsciously, is not disposed to resist: Another organ would allow the team to rectify what it may view as its earlier failure. Finally, the transplant team may feel that it has made a commitment to the patient in performing the initial transplant that is different and stronger than its commitment to help other potential recipients and that not to seek to secure another organ to replace the failed graft would constitute an ethically unjustified abandonment of the patient.

All of this may make it hard to resist giving priority to the patient with a failed graft. But when other candidates for the additional organ exist who will also die without that organ, in my view fairness requires that it go to a candidate who has not yet received an organ. This should certainly be so if the other potential recipients are at least as good candidates by the usual selection criteria but also even if the other potential recipients may not be so strong candidates as the patient with the failed graft. This is a place where fairness has some independent weight as against doing the most good with scarce resources, even if fairness results in doing less good than otherwise might have been done. If this policy is made clearly known at the outset to all patients considering transplantation, it need not constitute wrongful abandonment.

Notes

1. If ability to pay for transplantation surgery should not be used to select recipients, then neither should ability to pay be used for access to expensive immunosuppressive drugs like cyclosporine. This is a serious problem for many patients because funding programs for renal transplantation at present do not cover these large out-patient drug costs. See Task Force on Organ Transplantation, *Report to the Secretary and the Congress on Immunosuppressive Therapies* (Washington, D.C.: U.S. Department of Health and Human Services, October 1985).

2. Task Force on Organ Transplantation, *Organ Transplantation: Issues and Recommendations* (Washington, D.C.: Government Printing Office, 1986).

3. Task Force, *Organ Transplantation,* p. 9.

4. For an argument on the desirability of obscuring the nature of some of these choices and the value judgments that they require, see Guido Calabresi and Philip Bobbitt, *Tragic Choices* (New York: W. W. Norton and Company, 1978).

5. Massachusetts Task Force on Organ Transplantation, *Report,* Massachusetts, Department of Public Health, October 1984. See Chapter 12 of this volume for an overview of the report.

6. Task Force, *Organ Transplantation,* p. 87.

7. Task Force, *Organ Transplantation,* p. 86.

8. Present policy of most transplant centers seems to be that patients with past histories of alcoholism are not for that reason excluded from waiting lists for a liver transplant, but patients with active alcoholism within the recent past (say, two years) are excluded on the grounds of their reduced probability for a successful graft.

9. Task Force, *Organ Transplantation,* p. 87.

10. Task Force, *Organ Transplantation,* p. 95.

11. Task Force, *Organ Transplantation,* pp. 137–138.

12. Task Force, *Organ Transplantation,* pp. 137–138.

9

The Patient and Entitlement to Benefits

Thomas D. Overcast and Karen Merrikin

Patient Selection for Heart Transplantation and the Handicapped

Since the enactment of Section 504[1] of the Rehabilitation Act of 1973[2] and the promulgation of its implementing regulations,[3] violations of the civil rights of the handicapped have been increasingly recognized and litigated. Despite its broad prohibition of discrimination in any program or activity receiving federal financial assistance, most litigation under the Act has focused on discrimination in access to public transportation and buildings, employment, and education. Until the recent public furor over the "Baby Doe" case,[4] little attention was given to the potential impact of Section 504 on the activities of health care providers. The question of withholding treatment for handicapped newborns, however, is not the only area of medical practice that is affected by Section 504. Potential exists for charges of handicap discrimination in at least one other new and as yet unexplored area of health care—patient selection for medical treatments such as heart transplantations.

In the past two decades, scientific and medical research has developed remarkable new curative and restorative techniques. Heart transplantation and similar high technology medical procedures are being used with increasingly positive outcomes. However, procedures such as heart transplantation that involve resource scarcity of one type or another often impose a difficult duty on the health care provider—the necessity of choosing a few out of many in need for potentially lifesaving treatment. Each year as many as 75,000 people have conditions that require heart transplantation.[5] However, it is estimated that only 1,000–2,000 donor hearts may be available each year.[6] Moreover, because procedures such as heart transplantation are not yet fully within the realm of accepted therapy, physicians may well choose patients on the basis of factors other than ability to benefit from treatment. They may, for example, select patients with no other physical or mental abnormalities in order to facilitate

Reprinted by permission from R. W. Evans et al., *The National Heart Transplantation Study: Final Report* (Seattle, WA: Battelle Human Affairs Research Centers, 1984), pp. 32-1–32-119.

the assessment of the side effects of, or contraindications to, transplantation. In addition, the highly technological and quasi-experimental status of the procedure may also limit treatment availability, as only a few hospitals have active transplantation programs or are capable of undertaking them.

Resource scarcity, as well as the quasi-experimental nature of organ transplantation procedures, necessitates selection—and selection in the allocation of medical treatment presents some of the same thorny issues of handicap discrimination as those currently arising in the context of education and employment. Patient selection, no less than college admissions or hiring, may necessitate the selection of a few out of an applicant pool of many. As in education and employment decisionmaking, reliance on stereotypes or presumptions of unfitness in patient selection may often erect barriers for the handicapped person that do not exist for others. Similarly, facially neutral selection criteria may also unfairly exclude the handicapped.

Patient selection for medical treatment presents unique challenges for defining discrimination and for interpreting the Rehabilitation Act. Due to the novelty of the transplant procedure and the uncertainty of what the true contraindications to transplantation are, defining and detecting discrimination in patient selection poses problems. Is it a legitimate goal to select those candidates judged to have not merely a fair but the greatest probability of surviving transplantation? To what extent should patient selection decisions be based on evaluations of emotional stability, a factor in survival, or upon criteria such as the presence of a stable home life or past psychological history, criteria that may exclude some of the handicapped? When may patients with a secondary physical or mental disability claim that they have been unfairly denied entry into a transplantation program?

This section explores the potential impact of Section 504 of the Rehabilitation Act of 1973 in the patient selection process for heart transplantation, a provocative testing ground for application of the law. Application of the law against handicap discrimination to decisionmaking in this area can make at least two important contributions to policy discussion. First, it can alert governmental agencies and health care providers to the duties and limitations that the Act may impose on patient selection arising out of resource scarcity or research preference. Second, an analysis of the Act in the medical services context can also help to illuminate the difficulties of defining handicap discrimination in a setting in which the treatment program is still in its formative stages.

This section will survey the current patient selection practices of heart transplantation programs throughout the country. It will then focus on the Rehabilitation Act and the extent to which current methods for patient selection may be constrained by application of Section 504. The next section focuses on the crucial threshold questions concerning the applicability of Section 504 to heart transplantation practice: Is a heart transplantation program a "program or activity" under the Rehabilitation Act? Is it a "health benefit or service" within the meaning of the Section 504 regulations, or can it be excluded as an "experimental procedure"? The last section explores the applicability of the Age Discrimination Act's provisions with respect to choosing heart transplant patients.

Scope of the Problem: Heart Transplantation

Heart disease is and is likely to remain a catastrophic disease of major proportions—killing or crippling vast numbers of individuals. The leading cause of death in the United States is coronary heart disease, accounting for two-thirds of all cardiovascular deaths.[7] In 1978, it alone was responsible for nearly 650,000 deaths. More than 150,000 of these occurred in people less than 65 years old. It is currently estimated that nearly one-third of the deaths from all causes in persons between the ages of 35 and 64 years are due to coronary heart disease, and nearly 40 percent of all deaths in white males aged 55 years and over are caused by the disease. For more than half a century cardiovascular diseases have led the list of the nation's killers.

Cardiovascular disease has extensive economic and social costs. For example, it accounts for more bed days than any other single condition. The total economic cost of cardiovascular diseases is believed to be in excess of $60 billion annually.[8] At present, the only treatment for the end-stage cardiac disease (ESCD) patient facing imminent death is transplantation—the replacement of his or her damaged heart with a healthy heart from a person who has just died of other causes. At present, however, only a limited number of these individuals are viable candidates for cardiac transplantation because among persons with coronary heart disease, there is a critical limitation—sudden onset of death before the individual reaches the hospital. Patients suffering from other less serious heart conditions will probably supply a comparatively smaller percentage of potential transplantation candidates, because they are likely to have other diseased organs that preclude transplantation or have available to them alternate medical and surgical therapies that at the present time offer greater promise of success at a smaller risk. In addition to these problems, a major roadblock to widespread acceptance of transplantation as a therapeutic technique is the problem of rejection and its treatment through effective immunosuppression.[9] Problems associated with transplantation—infection, rejection, and malignancy—are all related to current methods of immunosuppression. Once the immunosuppression problem is solved, however, the demand for heart transplantation could rise dramatically.

For some time to come, only a small percentage of those who suffer from heart disease can be treated by having their damaged organ replaced by a healthy one. Yet the large number of persons with some form of cardiac disease still includes a substantial number who can benefit from transplantation.[10] Because of the relatively large number of potential applicants and the great need for selectivity, potential clashes with anti-discrimination laws are likely.

Current Practices for Patient Selection

Although some aspects of heart transplantation are still in the experimental stages, a consistent pattern has emerged with respect to patient selection. In one transplantation program, potential heart transplant candidates are assessed for treatment suitability by a group that includes a cardiologist, a social worker, and a cardiac surgeon, all of whom have significant responsibility for direct patient care. Typically, the group accepts a number of patients roughly equal to the number of transplants that can be performed in any given period.[11] While they are not labelled as such, the program eligibility standards seem to be that: (1) the patient have a critical medical need for the transplant; (2) there be no alternate medical or surgical means that allows greater survival; and (3) the procedure have a reasonable chance of successful outcome given the current state of transplantation technology.

Specifically, in order to be considered for transplantation, a patient must have a New York Heart Association Class IV cardiac disability (essentially a bed-to-chair existence) and/or have an estimated life expectancy of less than six months.[12] In addition, the patient must have no medical contraindications to treatment, such as a recent history of pulmonary embolism, and other major organ systems also must be free from disease and infection.

Heart transplantation specialists have also singled out several psycho-social characteristics as bearing on the patient's survivability. According to current practice, the patient should have a strong "will to live," as well as the ability to endure the stress and tension caused by the pain of treatment and the need for a serious adjustment in lifestyle during the treatment and rehabilitation period.

Transplantation teams have translated these general psycho-social requirements into several specific patient selection criteria. To assure the proper mental attitude and to facilitate the patient rehabilitation process, the patient must have a stable or rewarding family or vocational environment to return to after the transplant. In addition, the patient may be excluded if he or she has experienced a history of alcoholism, job instability, or antisocial behavior.[13]

When patients are found to be otherwise suitable for transplantation, they are subjected to a variety of blood and histocompatibility tests.[14] Over the past decade, an array of systems for matching cardiac donors to recipients has been investigated. Only three systems have been demonstrated to be useful and/or practical. These include ABO blood type compatibility, negativity of the lymphocyte crossmatch, and compatibility for the human lymphocyte antigen HLA-A2. Mismatch on the A2 antigen appears to increase the probability that a long-term survivor will develop allograft coronary athrosclerosis. Matching on the basis of other HLA antigens, including those of the D locus, has not proven practical since the number of people awaiting a transplant is small, making it difficult to attain a close match between donor and recipient. Other matching systems dependent on cell cultures, although of potential value, have proven impractical because cadaver donors cannot be maintained for the time period long enough to complete the assay. With more medical centers instituting heart transplant programs and with improved techniques of organ preservation, the recipient pools will become larger. With effective mechanisms for organ sharing, more precise histocompatibility testing may become realistic. In turn, better matching of recipients to donor hearts will markedly affect the process by which patients are selected, and no longer will ABO blood type and negative lymphocyte crossmatch be the major means of indicator histocompatibility. This section focuses on the first stage of the selection process—the initial determination of who is suited for treatment.

Patient Selection and the Handicapped

Currently utilized selection criteria and mechanisms may be subject to attack under the federal handicap discrimination law because they may place barriers between treatment and the handicapped individual. Much like employee and college applicant screening, the discretionary nature of the patient screening process may be affected by the screener's unconscious biases against, or unfounded perceptions of, the handicapped. Discriminatory attitudes toward the handicapped, much like attitudes toward racial or ethnic minorities, remain embedded in our culture. Unlike race or alienage, however, a handicap—the trait that gives rise to the individual's legally protected status—may actually be perceived as a medical contraindication to treatment or as an indicator of emotional or mental instability, even though it may not affect that person's ability to benefit from treatment.[15] In addition, disabled persons are sometimes considered less able to make rewarding contributions to the community through social interaction.[16] This factor may be crucial in the allocation of scarce medical resources, because those considered most likely to make a positive contribution to society may be consciously or unconsciously favored for selection as transplant recipients.[17]

Use of ostensibly evenhanded selection criteria may also weigh against the handicapped in several ways. First, some disabilities—correctly or incorrectly— are adjudged to be medical contraindications to treatment. A severe diabetic, for instance, would probably not be considered as a candidate for heart transplantation.[18] Second, resource rationing and research considerations often dictate that the decision maker choose candidates who are least likely to suffer debilitating complications. Physicians in a new field may often be playing the medical odds— and may be disinclined to choose a person for treatment who has any history of medical or psychological debilitation. Third, some handicaps may limit or be perceived as limiting the individual's ability to adhere to a strict regimen during post-transplant rehabilitation. A heart transplantation recipient, for instance, must follow a rigorous post-operative treatment regimen consisting of drug therapy and altered life style (e.g., diet, exercise, etc.). An applicant with a limited intellectual capacity may be excluded because of doubts about whether that individual could adequately maintain the necessary medication schedule. Fourth, the use of exclusionary criteria may reflect stereotyped assumptions about the emotional or mental characteristics of the handicapped.

Thus, there are several points in the patient selection process at which the implications for potential exclusion of handicapped individuals should be carefully considered. The next section explores the potential impact that the Rehabilitation Act may have on selection practices for heart transplantation.

Section 504 of the Rehabilitation Act of 1973

Section 504 of the Rehabilitation Act of 1973 prohibits discrimination on the basis of handicap in any program or activity receiving federal financial assistance. It provides:[19]

> No otherwise qualified handicapped individual in the United States, as defined in Section 706(7) of this title, shall, solely by reason of his handicap, be excluded from participation in, be denied the benefits of, or be subjected to discrimination under any program or activity receiving Federal financial assistance or under any program or activity conducted by any Executive agency or by the United States Postal Service.

While the statute itself amounts to a broad extension of civil rights protection to the handicapped, the bare language of the statute provides little guidance to its application in specific fact situations. To ameliorate this difficulty, the Secretary of Health, Education and Welfare issued regulations in 1979[20] to enforce the Congressional mandate of providing equal opportunity to the handicapped.[21] These regulations address some but not all areas of controversy under Section 504. This section will discuss briefly several of the most pressing questions concerning Section 504's applicability to patient selection for heart transplantation, drawing on both the regulations and case law dealing with Section 504 in other settings.

The questions that arise generally center on the scope and substance of the Act. First, what is the scope of the Rehabilitation Act? Is a heart transplantation program a "program or activity" under the statute? Must the heart transplantation program itself receive federal funds, or is it sufficient that the hospital receives them? Are experimental procedures within and thus subject to anti-discrimination laws? Second, what are the substantive issues? What does the term "qualified handicapped individual" mean in a transplantation setting? What limitations does the Act place on the use of selection criteria? What types of selection practices may violate the Act?

The Scope of Section 504

The initial inquiry in a Section 504 case is whether the alleged discrimination occurred in a program or activity that receives federal financial assistance. Included within the scope of the regulations are many programs to which the Department of Health and Human Services (HHS) provides assistance through many different kinds of recipients, including states, political subdivisions of states, and public and private agencies, institutions and organizations.[22]

In order to be subject to Section 504, health care providers must receive or benefit from federal financial assistance. The major controversy in this area has focused on the exclusion from coverage under Section 504 of "any federal assistance by way of insurance or guarantee contracts."[23] Providers of medical services have argued that Medicare and Medicaid are types of insurance and therefore do not constitute federal financial assistance. According to this argument, receipt of Medicare or Medicaid funds would not subject the actions of health care providers to federal scrutiny.

This issue was specifically addressed in the HHS regulations, where it was concluded that Medicare Part A[24] and Medicaid constituted federal financial assistance, but that Medicare Part B[25] did not. The merits of this approach have received little judicial attention,[26] but it remains the explicit policy of HHS.

Under the present interpretation, hospitals with transplantation programs will almost invariably meet the requirement of receipt of federal financial assistance, since nearly all hospitals receive Medicare Part A or Medicaid funds. Of course, receipt of other federal funds may also subject recipients to Section 504.

A second set of unsettled questions centers on whether the transplantation program itself must receive federal financial assistance in order to be subject to the Act. Health care providers have contended that the scope of Section 504 is limited to the specific program or activity receiving federal financial assistance and does not extend to the entire entity, or that general assistance to the hospital is insufficient to subject a particular program (that does not receive any separate federal financial assistance) to scrutiny under Section 504.

The applicable section of the HHS regulations suggests that a transplant program itself need not receive separate federal monies so long as it benefits from other sources of assistance to the hospital. It states that Section 504 applies to health programs that receive or *benefit* from federal financial assistance and to recipients that operate or that receive or benefit from federal financial assistance for the operation of such programs.[27] Whether or not the heart transplantation program itself is considered to be the "recipient," it appears sufficient that the hospitals receive some amount of assistance that benefits the heart transplantation program. As yet, however, the meaning of the term "benefit" has not been defined by the courts, and the directness and strength of the necessary benefit are unknown. . . .

Heart transplantation is still considered by some to be an experimental procedure,[28] while the regulations under Section 504 discuss only the provision of health benefits or services (in fact, most third-party insurers consider heart transplantations to be experimental). Thus, one could conceivably argue that transplantation programs are research endeavors rather than health services and are immune from the anti-discrimination provision of Section 504. However, this argument would in all likelihood be rejected, both because heart transplantation is in large measure a health benefit or service (even though it has experimental aspects) and because Section 504 extends beyond the programs listed in the HHS regulation to "*any* program or activity receiving federal financial assistance." This analysis is borne out by an examination of the Section 504 regulations issued by the National Science Foundation (NSF),[29] an agency that disburses scientific research funds. The NSF regulations define and discuss "qualified handicapped individual" with respect to participation in scientific and technical experimentation.[30] Thus, even if cast as a research activity, heart transplantation would still fall within the scope of Section 504 if it received federal financial assistance.

These arguments may arise out of concern that Section 504 will interfere with the ability of physician-researchers to select patients on the basis of factors relevant to research objectives. However, the Act does not prohibit the use of selection criteria or practices necessary to the fulfillment of legitimate research objectives.[31]

Thus, while several of the questions addressed in this section have not been definitely settled, heart transplantation programs do appear to be subject to federal scrutiny under Section 504. The next section describes the effect of the substantive provisions of the statute on patient selection procedures and practices.

Substantive Issues

Section 504 prohibits discrimination against otherwise qualified handicapped individuals. Before discussing what it means to be a "qualified" individual in the heart transplantation setting, it is useful to briefly describe who is considered handicapped under the statute. As will be seen, the definition is very broad and may apply to a relatively large number of potential transplant recipients.

The Rehabilitation Act provides a definition that has three criteria, any one of which may result in an individual being considered handicapped. A handicapped person is one who:[32]

- has a physical or mental impairment which substantially limits one or more major life activities; or
- has a record of such impairment; or
- is regarded as having such an impairment.

Neither the Act nor the regulations provide a list of the specific handicaps covered, but the regulations do supply broad definitions of disorders that will be considered impairments. Among these conditions are physiological disorders or conditions involving the neurological, musculoskeletal, cardiovascular, and respiratory systems, in addition to the special sense organs. Additionally, such mental or psychological disorders as mental retardation, organic brain syndrome, emotional or mental illness, and specific learning disabilities are included within the meaning of "impairment." Alcoholism and drug addiction are also impairments for the purposes of distribution of health benefits.[33] Moreover, if a cosmetic disfigurement of anatomical loss affects the specified body systems, such a condition is an impairment. The regulations also list additional systems and parts of the body that may be used as a basis for defining a handicap.[34]

Under the first part of the definition, it is not enough for an individual to have one of these conditions—the condition must limit one or more of the individual's major life activities. These include functions such as walking, seeing, hearing, speaking, breathing, learning, and working.[35]

The second part of the definition includes persons who have a history of handicapping condition but no longer have the condition, and persons who were once incorrectly identified as having a handicap. Examples of persons with a history of handicap are persons with a history of cancer or mental illness. These persons may have recovered, but their past records still provide the basis for discrimination against them. Examples of persons who have been misclassified are those who have been classified as mentally retarded because of ethnic or cultural bias rather than on the basis of accurate criteria.[36]

The last part of the definition encompasses persons who may not have a handicap or a record of such handicap, but who nevertheless encounter discrimination that indicates that they are considered handicapped. Examples of this category are individuals with limps or disfiguring scars. Some confusion may arise in the transplant situation over what constitutes the relevant "handicap." Persons with end-stage cardiac disease (ESCD) are all handicapped under Section 504 because they have a cardiovascular infirmity that substantially limits one or more of their major life activities. However, discrimination among these individuals can occur if a transplantation program eliminates from consideration persons with additional handicapping conditions that do not limit their ability to benefit from treatment (or some other essential eligibility requirement). By way of example, a blind ESCD victim may be impermissibly denied access to a transplantation program on the assumption that blindness limits his or her ability to benefit from treatment, even though every applicant is "handicapped" under the Act. Therefore, Section 504 can be applied in the patient selection setting to reduce discrimination among handicapped individuals based on a second handicapping condition.

Section 504 does not bar discrimination against the handicapped unless they are "otherwise qualified" to participate in or benefit from a program. In *Southeastern Community College v. Davis*,[37] the Supreme Court held that the term "otherwise qualified" refers to a person who is qualified *in spite of* rather than *apart from* his or her handicap. An institution is therefore not required to disregard the disabilities of the applicant if his or her handicapping condition is relevant to reasonable program acceptance standards. The Court's ruling in *Davis* indicates that a handicapped person may be excluded from a federally funded health program if he or she doesn't meet the program's essential physiologically or mentally based eligibility requirements.[38] Such physical or mental requirements must, however, be legitimate and necessary.[39] Thus, the Rehabilitation Act does not prohibit reasonable, necessary physiologically or mentally based requirements of a transplantation program, even if they result in the exclusion of some handicapped individuals. These individuals are not "qualified" for heart transplantation and are thus not protected by the Act. The Act can, however, be used to scrutinize selection standards and program requirements to see if they are legitimate and fairly applied.

With these principles in mind, it is useful to examine heart transplantation patient selection practices in the context of Section 504. If patient selection practices were challenged under Section 504, the following questions are likely to arise. First, may physicians exclude handicapped individuals with a reasonably good chance of successful clinical outcome if their handicap or some condition associated with it makes them less qualified than other applicants? Second, what selection standards and criteria may be legitimately employed without violating Section 504? Third, what types of screening practices other than use of biased criteria may violate Section 504? These questions are addressed in turn below.

To our knowledge, no court has addressed the issue of comparative medical evaluations in the allocation of scarce medical treatment under Section 504. However, an analogous problem has arisen in the context of medical school admissions, and the court in that case used broad language that is relevant to permissible patient selection practices. That language could be applied by analogy to sanction comparative medical evaluations that result in the exclusion of handicapped persons who meet all reasonable transplant program requirements, if other non-handicapped persons have a *better* prognosis.

The case, *Doe v. New York University*, involved Jane Doe, a woman with a long history of severe psychiatric disturbances, including several attempts at severe self-mutilation.[40] Ms. Doe was admitted into NYU medical school after falsely representing in her application that she did not have any chronic or recurrent illnesses or emotional problems. In 1976 during her second semester, she re-exhibited her previous self-destructive tendencies and was given a leave of absence with the understanding that she could apply for readmission. Shortly thereafter, she was diagnosed as a "borderline personality."[41] After undergoing treatment in California, she reapplied but was denied admission. She was, however, admitted into Harvard's School of Public Health where she earned a Master's degree. During the pendency of her Master's degree program at Harvard, she renewed her efforts to be re-admitted to NYU. After re-interviewing her and getting the opinion of a mutually agreed upon psychiatrist, NYU refused to re-admit her based on the psychiatrist's diagnosis. Ms. Doe then filed suit, claiming that the psychiatrist's report could not be validated as a predictor of success in medical school and that NYU had denied her readmission in violation of Section 504.[42]

Ms. Doe was required to exhaust her administrative remedies before the district court would hear her case.[43] However, when the court considered the case in 1981, it concluded that Ms. Doe was "otherwise qualified" since it was "more likely than not" that she could complete her studies and become a competent physician.[44] This finding was based in part upon the fact that she had not engaged in any self-destructive or anti-social behavior since 1977 and had been working in a stressful job where her performance had been evaluated as excellent. On the basis of its findings and its analysis of Section 504, the district court granted a preliminary injunction and ordered NYU to re-admit her in 1981.[45]

In reviewing the lower court's opinion, the court of appeals concluded that "n[o] deference was given to NYU's evaluation of Doe's qualifications as compared with those of other qualified first year students."[46] The court sanctioned the use of comparative psycho-social evaluations, stating that:[47]

> the qualification of a handicapped person for admission into an institution turns not only on whether he or she meets its *reasonable* program requirements, but on whether the individual, where a few must be chosen out of many, is *as well* qualified despite the handicap as others accepted for the limited number of openings.

In effect, the court stated that where there are more qualified applicants than openings, the institution is *not* required to accept a handicapped individual who meets all reasonable program standards if the handicap renders that individual less well qualified than other applicants.

In light of the opinion's broad wording, there is little reason to believe that the holding is confined to the school admissions context. Rather, it implies that where a medical or psycho-social characteristic is relevant to successful program participation, the institution can take it into consideration when weighing the candidate's relative merits and exclude those handicapped individuals who rank comparatively lower on this factor. The case is also significant because the same requirement of emotional ability to withstand stress is the basis for the imposition of psycho-social patient selection standards in both educational admissions and selection for heart transplantations.

Despite the likelihood that other courts may follow the lead of the Second Circuit Court of Appeals and hold that choosing those with maximum likelihood of successful clinical outcome will not violate the requirements of Section 504, patient selection ostensibly based on this goal may still violate the statute where the quality measured is relevant only up to a threshold level and comparative evaluations are made beyond that point. Distinctions between the handicapped and non-handicapped may become irrelevant after this threshold level is met. For example, if one needs to have some degree of emotional stability to undergo heart transplantation, does it matter that another individual is *more* stable, if emotional health only impacts on survivability on the lower end of the scale? If it does not matter, then such a characteristic is no longer relevant to reasonable acceptance standards and exclusion on the basis of emotional stability may violate both the spirit of the regulations and the holding in *Southeastern Community College v. Davis*.

Past history in the area of medical practice indicates that reliance on irrelevant factors in patient selection is possible, if not likely. Consider, for instance, the case of insulin distribution to diabetics when the drug first appeared on the medical scene and was in extremely short supply. Patients were often excluded ostensibly because they did not possess sufficient strength of character to maintain the treatment regime. This exclusionary policy undoubtedly adversely affected individuals who would now be protected under the Rehabilitation Act. However, it is now widely believed that most persons whose lives depend on taking insulin and reducing their sugar intake can do so. There is a strong possibility that the earlier view rested not so much on valid medical evaluation as on the pressure to invent some reasoned basis for the allocation decision, thereby avoiding the tremendous difficulties of rationally deciding whom to leave to the ravages of a lethal condition when medical science offers the hope of a cure.[48]

Questions of handicap discrimination may also arise when the medical or psychological reasons advanced for denying admission rest on hard to prove or unproven assumptions. One court, interpreting Section 504 in a case involving psychological employment screening, has stated that conclusions based on nothing more than psychological theory are "weak and inadequate threads where . . . (someone's) entire future . . . is at stake."[49] This reasoning can only apply more forcefully when it is life itself, rather than merely a career opportunity, that hangs in the balance.[50]

In summary, the only court case that addresses the issue of selecting the *most* qualified applicants suggests that Section 504 would allow selection of those with maximum likelihood of clinical success, even though this may result in the exclusion of qualified handicapped individuals. However, under the principles outlined by *Davis* and the regulations, such comparative exclusion cannot be continued after the factor loses significance as a predictor of outcome or survivability. Courts may also be more hesitant to exclude such individuals where denial rests on unsubstantiated medical or psychological theory.

Several principles may limit the types of criteria that transplant centers may utilize in selecting their patients. Under Section 504 and its implementing regulations, health care providers may not offer a handicapped individual who meets essential program eligibility requirements an opportunity to receive benefits that is not equal to that offered non-handicapped persons. Providers may not utilize patient selection criteria that have the effect of subjecting qualified handicapped individuals to discrimination on the basis of their handicapping conditions.[51] There have been no judicial interpretations of the applicability of Section 504 in the selection of patients for heart transplantation. Therefore, the analysis set out below is based on the analogy of Section 504's application in the education and employment settings.

Heart transplantation is an ordeal that is both arduous and risky. Transplant programs therefore seek individuals who are relatively healthy apart from their cardiac condition. In addition, they seek individuals with a strong will to live and the ability to cope with the stress and tension caused by the pain of treatment and the need for adjustment in lifestyle. These goals have been translated into a number of discrete patient selection criteria. Discussion of these criteria will illustrate both the possibility for discrimination on the basis of handicap and the implications of Section 504 in the patient selection context.

From the literature, it appears that the relevant psycho-social patient selection criteria fall into a group of contraindications and requirements. The major *contraindications* are a history of alcoholism, presence of psychiatric illness, job instability, and antisocial behavior. The major *requirement* is a stable or rewarding family or vocational environment to return to following transplantation.[52]

These criteria and requirements, along with the more physiologically oriented criteria, can be divided into two groups. First are those that explicitly deny services to individuals on the basis of handicap. Exclusions based on "history of alcoholism" and "presence of psychiatric illness" fall into this category. Second are those that may disproportionately affect the handicapped although they appear neutral on their face. Both "job instability" and "presence of a stable family or vocational environment" can be placed in this category. These two types of criteria present different problems for defining the content of Section 504's anti-discrimination provisions.

Some of the disability-specific selection criteria discussed above are considered to be either totally exclusionary or strongly adverse factors in the decision whether to admit the heart transplant candidate into the patient pool. For example, persons with irreversible and severe renal or hepatic dysfunction are either totally excluded or given very small hope of real consideration, as are persons with severe insulin-requiring diabetes. As mentioned above, some facilities may exclude or limit the participation of persons on the basis of histories of psychiatric illness or alcoholism. All of the conditions mentioned above are considered handicaps under the Section 504 regulations.[53]

Following the approach taken in other selection contexts, handicapped individuals legally may be excluded from heart transplantation on the basis of their handicapping condition if *all* persons possessing such a handicap could not benefit from treatment.[54] A blanket exclusion of this type is not discriminatory because no individual with a condition that always disallows any reasonable chance of successful clinical outcome can ever meet the essential eligibility requirements of the program. Such individuals therefore would never be qualified under the Act.

However, persons sharing a particular type of handicapping condition often do not share the same level of debilitation. For instance, included among epileptics are the 50% who are seizure free with the prescribed medication and the 30% who can control their seizures with the proper medication.[55] Similarly, the class of persons with a "history of mental illness" may include individuals who have experienced a nervous breakdown, persons diagnosed as acutely schizophrenic, and persons with intellectual disabilities of various types and degrees.[56] In short, the variation in types and levels of impairment among people with a specific handicap often disallows meaningful generalizations about their chances for successful clinical outcome following a heart transplantation. Categoric exclusions of classes of handicapped individuals might be considered overbroad if used to exclude persons who can benefit from treatment.[57] Of course, the individual's handicapping condition may nevertheless be relevant to the treatment decision. However, the admission decision would necessarily have to be based on an individualized consideration of that person's physical condition and prognosis.

Exclusionary criteria may be narrowed to focus on a small, uniformly affected group of handicapped persons. A refusal to admit because of a highly particularized handicap would be legitimate because of the inability of anyone in that class to meet the essential eligibility requirements of the program.[58]

Thus, criteria that excluded certain classes of handicapped individuals should pass muster under Section 504 as long as they are sufficiently narrowly tailored. A program might encounter difficulties if, for example, it excluded persons with all forms of diabetes unless none could meet the essential eligibility requirements of a heart transplantation program. By way of contrast, persons with insulin-requiring diabetes could probably legitimately be excluded as a class if they uniformly cannot meet the essential eligibility requirements.[59]

Section 504 prohibits both discriminatory actions that explicitly use handicap as criteria and actions that have the *effect* of discriminating on the basis of handicap.[60] Several of the recognized patient selection criteria that attempt to measure emotional stability may disproportionately affect the handicapped. For example, the presence of a stable family or work environment is often used as a measure of emotional stability. On its face, such a requirement does not exclude any group of the handicapped. However, the handicapped individual often may be without the type of stable family or work background that the screeners seek.

The Office of Civil Rights of the Department of Health and Human Services uses a three-part test to review health care policies or practices that may have a discriminatory effect on handicapped persons.[61] That test is outlined below, followed by a discussion of its application in the heart transplantation setting:

First, does the policy or practice have a disproportionate, adverse effect on handicapped persons? If the policy or practice does not have a disproportionate adverse effect, it does not violate Section 504. If the policy or practice does have a disproportionate adverse effect, the second part of the test must be applied: Is the policy or practice related to a legitimate objective unrelated to handicap? If the policy or practice has a disproportionate, adverse effect and does not further a legitimate objective, it violates Section 504. If the policy or practice has a disproportionate adverse effect and furthers a legitimate objective, the third part of the test must be applied: Are there alternatives that would further the same objectives but that would have a lower disproportionate effect? If such alternatives are available, the policy or practice violates Section 504.[62]

Several selection criteria, while facially neutral, may pose a risk of both disproportionately excluding the handicapped and violating Section 504. By way of example, some heart transplant programs may evaluate present and future emotional stability by reference to the candidate's ability to hold a job and by the stability of his or her family and work environment. While these indicia may accurately reflect emotional stability for some non-disabled persons, for the handicapped such factors may not be appropriate. Handicapped individuals who are mentally and emotionally able to handle the stresses of heart transplantation are often unable to keep or even obtain employment because of discriminatory attitudes among employers and fellow workers as well as unwillingness to accommodate the handicapped worker.[63] Similarly, the handicapping condition and the response of others to persons with such a condition may make it more difficult for the handicapped individual to attain the type of traditional stable family relationship sought by transplantation teams. The use of such selection criteria may therefore disproportionately exclude handicapped individuals from transplantation programs. Upon proof of such a disproportionate impact, the first prong of the test is satisfied.

The second prong of the test asks whether the standard or criteria is related to a legitimate objective unrelated to handicap. These criteria are all related to emotional stability, which in turn is presumed to impact upon survivability. Accepting for the moment that such objectives—choosing emotionally stable persons in order to assure survivability—is valid, then the criteria must be measured against the third prong: whether there are alternative standards that would further the same objectives with a lower disproportionate impact upon any class of handicapped individuals. In the heart transplantation context, that alternative may simply be to individually assess each candidate on the basis of that person's current emotional stability by considering the opinion of the individual's physician, mental health professional, or social worker if available and through personal interviewing.[64]

In sum, the following guidance can be offered to health care providers who seek to establish patient selection criteria that will pass muster under the Rehabilitation Act: first, any criteria that specifically exclude or limit the opportunities of handicapped individuals must be narrowly tailored to reach only those individuals whose disabilities would uniformly impact upon ability to meet the essential eligibility requirements; and second, facially neutral criteria may not be used if they have the effect of discriminating on the basis of handicap. . . .

Title VI and Heart Transplantation:
Discrimination in Patient Selection

Title VI of the Civil Rights Act of 1964 prohibits discrimination on the basis of race, color, or national origin in federally assisted programs.[65] Section 601 of the act provides that:

No person in the United States shall, on the ground of race, color, or national origin, be excluded from participation in, be denied the benefits of, or be subjected to discrimination under any program or activity receiving federal financial assistance.

While Title VI was enacted primarily to prohibit segregation in publicly funded schools, it applies equally to all recipients of federal funds, including institutions that provide health care. Because virtually all hospitals with transplant programs accept some form of federal financial assistance,[66] Title VI has implications for patient selection practices for heart transplantation. The potential impact of Title VI on patient selection for heart transplantation is difficult to assess because, to date, the Title VI enforcement program has not brought substantive issues of discrimination to the fore in even the most common areas of health care.[67] However, due to increasing concern over rising costs and the use of sophisticated technology, government scrutiny of all facets of health care and health care spending is likely to increase.[68] It is in this context that the issue of discrimination in the selection of patients for transplantation must be considered because the regulatory and allocative decisions that are currently being made with respect to heart transplantation may adversely affect racial and ethnic minorities.

The nature and extent of the problem of racially based inequities in heart transplantation programs are difficult to define precisely or to specify. However, substantial disparities may exist in the receipt of heart transplantation by race and ethnicity. In other areas of health care, evidence indicates that racial and ethnic minorities do not have equal access to medical services.[69] It is likely, particularly in light of the emphasis on selectivity in the heart transplantation setting, that this problem is or will be exacerbated in the heart transplantation patient selection process.[70]

The important question is whether any part of the disparity arises out of discrimination in the legal sense of the term and, if so, whether and when such discrimination can be legally attributable to the patient selection procedures of the government or specific health care facilities. While aspects of patient selection may raise Title VI issues, many cannot be definitively settled because of the difficulty in determining both the content and the scope of Title VI as it applies in this specialized area of health care.

The *content* issues concern the effect of Title VI on patient selection practices. They include choice of patient selection criteria, application of those criteria to the heart transplant candidate, and the impact of a range of environmental and socio-cultural factors on the representation of racial and ethnic minorities in the transplant recipient population. The *scope* issues involve the persons and institutions to whom the statute applies. Even a cursory examination of the complicated arrangements through which patients are referred to heart transplantation programs and chosen for treatment suggests a number of difficult issues that can only be briefly discussed here: Who is responsible if a private physician makes discriminatory referrals to a transplant program? May a federal agency write and enforce regulations that would violate Title VI, if written and imposed at the transplant program level? Is the transplant facility open to charges of discrimination if it utilizes discriminatory patient selection criteria that were promulgated by a federal agency?

The potential merit of many claims of discrimination in patient selection and referral rests on resolution of these scope and content issues. Yet these issues cannot be definitively addressed because they in turn reflect further uncertainties in two central areas of Title VI law. They are (1) whether a discriminatory effects or intent standard is appropriate for Title VI litigation and enforcement, and (2) the meanings of "federal financial assistance" and "recipient" as they arise under Title VI.

The applicable standard substantially impacts on the content issues because differential utilization of heart transplantation programs by racial and ethnic groups may arise out of facially neutral practices[71] actionable, if at all, only under the effects test. The second uncertainty—the meanings of federal financial "assistance" and "recipient"—is important to the scope issues because only health care providers who receive federal financial assistance, and are thus "recipients," are subject to Title VI.

Because the heart transplantation issues arising under Title VI are conceptually organized around these central areas of Title VI law, the remaining body of this section is structured to reflect this natural grouping into content and scope issues. Thus, we first address what patient selection practices may be affected by Title VI, and then take up who may be subject to the requirements of Title VI.

The Content Issues: Discriminatory Intent or Effects?

Federal courts have not yet established a uniform standard by which to identify actions or practices forbidden by Title VI. While the U.S. Supreme Court has not yet spoken on the subject,[72] lower federal courts have divided on which test is the appropriate one under Title VI.

The *effects* test requires the plaintiff to present evidence of a disproportionate and injurious impact of the defendant's facially neutral action on the members of a racial minority group as a class.[73] Upon an initial showing of discrimination by the plaintiff, the burden shifts to the defendant to establish a legitimate justification for its action and to show that a less discriminatory course of action is not available.[74] By comparison, the *intent* test requires the plaintiff to present evidence of the defendant's discriminatory intent in addition to showing the disproportionate impact of the defendant's action. Under this test, the plaintiff must present evidence—direct or circumstantial—establishing that the defendant acted with a specific discriminatory purpose. Thus, evidence of impact, by itself, is insufficient to establish an illegitimate purpose.[75]

The choice between these threshold tests has become increasingly important as the nature of Title VI cases has changed. It is increasingly rare to encounter the kind of direct and overt discriminatory practices that originally prompted Congress to enact the anti-discrimination laws. While openly discriminatory hospital admissions policies and regulations were documented in the 1960s,[76] it would be extremely unusual today for any minority group to be refused medical services explicitly on the basis of race. Recently, Title VI claims have tended to focus on stereotypical or facially neutral practices rather than overt racial bias.[77] In these types of cases, the legal test of discrimination chosen by a court significantly affects the outcome of a case because the plaintiff often may be able to prove discriminatory effect, but not discriminatory intent.

The standard used is important for our purposes because patient selection practices and selection criteria will be challenged more easily under the effects test. For this reason, and because it is the test currently used by the federal office primarily responsible for enforcing Title VI in the health care area,[78] the U.S. Department of Health and Human Services' (HHS) Office for Civil Rights (OCR), we will concentrate on exploring the ramifications of the effects test for patient selection.

The regulatory basis for the effects test under Title VI is found in 45 CFR §§80.3(b)(2). It provides that:

> A recipient, in determining the types of services, financial aid, or other benefits, or facilities which will be provided under any such program, or the class of

individuals to whom, or the situations in which, such services, financial aid, other benefits, or facilities will be provided under any such program, may not, directly or through contractual or other arrangements, utilize criteria or methods of administration which have the *effect* of defeating or substantially impairing the objectives of the program as respects individuals of a particular race, color or national origin. (emphasis added)

However, neither this nor other explanations of Title VI's substantive provisions are specific enough to guide OCR staff and the courts, as well as recipients and beneficiaries, in determining compliance.[79] Civil rights enforcement actions have therefore frequently relied on interpretive rules that interpret those general obligations in specific factual contexts.[80] One of the most important areas in which the OCR developed policy was in specifying how the effects test was to be applied. As noted in the previous section, OCR evolved a three-part test for determining when a Title VI violation has occurred.[81] Although the test itself is rather simplistic, it does offer some guidance in determining when facially neutral policies or practices will violate Title VI.

The first part of the test asks whether the proposed criteria or action will have a disproportionate adverse effect on persons of a particular race, color, or national origin. If the action does not have such a disproportionate effect, it does not violate Title VI. If the action will have such a disproportionate adverse effect, the second part of the test asks whether the action is necessary to further legitimate governmental objectives unrelated to race, color, or national origin. If the action is not necessary to further such legitimate objectives, it will violate Title VI. Even if the action furthers legitimate objectives, if alternatives exist that would further those objectives with a lesser disproportionate adverse effect, Title VI is violated under the third part of the test.[82] After briefly describing some current patient selection practices, we will discuss how the effects test may be applied in the patient selection setting.

Several of the recognized patient selection criteria currently used in heart transplant programs may disproportionately affect racial and ethnic minorities under the first part of the effects test. Our intent here is not to analyze exhaustively every patient selection criterion or practice that could be challenged under Title VI; rather, it is to indicate how OCR's effects test can be applied to patient selection practices for heart transplantation. To do this, we will focus on two patient selection criteria that may disproportionately affect racial or minority groups and indicate how they may be analyzed under the effects test. The reader should be cautioned that in so doing we are forced to paint with a very broad brush. With that caution in mind, the remaining portion of this section concentrates on two specific selection criteria for heart transplantation; one medical, one psycho-social. The first is exclusion because of severe renal dysfunction; the second is exclusion based on lack of a stable family environment to return to after transplantation.

As noted above, the first part of the effects test asks whether facially neutral criteria or practices disproportionately affect a racial or ethnic minority. If the presence of severe renal dysfunction is used as a basis for exclusion from heart transplantation, this first part of the effects test will be met, because such a criterion will tend to disproportionately screen out racial and ethnic minorities, particularly blacks. While blacks constituted slightly more than 11.3% of the population as measured by the 1970 census, as of March 1977 the End-Stage Renal Disease (ESRD) Medical Information System indicated that blacks constituted 24.1% of the ESRD population.[83] Clearly blacks would likely be disproportionately excluded from heart transplantation by a criterion focused on renal dysfunction.

Similarly, an exclusionary criterion based on lack of familial support mechanisms could disproportionately affect blacks and other minority groups, especially if the criterion focused on factors such as the presence of the spouse in the household. The 1980 census figures indicate that married minority group members, particularly blacks, are disproportionately likely to have their spouse absent from the household.[84] Thus, any criterion that focuses on the presence of the spouse in the home may also disproportionately affect racial or ethnic minority groups.

However, a disproportionate effect on racial or ethnic groups, in and of itself, does not establish a Title VI violation. The second part of OCR's effects test proceeds to ask whether the action or criterion is necessary to further a legitimate government objective. Under a system of Medicare reimbursement for heart transplantation, strict patient selection criteria would relate to at least the following two objectives: (1) assuring that those most likely to benefit from treatment undergo the procedure, and (2) controlling costs by keeping the number of potential recipients low.

While the question has not arisen in Title VI case law, selecting those transplant candidates most likely to benefit from the procedure is probably a legitimate objective.[85] Moreover, OCR has specified that realizing necessary fiscal savings is a legitimate objective unrelated to race or national origin.[86]

If renal dysfunction limits the ability of individuals to benefit from heart transplantation, exclusion of individuals with that condition would further a legitimate objective and thus the criterion would pass the second part of the effects test. Similarly, the exclusion of persons without recognized familial support systems would probably pass muster under the second part of the test, since it would serve the same legitimate objective of aiding in the selection of those most likely to benefit from treatment, because interpersonal support systems have been shown to be important to successful rehabilitation from serious illnesses.[87]

The crucial issues surrounding any criteria used to select those eligible to receive heart transplants will probably focus on the third element of the test: whether alternative methods or criteria exist that will further the same objective with a lesser disproportionate effect. Exclusion because of severe renal dysfunction probably is not discriminatory under Title VI. If renal dynsfunction is a true contraindication to heart transplantation, then no alternative method or criterion could be devised that could have a lesser disproportionate effect on blacks while still meeting the legitimate programmatic objective of excluding those unlikely to benefit from treatment. Absent unforeseen factors, then, the exclusion would survive a Title VI challenge.

However, an exclusion focused on particular types of family support systems is more troublesome. Members of racial and ethnic groups may disproportionately vary from the predominant middle-American norms of living patterns, but the alternatives adopted may be just as likely to provide the strong interpersonal support necessary for successful recovery following the transplant procedure. Thus, there may well be alternative criteria or methods of selecting patients that would have a lesser disproportionate effect on racial or ethnic groups. For instance, an alternative policy of individually assessing the degree and extent of all forms of interpersonal support mechanisms could be used. Since an alternative method exists to further the presumably legitimate objective of choosing those who will rehabilitate quickly and successfully, the practice of excluding persons who vary from the traditional nuclear family norm may violate Title VI.

Another type of discrimination may surface in admissions decisions even if the transplant program standards and criteria for patient selection do not violate Title VI. The screeners'[88] conscious and unconscious perceptions of members of racial and ethnic groups may influence their assessment of minority transplant candidates. If discriminatory intent need not be proven, Title VI is also violated when the applicant, on the grounds of race, is rejected or treated differently from others in determining whether he or she meets any of the selection criteria.[89] While no systematic data in the heart transplantation setting are available, studies have noted racial/ethnic sorting processes in mental health care settings.[90] In light of the greater emphasis on selectivity in the heart transplantation setting than in most health care settings, the same kind of practices probably exist to a more significant degree in patient selection for heart transplantation. While such practices have never received formal legal attention, they may not conform to the mandates of Title VI.

The Scope Issues

The analysis above concentrated on *what* types of actions may violate Title VI. The remaining analysis examines *who*, in the chain of persons who refer and select heart transplant candidates, is subject to the substantive provisions of Title VI.

Absent complicating factors, if the transplant facility utilizes discriminatory methods or criteria in patient selection, it may be held in violation of Title VI under the effects test. Yet other factors may account for low minority representation in the transplant recipient population.[91] For example, discrimination may have occurred further back in the chain of patient referrals to a transplant program. Who may be held in violation of Title VI if the referring physician discriminates and refuses, for example, to refer black individuals to a transplantation program on the basis of race? Is this a violation of the transplantation facility's Title VI obligations? Can the individual physician be found in violation of Title VI? Second, is the Health Care Finance Administration (HCFA) subject to Title VI when it makes reimbursement decisions for the Medicare program? Could it impose patient selection criteria that would ordinarily violate Title VI on transplant facilities as a condition of their participation in a Medicare heart transplant reimbursement system? . . .

. . . Although the unsettled nature of Title VI law in this area precludes the formation of definitive conclusions, it appears that Title VI may impose limitations on: (1) the permissible range of patient selection criteria; (2) physician and hospital referral practices; and (3) federal agency standard setting for provider inclusion in Medicare heart transplantation reimbursement plans.

. . . Choice and use of patient selection criteria may be circumscribed under Title VI if they result in discrimination against racial or ethnic minorities even if they were not intended to have that effect. These limits may apply to both the transplant facility and the referring physician. In addition, it may be advisable for HCFA to assure that any standards for patient selection it may impose on transplant facilities as a condition of participation in a Medicare reimbursement program for heart transplantation do not conflict with the mandates of Title VI in order to avoid the creation of possible noncompliance issues for the transplant facility, if not for HCFA itself.

Age Discrimination in Patient Selection
for Heart Transplantation

The Health Care Financing Administration (HCFA) recently[92] solicited applications from hospitals and medical centers to participate in a general study to examine all aspects of heart transplantation. Included in the solicitation were the procedures and criteria to be used for selecting institutions to be reimbursed for heart transplantations under the study. The second of four criteria required that applicant institutions have adequate patient selection criteria, evidenced by (among others) criteria that give consideration to those factors that are recognized at the present as exerting an adverse influence on the outcome after cardiac transplantation. Such "strongly adverse factors" include "Advancing age—e.g., beyond the age (normally about 50) at which the individual begins to have a diminished capacity to withstand postoperative complications."[93] The purpose of this section is to examine, through the lens of the Age Discrimination Act of 1975 (ADA),[94] the legal viability of "advancing age" as a "strongly adverse factor" in the selection of patients for heart transplantation.

The basic structure of the ADA is simple. The Act prohibits discrimination on the basis of age in all federally assisted programs and activities and then excludes from coverage those programs or activities "established under authority of any law" employing age criteria to condition benefits or participation. In addition, the statute contains several broadly worded "reasonableness" exceptions from the general prohibition. Finally, the Act requires each federal agency or department to issue implementing regulations. Enforcement of the ADA is to be through governmental agencies and departments and, following the 1978 amendments, by private individuals through the courts. . . .

Because of both the lack of precision in its legislative history and the paucity of judicial experience with its interpretation, it is difficult to assess the extent to which the ADA may affect the use of age as a patient selection criterion. The controversies over the intended interpretation of the ADA remain to be resolved. The importance of these controversies, however, lies in the fact that their resolution will determine the scope of application of the statute; to the extent that the exclusions and exceptions are broadly construed, the range of permissible uses of age distinctions will be constricted. At this point the best that can be done is to identify those issues upon which there is some consensus and to point out issues that remain unresolved. The material in the following section will briefly discuss some of these considerations in specific reference to the use of age as a patient selection criterion in heart transplantation programs.

Defining Discrimination

A question of fundamental importance is whether age is or should be considered in the same vein as race, sex, or religion, meriting special attention and protection in the law. The arguments on both sides of this question are presented elsewhere,[95] but it should be noted that there are persuasive legal and policy considerations from both perspectives.

In general, though, it is difficult to imagine any procedure for rationing limited program benefits among a large pool of applicants (a necessary condition for the current operation of a heart transplant program) that would not have differential age-related impacts. For example, a means test or fee schedule will certainly work to the detriment of the less affluent (i.e., the retired elderly). Age groups are not uniformly distributed geographically, thus location criteria will tend to favor age groups living in proximity to transplant centers (be they young or old). Finally, a first-come-first-served procedure will tend to favor those age groups who are most mobile and better informed, to the detriment of the elderly. The question remains, though, whether such differential age impacts are "discrimination" or merely inadvertent by-products of administrative convenience in the distribution of government benefits.

Even a cursory examination of the law reveals that age distinctions arise in numerous different contexts, where they are used as proxies for, or predictors of, many factors thought to be correlated with age.[96] All such classifications treat one age group differently than another and frequently exclude one or more age groups from benefits altogether. In general, the reasonableness of any particular age classification will hinge on the consequences of using age as a proxy or a predictor in the specific context in which it is used. The legal viability of age distinctions in patient selection for heart transplantation, however, will depend upon the resolution of as yet undecided questions about the scope of the ADA.

"Any Law" Exclusion

The courts have yet to determine whether the provisions of the ADA apply only to federal law or also encompass state and local law. It seems unlikely, however, that the courts would permit (or Congress intended) the ADA to be used to invalidate the myriad of legitimate uses of age distinctions in state and local law. In any case, regulations established under the authority of the federal Medicare program would be exempt from the ADA under the "any law" exclusion of Section 304(b)(2). Thus, it is likely that a strict age criterion for heart transplantation patient selection would be excluded from scrutiny under the ADA.

"Normal Operation" Exception

For an action such as the use of a strict age criterion to be sustained under the normal operation exception, there are two operative questions: (1) does the criterion "reasonably" take age into account? *and* (2) is the use of the age criterion "necessary" to the normal operation of a heart transplant program?

The first leg of the test may be satisfied merely by a showing that age is in some way correlated with physical hardiness or survivability. Under analogous tests of reasonableness, this requirement could be met upon a showing of only the most minimal relationship between age and survivability; the use of the criterion would be unreasonable only if there was *no* relationship between the two.

The second leg of the test, however, is more difficult to meet. The question is whether the use of an age criterion is "necessary" to the normal operation of a heart transplant program. In the first instance, it should be apparent that an age criterion is not necessary to the normal operation of a heart transplant program—transplanting 60-year-olds would merely reduce the success rate of the program. The more appropriate question is whether an age criterion is "necessary" to the *cost-effective* operation of the program; that is, does the normal operation of a heart transplant program encompass targeting scarce resources on those individuals who are most likely to benefit from the program? The answer is not entirely clear, but there is language in the regulations that suggests that notions of efficiency and cost-benefit favorability cannot be equated with "necessary," and thus a strict age criterion may not meet this leg of the exception.

"Statutory Objective" Exception

A strict age criterion in patient selection may be exempt from the provisions of the ADA if its use is necessary to "the achievement of any statutory objective" of a heart transplant program. Although the exact nature of a statutory objective is unclear, the regulations specify a four-part test for the exception. Thus, in order for a strict age criterion to be exempt under the statutory objective exception it must be shown that:

1. age is used as a measure or approximation of survivability;
2. survivability is an important factor for the normal operation or the achievement of a statutory objective of the heart transplantation program;
3. survivability can be reasonably measured or approximated by the use of a strict age criterion; *and*
4. survivability is impractical to measure directly on an individual basis.

The burden of meeting these requirements will be placed on the transplant program asserting the need for using the strict age criterion.

Conclusion

With the caution that there is a woeful lack of law supporting any interpretation of the ADA, several tentative conclusions can be made:

1. Discrimination on the basis of age is not viewed with the same degree of alarm as discrimination on the basis of race, sex, or religion. In general, the use of age distinctions will be subject to fewer legal restrictions than other forms of discrimination.
2. Regardless of the ultimate determination of the meaning of "any law," the use of a strict age criterion in patient selection for heart transplantation will be excluded from the ADA's general prohibition against age discrimination.
3. Because the use of a strict age criterion is not "necessary" to the normal operation of a heart transplantation program, its use would not meet the requirements of the "normal operation" exception of the ADA.
4. If the relationship between age and survivability is demonstrably strong, the use of a strict age criterion will be exempt from the ADA under the "statutory objective" exception.

In summary, the ADA and its prohibition against age discrimination are unlikely to seriously impede the use of a strict age criterion in patient selection for heart transplantation.

Notes

1. 29 U.S.C. Section 794 (1976) (as amended by Rehabilitation, Comprehensive Services, and Developmental Disabilities Amendments of 1978, Pub. L. No. 95-602, Sections 119, 122, 92 Stat. 2955, 2982).

2. 29 U.S.C. Section 701-794 (1976) (as amended by Rehabilitation, Comprehensive Services, and Developmental Disabilities Admendments of 1978, Pub. L. No. 95-602, tits. I–IV, 92 Stat. 2955–3003).

3. See, 45 C.F.R. Section 84 et seq. (1979).

4. See, e.g., *United States v. University Hospital, State University of New York at Stony Brook*, No. C.V. 83-4818, (D.C. E.D.N.Y. Nov. 17, 1983).

5. Schroeder, *Current Status of Heart Transplantation*, 241 Journal of the American Medical Association 2069 (1979).

6. Penneck, Oyer, Reitz, Jamieson, Bieber, Wallwork, Stinson & Shumway, *Cardiac Transplantation in Perspective for the Future: Survival, Complications, Rehabilitation and Cost*, 83 Journal of Thoracic Cardiovascular Surgery 168 (1982) (Hereinafter cited as Penneck, et al.), 1982.

7. Levy and Moskowitz, 1982.

8. Levy and Moskowitz, 1982. Of this amount, $20 billion represents health expenditures, $10 billion productivity lost due to illness, and $30 billion potential productivity lost due to early death. This $60 billion accounts for more than one-fifth of the total cause of illness in the United States.

9. For example, among heart transplant recipients, major causes of death include infection (58%), acute rejection (18.3%), graft arteriosclerosis (10.7%), and malignancy (4.6%). Penneck, cited supra n. 6. Infection, rejection, and malignancy are all related to current methods of immunosuppression.

10. Christopherson, *Heart Transplants*, The Hastings Center Report 12, February 1982. There is already some evidence that the pressure of referrals is causing criteria other than expected outcome to be used for patient selection. *Id*. This pressure could conceivably result in more handicapped individuals being excluded from transplantation programs because of their perceived or actual limitations or because of the interviewers' personal biases.

11. *Id*. at 19.

12. See, Copeland & Stenson, *Human Heart Transplantation*, 4 Current Problems in Cardiology 1 (1979); Evans, *Economic and Social Costs of Heart Transplantation*, 1 Heart Transplantation 243 (1983).

13. Knox, *Heart Transplants: To Pay or Not to Pay*, 209 Science August 1, 1980, at 570, 572. Note that these psycho-social requirements, like the physical contraindications to heart transplantation, to the extent that they are currently valid, are subject to change as the technology of transplantation changes. For instance, improvements in transplantation may make continuous treatment unnecessary following a successful operation and therefore "cooperativeness" and ability to adjust to treatment may become less significant. See Eschbach, Barnett, Daly, Cole and Schribner, *Hemodialysis in the Home*, 67 Annals of Internal Medicine 1167 (1967).

14. Environmental factors serve to exclude many from consideration. The cardiac patient may live in a rural area and thus never be referred to an urban transplant center. Inability to pay for treatment also results in the exclusion of many.

15. See, Amos, "Transplantation—Opportunities and Problems," in *Research in the Service of Man* 177, 179; P. E. Oyer, E. B. Stinson, B. A. Reitz, et al., *Cardiac Transplantation: 1980*, 13 Transplantation Proceedings 199–206 (1981).

16. See, Karst, *Equal Citizenship under the Fourteenth Amendment*, 91 Harvard Law Review 610 (1977). For example, the language difficulties of hearing impaired persons are often assumed to be an indication of lack of intelligence. A. Crammate, *Deaf Persons in Professional Employment* (1968).

17. One of the most widely discussed allocation crises arose during the 1960's and early seventies, when the artificial kidney became a practical reality. At the Seattle Artificial Kidney Center at the University of Washington, explicit "social worth" distinctions were utilized to choose among medically suitable dialysis candidates. No moral or ethical guidelines were given the committee; the members were left to be guided by their individual consciences. The deliberations and criteria of the committee were as follows:

All candidates for treatment must be under 40 years of age. They must be self supporting and residents of the state of Washington. A first panel, composed of physicians, eliminates the medically unfit. . . . These include heart patients, diabetics . . . and those with other chronic illnesses.

The second panel consists of seven persons. At present they are a clergyman, a banker, a labor leader and two physicians. This group makes the final decision, and they remain anonymous in order to be protected from public pressures. . . .

This civilian group bases its decisions on social and economic criteria. Other factors equal, the group chooses those with dependents. It favors patients who are stable in their behavior, and appear to be emotionally mature. To have a record of public service is a help—scout leader, Sunday school teacher, Red Cross volunteer. They frown on those who have a record of skipping appointments.

This type of "system would result in the elimination of many handicapped individuals. For an interesting account of these early decisionmaking processes and some of the early legal arguments advanced against them, see, Sanders & Dukeminier, *Medical Advance and Legal Lag: Hemodialysis and Kidney Transplantation,* 15 U.C.L.A. Law Review 267 (1968).

Societal discomfort with these rationing choices may have been one major reason that federal legislation was soon enacted to provide almost universal funding for kidney dialysis. On July 1, 1973, Section 299-1 of the Social Security Amendments of 1972, termed H.R.-1, provided for the payment of maintenance hemodialysis and kidney transplantation for over 90 percent of the population. See Friedman & Kountz, *Impact of HR-1 on the Therapy of End Stage Uremia,* 288 New England Journal of Medicine 1286 [1973] For an enlightening discussion of the political debate surrounding the enactment of HR-1, see Rettig, *The Policy Debate on Patient Care Financing for Victims of End Stage Renal Disease,* 40 Law and Contemporary Problems 196 (1976).

18. This is because severe insulin requiring diabetes mellitus is exacerbated by the long-term use of immunosuppressive drugs, primarily steroids such as azatheoprine and prednisone.

19. 29 U.S.C. Section 794 (1976), (as mentioned by Rehabilitation, Comprehensive Services, and Developmental Disabilities Amendments of 1978, Pub. L. No. 95-602, Section 119, 122, 92 Stat. 2955, 2982).

20. 45 C.F.R. Section 84 (1979).

21. Pursuant to Executive Order No. 11,914, 3 C.F.R. 117 (1977), reprinted in 29 U.S.C. 794 app., at 88 (1976). The Secretary also promulgated 45 C.F.R. Section 85 (1979) to coordinate enforcement of Section 504 with respect to all federal agencies and programs providing federal financial assistance. Each federal agency must issue its own regulation enforcing Section 504. Executive Order No. 11,914, supra. See also Rehabilitation, Comprehensive Services, and Developmental Disabilities Amendments of 1978, 29 U.S.C. 794 (1978). These regulations must be consistent with the standards and procedures established by HEW (now Health and Human Services [HHS]). Executive Order No. 11,914, supra. Because of the supervisory authority granted to HHS, this article discusses primarily the HHS regulation.

22. The term "recipients" is defined to include those entities that receive the assistance from HHS, not the persons served by the programs; they are termed the "beneficiaries." Section 504 applies whether recipients receive assistance directly or through another recipient.

23. 42 U.S.C. Section 2000d-4 (1974) (Title VI). Although a comparable provision was not included in the Rehabilitation Act of 1973, the Secretary of HEW concluded that its omission was inadvertent. 42 Fed. Reg. 22,685 (1977). The Section 504 regulations are therefore similarly limited in application.

"Federal financial assistance" is defined in the HHS regulations as: "any grant, loan, contract (other than a procurement contract or a contract of insurance or guaranty), or any other arrangement by which the Department provides or otherwise makes available assistance in the form of: (1) funds; (2) services of federal personnel; (3) real or personal property or any interest in or use of such property, including (i) transfers or leases of such property for less than fair market value or for reduced consideration; and (ii) proceeds from a subsequent transfer or lease of such property if the federal share of its fair market value is not returned to the Federal Government." 45 C.F.R. Section 84.3(h) (1979).

24. Medicare Part A provides reimbursement for inpatient hospital services and certain post-hospital extended care services and home health services for qualified individuals. 42 U.S.C. Section 1395c *et seq.* (1976).

25. Medicare Part B is the program of supplementary medical insurance benefits for the aged and disabled and provides reimbursement for physicians' services and other enumerated outpatient services for qualified individuals. 42 U.S.C. Section 1395j *et seq.* (1976).

26. See, e.g., *Cook v. Ochsner Foundation Hospital*, No. 70-1969 (E.D. La., Memorandum and Order on Defendant's Motion to Dismiss entered Jan. 30, 1981), at 9.

27. 45 C.F.R. Section 84.51 (1979).

28. Historically, as noted in Katz and Capron, *Catastrophic Diseases: Who Decides What?* (1975) at 8–9 (hereinafter referred to as "Katz and Capron"), some leading surgeons felt strongly that the procedure was investigatory (and therefore should be carried out only on a limited scale). They dissuaded others from joining the cardiac transplantation sweepstakes of 1968–69. See also, F.D. Moore, *Transplant: The Give and Take of Tissue Transplantation* 255 (1972). In fact, in February, 1969, in light of poor survival rates and failure to resolve the rejection problem, an informal moratorium on heart transplantation was called. This is evidenced by the substantial decrease in the number of procedures performed. Worldwide there were two heart transplants performed in 1967, 101 in 1968, 47 in 1969, 17 in 1970, 17 in 1971, and 16 in 1972. More recently, however, as the survival rates of heart transplant recipients have approximated those for cadaver kidney transplant recipients, the therapeutic potential of heart transplantation is increasingly being recognized.

29. 45 C.F.R. Part 605, 47 Fed. Reg. 8570 (1982).

30. 47 Fed. Reg. 8570, (1982). [A qualified handicapped individual is one who . . .] "with respect to scientific and technical experimentation, observation or field work, a person who meets the academic, scientific, and technical standards for admission and any reasonable physical qualifications for participation."

31. This in fact is the approach taken by the NSF regulations, supra, n. 25. While the NSF admits its recipients' obligation "to provide for the participation of handicapped persons who are qualified to participate in the research so designed," the NSF regulations provide that "factors such as costs, risk, or *sacrifice of legitimate program objectives may be considered*" when determining the reasonableness of any physical requirements.

32. 45 C.F.R. Section 84.3(j).

33. 45 C.F.R. Section 84.53.

34. While neither the Act nor the regulations list specific conditions considered to be handicaps, the departmental analysis accompanying the regulations notes that clearly included are such diseases and conditions as orthopedic, visual, speech and hearing impairments, cerebral palsy, epilepsy, muscular dystrophy, multiple sclerosis, cancer, heart disease, diabetes, mental retardation, and emotional illness.

35. HHS rejected the suggestion that it should limit coverage to the more common handicaps. Its position has been that the statutory language of Section 504 requires the expansive approach taken. The regulations also include specific learning disabilities such as dyslexia and developmental aphasia.

36. It should be noted that environmental, economic, and cultural disadvantages are not in themselves considered handicaps within the meaning of Section 504. Characteristics such as homosexuality, age, or prison record are therefore not considered handicaps.

37. 442 U.S. 397 (1980). While *Davis* set forth these principles in the context of nursing home admissions, they appear to be equally applicable to all Section 504 cases involving admissions processes and standards since it defines "otherwise qualified," the critical term of the statute, which applies in all settings.

38. With respect to health services, a qualified handicapped individual is one who meets the essential eligibility requirements for receipt of such services. 45 C.F.R. Section 84.3(k)(4).

39. 442 U.S. at 408.

40. 666 F.2d 761 (2d. Cir. 1981).

41. According to the opinion, the American Psychiatric Association's Diagnostic and Statistical Manual (3rd Ed.) notes that a person suffering from this disability is likely to

continue to have it through most of his or her adult life, subject to modification only by treatment by well-trained therapists over a period of years and adoption of a lifestyle that avoids situations that subject the person to types of stress with which he or she cannot cope. 666 F.2d at 768.

42. 666 F.2d at 770.

43. *Doe v. New York University,* 442 F. Supp. 522 (S.D.N.Y. 1978).

44. *Doe v. New York University,* No. 77 Civ. 6285 (GLG) (slip opinion) (S.D.N.Y. Sept. 25, 1981, as amended October 2, 1981).

45. *Id.*

46. 666 F. 2d 761, 777 (1981). Before reaching the merits of the case, the court of appeals noted that there were two basic elements that needed to be demonstrated before a preliminary injunction could be issued. The first element, irreparable harm, was dispatched with quickly. The court found that a further delay in going back to school was insufficient harm to justify the issuance of a preliminary injunction. The second factor, likelihood of success on the merits, was also dismissed because the plaintiff had already entered NYU and the issue was relevant to motions for summary judgment.

47. 666 F. 2d at 776. (Emphasis added.)

48. See, H. K. Beecher, "Scarce Resources and Medical Advancement," in *Ethical Aspects of Experimentation with Human Subjects* (1969).

49. *Pushkin v. University of Colorado,* 658 F.2d 1372, 1391 (10th Cir. 1981).

50. Some courts, however, are far more willing to defer to the opinions of the specialist. See note 49 supra.

51. 45 C.F.R. Section 84.52(a)(4).

52. Knox, *Heart Transplants: To Pay or Not to Pay,* 209 Science, August 1, 1980, at 570, 572.

53. The reader is cautioned that this discussion is made by analogy to the use of selection criteria in education and employment. Not surprisingly, the literature on handicap discrimination is simply devoid of discussion about patient selection. This section draws in particular on Gittler's discussion of the use of handicap-specific exclusionary criteria in employment contexts. See, Gittler, *Fair Employment and the Handicapped: A Legal Perspective,* 27 DePaul Law Review 953 (1978).

54. *Id.* See also the HHS regulations on employment, 45 C.F.R. Section 84.13(a): "A recipient may not make use of any employment selection criteria that screens out or tends to screen out handicapped persons or any class of handicapped persons unless (1) the . . . selection criterion, as used by the recipient, is shown to be job-related for the position in question, and (2) alternative job-related criteria that do not screen out or tend to screen out as many handicapped persons are not shown by the director to be available."

55. Epilepsy Foundation of America, *Answers to the Most Frequently Asked Questions People Ask About Epilepsy,* at 8–9 (1975), cited in Gittler, *Fair Employment and the Handicapped: A Legal Perspective,* 27 DePaul Law Review 953, 967 (1978).

56. Gittler, cited n. 53 supra, at 967.

57. Several lower courts have ruled that Section 504 bars employers from excluding the handicapped through use of blanket presumptions of incompetence. See, *Duran v. City of Tampa,* 451 F. Supp 954 (M.D. Fla. 1978). (Section 504 prohibits police department from disqualifying plaintiff for employment because he suffered from epilepsy during childhood); *Gurmankin v. Costanzo,* 411 F. Supp. 982 (E.D. Pa. 1976)(dictum), aff'd 556 F.2d 184 (3rd. Cir. 1977). Compare *Davis v. Butcher,* 451 F.Supp. 791 (E.D. Pa. 1978)(absolute exclusion of former drug users for city employment violates Section 504) with *New York Transit Co. v. Beazer,* 440 U.S. 568 (1978) (transit authority policy of excluding participant in methadone maintenance programs from employment did not violate the Equal Protection clause or Title VII).

One must bear in mind, however, the definition of handicapped individual set out by the regulations; often, persons with slight handicaps are not handicapped within the meaning of the statute because such handicaps do not impinge on that person's ability to carry out major life functions. See 45 C.F.R. Section 84.3.

58. For a discussion of these principles in the employment setting, see Gittler, cited in n. 53 supra, at 978–80.

Since the Section 504 standard rests on an individualized assessment of performance capabilities, it does not involve the concept of "bona fide occupational qualification" (BFOQ). A BFOQ permits an employer an exemption from the general prohibition against policies that discriminate against a designated class and allows a policy that absolutely excludes all members of a protected class from a particular job regardless of any individual's qualifications or abilities. BFOQ provisions are contained in the Age Discrimination Act of 1967, 29 U.S.C. Section 623 (f)(1)(1970), and in Title VII, 42 U.S.C. Section 2000(e)(2)(1)(1970).

59. This example is offered merely to illustrate the analytical approach; it does not rest on any knowledge of the ability of diabetics to meet the essential eligibility requirements of a heart transplantation program.

60. OCR Memorandum, December 22, 1980; see also 45 C.F.R. Section 84.(b)(4): "A recipient may not . . . utilize criteria that have the *effect of* subjecting qualified handicapped persons to discrimination on the basis of handicap"; and Section 84.52(a)(4), "[A recipient may not] provide benefits or services in a manner that limits or *has the effect of limiting* participation of qualified handicapped persons."

61. OCR Memorandum, December 22, 1980. This test is adapted from *Griggs v. Duke Power Co.*, 401 U.S. 424, 431 (1971) and *Dothard v. Rawlinson*, 433 U.S. 321 (1977). Under these cases, a plaintiff need only show that the facially neutral standards in question select applicants for hire in a significantly discriminatory pattern to establish a prima facie case of discrimination. Once it is thus shown that the standards are discriminatory in effect, the employer must meet the burden of showing that any given requirement has a manifest relation to the employment in question. If the employer proves that the challenged requirements are job-related, the plaintiff may then show that other selection devices without a similar discriminatory effect would also serve the employer's legitimate interest in "efficient and trustworthy workmanship." See, *Albermarle Paper Co. v. Moody*, 442 U.S. at 425, quoting *McDonnell Douglass Corp. v. Green*, 411 U.S. 792, 801.

62. The burden shifting scheme in a case before the OCR places the same evidentiary burdens on the recipient as those enunciated in *Griggs* except that the recipient also must show that no selection devices with a lesser discriminatory effect are available. OCR Memorandum, December 22, 1980.

63. Under the regulations, employers as well as educational institutions are required to make reasonable accommodations to the known physical or mental limitations of an otherwise qualified handicapped applicant or employee unless the recipient can demonstrate that the accommodation would impose an undue hardship on the operation of its program. Reasonable accommodation may include making facilities accessible to the handicapped, job restructuring, modified work schedules, provisions of readers, etc. See, 45 C.F.R. Section 84.12.

The extent of the recipient's duty to accommodate the handicapped has stirred much controversy. For a thorough discussion of the topic see, Note, *Accommodating the Handicapped: Rehabilitating Section 504 After Southeastern*, 80 Columbia Law Review 171 (1980).

64. Caution must be taken even with individualized interviews, however, for the interviewer may fail to apply the established standards, due to misconceptions about the individual's handicapping condition. See, for example, *Pushkin v. University of Colorado*, 658 F.2d 1372 (10th Cir. 1981).

65. Pub. L. No. 88-352, tit. VI, Section 601–605, 78 Stat 752–53 (codified at 42 U.S.C. Sections 2000(a)–2000(d)4 (1970)).

66. The major sources of federal financial assistance to hospitals are funds received under the Hospital Survey and Construction Act (Hill-Burton Act), 42 U.S.C. 291–290 (1976), as well as the Medicare and Medicaid programs.

67. For a discussion of this issue, see Wing, *Title VI and Health Facilities: Forms without Substance*, 30 Hastings Law Journal 145 (1978); and Chavkin, *Health Access and the Civil Rights Laws: The Smoking Gun and Other Sorrows*, 15 Clearinghouse Review 561–566 (Nov. 1981).

68. Evans, *Health Care Technology and the Inevitability of Resource Allocation and Rationing Decisions: Notes of a Technology Watcher*, Update No. 10, National Heart Transplantation Study, Battelle Human Affairs Research Centers, August 1982; Cooper, *Rationing*

Health Care, London: Croom Helm Ltd., 1977; Golding, Tosey, *The Case of High-technology Medicine,* The Lancet, 195–197 (July 1980); Cochrane, *Effectiveness and Efficiency: Random Reflections on the National Health Service,* London: Nuffield Provincial Hospitals Trust, Burgess and Son, Ltd., 1971; Fuchs, *Who Shall Live?: Health, Economics, and Social Choice,* New York: Basic books, 1974; and Weinstein and Stason, *Foundations of Cost-effectiveness Analysis for Health and Medical Practices,* 296 New England Journal of Medicine 716–721 (1977).

69. See, e.g., Aday, Achieving Equity of Access to the American Health Care System: An Empirical Look at Target Groups, in U.S. Commission on Civil Rights, *Civil Rights Issues in Health Care Delivery* (1981), p. 252; Institute of Medicine, *Health Care in a Context of Civil Rights,* National Academy Press: Washington, D.C., 1981, pp. 20–71; and DHEW, Health Status of Minorities and Low Income Groups, 1980, Pub. No. (HRA) 79-625.

70. The current availability of heart transplantation is somewhat similar to that of dialysis in the late 1960s and early 1970s before the extension of Medicare coverage for all End-Stage Renal Disease (ESRD) victims resulted in widespread availability of dialysis treatment. Heart transplantation is, as dialysis was then, both scarce and extremely financially burdensome for the individual. Evans, et al., *Implications for Health Care Policy: A Social and Demographic Profile of Hemodialysis Patients in the United States,* 245 Journal of the American Medical Association 487 (1981); see also, Evans, *Defining the Need for Heart Transplantation,* Update No. 5, National Heart Transplantation Study, Battelle Human Affairs Research Centers, 1982.

In the early years, the available data indicate that blacks were severely underrepresented in the dialysis population. The current dialysis care levels indicate that blacks suffer disproportionately from ESRD; although blacks in 1970 (U.S. Census) comprised only 11.3% of the U.S. population, as of 1977 blacks constituted 24.1% of the Medicare dialysis population. Despite the prevalence of ESRD among blacks, only 7% of the 1967 (pre-Medicare) dialysis population was black (Evans, "Implications for Health Care Policy," cited supra).

Due to the expense, differential access to health care, and possible biases in the selection procedures, as well as other factors, it is very likely that minorities are also underrepresented among the heart transplant recipient population, despite higher incidence of death due to cardiac diseases among blacks. Health, United States, 1981, DHHS Pub. No. (PHS) 82-1232.

71. A facially neutral practice is one that, while appearing nondiscriminatory on its face, will tend to exclude minority group members. For instance, some hospitals that participate in the Medicaid program require that patients be admitted by physicians with staff privileges. Minorities are less likely to have access to physicians with staff privileges than are whites in the same income groupings. Thus, the admission practice is one that tends to exclude minorities from treatment although it makes no reference to race. See, Ivie, *Ending Discrimination in Health Care: A Dream Deferred,* in U.S. Commission on Civil Rights, *Civil Rights Issues in Health Care Delivery* (1981) pp. 282–317.

72. The Supreme Court soon may address this issue in *Guardians Association of NYPD, Inc. v. Civil Service Commission,* 633 F.2d 232 (3d Cir. 1980), cert. granted 50 U.S.L.W. 3547 (U.S., Jan. 11, 1982, no. 81-431).

73. See, e.g., *Lau v. Nichols,* 414 U.S. 563 (1974); *Board of Education v. Califano,* 584 F.2d 576 (2d Cir. 1978) (aff'd on other grounds sub nom *Board of Education v. Harris,* 444 U.S. 130 (1979).

74. See, *Resident Advisory Board v. Rizzo,* 564 F.2d 126, 147–49 (3d Cir. 1977). See, generally, Perry, *The Disproportionate Impact Theory and Racial Discrimination,* 125 University of Pennsylvania Law Review 540, 544–48 (1977). As stated, the effects test is adopted under the HEW regulations implementing Title VI. The regulations prohibit discrimination that *restricts* an individual's enjoyment of any advantage or privilege enjoyed by others receiving any service, financial aid, or other benefit under the program. 45 C.F.R. Section 80.3(b) (3) (1979) (emphasis added). The regulations further state that a recipient may not, "in determining the types of services . . . or other benefits which will be provided under such programs . . . or the class of individuals to be afforded an opportunity to participate in any such programs, directly or through contractual or other arrangements,

utilize criteria or methods of administration which have the *effect* of subjecting individuals to discrimination because of their race, color, or national origin. . . ." *Id.* at Section 80.3(b)(2).

75. See, *Village of Arlington Heights v. Metropolitan Hous. Dev. Corp.*, 429 U.S. 252 (1977); *Washington v. Davis*, 426 U.S. 229 (1976).

Several recent lower federal court decisions have required a showing of purposeful discrimination under Title VI. See *Guardians Assn. of NYC Police Dept. Inc. v. Civil Service Commission*, 633 F.2d 232 (3rd Cir. 1980) cert. granted 50 U.S.L.W. 3547 (U.S., Jan. 11, 1982)(no. 81-431); *Lora v. Board of Education of New York*, 603 F.2d 248 (2d Cir. 1980); *Parent Assn. of Andrew Jackson High School v. Armback*, 598 F.2d 705 (2d Cir. 1979).

However, the Supreme Court in the past has not required proof of discriminatory motive in Title VI cases. The Court in *Lau v. Nichols* based its decision on the government's power to establish the terms upon which it would disperse money. The Court cited Sen. Humphrey, quoting from Pres. Kennedy's message to Congress, June 19, 1963: "Simple justice requires that public funds, to which all taxpayers of all races contribute, not be spent in any fashion which encourages, entrenches, subsidizes, or results in racial discrimination." 414 U.S. at 569.

In *Board of Education v. Califano*, the Court reasoned that Congress has the power to enact stricter statutory standards than the constitutional minimum required by the 14th Amendment. The Supreme Court expressly declined to decide whether Title VI required a showing of discrimination or effectual discrimination. 444 U.S. at 149. Writing for the dissent, Justice Stewart relied on dicta in *Regents of California v. Bakke*, 438 U.S. 265, 281–87, 328–55 (1978) (Powell, J., at 281–87 and Brennan, White Marshall & Blackman, J.J., at 228–55) to support his position that: "Title VI, which prohibits discrimination in federally funded programs, prohibits only discrimination violative of the 5th Amendment and the Equal Protection clause of the 14th." 444 U.S. at 160.

The Court in *Bakke*, however, did not overrule *Lau* and, in fact, cited it to support the position that Title VI embodies constitutional definitions of proscribed racial classifications. 438 U.S. at 284, 341, 350–51. Moreover, the Court was not deciding the *type* of discrimination proscribed by Title VI; it was deciding whether Title VI prevented the use of all racial criteria.

More recently, the Court in *Fullilove v. Klutznick*, 448 U.S. 448 (1980) employed *Lau* to support its holding that federal law requiring that at least 10 percent of federal funds granted to states for local public works projects be allocated for minority businesses did not violate the Equal Protection clause of 14th Amendment or the Due Process clause of the 5th Amendment. The Court stated: "There are relevant similarities between the MBE [Minority Business Enterprise] program and the federal spending program reviewed in *Lau v. Nichols*, 414 U.S. 563 (1974). In *Lau*, a language barrier "effectively foreclosed" non-English speaking Chinese pupils from access to the educational opportunities offered by the San Francisco public school system. *Id* at 564–66. It had not been shown that this had resulted from any discrimination, purposeful or otherwise, or from other unlawful acts. Nevertheless, we upheld the constitutionality of a federal regulation applicable to public school systems receiving federal funds that prohibited the utilization of criteria or methods of administration which have the effect of defeating or substantially impairing accomplishment of the objectives of the [educational] program as respect individuals of a particular race, color or national origin." *Id* at 568. Several lower courts have found *Lau* to be controlling and have used the effects test in Title VI cases. See, e.g., *Guadalupe Org. Inc. v. Tempe Elementary School District No. 3*, 687 F.2d 1022, 1029 (n. 6) (9th Cir. 1978); *Serna v. Portales Mun. Schools*, 499 F.2d 1147, 1154 (10th Cir. 1974); *Wade v. Mississippi Coop. Extension Serv.*, 528 F.2d 508 (5th Cir. 1976); *Shanna v. HUD*, 436 F.2d 809, 816–17 (3rd Cir. 1970); *NAACP v. Medical Center Inc.*, 657 F.2d 1322, 1328–30 (3rd Cir. 1981); *De La Cruz v. Tormey*, 582 F.2d 45, 61 and n. 16 (9th Cir. 1978), cert denied 441 U.S. 965 (1979); *Larry P. v. Riles*, 495 F.Supp. 926, 964–5 (ND Cal 1979).

76. For a full discussion of these issues, see Institute of Medicine, *Health Care in a Context of Civil Rights*, National Academy Press (1981).

77. See Schwemm, *Washington to Arlington Heights and Beyond: Discriminatory Purpose in Equal Protection Litigation*, University of Illinois Law Review, 961, 974 (1977).

78. Various agencies of the federal government provide financial assistance and therefore administer aspects of Title VI. However, as stated, the principal agency with responsibility for health programs is the Department of Health and Human Services through the Office for Civil Rights.

79. Title VI establishes specific procedures for agencies to follow in enforcing the civil rights obligations of recipients. The enforcement process encompasses two basic procedures—complaint investigations and compliance reviews. Complaint investigations are initiated in response to specific complaints of discrimination filed by parties or their representatives. 45 C.F.R. Section 80.7(b). Compliance reviews are initiated by the OCR in order to monitor ongoing compliance and do not depend on the filing of a complaint. 45 C.F.R. Section 80.7(a).

80. Chavkin, cited n. 67, supra, p. 565.

81. The test was set forth in a memorandum in 1 OCR Policy Digest No. 2, at 10. For an example of an application of the effects test in a specific factual setting, see, OCR Memorandum to Carolyn Russell from David Chavkin dated December 11, 1980, 1 OCR Policy Digest.

While the Digest and the policy interpretations in it are approved before issuance by the Director of the Office of Civil Rights and by the Assistant General Council for Civil Rights as the official policy of the office, they are not subject to the notice and comment provisions of the Administrative Procedure Act, 5 U.S.C. Section 53(b), and are not strictly binding on the courts, National Nutritional Foods Assn. v. Weinberger, 512 F.2d 688 (2d Cir. 1975); National Assn. of U.S. Agents Inc. v. Bd. of Governors of Fed Reserve System, 489 F.2d 1268 (D.C. Cir. 1974). They are deferred to, however, in enforcement actions as the official position of the agency. See, e.g., Lau v. Nichols, 414 U.S. 563, 568 (1974).

82. OCR memorandum, cited n. 81, supra. One of the key issues that frequently arises in enforcement actions is which party bears the burden of persuasion on each of these elements. For example, must the OCR demonstrate the availability of alternatives or must the recipient demonstrate the absence of alternatives?

The OCR interpretive rules set forth OCR policy in this area as well. In applying the three-part test, the burden is on OCR to establish that the proposed action will have disproportionate, adverse effect. The burden is on the recipient to demonstrate that a legitimate objective would be furthered and that no alternative course of action could be adopted that would further that objective with a lesser disproportionate impact. In NAACP v. The Medical Center, Inc., 657 F.2d 1327 (3rd Cir. 1981), the Third Circuit Court of Appeals disagreed with this allocation of responsibility and concluded that the burden of persuasion on all elements must ultimately be met by the plaintiff.

83. Evans, Implications for Health Care Policy, cited no. 70, supra. See also, Rostand, et al., Racial Differences in the Incidence of Treatment for End-Stage Renal Disease, 306 New England Journal of Medicine 1276 (1982).

84. U.S. Bureau of the Census, Statistical Abstracts of the United States: 1981 (102d Ed.) Washington, D.C., 1981. These are raw figures and thus are not controlled for income.

85. See, Doe v. New York University, 666 F.2d 761 (1981). This case involved selection of best possible candidates for medical school and a claim of handicap discrimination. It suggests that maximum likelihood of clinial success would be a legitimate programmatic goal under Section 504 of the Rehabilitation Act of 1973, 29 U.S.C. Section 794 (as amended 1978). Since it would survive analysis under Section 504, it would also likely survive analysis under Title VI, because the antidiscrimination provisions of Section 504 were explicitly modeled after those of Title VI.

86. Among the objectives that have been accepted by the OCR in the health area are improving accessibility of services, improving quality of services, and realizing necessary fiscal savings. See Chavkin, cited n. 67 supra.

Of course, any transplant selection program can have objectives beyond selecting those most likely to benefit from treatment. For example, the hospital or government may have research objectives which limit the types of patients it selects. Under Title VI, these must be assessed for their legitimacy. If the courts or if OCR find them legitimate, then they may be utilized by recipients.

87. Bellock and Hazelkorn have noted that "satisfying, cohesive, and supportive relationships" facilitate the patient recovery process. Bellock and Hazelkorn, *Psychological Aspects of Cardiac Illness and Rehabilitation*, 37 Social Casework 483 (1956), cited in Evans, *Dimensions of Family Impact Pertinent to Heart Transplantation*, Update No. 8, National Heart Transplantation Study, Battelle Human Affairs Research Centers, June 22, 1982.

88. While the process of elimination of potential heart transplant candidates may start well before the patient is ever assessed at a transplant facility, we use the term "screeners" here to indicate the professionals on the transplant facility's staff who formally assess patients for treatment suitability. At Stanford University's transplant facility, this group consists of a cardiologist, a social worker, and a cardiac surgeon. See, Christopherson, *Heart Transplants*, The Hastings Center Report (February 1982), p. 20.

Of course, the population actually interviewed by the transplant program has already been considerably narrowed through socio-cultural and geographic factors, which can result in lack of access to physicians who actively refer patients to transplant programs, and informal screening by physicians. While discussion of these factors is beyond the scope of this paper, they are noted with reference to access to health care in *Civil Rights Issues in Health Care Delivery*, cited n. 69, supra.

89. 45 CFR Section 80.3(b)(1)(v) "a recipient may not on grounds of race, color or national origin: (v) Treat an individual differently from others in determining whether he satisfies any admission, enrollment, quota, eligibility, membership or other requirement which individuals must meet in order to be provided any service, financial aid, or other benefit under this program. . . .

(1)(i) Deny an individual any service, financial aid, or other benefit provided under the program."

90. In its 1981 report, the Institute of Medicine reviewed data on racial differences in health care utilization and noted that they were consistent with the hypothesis that minority groups' use of health care is influenced by patterns of discrimination by physicians. *Health Care in a Context of Civil Rights*, p. 44. As they noted, despite reports of physician discrimination in the form of segregated waiting rooms or office hours, there currently are no data on the extent to which racial discrimination exists in actually accepting or referring patients for treatment. *Id.* However, the possibility remains that racial-ethnic minorities are not being referred to heart transplantation (or accepted) for reasons unrelated to health or income status.

Flaherty and Meagher, in a study of 66 black and 36 white male schizophrenic inpatients, found blacks more likely than whites to have been given medications on an "as needed" basis, less likely to have received recreation and occupational therapy, and more likely to have been put in seclusion and to have restraints used. Flaherty and Meagher, *Measuring Racial Bias in Inpatient Treatment*, 137 American Journal of Psychiatry 679 (June 1980). These differences appear to have been due to subtle racial stereotyping among staff members and their greater familiarity with white parents, rather than to racial differences in pathology. *Ibid.* Similarly, in a study of racial differences in the treatment of children in five mental health clinics, Jackson, Berkowitz, and Farley found that black children were less likely than white children to be accepted for treatment, less likely to receive individual eligibility treatment, and (at two clinics) likely to be seen for a lesser length of time. Jackson, Berkowitz, and Farley, *Race as a Variable Affecting the Treatment Involvement of Children*, 13 Journal of the American Academy of Child Psychiatry 20 (1974).

91. Studies indicate that a variety of factors affect low minority utilization of all forms of health care. They include residential patterns, differences in socioeconomic status, ethnic differences in concepts and values associated with disease and treatment, constraints and incentives that are built into federal health programs, and, possibly, discrimination.

These same factors apply with special force to access to heart transplant programs, since we must first gain access to referral physicians, typically specialists, before being formally considered at all. In addition, lowered health status associated with poverty may eliminate many more minorities from active consideration as heart transplant recipients. For a review of the studies mentioned above, see *Health Care in a Context of Civil Rights*, cited n. 69, supra.

92. Health Care Financing Administration. *Medicare Program: Solicitation of Hospitals and Medical Centers to Participate in a Study of Heart Transplants,* 46 Federal Register 7072–7074, January 22, 1981.

93. 46 Federal Register 7073, January 22, 1981. The distinction between age as a "strongly adverse factor" as used in the Federal Register notice and its use as an absolute exclusionary criteria is not clear. Functionally, an individual apparently could present evidence overcoming a strongly adverse factor, while an exclusionary criterion would be deemed conclusively presumptive of his or her ineligibility.

94. 42 U.S.C. Sections 6101–6107 (1976) *as amended by* Amendments to the Older Americans Act of 1965, Pub. L. No. 95–478, 92 Stat. 1555 (1978).

95. Alexander, *Shucking Off the Rights of the Aged: Congressional Ambivalence and the Exceptions to the Age Discrimination Act of 1975,* 57 Chicago-Kent Law Review 1009 (1981).

96. Thus age is commonly used as a measure of the likelihood of experiencing particular kinds of medical problems, as in medical programs that specialize in serving certain age groups. In addition, however, age is used to measure (1) intellectual, physical and/or emotional maturity in minimum age requirements for certain educational programs; (2) readiness to assume adult responsibilities in minimum age requirements for voting, alcohol consumption, and possession of firearms; (3) the likelihood of possession of certain risk factors as in concentrating breast cancer screening programs on women above a certain age; (4) certain physical abilities as in separating sports leagues by age; and (5) the expected duration of future employability or service as in concentrating job-training programs on younger aged workers.

PART THREE

Costs, Funding, and the Diffusion of Technology

10

Introduction

Deborah Mathieu

Experiment or Therapy?

In our health care system, the difference between an *experiment* and a *therapy* is a very significant one indeed. If a drug, device, or procedure is considered to be experimental, government programs (such as Medicare and Medicaid) and most private insurance carriers will not offer it as a covered benefit, and only the comparatively small number of patients who have been accepted into specific research protocols will receive it. The designation of a medical intervention as therapeutic, in contrast, may change the situation dramatically for everyone involved: Many more patients will have access to it, physicians are free to use it without first seeking peer review, and third-party payers (including the federal government and private insurance carriers) will probably pay for it.[1] The change in the status of a medical device, procedure or drug thus may save thousands of lives, but it also may create many difficulties.

In principle, determining that a medical intervention is still in the experimental stage is easy: It is experimental if the main purpose in using it is to increase scientific knowledge. Deciding that a medical intervention has become accepted as therapeutic is also relatively straightforward in principle: It is therapeutic if its risks and benefits are known and if it has been demonstrated to benefit patients with a particular ailment. The real difficulty lies in the fact that new medical interventions do not suddenly graduate from the experimental stage to the therapeutic. Instead they advance along a continuum, with experimental procedures shading off into therapeutic ones. As Renee Fox and Judith Swazey explained:

> Therapeutic innovation is more accurately viewed as a process on a continuum that moves from animal experiments to clinical trials with terminally ill patients, then to the use of conventional therapies, then to the use of the treatment on less and less critically ill patients. This evolution is not necessarily unbroken and in one direction. . . . But whatever its stage of development, clinical investigation entails an interplay between research and therapy, and the balance shifts as the new treatment evolves.[2]

Determining exactly where along the continuum a certain treatment falls is problematic, as there is no clear-cut method for deciding when an experimental procedure becomes therapeutic. This is largely because the decision is not a factual or scientific one, following unavoidably from the details of the case. It is, instead, a value judgment. And as Daniel Wikler pointed out in Chapter 2, it is a value judgment that may vary depending on who is doing the assessing: A dying patient, for instance, may be more willing to accept a potentially life-prolonging technology as therapeutic than would the chief executive of a private insurance company that is asked to pay for the technology. Because of their varying interests and perspectives, different parties may disagree as to when a procedure has been shown to be sufficiently safe and sufficiently beneficial to be awarded the status of a therapy.

It is equally a value judgment even for the "experts": the researchers and physicians who utilize the technology. When *is* something safe enough and effective enough to be offered to patients as therapy? When the benefits barely outweigh the risks? When the risk of death from the procedure is 1 percent, 10 percent, 50 percent? When enough physicians use the procedure to make it common practice? And in determining how beneficial a procedure is, what role (if any) should be given to the quality of life of the patient receiving the treatment?

Take, for instance, the case of liver transplantation. A consensus development conference, which is one of the methods developed by the National Institutes of Health to determine the status of medical procedures, devices, and drugs, was held in June 1983 to discuss liver transplantation.[3] The panel of experts convened concluded that "sufficient data for thorough assessment of liver transplantation are not available."[4] The best the panel could do was to agree that "one-year survival among transplant recipients since 1980 is favorable when compared with their expected course in the absence of transplantation," (the expected course in the absence of transplantation for end-stage liver disease patients is death). So a liver transplantation may save the life of someone whose only alternative is death. But it may not: Between 20 and 40 percent of liver transplant patients died within the first month after surgery.[5] Moreover, the quality of life of those who survived longer was often dubious. Nonetheless, the panel concluded that "liver transplantation is a therapeutic modality for end-stage liver disease that deserves broader application." To conclude on the basis of this sketchy and not entirely encouraging data that liver transplants "deserve broader application" because they are "therapeutic" is clearly to make a value judgment with which others may reasonably disagree. The Health Care Financing Administration (HCFA) is one group that dissented from this assessment, and liver transplants—except for selected pediatric cases—are not covered by Medicare.

Complicating the determination of whether specific organ transplantation procedures are experimental or therapeutic is the fact that the skill of the individual practitioner has an enormous influence on the outcome. In assessing liver transplantations, for instance, the Blue Cross/Blue Shield Association noted that "The link between procedure and outcome, even for a narrowly specified set of diagnoses, is unusually dependent on the qualifications of the practitioners, and their institutional settings, and there are only a few practitioners and settings recognized as having the requisite qualifications."[6] The uneasy conclusion to draw from this fact, Blue Cross/Blue Shield reluctantly admitted, is that

> Liver transplants may currently be experimental or investigative when performed at most centers, but have arguably become accepted medical practice for certain diagnoses when performed at a select few. . . . This variation from site to site

complicates our traditional method of technology assessment. Liver transplantation, for example, seems to demand that the skills, resources and ability of the practitioners and their institutions be considered in the assessment process.[7]

Blue Cross/Blue Shield did conclude that liver transplantation is therapeutic for congenital diseases in children and for a few acquired diseased in adults, and almost all Blue Cross/Blue Shield plans pay for the surgery on a limited basis. Indeed, liver transplants are covered by most insurers today: Approximately 80 percent of commercial insurers and health maintenance organizations cover liver transplants, as do approximately 66 percent of Medicaid programs.[8] The Medicare program is a notable exception.

Diffusion of the Technology

Medicare is mandated by law to cover all "reasonable and necessary" medical services received by its beneficiaries (those who are sixty-five years old or older, the permanently disabled, and sufferers of end-stage renal disease). But the interpretation of this mandate has been kept vague. Indeed, one commentator has noted that the National Heart Transplantation Study was "the first time in the fifteen-year history of Medicare the government has attempted to define what is meant by the statutory requirement that the program pay only for 'reasonable and necessary' medical care—including such controversy-fraught issues as 'necessary for whom' and 'reasonable under what circumstances.'"[9] The mandate is usually translated to mean that Medicare should cover those health care goods and services that are safe, effective, and accepted within the medical community as appropriate treatment. In other words, once a treatment was considered to have graduated from the experimental to the therapeutic stage, it would fairly automatically be offered by Medicare as a covered benefit. In large part, private health insurance companies operate in a similar manner.

The decision to move a medical procedure from the experimental to the therapeutic stage, however, does not entail the conclusion that the treatment should be used on a widespread basis, or the conclusion that the treatment should be covered by third-party payers. These are entirely separate decisions. Unfortunately, this is often not recognized, and the most common decision-making procedure is a circular one, conflating the various decisions in the process. As Roger Evans noted,

> In the final analysis, it is clear that the diffusion of a technology (e.g., surgical procedure) hastens its achievement of therapeutic status. As more procedures are performed at a larger number of institutions, there is a paradoxical reassurance that coverage is appropriate. Furthermore, following a favorable coverage decision, diffusion provides support for the initial payment decision.[10]

In addition, new procedures are introduced, adopted, and covered by insurance plans with little regard for their efficacy when widely employed. The Office of Technology Assessment has estimated that only between 10 and 20 percent of all medical techniques have been demonstrated to be efficacious by controlled clinical trials.[11] And even the results of the few studies that have been conducted are often ignored. Some recent studies, for instance, have indicated that widespread use of some of the most common surgical techniques, such as cardiac bypass surgery, is *not* appropriate,[12] yet these procedures continue to be performed in large numbers, and the question of whether they should continue to be covered by third-party payment is hardly ever raised.

Issues of Cost and Efficiency

Although the efficacy of a treatment is a significant factor, it is important to note that the decision to make a technology widely available should not be made on the basis of the efficacy of the treatment alone. Showing that a procedure is efficacious in the sense of producing some net benefit would only be sufficient for establishing the desirability of using that procedure if the procedure were costless. But no procedure is costless: Each involves an outlay of scarce resources, resources that could have been used to produce other benefits, perhaps even greater ones. Hence, efficacy is not enough and efficiency must also be assessed. We must decide who can best benefit from the therapy and whether we can afford it without jeopardizing other goods we wish to support.

In other words, the cost-effectiveness of the therapy must be evaluated. It is not simply that there may be other forms of health care that produce more benefit for the same expenditures, although this is very important. We must also consider competing non–health care goods. After all, health care is not the only good in life, and there may be some efficacious therapies that are not worth pursuing at all.

The costs of a therapy are not easy to determine, however. Although heart transplantation, for instance, has been very widely studied and analyzed, no two analysts seem to agree on the monetary cost of the procedure. The Task Force on Organ Transplantation estimated the average cost of a heart transplant to be $90,000;[13] an analyst for the National Center for Health Care Technology estimated that the operation costs $70,000;[14] an analyst for the Department of Health and Human Services estimated that the operation costs $80,000.[15] Of course, the cost of the operation itself is not the only factor: One must also include the costs of presurgical treatment and postsurgical treatment (including, for instance, the $5,000 to $7,000 per year cost of immunosuppressant drugs and the costs associated with transplant failure).

But it is not only the relatively simple calculation of the cost of the medical care that is in doubt. The number of procedures that are likely to be performed also is a matter of great controversy. Take again the case of heart transplants. One must calculate first how many people are likely to suffer from end-stage heart disease each year. This may be a very large number indeed, as coronary disease is the leading cause of death in the United States and accounts for two-thirds of all cardiovascular deaths. But not all of these people are candidates for heart transplants: Some heart attacks kill instantly, some patients are too ill with other diseases to be able to survive a transplant, and some patients can be treated by other means. Hence it is difficult to determine with any precision how many people are appropriately considered to be potential candidates for transplant. One must then take this speculative figure and subtract the number of cadaver hearts in good condition that are likely to become available in time to save the patients' lives—another unknown quantity.

Putting these dubious figures together with the uncertain estimates of the costs of the procedure itself creates widely disparate estimates of the total annual costs of heart transplants. For instance, one analyst calculates that it is from $2 to $3.5 million;[16] another calculates the range as between $150 million and $4.5 billion;[17] while a third suggests that $2.5 billion might be more accurate.[18]

Another significant and equally speculative figure is the cost of each life-year saved. This figure is calculated by dividing the above uncertain costs by the length of time the transplant recipients live after transplantation (which may vary a good deal). These estimates too range widely: $35,340 per life-year,[19] $30,000 per life-year,[20] $23,000 per life-year.[21] These daunting complexities are quite independent of the even more controversial character of attempts to take quality-of-life estimates into account in the cost-effectiveness analysis of transplantation.

There are also other complicating factors that must be taken into consideration before a responsible policy decision can be made with regard to the dissemination of a particular medical technology. For instance, once the decision is made that a certain technology is worth pursuing, the further decision arises regarding what levels of support we wish to give to different aspects of the therapy. Hence the costs of providing the therapy in question must be considered in relation to the costs of promoting other complimentary facets of the technology. H. David Banta pointed out the assortment of ways to distribute money set aside for an organ substitution program:

- Basic research;
- Applied research and technology development;
- Development of technologies' benefits, risks, costs;
- Health services research to improve delivery systems and financing of treatment;
- Development and operation of communications/data handling systems and creating and disseminating data on the technologies, delivery systems, individuals in need, and potential donors;
- Treatment of disease through organ transplantation;
- Treatment of disease through artificial organs or through other alternatives to transplantation;
- Efforts to increase public understanding of transplantation and organ donation.[22]

These are just various ways to spend money within one program; they must be compared with all the other ways we have of spending money, including other health care goods as well as non–health care goods. That is, we need to consider the opportunity costs of a wide dissemination of the technology. This is an enormously difficult task indeed and one that our society has consistently attempted to avoid. But given that the technologies in question are so expensive—and that they are largely funded with public monies—it makes sense at least to begin reflecting on their importance vis à vis other goods and services. The point, of course, is that we want to get the most (e.g., save the most lives, relieve the most suffering) for our money.

This is not to say that the allocation of health care goods and services is a zero-sum game and that the object of our deliberations is to distribute a fixed amount of money in the most efficient way possible. It would be naive to assume that the supply of the resources is fixed (even though it is, of course, limited at any point in time at which a decision concerning the allocation of resources is made). Indeed, once the effects of incentive structures on the production and delivery of goods to be allocated is understood—what economists call the interdependence of production and distribution—it may be possible to relieve some allocational strains by increasing the size of the pie and thus reducing the range of difficult choices we are forced to make. But it would be equally naive to believe that if more money were poured into the health care system, all of our problems of allocation would disappear. It is unlikely that enough money to provide for all health care needs and preferences ever would materialize, much less that it could do so without imposing unacceptable constraints on our ability to produce other valuable things. Hence questions regarding the proper allocation of health care goods and services will always exist.

Federal Funding for End-Stage
Renal Disease (ESRD)

Before turning to the question of how the more recently developed technologies, such as heart and liver transplants, should be allocated, it would be instructive to take a brief look at the course taken by a set of older, more established technologies: renal dialysis and transplantation.

In 1972, end-stage renal disease, the permanent failure of the kidneys to collect and dispose of bodily wastes, became a very special condition indeed, for in September of that year Congress decided that the Medicare program should pay for the health care of virtually all individuals with that life-threatening condition.[23] The Medicare program had already been paying for some ESRD care—patients who were eligible for Medicare benefits could receive treatment for end-stage renal disease—but now Congress widened Medicare's eligibility criteria to include almost all sufferers of this condition, regardless of their age. Congress did not undertake to pay for all care for all sufferers of the disease: Those patients who had not worked long enough to be covered by Social Security were excluded, and patients included in the program were still responsible for some costs (deductibles, copayments, drugs, and the first three months of dialysis treatment in a hospital). But the bulk of medical care for about 90 percent of patients did become the responsibility of the federal government through the Medicare program.[24]

There is a widespread misconception that Congress's original decision to fund medical care for end-stage renal disease was made precipitously and without knowledge of the issues. The picture many people have is of members of Congress who were emotionally overcome one day by the sight of a few dialysis patients in wheelchairs, and when the legislators were told by special-interest-group lobbyists that these individuals would surely die unless the federal government agreed to pay for their medical care, Congress voted immediately to save their lives by instituting the End-Stage Renal Disease Program.

Although this scenario is not entirely inaccurate (the actual vote was preceded by a very brief formal discussion) the reality of the situation is more complex. Indeed, the debate about appropriate federal policy regarding end-stage renal disease had been active for over a decade, and the move by Congress to allocate funds was the culmination of a long-standing concern. Between 1965 and 1972, for instance, more than one hundred bills had been submitted to Congress regarding funding for ESRD,[25] and there were already a variety of other public programs prior to the enactment of Public Law 92-603, which paid for the medical care of patients with end-stage renal disease: the Veterans Administration, some Medicaid programs, the vocational rehabilitation program, and state crippled children's services. In addition, the federal government had allocated $15 million to cover the cost of renal dialysis at several regional kidney centers. Therefore, as Richard Rettig pointed out:

> The proponents of a treatment payment program were only able to achieve their goal as a result of a complex and gradual process. A sequence of federal government

actions—involving financing of research and development, demonstration, and capacity-building within HEW, and patient-care financing of eligible veterans by the V.A.—set the stage for passage of section 2991. The deepening federal role was, in turn, the product of a number of other processes, including the development of an identified group of physicians, the cumulative effects of publicity, and the evolution of the federal role in health in general. In short, although society is reluctant to sacrifice lives for dollars, this reluctance did not swiftly and by its strength alone win federal financing for the victims of end-stage renal disease.[26]

However, there is another widely held view of the way Congress decided to adopt the end-stage renal disease program that is a bit more accurate: the view that Congress did not know how much money the program would cost. The enormous increase in the size of the ESRD population had not been anticipated in 1972 nor had the dramatic escalation in expenditures. Original estimates of the first-year cost of the ESRD program ranged from $35 million to $75 million, anticipating an increase to $250 million in the fourth year.[27] Instead, the ESRD program cost the federal government approximately $200 million a year in the first few years of the program (for about 15,000 patients); and by 1976 the costs were already approximately $600 million (for about 35,000 patients). The annual costs to Medicare currently are around $2 billion (for approximately 75,000 patients), and the cost of income maintenance of ESRD patients adds another $500,000 to $1 million to the overall cost of caring for this patient population.[28]

Costs of the program continue to escalate, and it is predicted that unless rather drastic measures are taken, they will persist in doing so. One reason for this is the growth in the patient population; another (and related) reason is the change in patient selection criteria. Patients who are very elderly and/or who are ill with other serious conditions are now often considered to be suitable candidates for dialysis, whereas in the early stages of the ESRD program they were not. The extra care required by these patients increases the cost to Medicare in several ways: These patients are unable to be dialyzed at home, so they must use the more expensive means of institutional dialysis; they cannot survive a kidney transplantation procedure, so they must remain on dialysis all their lives; they require more medical services in general. Indeed, the cost to the ESRD program of caring for these patients must be added to other social costs. "Considering that these patients are among the least likely to be rehabilitated, the disability benefits they receive also add greatly to the total cost of their care. Thus, the cost of dialysis per se is but only one component of the total health care and social welfare dollar expended for patients in this category."[29]

Although the ESRD program is considered to be a success insofar as it pays for the care of a certain class of patients, the increasing medical and social costs involved have created certain anxieties regarding the future of the program. This has had an enormous influence on the reluctance of the federal government to include other catastrophic disease programs within Medicare, particularly those involving transplantation of other organs.

It is ironic that this is the case, as the institution of the end-stage renal disease program was initially viewed by many to be the first step toward a general federal catastrophic disease program, and it was believed that the success of the ESRD program would facilitate the institution of a larger, more comprehensive national insurance program in the near future. Instead, concerns over the high costs of paying for the care of this one patient population, as well as concerns over the ethical and public policy dilemmas such a program engenders, have made the federal government and the public even more wary of expanding the program to include other sorts of very expensive care, such as heart and liver transplants. Of course, some of these concerns existed from the beginning of the end-stage renal disease program. A panel convened by the Institutes of Medicine in 1973, for instance, expressed a distinct lack of enthusiasm for dealing with catastrophic diseases in a piecemeal manner and declared its "unanimous agreement that coverage of discrete categories similar in kind to end-stage renal disease would be an inappropriate course to follow in the foreseeable future for providing expensive care to those who are unable to afford it."[30]

The history of the federal ESRD program raises two important questions that apply with equal force to the recent extension of private insurance and Medicare coverage to heart transplants: (1) Is this piecemeal approach—the selection of one particular disease and treatment modality for special consideration—cost-effective? and (2) Is it fair, or does it represent an arbitrary and discriminatory bias in the expenditure of public resources?

Federal Funding for End-Stage Heart Disease (ESHD)

Medicare

In 1980, a panel of experts convened by the National Heart, Lung and Blood Institute at the request of the National Center for Health Care Technology (NCHCT) submitted its recommendations regarding Medicare coverage of heart transplants.[31] Although the panel refused to make any statement about the efficacy of heart transplantation in general, it did conclude that those transplants performed at Stanford University Medical Center were indeed therapeutic. The committee recommended that heart transplants performed at that institution and at other institutions with comparable standards of expertise should be covered by Medicare.

But for a number of reasons, the Secretary of the Department of Health and Human Services (DHHS) did not recommend including heart transplants under Medicare. One of the reasons was her concern that too many social issues remained to be evaluated. The NCHCT panel, which consisted of eighteen cardiologists and transplant specialists, had not addressed any of the myriad ethical, legal, or public policy issues, and thus their recommendations were limited in scope. In addition, although the members of the panel were eminently qualified to assess the efficacy of heart transplantation procedures, their conclusion that Medicare should cover the procedure was at least slightly suspect because they would benefit enormously from increased government funding.[32] So the secretary of DHHS commissioned a group with no apparent conflicts of interest, the Battelle Human Affairs Research Centers, to examine a plethora of issues regarding heart transplants: estimates of potential need for heart transplants and the potential availability of donor hearts, the survival and quality of life of heart transplant recipients, costs of the program, access to care, and a variety of other issues.

The scope of this study was most unusual: As mentioned earlier, if a medical intervention was generally regarded as net-beneficial to patients, then it was usually covered by Medicare—and no consideration was given to social and ethical issues in making that decision. Even the decision to commission a national study was unusual. Although a few Medicare coverage determinations are made on the national level, the large majority of them are made by Medicare intermediaries and carriers (the commercial insurers who process the claims and pay the bills for Medicare). Hence there is a great deal of variation among the benefits offered by the different Medicare contractors.

Because the national heart transplantation study was unprecedented, it met with a good deal of opposition. Although those responsible for the Medicare program maintained that the new study was required in order to address the cost-effectiveness of heart transplants, as well as the legal, ethical, and policy issues involved in including heart transplants in the Medicare program, some critics charged that HCFA was overstepping its bounds in doing so, because it "does not have, and has not requested, the authority to base payment decisions on such broader considerations."[33] Other critics have charged that the main impetus behind the study was to permit Medicare to save millions of dollars by delaying coverage of heart transplants.

The Battelle study was completed in the fall of 1984, and it reached basically the same conclusions that the NCHCT had reached several years earlier: Heart transplantation had passed the experimental stage and was indeed therapeutic. As Robert Evans, the principal author of the report, later stated, "The outcomes of heart transplant recipients were impressive, all things considered. . . . In general, it was found that on nearly all objective and subjective quality of life measures, heart transplant recipients compared favorably with other patients undergoing life-saving therapy."[34] In particular, the quality of life of heart transplant patients was compared to the quality of life of patients in the End-Stage Renal Disease Program. Although kidney transplant patients enjoyed the highest quality of life according to most indications, the study concluded that heart transplant patients were not far behind: "On many indicators, heart transplant recipients were very comparable with home hemodialysis patients and on all indicators with the exception of ability to work they equaled or surpassed in-center hemodialysis patients. Moreover, on all indicators but life satisfaction they surpassed continuous peritoneal dialysis patients."[35]

But Medicare still hesitated to pay for heart transplants. Finally, in June 1986, the new secretary of DHHS announced that Medicare would begin to include heart transplants as a covered benefit for those already meeting Medicare eligibility criteria, but only if the transplants were performed at a few designated transplant centers throughout the country. (In order to qualify, a transplant center must perform at least a dozen transplants a year and have a one-year patient survival rate of 73 percent and a two-year patient survival rate of 65 percent). The federal regulations, which became final in November 1987, were expected to add about $5 million to the Medicare bill during the first year of the program—for approximately sixty-five transplants.

Medicaid

Medicaid was established to provide health care for the poor, although it does not pay for the health care of all of the poor (it is estimated, for instance, that only about one-half of people below the federal poverty line are eligible for Medicaid benefits). Unlike Medicare, which is one federal program, Medicaid is a conglomerate of separate state programs financed in part with federal dollars and adhering to general federal standards for benefit coverage. Although these standards outline a minimum set of benefits that must be offered by state Medicaid programs, they do not delimit the maximum set, and states are free to offer additional benefits. Each state, for instance, has the authority to decide whether or not to provide coverage for organ transplants.

Until recently, most states refused to cover organ transplants—except those involving kidneys and corneas—claiming that these other transplants were still experimental and therefore not appropriately included in the benefit package. Many states, though, while refusing to pay for organ transplants in general, made exceptions in particular cases and paid for some individual transplantations. Now, however, more and more states are accepting various organ transplant procedures as therapeutic. Approximately 66 percent of state Medicaid programs have paid for liver transplants; 50 percent have paid for heart transplants; 26 percent have paid for heart-lung transplants; and 6 percent have paid for pancreas transplants.[36]

U.S. Congress

In the meantime, Congress was considering the plight of patients who require organ transplant surgery. In 1984, Congress passed the Organ Procurement and Transplantation Act, which provides the following: (1) the creation of a task force to "conduct comprehensive examinations of the medical, legal, ethical, economic, and social issues presented by human organ procurement and transplantation"; (2) authorization of $2 million each year to support a national computerized system for matching organs with patients; (3) authorization of increasing amounts of money (from $5 million in 1985 to $12 million in 1987) to improve local organ procurement agencies; (4) prohibition of the sale or purchase of human organs; (5) creation of a national registry of transplant patients as a necessary step in monitoring the efficacy of transplantation as a therapy. (See Appendix D for a copy of the bill.)

What Congress decided to *exclude* is as interesting as what it decided to include. Although it was well aware that most people who require organ transplants cannot afford them, Congress decided not to provide any direct aid to them. Instead, the bill sets aside funds to streamline and upgrade the procurement of organs and the system of matching them with potential recipients. It does not authorize funds to pay for transplants, for postoperative care, or for immunosuppressive drugs (which are essential in helping to prevent the rejection of the organ and which cost a patient between $5,000 and $7,000 each year).

It did not take Congress long to reconsider its decision, and in the fall of 1986 it once again passed legislation pertaining to organ transplants. Although Congress remained firm in refusing to cover organ transplants in general, it relented somewhat in its refusal to pay for the drugs needed to prevent organ rejection. Hence as of October 1987, Medicare is authorized to pay for one year of a recipient's immunosuppressive drug therapy. After the first year, however, and for the rest of his or her life, the transplant recipient must find other means of paying for immunosuppressive drug treatments.

Support on the Executive Level

President Reagan has shown considerable support for organ transplantation, even going so far as to aid personally in the search for organs needed by certain individuals. Yet when it came time to spend federal money to procure organs, the executive branch demonstrated an altogether different attitude. Although Congress authorized millions of dollars to be given to organ procurement agencies over a three-year period, the president's 1986 budget provided no money at all to organ procurement agencies. The explanation was, it seems, that organs could best be procured on a voluntary basis, using charitable donations and state funds. This, of course, is pretty much the status quo—one that most people would agree is not working. Senator Albert Gore, one of the sponsors of the law, was justifiably angry with the administration's position, and he complained that it missed the point: "Their foot-dragging in implementing the law, and their continued insistence that voluntary groups and private organizations can solve this societal problem—a problem that requires a national solution—is inexcusable."[37]

Issues of Fairness

The administration's inclination to withhold federal dollars from organ procurement agencies is not really surprising because it is consistent with other administration views about limited federal involvement, the importance of private enterprise and charity, and so on. The position adopted by Congress, however, is considerably more interesting. That Congress refused to cover the cost of heart transplants for all who need them is especially noteworthy in the light of the fact that all of the ingredients that Rettig identified as swaying an earlier Congress to provide funding for most sufferers of end-stage renal disease were present also in the case of end-stage heart disease: The federal government had been involved in funding heart transplantation research, a group of physicians had been identified as experts in the field, sufferers of the disease had been identified and their plight had received considerable publicity. This time, however, Congress was very much concerned with the costs of the program and seemed to be unwilling to spend the billions of dollars required to save relatively few human lives. Indeed, politicians currently are not even proposing in any serious manner that the federal government cover heart and liver transplants on the same basis as kidney transplants.

The decision is also interesting in light of an important difference between the debate about federal responsibility for sufferers of end-stage renal disease and for sufferers of end-stage heart disease: The former was considered to be an act of beneficence, the latter has been discussed chiefly as an issue of fairness. There are two primary reasons for this difference. The first is due to the simple fact that the end-stage renal disease program was the first of its kind, so it had no precedent to follow. But because it already existed by the time the end-stage heart disease program came to be considered, a natural question of fairness arose: If the government funds kidney transplants, why not heart transplants? It is unfair, some claim, for the federal government to withhold funding for heart transplants when it pays for kidney transplants. The argument is that there is no morally relevant distinction between the two groups of patients, thus treating them unequally is tantamount to unfair discrimination against the sufferers of end-stage heart disease.

Although forceful, this argument has an important limitation. If we commit ourselves to continuing and/or expanding certain programs—on the grounds that because we did something in the past we should do it in the future—then we may commit ourselves to making the same mistakes over again. We must be careful not to embrace an existing program simply because it exists: It might have been a bad idea. And even if doing something once made sense, doing it twice may not. Thus although there may be no morally relevant distinction between ESRD patients and ESHD patients, it does not follow that ESHD patients should be included in federal reimbursement programs to the same extent as ESRD patients. Other arguments are needed to buttress this claim.

An examination of what exactly was being funded in the Medicare ESRD program highlights another difference in focus between an issue of beneficence and an issue of fairness. In the late 1960s, kidney transplantation was not nearly so successful as it is today. In 1968, for instance, the one-year survival rate for patients receiving transplants from cadavers was 65 percent; it is as high as 95 percent today.[38] Thus when the program was being considered, it was assumed that the vast majority of patients would be dialyzed instead of receiving transplants. But the assumptions regarding patients with end-stage heart disease are different. Because there is no well-functioning artificial heart available, it is assumed that sufferers of end-stage heart disease will receive organ transplants. And it is the fact that transplants require organ *donations* that makes this an issue of justice.

This is because all citizens—not just the affluent—are asked to donate their organs. It does not seem fair to ask the poor to donate organs that will then only be used to aid the affluent portion of the population. And, more importantly, as Mary Ann Baily points out in Chapter 15, it does not seem fair to use public funds to develop and implement a technology (and to pay for advertising campaigns that encourage the public at large to donate) when the technology will be available *only* to the wealthy. Indeed, no matter how much a patient is willing to pay, he or she still will not cover the full cost of the operation, as publicly subsidized facilities and resources will be utilized. In addition, we must take into account the fact that the organ transplantation technology used was developed in large part through grants from the federal government, grants that were underwritten by tax dollars.

Ability to Pay

The question of what role the ability to pay for the transplant should play in decisions regarding the allocation of organs remains an important one. One view is that we should not worry about developing distributive policies, we should just let the market take care of the situation. The argument for the market solution is often based on a libertarian view of the state: The only legitimate role of the state is to protect the negative rights of individuals, and this does not include the conferral of positive benefits such as health care. Because the only social structure compatible with this view of the state is the competitive market, there is no need for a theory of resource allocation: Resources should be distributed by free market processes. Champions of this method conclude that the resulting allocation of benefits and burdens—whatever it is— will be just because it will have arisen out of voluntary exchanges.[39] Hence those who find themselves unable to purchase something, such as lifesaving health care, have no cause to claim that they are victims of an unjust system or that their rights are being violated. They are victims of misfortune, not of injustice.

But is it true that injustices will not arise from the interplay of legitimate voluntary exchanges in the marketplace? Those who take seriously the problem of cumulative harms do not think so. One argument against the libertarian stance, then, is that cumulative harmful effects on welfare and liberty created by unfettered market processes may be serious enough to provide strong ethical grounds for challenging the virtually unlimited right to private property and free exchange championed by libertarians.[40] A second major argument against the unfettered market is that because everyone has an extended period of dependence in childhood, how well one fares will be determined to a large extent by the voluntary exchanges of one's parents, *not* by one's own voluntary exchanges. In extolling the market virtues of voluntary exchange and individual responsibility, libertarians often fail to appreciate the significance of the fact that human beings are children before they become "market people." A final argument against the libertarian position is that the market simply transmits the unfairness of the initial distribution of assets that people bring to the market. For all of these reasons, the moral and social costs of an unchecked market may be too high, and interference may be warranted in some circumstances.

Something that is frequently invoked as a legitimate exception to allowing market forces to operate freely is the allocation of health care goods and services. There is a strong feeling in this country that health care is not merely another commodity, like sport cars and fishing rods, and that it has a special importance in our lives that mere commodities do not. The President's Commission for the Study of Ethical Problems in Medicine documented the persistence and prevalence of this view in U.S. public life and then argued that it is a reasonable one:

Society has an ethical obligation to ensure equitable access to health care for all. This obligation rests on the special importance of health care: its role in relieving suffering, preventing premature death, restoring functioning, increasing opportunity, providing information about an individual's condition, and giving evidence of mutual empathy and compassion. Furthermore, although life-style and the environment can affect health status, differences in the need for health care are for the most part undeserved.[41]

Using ability to pay to decide which patients receive health care is, some argue, to discriminate unfairly against the poor. Need for health care, then, not ability to pay, is often championed as *the* relevant distributive criterion. This position is subject to serious limitations, of course, because resources are finite and health is not the only good. Hence the argument is generally considered to be most forceful when applied, not to all available health care, but to a decent minimum of care.

It is a matter of great debate, however, whether organ transplants should be included as part of the decent minimum—at least under the current circumstances. One reason for doubt is the very high cost of the procedure; another is the efficacy of treatment. But the major problem is that there is no clear-cut definition of a "decent minimum": It is a concept many people are comfortable espousing when left vague, but which dissolves into controversy when probed.

Of course, there are those who claim that a decent minimum does not go far enough, and that *equality* is the appropriate distributive criterion for health care. The argument here is that people have a right to receive health care, a right that goes beyond a mere decent minimum or core set of basic health services. Instead, it is argued, the claim on health care resources is much stronger: Everyone who has an equal need for health care should have equal access to it.[42]

Although attractive to some, this position seems to lead inevitably to unappealing results, depending on where the level of health care to which everyone is entitled is set. If it is set as high as is technically feasible, then the commitment to providing everyone with the very best and most expensive health care will place an unbearable burden on social resources and may even require the elimination of other important social goods. However, if the level is set considerably below the maximum—in order to avoid swallowing the entire gross national product—then some people will be prohibited from purchasing the health care they desire. Do we really want a society in which people may spend money on frivolous objects and idle pursuits, but may not purchase lifesaving medical care? Such a system seems to involve too much interference with individual liberty.

So what does justice require here? Approximately 37 million people in the United States have no private or public health care insurance, and these people are truly at risk of being left out of the system. But the poor lack a great many goods. Perhaps they would prefer to have some of their other needs met with the money that could be set aside for organ transplants. And if only a fraction of the amount to be spent on organ transplants were used to purchase other goods for the needy: nutrition, shelter, and early diagnosis of disease, for instance, the long-term impact on the nation's health would be much greater.

One difficulty with attempting to answer questions about how best to allocate resources among various forms of health care is that it is reasonable for the rich and the poor to prefer different allocational systems. The better-off, who already enjoy acceptable levels of basic health care as well as acceptable levels of nonmedical goods, would probably opt for including organ transplants in their health plan. It would make sense for the poor, however, who suffer from the lack of access to basic medical care as well as from the lack of material goods, to forgo these extreme lifesaving measures in favor of other forms of medical care and other nonmedical goods. If allocation policy is based on the preferences of the better-off, then not only will allocations fail to maximize welfare, they will also be open to the charge that they are paternalistic toward the poor.

In sum, the case for including organ transplantation in the decent minimum of health care that justice ideally requires is problematic. Yet the case for a legal entitlement to organ transplants—at the cost of failing to provide coverage for other more efficacious and widely needed treatments that are less controversially components of the decent minimum—is even more dubious. And leaving organ transplantation as a commodity to be purchased on the unrestrained market also seems unsatisfactory.

Finally, it should be noted that there is no law in the United States mandating that medical benefits be offered to everyone, regardless of ability to pay. Instead, the government may choose to offer benefits to almost everyone who needs them (as in the end-stage renal disease program), or it may choose to exclude from its benefit program those who cannot pay. As the National Heart Transplantation Study noted:

> Assuming that procedural requirements are otherwise met, no legal doctrine prevents the government from requiring program participants to contribute some amount to defray the expense of providing the service, even though this means that some individuals will be excluded from the program. Thus, a government heart transplant program would be free to establish rules that required financial participation— there is simply no law or policy that requires the government to provide a service to every person who might need or benefit from it.[43]

Allocational Issues Raised
by Organ Transplant Technology

The chapters in this section deal with the formidable allocational issues raised by organ transplantation technology and address considerations of both efficiency and justice. All of the authors are concerned with attempts to gain control over the technology, to deal with it in a rational and responsible manner. Decisions about the distribution of health care goods and services are made on many levels, and the chapters reflect this: The initial chapters explore concrete proposals for dealing with organ substitution technology on two important levels, the individual health care organization and the individual state, whereas the latter chapters discuss the diffusion of the technology on the national level.

Levels of Decision Making

In Chapter 11, Paul Menzel tackles the issue of the fair and efficient allocation of organ substitution technology in the context of the decisions of one of the nation's largest and most successful prepaid health care plans, Group Health Cooperative of Puget Sound. Menzel's aim is to draw lessons for general social and institutional policymaking from this organization's experience in imposing a rationing system for life-prolonging technology. In doing so, he advocates consumer choice as the basic decision-making force regarding health care coverage, and he also analyzes some fundamental issues of health policy, such as arguments regarding what sort of relative weight prior preventive care should have in relation to remedial crisis care, such as organ transplants.

One of Menzel's main concerns is the difficulty experienced by health insurance companies (including HMOs) in trying to avoid attracting those *most* likely to become ill (adverse selection) without at the same time overtly attracting those *least* likely to become ill (cream skimming). He argues that avoiding adverse selection is good business, whereas cream skimming is morally pernicious; hence it is important for a plan to achieve the former without succumbing to the latter. The danger here is the likelihood of unfair discrimination against those people who are more apt to become ill—a very real danger, given the market incentives involved in a system based on consumer choice.

There is a way in which it may be possible for third-party payers to avoid both the danger of being a victim of adverse selection and the temptation to be a cream skimmer, but this involves an appeal to a force other than consumer choice and the market. If a system can be developed (and enforced) in which the burden of paying for sicker, more expensive patients is distributed fairly among competing payers, then no payer will be able to rationalize its refusal to enroll costly patients on the grounds that it cannot do so and remain competitive.

Such a system could be generated by the health care institutions and payers themselves: They could all agree to share on a voluntary basis the burden of caring for the more expensive patients. This method of proceeding, however, is not likely to be successful, for it is open to the familiar free-rider problem: It would be to each plan's economic advantage *not* to participate and to leave the burden for the others to share. The problem seems unavoidable in a voluntary system. But even if payers did not attempt to be free-riders, voluntary compliance with a scheme to distribute the burden of caring for the more expensive patients may succumb to the assurance problem. Unless an individual plan can be assured that its competitors are all sharing the burden—assurance that is difficult to obtain in a voluntary scheme created in a competitive free market situation—then the plan might be putting itself at a competitive disadvantage by keeping its end of the bargain. Thus an enforcement mechanism may be needed. This would most likely come from outside the competitors themselves, and the state is the most plausible candidate. Hence a plausible argument can be made for the state's putting some limits on consumer choice and market forces, at least to see that high-risk groups are not discriminated against.

Chapters 12 and 13 discuss the attempts of an individual state to control the dissemination of organ transplantation technology and especially its attempts to make its health care system both fair and efficient. In the past, a state would have looked to the federal government for guidance regarding coverage for organ transplantation, but as Medicare continues to delay coverage of organ substitution technology and as states continue to receive pressure from patients and health care professionals to support it, individual states are increasingly moving to develop their own methods of controlling the diffusion of this expensive technology. The Commonwealth of Massachusetts, which has taken a leadership role in regulating the introduction of organ transplantation, offers a good case study.

The Massachusetts Experience

In 1983, Massachusetts formed a multidisciplinary panel—consisting of physicians, lawyers, economists, insurers, members of the clergy, public health officials, and consumer advocates—to examine the social issues involved in transplantation technology and to make recommendations concerning how it should be disseminated in Massachusetts. George Annas headed the Massachusetts Task Force on Organ Transplantation, and Chapter 12 is his overview of its report.

The task force did not give a resounding vote of support for the widespread use of organ transplantation technology, but rather cautiously gave permission for its dissemination on a limited and controlled basis. As Annas explains, the basic conclusion of the task force was the following:

> Because transplants are extreme and expensive procedures that nevertheless do not cure disease but replace the patient's underlying disease with a lifetime of immunosuppression, and because introducing transplantation into the current cost-constrained health care system threatens to displace other, higher priority health care services (including services to the Medicaid population and the poor), transplants should not be performed at all unless they are done on those who are likely to benefit from them, unless the total cost is controlled, and unless resources are not diverted from higher priority care.

"Higher priority care" was interpreted by the task force to mean those forms of clearly beneficial medical care that already were being provided.

The recommendations of the task force were adopted as policy by the Massachusetts Department of Public Health in 1984. Among the recommendations were the following: (1) if organ transplantation is offered in Massachusetts, then it should be offered to all who need it, regardless of ability to pay; (2) organ transplantation should be introduced in a controlled and carefully monitored fashion, and during the initial phase it is expected that only a few procedures will be performed in order to allow for close study; (3) patient selection criteria should be public, strict, and fair, and transplants should be offered only to those who will clearly benefit; (4) a hospital wishing to perform transplants must demonstrate that resources will not be diverted from other beneficial health care services already offered by the hospital; (5) hospitals must agree to collect data on costs and outcomes; (6) all clinical protocols, organ procurement methods, patient selection criteria, and informed consent processes must be submitted for review (either by the hospital's own institutional review board or by a Department of Public Health review board).

In Chapter 13, Mark Pauly offers some criticisms of the task force's plan. One of his concerns is about the opportunity costs of permitting only a limited transplantation program: the lives that will be lost because transplants are not available. A person in Massachusetts dying of end-stage heart disease could fritter millions of dollars away but would not be able to purchase a heart transplant in the commonwealth. "In effect," claims Pauly, "the Task Force finds objectionable a family's decision that it is willing to sacrifice other things it might consume in order to prolong the life of one of its members." But it is likely that the rich will not accept this status quo, and instead will seek transplantation elsewhere. Hence, Pauly concludes, in attempting to provide equitable access to this costly technology, the plan of the task force really has the opposite effect: It widens the gap between the haves and the have nots. This is because the rich can go to another state for transplantation, whereas the poor must queue for the few available openings in the Massachusetts program.

Thus Pauly argues that the goal of the task force to narrow the gap between the rich and the poor is doomed to failure because the rich will go elsewhere. But Pauly also offers a more fundamental criticism of the whole enterprise. He contends not only that the task force plan fails on its own terms, but also that the terms it chooses are wrong: The task force seems to have misinterpreted its fundamental principle of distributive justice.

In introducing its recommendations, the task force stated:

> On the issues of equity and fairness, we concur with the conclusions of the President's Commission for the Study of Ethical Problems in Medicine and Biomedical and Behavioral Research: society has an ethical obligation to ensure equitable access to health care for all; and the cost of achieving equitable access to health care ought to be shared fairly.[44]

The President's Commission was careful to point out the important distinction between *equity* and *equality*. Treating people equitably, that is, fairly, does not necessarily involve treating them equally. The basic principle of equity is: Equals should be treated equally, and unequals should be treated unequally, in proportion to their relevant differences.[45] The President's Commission held that ability to pay is a relevant difference with respect to access to health care insofar as prohibiting the wealthy from purchasing health care services would infringe too much on their liberty and freedom of choice.[46] Thus the commission concluded that a right to health care services need not—and indeed should not—be seen as a strongly egalitarian right that requires (or even justifies) a ceiling on benefits.[47] Yet this is precisely what the Massachusetts task force attempted to do. In setting a ceiling on health care services, rather than a floor (or basic minimum) as recommended by the President's Commission, the task force thus misconstrued the thrust of its professed distributive principle.

Many of Pauly's complaints rest on the ability of the Commonwealth of Massachusetts to implement the recommendations of the task force, that is, the state's ability to limit the dissemination of the technology. And this was very difficult to do. The pressure came not just from patients who wanted the technology to be made available, but also from hospital administrators who wanted transplantation programs in their institutions.

While the task force was still deliberating, several hospitals in Boston sought permission from the Public Health Council (via certificates of need) to perform liver transplantations.[48] Another panel was convened by the state (this one composed of physicians and public health experts) to study the request for a three-year demonstration project. The panel recommended that in order to provide for adequate assessment of the technology and to assure quality of care, permission to perform the procedure be given only to one or two hospitals (to form one pediatric program and one adult program). The four hospitals that wished to institute liver transplantation programs offered a compromise counterproposal: If all four of them were allowed to perform liver transplantations, they would work together as a consortium. The Public Health Council accepted their proposal, and the liver transplantation consortium became a reality in January 1984.

Later that same year, the Public Health Council, with the agreement of the task force, gave permission to Brigham and Women's Hospital to perform heart transplants for a year, as part of another three-year demonstration project. But other hospitals were also eager to institute heart transplantation programs and convinced Brigham and Women's to join with them in another consortium.[49] This group of hospitals (some members of the liver consortium, some new members) then applied for a certificate of need to perform heart transplants, and their application constituted the real test of the strength of the recommendations of the task force. At stake was the proposal that organ transplantation be introduced on a very limited and controlled basis, allowing for careful study and quality control.

Opponents of the heart consortium (including Annas) contended that the four hospitals would not be able to meet the standards of efficacy set by the task force. The problem, critics contended, is that the few heart transplants predicted to be performed each year in Boston will be divided among four different hospitals, so no single hospital would be able to gain sufficient experience to warrant its having a transplantation program. Charles Donahue, the executive director of the Health Planning Council, argued that according to his projections, the hospitals could not perform the "minimum number of procedures [needed] to maintain their skills"—especially those involved in posttransplantation care.[50]

Despite the opposition, the Public Health Council gave the consortium of hospitals permission to proceed with the trial heart transplantation programs. The recommendation of the task force that the technology should be introduced on a limited and carefully controlled basis were overwhelmed by the strong desire of these hospitals to have the power and prestige associated with organ transplantation centers.

Unfortunately, the fears of the opponents of the consortium seem to have been borne out. During the first two years of operation (1985 and 1986), the consortium of four hospitals performed only a total of eighteen heart transplants, and six of the patients died. The record is not too bad—a 67 percent survival rate—but it pales in comparison with other transplant centers, such as the one at Stanford University, which had an 88 percent patient survival rate in 1986. And some hospitals in the consortium had fairly low rates of patient survival: Two of the four heart transplant patients at Massachusetts General Hospital died, and two of the three transplant patients at New England Medical Center died.[51]

The Massachusetts experience with controlling heart transplantations high-lights two fundamental obstacles in dealing with lifesaving technology on the state level. The first is the difficulty of limiting expansion, both in determining the proper scope of the limits and in obtaining compliance with the limits set. When good intentions to circumscribe development—even in the form of state regulations—meet with powerful pressures to expand, it is not clear that the limits will (or even should) win. In Massachusetts, a "consortium" of hospitals was created in order to undermine the limits set; in other states there will no doubt be other methods.

The second obstacle is a basic problem for any transplantation program that is not part of a national plan: Patients who are dissatisfied with their lack of access to the technology will go elsewhere. Hence, despite all efforts to the contrary, ability to pay will still play a large role in the dissemination of the technology. This fact indicates that piecemeal allocational programs are doomed to failure and that only a national plan can come close to assuring equitable access. It is to the possibility of developing a coherent and just national allocational system for organ substitution technology that we will now turn.

The Allocation of Organ Substitution Technology on the National Level

The next three chapters deal not only with the most fundamental theoretical questions regarding society's obligation to provide access to this costly technology, but also with the practical aspects of the issues and the implications of their views for health care in general.

Roger Evans and Christopher Blagg begin by examining the use of organ substitution technology within Medicare's End-Stage Renal Disease Program and analyzing the implications for end-stage heart disease. On the basis of their study, they conclude that certain aspects of heart transplantation are likely to follow the path of kidney transplantation: Patient selection criteria will be loosened, for instance, so the success rate of the procedure will worsen and the quality of life of the survivors will decline, yet costs will escalate.

In Chapter 15, Mary Ann Baily widens the focus a bit to include a variety of transplantation technologies: kidney, heart, and liver. She first discusses the difficulties of ascertaining how much money really is at stake here—that is, how much money the wide dissemination of heart, liver, and kidney transplants would cost. Baily then turns to the question of what role the ability to pay should have in the allocation of these technologies. In doing so, she examines three possible future scenarios: (1) the ability to pay will have no role (which she thinks is unlikely); (2) only those patients who have the ability to pay will have access to the technology (another unlikely outcome); and (3) the ability to pay will play some role in determining access to the technology (the most likely, and for Baily, the least satisfactory alternative).

In Chapter 16, Norman Daniels considers the allocation of organ substitution technology in light of a specific theory of justice. He argues that the principle of justice that should govern the design of health care institutions is a principle that calls for guaranteeing fair equality of opportunity and that this principle prohibits financial, geographical, and discriminatory barriers to the level of health care that promotes normal functioning. This does not include all health services, for Daniels recognizes the scarcity of resources, but it does include those services that are part of the design of a system that, on the whole, protects equal opportunity.

The next question, of course, is whether or not organ substitution technology should be included as one of those services. In an ideally just world, the answer might be no—if providing the technology had unacceptable opportunity costs. But Daniels points out that policymakers do not have the luxury of working within completely just institutions and that the constraints imposed by the current state of U.S. health care policy complicate the answer. This leads him to an analysis of those features of the health care system that make it especially difficult for policymakers to respond to efficiency arguments and arguments based on claims of justice. Daniels's basic conclusion is similar to that of Mary Ann Baily: The only possibility for providing a fair and efficient allocation of health care goods and services lies in a fundamental revamping of our social institutions.

In Chapter 17, H. Tristram Englehardt, Jr., takes a tack different from that of Baily and Daniels. He argues that the dissemination of organ substitution technology may not be a matter of justice at all, but a matter of charity. Although it is unfortunate that some individuals do not have access to this costly technology, he claims, it may not be unfair. As Englehardt explains, "It must be understood that though unfortunate circumstances are always ground for praiseworthy charity, they do not always provide grounds, by that fact, for redrawing the line between the circumstances we will count as unfortunate but not unfair and those we will count as unfortunate and unfair." His argument is based on the importance of free choice and the value of living with the consequences of those choices.

Notes

1. Although this is true in most circumstances, there are instances in which drugs or devices have been deemed to be too expensive to market to the few patients who need them, and companies have not made them available. This is known as the "orphan drug" syndrome.

2. Renee C. Fox and Judith P. Swazey, *The Courage to Fail: A Social View of Organ Transplants and Dialysis*, 2d ed. (Chicago: University of Chicago Press, 1978), p. 64.

3. For a discussion of the consensus development conference, see S. Perry and J. T. Kalverer, Jr., "The NIH Consensus Development Program and the Assessment of Health-Care Technologies: The First Two Years," *New England Journal of Medicine* 303: 169–172, 1980. See also D. Rennie, "Consensus Statements," *New England Journal of Medicine* 304: 665–666, 1981.

4. National Institutes of Health, "Liver Transplantation," *Journal of the American Medical Association* 250: 2961–2964, 1983.

5. National Institutes of Health, "Liver Transplantation."

6. Lawrence Morris, senior vice president of Blue Cross/Blue Shield Association, Testimony Before the Committee on Labor and Human Resources, U.S. Senate, October 20, 1983.

7. Morris, Testimony.

8. Samuel Korper, Johannes Vang, Norman Weissman, "Status of Insurance Coverage for Organ Transplants in the United States: A Review of Recent Surveys," *International Journal of Technology Assessment in Health Care* 2: 563–570, 1986.

9. R. A. Knox, "Heart Transplants: To Pay or Not to Pay." *Science* 209: 570–575, 1980.

10. Roger W. Evans, "Coverage and Reimbursement for Heart Transplantation," *International Journal of Technology Assessment in Health Care* 2: 425–449, 1986, p. 429.

11. Office of Technology Assessment, *Medical Technology and the Costs of the Medicare Program*, Report No. OTA-H-227 (Washington, D.C.: Government Printing Office, 1984).

12. "Myocardial Infarction and Mortality in the Coronary Artery Surgery Study (CASS) Randomized Trial," *New England Journal of Medicine* 310: 750–758, 1984. See also Judith Randal, "Coronary Artery Bypass Surgery," *Hastings Center Report* 12: 13–18, 1982.

13. Task Force on Organ Transplantation, *Organ Transplantation: Issues and Recommendations* (Washington, D.C.: Government Printing Office, 1986).

14. P. L. Frommer, "Medicare Coverage of Heart Transplants," Memorandum to Director, Coverage Assessment Staff, National Center for Health Care Technology (Bethesda, MD: National Heart, Lung, and Blood Institute, 1980), cited in Evans, "Heart Transplantation," p. 430.

15. J. B. Reiss, J. Burckhardt, and F. Hellinger, "Cost and Regulation of New Medical Technologies: Heart Transplants as a Case Study," in *Critical Issues in Medical Technology*, B. J. McNeil and E. G. Cravalho, eds. (Boston: Auburn House Publishing, 1982), pp. 399–417.

16. Evans, "Heart Transplantation," p. 431.

17. Reiss et al., "Cost and Regulation."

18. Ward Casscells, "Heart Transplantation: Recent Policy Developments," *New England Journal of Medicine* 315: 1365–1368, November 20, 1986.

19. Reiss et al., "Cost and Regulation."

20. Frommer, "Medicare Coverage."

21. Evans et al., *National Heart Transplantation Study: Final Report* (Seattle, WA: Battelle Human Affairs Research Centers, 1984).

22. H. David Banta, Statement Before the Subcommittee on Investigations and Oversight of the Committee on Science and Technology, U.S. House of Representatives, April 1983.

23. Section 2991 of Public Law 92-603, Social Security Amendments of 1972, effective July 1973.

24. Basically, three types of treatment for end-stage renal disease are available: hemodialysis, peritoneal dialysis, and organ transplantation. Hemodialysis—which involves filtering the patient's blood through an artificial kidney machine and then returning it to the body—is the most widely utilized treatment method. Peritoneal dialysis has been gaining in popularity since the development of continuous ambulatory peritoneal dialysis: Rather than being hooked to a machine, the patient continually dialyses himself by infusing dialysate from a flexible plastic container (which can be kept in a pocket) into his or her peritoneum. With organ transplantation, the diseased kidneys are removed and a healthy kidney, obtained either from a cadaver or from a living donor, is put in their place.
    Medicare coverage through the End-Stage Renal Disease Program begins at different times, depending on the type of treatment. If the treatment is administered in a dialysis facility, Medicare coverage begins three months after the start of the program; if dialysis is administered at home, Medicare coverage begins one month after treatment begins; and coverage begins immediately if the patient has a kidney transplant. Patients continue to receive Medicare benefits as long as they receive dialysis, although benefits end thirty-six months after a successful kidney transplant.

25. No hearings were held on any of the bills, and only one piece of legislation on ESRD was passed prior to Public Law 92-603: The Heart Disease, Cancer, and Stroke Amendments of 1965 were amended in 1970 to include kidney disease. Richard A. Rettig and Ellen Marks, *The Federal Government and Social Planning for End-Stage Renal Disease: Past, Present, and Future* (Santa Monica, CA: The Rand Corporation, 1983), p. 2.

26. Richard A. Rettig, "The Policy Debate on Patient Care Financing for Victims of End-Stage Renal Disease," *Law and Contemporary Problems* 40(4): 196–230, Autumn 1976, p. 229.

27. These costs cover the expenses of only 60 percent of end-stage renal disease sufferers—those who are under the age of 65. Although Congress greatly underestimated the costs of the ESRD program, the Department of Health, Education and Welfare's estimates were considerably more accurate. Rettig and Marks, *Social Planning*, p. 3.

28. Jerome Aroesty and Richard A. Rettig, *The Cost Effects of Improved Kidney Transplantation* (Santa Monica, CA: The Rand Corporation, February 1984), p. 1.

29. R. W. Evans, C. R. Blagg, F. A. Byran, Jr., "Implications for Health Care Policy: A Social and Demographic Profile of Hemodialysis Patients in the United States," *Journal of the American Medical Association* 245: 487–491, 1981, pp. 490–491.

30. National Academy of Sciences, Institute of Medicine, *Report of the Panel on Implications of a Categorical Catastrophic Approach to National Health Insurance*, Washington, D.C., 1973.

31. The National Center for Health Care Technology (NCHCT) was established by Congress in 1978 to analyze medical procedures not falling under the mandate of the Food and Drug Administration. Because of federal budget cuts in 1981, however, NCHCT was terminated. The National Center for Health Services Research and the Congressional Office of Technology Assessment have taken up this responsibility.

32. Dale Jamieson discusses a similar issue with regard to the artificial heart in Part Four of this volume.

33. H. David Banta, assistant director for health and life sciences, Office of Technology Assessment, Statement Before the Hearings Before the Subcommittee on Investigations and Oversight of the Committee on Science and Technology, U.S. House of Representatives, April 1983.

34. Evans, "Heart Transplantation," p. 431.

35. Evans et al., *Heart Study*, pp. 24–26.

36. Samuel Korper, Johannes Vang, Norman Weissman, "Status of Insurance Coverage for Organ Transplants in the United States: A Review of Recent Surveys," *International Journal of Technology Assessment in Health Care* 2: 563–570, 1986, p. 569.

37. Senator Albert Gore, quoted in Jane K. White, "Update," *Health Affairs* 4: 109–114, 1985, p. 112.

38. Task Force, *Recommendations*, p. 17.

39. See, for instance, Robert Nozick, *Anarchy, State and Utopia* (New York: Basic Books, 1974).

40. Some critics argue, for instance, that strictly voluntary exchanges of property may lead to such extreme concentrations of wealth that the rich are able to undermine the civil liberties of the poor. See G. A. Cohen, "Robert Nozick and Wilt Chamberlain: How Patterns Preserve Liberty," in *Justice and Economic Distribution*, John Arthur and W. H. Shaw, eds. (Englewood Cliffs, N.J.: Prentice-Hall, Inc., 1978).

41. President's Commission for the Study of Ethical Problems in Medicine and Biomedical and Behavioral Research, *Securing Access to Health Care* (Washington, D.C.: Government Printing Office, 1983), p. 4.

42. See Robert M. Veatch, *A Theory of Medical Ethics* (New York: Basic Books, 1981), pp. 264–268.

43. Evans et al., *Heart Study*, p. ES-77.

44. "Report of the Massachusetts Task Force on Organ Transplantation," *Law, Medicine and Health Care* 13: 8–26, 1985, p. 10.

45. See Joel Feinberg, *Social Philosophy* (Totowa, N.J.: Prentice-Hall, 1973).

46. The president's commission would allow such prohibitions if they were needed to ensure an "adequate level" or "decent minimum" of health care for all.

47. President's Commission, *Securing Access*, pp. 11–47.

48. Much of the information regarding the liver and heart consortia was taken from three articles: Ward Casscells, "Heart Transplantation"; Rene Becker, "Heart Failure," *Boston*, March 1987, pp. 111–156; George Annas, "Regulating the Introduction of Heart and Liver Transplantation," *American Journal of Public Health* 75: 93–95, 1985.

49. One of these, Massachusetts General Hospital, had received a great deal of publicity in 1980 when it decided not to perform heart transplants. The decision was swayed by such factors as: "the unproved ability of the procedure to benefit a large number of the many patients at risk, the unsolved problem of tissue rejection, and the diversion of limited resources to a procedure that at present has little impact on the all-too-common health problem that it addresses." "The Massachusetts General Hospital Trustees Say No to Heart Transplants," *New England Journal of Medicine* 302: 1087, 1980.

50. Becker, "Failure," p. 153.

51. These figures were reported by Becker, "Failure," p. 153.

11

Scarce Dollars for Saving Lives:
The Case of Heart and
Liver Transplants

Paul T. Menzel

Any society draws a functional distinction between people's merely unfortunate disasters on the one hand and their unfair as well as unfortunate ones on the other. If a person draws bad luck in the natural lottery of accident and disease, sometimes we will, and sometimes we will not, think it unfair then to compound his or her misfortune in the natural lottery with more bad luck in the social lottery. From an individual perspective, this person will see not only the natural but also the social lottery as indeed bad luck—through no fault of his or her own, someone hits not only a bad disease, but on top of it all, a disease for which others do not collectively fund the remedy. When is this just bad luck, and when is it socially unfair?

Assuming that people are not going to pay literally unlimited amounts of money to save a life, one important basis among others on which this line between the unfair and the merely unfortunate will inevitably get drawn is expense. Sometimes, when things just cost too much to repair, people will not regard their lack of repair as unfair. But what, of course, is "too much"? In the realistic context of health care finance, the important question to ask is, What care is so expensive in relation to its benefits that we should not cover it by insurance? In the case of heart and liver transplants in particular, how can that line be fairly drawn?

In this chapter, I will explore this issue by doing four things:

1. Relate a few observations about how one prepaid health care plan, Group Health Cooperative of Puget Sound, has handled its discussion of heart and liver transplant coverage in the last year and attempt to see what lessons for social and institutional policy can be drawn from this organization's experience.

2. Draw some implications about the basic ethic of the health care professions both from that experience and from the recent use of temporary artificial heart implants to tide patients over until a more permanent donor heart becomes available for transplant. The features of the basic ethic of the health care professions will have to be taken into account in any reasonable policy for dealing with the question of what should be covered by health care insurance.

3. State and assess several arguments about what sort of relative weight prior preventive care should have in relation to remedial crisis care in allocating health care resources and apply some of my conclusions to the case of coverage for heart and liver transplants.

4. Morally scrutinize decisions to exclude high-ticket items—such as organ transplants—from coverage because of a plan's desire to avoid attracting members with a greater than average likelihood of needing transplantation (avoiding "adverse selection") or because of its desire positively to attract more people with a less than average likelihood of needing them ("cream skimming").

One Prepaid Plan's Discussion
of Organ Transplantation Coverage

Group Health Cooperative of Puget Sound (hereafter GHC) is a 325,000-member consumer-governed health maintenance organization (HMO) in Washington State. In January 1986, GHC's Organ Transplantation Subcommittee reported its specific recommendations on heart and liver transplantation coverage to the cooperative's Board of Trustees. Concurrently, GHC's Ethics Council issued its own report of a somewhat different nature. This second report did not recommend any specific action on covering heart and liver transplants but did note the more important ethical principles and considerations in any decision regarding them. Later in the spring, a poll was taken of randomly chosen GHC members and prospective members (equal numbers of each) regarding their preferred priorities for different services, their willingness to increase dues to pay for new services covered, and so on. In June 1986, five public membership forums on coverage priorities were held in different parts of the region, with more than 300 people attending.

All of these discussions took place against an acknowledged background of commitment to certain traditional principles of the organization: excellence in health care, serving the needs and desires of its consumers, providing good preventive medicine integrated into the general system of care, giving all members equal access to benefits, reducing cost as a barrier to access, and respecting the autonomy of members both in their informed consent as patients and their role in cooperative governance. Furthermore, GHC was already covering bone marrow transplants, and in November 1985, it had decided on an ad hoc basis to cover the headline-generating first heart transplant performed in the Pacific Northwest, at the University of Washington Hospital.

The Organ Transplantation Subcommittee's estimate of the 1986 cost of heart transplants was $148,201 for each patient receiving a transplant, including all costs incurred in the year after the transplant as well as the transplant evaluation costs of other candidates accepted, but expected to die while waiting unsuccessfully for donor organs.[1] This estimate did not include the cost of immunosuppressant drugs for patients after their first year. The parallel cost for livers was $320,723 per recipient, including children with biliary atresia as well as adults. Annualized costs to the cooperative in the first five years of covering heart transplants, including follow-up immunosuppressant drugs, were estimated to be $629,836; for liver transplants, $837,699; for liver transplants only to children with biliary atresia, $205,151; for both heart and liver transplants, $1,467,535. These estimates are based on a projection of transplants of two to three livers and three to four hearts per year and one liver transplant for a child with biliary atresia every other year.[2]

The subcommittee almost immediately saw one problem as the crux of the matter: GHC's principles are challenged when the needs or desires of a very few consumers make unusually costly claims upon the cooperative's resources. The mere fact that this is a high expense incurred by the few and paid for by the many is not itself a problem; that, of course, is what any insurance for catastrophes involves. But it became a problem in the cooperative's discussion because of three further considerations:

1. How much life, health, and quality of life would we really be buying with this money? At somewhere from $200,000 to $1 million for five to forty years of life saved (in the case of adults), both heart and liver transplants appear to be near the ballpark of acceptable cost for benefits produced. But neither is any shoo-in, either. Whereas heart transplants are considerably less expensive than liver transplants, livers appear to have a better record than hearts in the final occupational and general health status of their recipients. For example, 80 percent of patients with transplanted livers surviving more than one year resumed their former occupations, but roughly only one-half of heart transplant recipients did.[3]

2. What competing services would have to be forgone if transplants were covered? Immediately competing projects and proposals in GHC included increased coverage of diabetic supplies, of orthopedic supplies, and of in-patient psychiatric care, as well as new programs in breast cancer screening and cardiovascular health promotion.

3. If dues were increased to pay the cost of covering organ transplantation, how would GHC's market position be affected? If no other services were cut, dues would have to be increased by 42 cents a month per enrollee, a 0.67 percent increase. That was judged by many to be significant in the cooperative's market situation.

In the initial deliberations, the expectations of most people seemed to be that heart and liver transplants had entered the therapeutic stage and thus would be recommended for coverage. However, the final (albeit not unanimous) recommendation of the Organ Transplantation Subcommittee was *not* to cover heart or adult liver transplants, but at the time only liver transplants for children with biliary atresia. The subcommittee did recommend annual reconsideration pending future medical and financial developments. Subsequent forums and a consumer survey showed that people value routine and preventive services more highly than coverage of organ transplantations. However, consumers were equally divided in their opinion about the importance of coverage for transplantation, and those who preferred it appeared willing to pay the additional premium.

The cooperative's Board of Trustees quickly accepted the subcommittee's recommendation to cover liver transplantation for children with biliary atresia but singled out the recommendation not to cover heart transplants for particular reservation. Later, in July 1986, after the member forums and consumer survey and after contentions by the University of Washington Hospital that heart transplantation costs were roughly half of the subcommittee's estimates, the board decided finally, in a divided vote, to accept its medical staff's recommendation to cover heart transplants. A key point in the board's reasoning was expressed by its chairman: Heart transplants are "quite expensive by any standard, but we have not excluded other care because it is expensive."[4] Nor had GHC excluded other care that is as expensive in relation to its projected benefits. It was also thought by some that no boost in premium rates would be needed, as administrative costs could be shaved to make up for the cost of coverage hoped to be lower than the subcommittee had projected. Meanwhile the policy of explicitly *not* covering adult liver transplantation was extended.

Needless to say, this whole matter has caused considerable controversy. The cooperative has ended up covering heart transplants and some liver transplants. What at first appeared to be a nearly foregone conclusion that the now therapeutic organ transplants would be covered has been dissected, almost torturously discussed, and restructured. A combination of scarce internal resources and external market considerations made a decision for coverage much more difficult than it would have been otherwise.

The New Ethic: Rationing

To this observer, it seems clear that the cooperative's discussions represented the recognition by diverse groups of people—consumers, health care administrators, physicians, nurses—that there is a need to ration some health care resources. This included both the need for rationing among GHC resources (allocation within the organization) and the need for rationing members' general resources between health care and other goods (the dues and market issues). What is especially significant in this case is that a group was prepared to impose upon itself a rationing system for life-prolonging technology. Furthermore, any self-imposed rationing policy would be decided upon prospectively. Although the parties discussing these questions were often imagining the possibility that they themselves would need a transplant, they were finally making a decision while *imagining* being the person needing it, not *being* that person. They were taking control of the individual and collective resources at their disposal should they themselves get in dire trouble, but they were doing that before they themselves got in trouble. This is simply the consumer's rationing perspective, as distinct from the patient's perspective. From this former perspective *it is strictly necessary to compare uses of resources in order to respect people's right to control what is done with their group's collective assets.*

In the end this will strain the traditional ethic of provider loyalty to the interests of the individual patient, but rationing of some sort is nevertheless absolutely morally essential. Without it we would be ignoring the choices people will make to control their resources for their own perceived welfare. That is a diminishment of their autonomy, and in the long run will undoubtedly reduce their total well-being. Respect for autonomy, concern for welfare, and a commitment to fairness all support the need for rationing. Without a rationing policy, the allocation of the group's resources may not reflect its members' priorities, it may yield an inefficient or wasteful use of those resources, and it may discriminate in a morally arbitrary way among potential recipients.

A much more dramatic example of the same necessity for addressing the issue of the type of policy one wants before one actually faces a crisis can be found in the use of artificial heart implants to tide patients over until an organ donor for transplant can be found. As George Annas has eloquently pointed out, the transplant surgeon and anyone else trying to tide a patient over until a suitable donor is found must take account of one very important fact: With the rather extreme shortage of donor hearts, any heart that the physician later gets for his or her patient will very probably in turn leave some other transplant candidate short a heart.[5] Thus, in the last analysis, temporary heart implants very seldom have any net life-saving effect; they only save one life rather than another, and usually at considerable extra expense over and above just waiting and saving the other life when a donor is found.

Does it then make any moral sense at all for the physician in this case to act exclusively out of loyalty to his current, individual patient, a loyalty that almost always comes at the expense of saving someone else, and someone else more cheaply? It seems quite clear that all potential heart transplant recipients would be better off if they could actually bind and tie physicians' hands in order to prevent them from indulging in their fantasy of saving lives with temporary implants. Although I am not speaking here of what actual patients (at the point of knowing that they are being considered for an implant as a bridge to transplant) would choose, I am also not speaking here only of what general consumers beforehand would choose. I am speaking of what policy actual heart failure patients awaiting transplant would vote for if they controlled policy. None would be able to guess that he or she is more likely to be saved by use of the artificial implant or more likely to languish and die without a donor heart because supply was just a bit too short. Yet each would know that a system that uses artificial hearts as a temporary bridge to human heart transplantation does involve more expenditures and hence drives up the price of transplantation for everyone—without saving any additional lives. Upon serious consideration of all of these realities, it is very likely that patients awaiting heart transplants would vote for a policy of not using the artificial heart as a temporary bridge to transplantation.

The next question we need to ask concerns the type of physician we want to have. Do we want a physician who will use the temporary implant to save someone who happens to be his or her patient (even though this saves no additional lives and is more costly)? Or do we want a physician who will forgo saving his or her patients in order to allow other patients to be saved and who will use the monetary resources saved to help still other patients? The latter choice, I believe, is preferable. In defending this choice I do not rely on the reason usually believed to underlie the claim that a physician should become a cost-conscious agent: the interests of society at large. Instead, I am relying on the prior consent of the patient. Thus my claim that the physician should become cost conscious is not open to the usual objections raised against the physician's becoming a cost-conscious agent of society.[6]

This is, unquestionably, the psychologically tougher course of action: The traditional ethical outlook of the physician, that is, loyalty to the current individual patient, is being superceded by a higher, more ethically sophisticated level of moral reasoning. Consideration of what polilcy these patients would adopt beforehand is correctly regarded as more sophisticated moral reasoning because it represents respect for patients' taking control over their scarce resources. It is important to note, however, that there is a certain danger in deciding an allocational policy beforehand: We must be careful to do so only with sufficient imagination of the human realities of the perceived crises as well as sufficient understanding of the odds that such crises will occur.

Our task, then, is to ascertain what allocations of scarce resources informed consumers of health care would choose for themselves when they are deciding beforehand with accurate imagination and understanding of the realities at stake. With regard to the question of "amount of money for results achieved," we should recognize that health care is not the only thing that people value; therefore, we should respect people's willingness to take risks in health care and health care coverage in order to save money for other things. And on the particular matter of the price tags for heart and liver transplantation—$200,000 to $1 million per successful operation (total treatment for the lifetime of the patient), to save from five to forty years of life—the conclusion is far from certain. Confronted with a real choice, many people will be willing to pay beforehand for the security of knowing that if they are among the unlucky heart or liver failure patients, they will be saved; but likewise, many people will *not* be willing to pay that extra cost. In particular, many would probably be inclined to exclude the less cost-effective cases (for instance, those heart transplants that statistically gain only a few years of life at a cost of over $200,000). The incidence of this type of case is not infrequent, and unless certain limitations on patient selection criteria hold firm, it is likely to increase in number.

Factors other than cost per benefit produced are also liable to enter the discussion. One is the relative weight of prevention and crisis care. Some will observe that if we only spend, for instance, $10 million more on prevention, we could save forty lives; this would be $250,000 per forty-year life span, let us say, compared to $500,000 for fewer years by transplantation. Others will argue that we cannot compare the two resource uses that way: We are saving identifiable lives by transplantation, but not by prevention, and that makes not only a great psychological difference but an important moral difference as well. Let me turn now to this prevention/rescue trade-off.

Prevention and Rescue

Two common arguments for giving crisis care priority are bad:[7]

1. We are told that prevention saves only statistical lives; crisis care saves identifiable lives. This argument begs the question: It still leaves unexplained why a real life should be less important simply because it is statistical. Furthermore, the distinction itself is confusing. Acute care patients are statistical beneficiaries of the care, too: Not all will live; and of those who do survive, some would have done so even without medical intervention. So are their lives, when saved, merely statistical lives? And preventive care patients are often themselves just as identifiable as recipients of the care as are acute patients.

2. It is said that by giving moral priority to crisis care over preventive measures, we symbolize our belief that life has no price, or nearly none. But we want to symbolize only what is right. That is, this symbolism is correct only if identifiable, known, high-risk lives really are worth *more*, while less identifiable, low-risk lives really are worth *less*. But are they?

There are two distinctly better arguments for giving some priority to crisis care, but they yield only sharply qualified priority.

1. Even when the proper question in allocating resources is seen to be what we would choose beforehand, not when we are already in crisis, we will still choose to give some priority to crisis care. We know, after all, that generally we are willing to pay at a higher rate per life saved to reduce risk in high-risk situations than in low-risk ones. We know this both intuitively from common sense, and also from what researchers tell us regarding studies of how much people want to pay. This pattern is illustrated by Table 11.1. The point to be gained from the table is not the particular dollar figures, but the pattern and order among them: People's willingness to pay to reduce risk drops more than proportionately with the drop in the risk they are paying to avoid.

TABLE 11.1
People's Pricing of Their Own Lives in Different Risk Situations

Risk of Death	Amount Paid to Reduce Risk to 0 (dollars)	Implied Monetary Value of Life (dollars)
1	1,000,000	1,000,000
1:10	80,000	800,000
1:1000	300	300,000
1:10,000	30	300,000
1:10,000,000	0	0 (?)

Source: Author's calculations.

Furthermore, people will think ahead. In choosing a policy for allocating between preventive and crisis care, they will take into account the higher-risk situations to which crisis care is naturally directed. The main qualification of this argument is that the amount of risk reduction in even a high-risk situation may be very small—indeed, as small or smaller than in many preventive care situations. Although this caution is important, it detracts little from the appropriate pull of crisis care in nonexperimental transplantation contexts, where usually the risk of death can be lowered drastically.

2. Suppose that generally we believe that statistically we will benefit in the long run if prevention takes precedence over crisis care when it saves a few more lives for the same amount of money. If a person has not had the chance of benefiting from such a policy because the society has not had it long enough, then it cannot be fair to that person *now* to shift some acute care resources to prevention. He or she, after all, never had the real opportunity to benefit from such an emphasis on prevention. This argument for giving priority to crisis care, then, is based on a view of fairness to people who are already ill.

Although this is a sound argument for giving priority to crisis care, it harbors an extremely important qualification on any such priority. In direct contrast to the facts necessary in order for this argument to work, many crisis patients in current transplant contexts may have had a very real opportunity to benefit from an emphasis on prevention—at least if we count the considerable public resources that have been spent to educate the public about the importance of diet, exercise, refraining from excessive consumption of alcohol, and so on. But this does not apply to all transplant patients, of course: Children with biliary atresia as well as some adults afflicted with cardiomyopathy due to infections almost certainly have not benefited from preventive measures. Clearly this latter group, but not so clearly others, deserves some priority for their crisis care on the basis of this argument.[8]

The conclusion is that rational, reflective individuals will vote beforehand for a *limited* priority for crisis care. After all, they already know two things about their willingness to pay: (1) They are willing to pay more per life saved in high-risk (crisis) situations than in lower-risk (preventive) ones; and (2) they are willing to pay more per life saved for large reductions in that risk than for small reductions. In addition, people who have never had the real opportunity to benefit from preventive measures will give some priority to crisis care, although when this point is applied to the issue of heart and liver transplantation, it perhaps only applies to children with biliary atresia and adults with heart infections. The legitimate moral priority that rescuing people in crisis does have over preventing crises from developing is only a partial one. It in no way supports a blank check for crisis care in general or for organ transplantation in particular.

Adverse Selection and Cream Skimming

If you leave the allocational question of "How much should we spend on health care?" up to consumers and the market, then consumers trying to find what they need and insurance plans that cater to those demands will try to carve out less expensive niches for themselves. In an atmosphere of heated economic competition, every payer will want to avoid attracting less healthy subscribers than its competitors. Thus an individual plan may want to avoid covering certain transplant procedures, at least until almost all other plans cover them. The factual assumption here is that healthier subscribers will not be willing to pay the marginal additional premiums created by their plan's attracting a higher than average portion of the more likely ill and thus that many of them will leave to join other, less expensive, plans. The result of this, of course, is that dues would have to go up even more for the remaining membership.

This factual assumption is undoubtedly correct: The healthier do flee the plans with more likely ill subscribers. But the moral question is whether they ought to; and the policy issue is whether they should be allowed to. Shouldn't we be willing to accept adverse selection? Shouldn't we be willing to pay higher dues to support the more likely ill?

In some respects, the proper answer to these questions is yes. Part of what we mean by equitable access to health care is simply that those who have had the sheer misfortune of being likely to need care should not have to pay considerably more for health care than others. The moral force of this simple idea is strengthened by the fact that those most in need of care are less likely to be able to afford it because the illness limits earning capacity. Health insurance generally tries to compensate for precisely these differences. But we need also to note a different sort of consideration: We ought not to have to pay *more* to support those in our group who are more likely ill than other likely well subscribers in society are paying to support the likely ill in their groups. This means that we are under no moral pressure to accept truly "adverse selection": the attraction to our group of more than a proportionate share of likely ill, more expensive subscribers.

One way in which the first moral principle is often conveyed is through the use of a pejorative label for the reverse of adverse selection: "cream skimming." A plan is accused of cream skimming if it deliberately attempts to attract the healthiest members of the community, regardless of whether it is to their personal credit that they are healthier. The first moral principle condemns cream skimming; the second principle, in contrast, says that it is perfectly permissible to avoid adverse selection.

When we balance off objectionable cream skimming with legitimate avoidance of adverse selection in the same case, we can observe another point: A plan ought not to do what it would otherwise be perfectly acceptable to do—avoid adverse selection—*if* it is objectionably helping itself by cream skimming. In the heat of competition, it may be very difficult to resist the temptation to attempt to skim off the cream of the most likely well (for instance, by not covering heart and liver transplants). But it is imperative for a plan to resist that temptation if it is going to preserve its moral integrity in avoiding adverse selection.

As complex as this may seem, it is the relatively easy part of the matter. The most interesting disputes are likely to break out as soon as we apply these convictions. In many cases it will be very difficult in practice to tell the difference between objectionable cream skimming and legitimate fear of adverse selection. For example, if we put more resources into better preventive care and less into remedial heart or liver transplants, are we avoiding the adverse selection of a higher than average number of potential heart and liver failure patients, or are we skimming the cream of subscribers least worried about their hearts and livers?

One of the first considerations might appear to be whether other insurers are covering such transplants; if they are, well then, one plan's omission of the standard coverage is simply cream skimming. That, however, can hardly be our final answer. Suppose that most other plans do cover these expensive procedures, and suppose that few of them aggressively offer as well-integrated preventive services as the plan in question. Would it be wrong for that plan to choose not to cover organ transplants and instead upgrade preventive programs, which *it* very plausibly judges to be, dollar-for-dollar, more beneficial?

I think the answer is clear. *If* the group's emphasis on prevention and its de-emphasis of some high-tech remedial services reflect the genuine beliefs and values of its members about what is the best overall balance of medicine, *if* it does not reflect the group's desire to shirk its share of paying for the legitimate health care of those less healthy, and *if* those who opt for other insurers do so because they differ from the group in those very values and beliefs, then how can anyone—even people most likely to need these high-tech procedures—plausibly claim that the group's decision not to cover them is merely cream skimming?

These are, of course, big ifs. The difficulty is telling the difference between legitimate reflection of different values and beliefs on the one hand and objectionable cream skimming on the other, especially amid the often haze-creating heat of competition. But this may not be a disadvantage. I suspect, instead, that it may be useful for a plan to be uncertain which of these two things it is doing: The uncertainty may properly serve to keep it on its moral toes.

Not covering some care when almost everyone else is covering it is not objectionable by itself. Thus, what may look like cream skimming or morally mindless scrambling to avoid adverse selection is not always objectionable. Certainly, however, there is a significant danger of discrimination against the more likely ill once we are operating in a market where individual consumer preference is the basic force in making decisions on what care is worth the money it costs.

Conclusion

Three broad conclusions can be reached from the above. First, consumers should be thought of as sitting down to decide beforehand what coverage policy they want for expensive organ transplants. There is no way to determine in abstraction based on who those actual people are whether they should or should not want transplants covered. The expense level of heart and liver transplants usually makes them borderline cases in terms of money spent for results achieved;

different rational individuals and rational groups can decide in different ways. Indeed, it may be that the most sensible coverage is not all-or-nothing, but rather a more limited coverage of those expensive procedures needed by those with the most years of likely healthy life to gain from them. Such an approach can be approximated either through the operations of consumer-governed health care cooperatives (such as GHC) or by allowing consumers to choose from an array of alternative health care policies that represent a range of different attitudes to risk and different priorities concerning prevention versus crisis care.

Second, crisis care has *some* legitimate priority over prevention in terms of dollars spent per life-year saved, but not much priority in the case of organ transplantation (except for cases of biliary atresia and cardiomyopathy due to infection).

Third, the permissible avoidance of adverse selection does not automatically justify a plan's excluding coverage for high-ticket transplants. However, even if almost all other plans cover these procedures, a plan should not be accused of objectionable cream skimming merely because it continues to refuse coverage.

Notes

1. In subsequent months this estimate was strongly disputed by University of Washington Hospital transplant surgeons. They insisted that the hospital's experience pointed to an average of roughly $60,000 for the first year after transplantation: (*Seattle Times,* July 24, 1986, pp. B1–B2). I will conservatively suppose this to be $80,000 when the evaluation costs of candidates not receiving transplants are included. Later, as we shall see, this figure—roughly half of the subcommittee's $148,201 estimate—played a significant role in the cooperative's final decision.

2. Organ Transplantation Subcommittee, Group Health Cooperative of Puget Sound, "Benefit Analysis for Coverage of Heart and Liver Transplantation" (Seattle, WA: Group Health Cooperative of Puget Sound, January 1986).

3. Subcommittee, "Benefit Analysis"; Bruce F. Scharschmidt, "Human Liver Transplantation: Analysis on Data of 540 Patients from Four Centers," *Hepatology* 4: Suppl: 95S–101S.

4. *Seattle Times,* July 24, 1985, pp. B1–B2.

5. See Chapter 12 by George Annas in Part Three of this volume; see also his article, "No Cheers for Temporary Artificial Hearts," *Hastings Center Report* 15: 27–28, 1985.

6. See, for example, the objections raised by Robert M. Veatch, "DRGs and the Ethical Allocation of Resources," *Hastings Center Report* 16: 32–40, 1986.

7. Except for the particular application to organ transplantation, this analysis is similar to my general discussion of the prevention/treatment distinction in Menzel, *Medical Costs, Moral Choices: A Philosophy of Health Care Economics in America* (New Haven: Yale University Press, 1983), Chap. 7.

8. Yet it is also important to note that prevention of congenital or early-onset problems— problems that preclude people from ever being in a position to vote self-interestedly for as much emphasis on prevention as on treatment—is surely as important as treatment. Thus it is wrong, as well as an inefficient use of resources, not to fund prenatal care programs at the same dollar-per-benefit rate as neonatal intensive care units.

12

Regulating Heart and Liver Transplants in Massachusetts: An Overview of the Report of the Task Force on Organ Transplantation

George J. Annas

Organ transplantation has been a favorite topic of health lawyers since its inception. Organ procurement was addressed with the adoption of the Uniform Anatomical Gift Act in all fifty states, and "brain death" has been recognized both judicially and legislatively across the country. Nonetheless, it is now apparent that the major problems in organ transplantation are not legal and thus neither are their solutions. Heart and liver transplants are extreme and expensive interventions that few individuals can afford and few hospitals can offer. In an era of economic scarcity, how (if at all) should organ transplant procedures and other extreme and expensive treatment be introduced into the health delivery system?

Although it seems reasonable to expect federal leadership to establish a limited number of high-quality transplant centers, federal efforts to date have focused almost exclusively on trying to help the scattered organ procurement agencies become more efficient. By default, the individual states have had to develop their own policies. A number of them, like California and Connecticut, have concentrated on Medicaid reimbursement requirements. Ohio has worked to develop a statewide "consortium" approach. But until late 1984, only Massachusetts had established a statewide public task force to make recommendations concerning how heart and liver transplants should be introduced. The Massachusetts Task Force grew out of a recommendation, made by Dr. Harvey V. Fineberg's earlier Liver Transplantation Task Force, that a broadly based public group examine the social issues involved with transplantation technology. The Massachusetts experience is important not only because it is the first state to utilize the strategy of a public task force, but also because of the strong medical institutions in Massachusetts, the vigorous use of determination-of-need mechanisms to regulate the introduction of liver and heart transplants, and the almost

---

Reprinted by permission from G. J. Annas, "Regulating Heart and Liver Transplants in Massachusetts," in *Law, Medicine & Health Care*, vol. 13, no. 1, pp. 4–7, 1985.

overwhelming desire of at least four Boston hospitals to do liver transplantation and of four Boston hospitals to do heart transplantation. Indeed, at times the political aspects of whether one hospital or more than one hospital should do either of these procedures have eclipsed all of the other critical issues involved in using these extreme and expensive technologies. . . .

The recommendations [of the Task Force] went to public hearing on November 5, 1984, and on November 27, 1984, the policy-making body of the Massachusetts Department of Public Health, the Public Health Council, unanimously adopted the recommendations as official Policy Guidelines and used the Report itself as explanatory text for the Department in reviewing determination-of-need applications for organ transplantation.

Major Conclusions

Although sometimes lost in bland prose, several significant conclusions were reached by the Task Force, which structured its set of recommendations. The basis of the Report can be stated in one long sentence. Because transplants are extreme and expensive procedures that nevertheless do not cure disease but replace the patient's underlying disease with a lifetime of immunosuppression, and because introducing transplantation into the current cost-constrained health care system threatens to displace other, higher priority health care services (including services to the Medicaid population and the poor), transplants should not be performed at all unless they are done on those who are likely to benefit from them, unless the total cost is controlled, and unless resources are not diverted from higher priority care. In fleshing out this basic principle, the Task Force concluded that public regulation would be ineffective if the burden of proving health care priorities was placed on the Department of Public Health. Accordingly, the Task. Force recommended that the analysis of health care priorities begin with a *presumption that all currently offered health care services have a higher priority than organ transplantation.* Therefore, any hospital applying to perform transplants should have the burden of demonstrating that "transplantation has a higher priority than any other currently available health service from which organ transplantation diverts funds and/or support systems."

On the underlying value issues of fairness and equity, the Task Force concluded that access to a transplant must be "independent of the individual's ability to pay for it." Thus, if offered at all in the system, heart and liver transplants must be considered part of the "minimum benefit package" to which all are entitled. But how could the health care system, which arguably could not handle organ transplants at all, introduce them in a manner that would make them available to everyone? They key is to *restrict the total number of transplants done.* However, this must be accomplished in a manner that optimizes the quality of care and benefit of those procedures actually performed, eliminates arbitrary patient selection excluders (such as income, age, and personal habits), and provides an equitable manner of selecting among suitable candidates when not all can be served. The most crucial element is to define "clinical suitability" for transplantation in a manner that concentrates on benefit to the patient in terms of life style and rehabilitation rather than simple survival. In the words of the Task Force, medical suitability should be an attempt to predict "those who can benefit the most from [transplants] in terms of probability of living for a significant period of time with a reasonable prospect for rehabilitation." Critical to maintaining a strict definition of "clinical suitability" is the restriction of total system capacity to perform transplants, as explained in the summary of the economics section later in this article.

Application of the Report

The utility of the Task Force Report, its recommendations, and the new Policy Guidelines of the Massachusetts Department of Public Health will face their first test when they are used to determine the public need for a four-hospital consortium to do heart transplants in Massachusetts in early 1985. A separate four-hospital consortium was approved to do liver transplants for a three-year period in January 1984. Conditions were placed on that determination of need, including requirements that the hospital not consider ability to pay or insurance status in patient selection, not reduce Medicaid services as a trade-off for liver transplantation, not reduce free care for non-transplant services below that provided in the most recent fiscal year, and have its liver transplantation protocols reviewed and approved by an institutional review board. The members of the Consortium objected to these conditions, and appealed them to the Health Facilities Appeals Board, which ordered a remand on procedural grounds. On remand, the Public Health Council explicitly adopted the conditions, with some modifications, over the objections of the Consortium. The IRB [Institutional Review Board] review requirement was modified most significantly to read:

> The hospital will have its liver transplant protocols, including consent and withdrawal of consent policies, organ procurement policies, recipient selection policies and confidentiality policies, reviewed and approved by an ethics committee of the Boston Center for Liver Transplantation, which will contain significant public representation, or by a special board set up for this purpose by the Department of Public Health.

It remains to be seen whether the Liver Consortium can live up to the Policy Guidelines. While the hospitals did not have to satisfy the Guidelines originally, they will serve as minimum requirements for any renewal of their DONs [determinations of need] two years from now. . . .

As previously mentioned, the consortium approach is primarily a political issue. It was grafted onto the original draft of the Report at the request of the Commissioner of Public Health. In March 1984, Commissioner Bailus Walker asked the Task Force's opinion about the advisability of granting a temporary exemption from determination of need to the Brigham and Women's Hospital, a tertiary care hospital, to do heart transplants. Such a single-hospital exemption was seen as preferable to having multiple hospitals request "emergency waivers" for individual patients while they pursued an institutional DON (this procedure was used for liver transplants in the Commonwealth by the Deaconess Hospital for more than six months). The Commissioner found it impossible to refuse such requests, and the use of emergency waivers in heart transplantation would have undercut any reasonable planning efforts.

The Commissioner's request for advice quickly became politicized, and a loose "consortium" of hospitals was thrown together to provide an alternative to the single-hospital exemption. The Task Force met three times on this issue. At its final meeting on this subject, May 15, 1984, the Task Force appeared for the first time in its entirety. Following a two-hour discussion, which was highlighted by a comment from State Senator Ed Burke that the paper consortium looked more like a "fig leaf" to cover "naked rivalry" among the hospitals, rather than a serious effort at cooperation, the Task Force voted unaminously to recommend a DON exemption for heart transplants in Brigham and Women's Hospital until the end of 1984. In addition, the Task Force voted to attempt to develop guidelines for a "truly cooperative consortium." A summary of guidelines for a "worthwhile consortium" appears in the group's final recommendation.

Economics

Since it was the cost of these extreme and expensive procedures that initially led to the formation of the Task Force, the Report's economic section and its conclusions are critical to any understanding of the recommendations. The analysis describes the many different ways of determining "costs" of transplants, and uses the specific figures generated by various agencies as examples of how divergent figures are calculated.

In general, hospitals have used only direct costs in the figures they have relied on to support their applications for determinations of need. Figures from the Massachusetts Liver Transplantation Task Force and Massachusetts Blue Cross, on the other hand, utilized fully allocated average costs. While arguments can be made for both views, the Task Force decided to use fully allocated-average-costs-for-one-year-of-survival as a benchmark for determining the cost of transplants and comparing it to the costs of other extreme and expensive medical procedures. In computing the costs of heart and liver transplants, the cost of the surgery itself is generally the smallest item, amounting to only about five percent of the cost, for example, of a liver transplant. About one-fourth of the cost is attributable to readmission to the hospital due to complications, and almost one-half of the total is attributable to ancillaries such as laboratory, blood, intravenous lines, radiology, social work, and physical therapy. The most important cost determiners are the number of ICU days that will be used by the patient and the cost of these days. Fully allocated, average costs will be a function not only of this, but also of the probability of surviving for one year and thus using the ICU bed for a longer period of time (and for additional years, if we want to arrive at average total costs).

Using this model, the Task Force derived costs of $230,000 to $340,000 per liver transplant patient alive at the end of one year (using a 70 percent survival rate), and $170,000 to $200,000 per one-year survival for heart transplant patients (also using a 70 percent survival rate). Additional years of survival would add from $10,000 to $20,000 in costs per year to these figures. Compared to other extreme and expensive medical care examined by the Task Force (including neonatal ICU care, adult ICU care, end-stage renal disease care, hemophilia, bone marrow transplants, and variceal bleeding) on the basis of fully allocated average one-year costs, the cost of heart and liver transplantation is 4 to 10 times more expensive than any of these. That's the bad news.

The good news is that these procedures can be performed for substantially less than this fully allocated cost to the health care system at least in a state like Massachusetts, which utilizes a prospective revenue cap on individual hospital budgets. Indeed, this cap on prospective total revenue may actually make innovation easier by limiting the costs to the system. A summary of the argument, which is the economic underpinning of the Report, runs like this. First, a significant portion of fully allocated costs goes toward amortization of the physical plant. Thus, if procedures can be "squeezed into" existing capacity without displacing other procedures, this cost will not have to be borne by the system. Second, and most important, since cost is primarily a function of ICU days, and since ICU days are a function of readmission and complications, the cost will be less if readmissions can be lowered. This is likely only if patient selection is kept very strict, i.e., if transplants are given to only those patients with strong clinical suitability, in the sense of being able to survive the transplant for a significant period of time with reasonable prospects for rehabilitation. Thus, cost becomes a function of patient selection criteria.

Patient selection criteria, however, tend to expand to include almost everyone in the absence of restraints on the system. This was well demonstrated in the end-stage renal disease program in which universal entitlement has led to universal treatment, whether medically beneficial or not. No one wants to repeat this experience with heart and liver transplantation, and thus no national politician has even suggested that heart and liver transplants be covered by Medicare. Indeed, even though he has made nationwide appeals for livers for children, President Ronald Reagan threatened to veto an organ transplant bill that would have provided federal money to pay the $6,000 needed annually for cyclosporin to immunosuppress transplant recipients, unless this portion of the bill was deleted—which it was.

Clinical suitability is not an immutable scientific fact, but one that is highly influenced by the environment. It is the Task Force's view that clinical suitability criteria will depend to some significant degree on system capacity. Thus, if system capacity is restricted, the clinical suitability criteria would remain relatively stringent. This would help ensure that only good candidates received transplants, and thus that the health care system would not have to be expanded to accommodate large numbers of patients. This would, in turn, ensure a cost-effective transplant program. The conclusion is that in order to maintain a cost-effective program, one must limit volume. And this, of course, makes determination of need a logical regulatory mechanism, one in which demand is adjusted to system capacity, rather than system capacity being adjusted to demand. The chief architect of this model, and author of the Economics Section of the Final Report, is Professor Marc Roberts of the Harvard School of Public Health.

It should be noted that limitation is a fair policy so long as we make transplants available in an equitable manner to all who are clinically suitable. In this way, we can permit organ transplants to become part of the "minimum benefit package" for Medicare and Medicaid recipients and even for the uninsured, without "breaking the bank. . . ."

Conclusions

Is all this merely an academic exercise? Won't the public demand expansion of the health care system to accommodate all who can obtain any conceivable benefit from transplants, no matter what the system costs? Possibly, but the experience with end-stage renal disease has been radicalizing. There are, for example, 80,000 individuals on dialysis in the United States today, yet only about 7,000, or less than 10 percent, are on waiting lists for kidney transplants. Because of the shortage of available organs, physicians have determined that more than 90 percent of all possible kidney transplant candidates are not "clinically suitable." Capacity of the system plays a critical role in this, and if we can directly limit the system's capacity, we not only can limit the system's costs, but also can provide the service to those who can benefit the most from it. A national system which limited heart and liver transplants to perhaps 20 high-quality centers is preferable. But in the absence of any national leadership on this subject, states will be forced to make their individual ways as best as they can. There will be tremendous pressures on the states from the hospitals, the media, and the public who cannot understand why such restrictions on capacity are being imposed. These pressures may be irresistible. But it may also be that these pressures can be resisted, at least during the 3-year "Phase I" envisioned by the Task Force, and that after this period of limited transplantation and data gathering, we will have learned enough about this issue to be able to make sound public policy that can be persuasively articulated to the public so that the policy is acceptable. So long as the entire procedure is public and perceived as fair, the potential for regulatory success should not be discounted.

My physician friends are fond of quoting the following line from *Hamlet* in describing organ transplantation. "Diseases desperate grown by desperate appliances are relieved, or not at all." The more appropriate passage for the regulator appears seven lines earlier in the King's declaration: "How dangerous is it that this man goes loose! Yet must not we put the strong law on him. He's loved of the distracted multitude . . . " (IV.iii). In this context, the man is organ transplantation. The challenge is to put "the strong law on him" long enough to persuade the public that a free-for-all in organ transplantation is reckless, while a controlled system has pay-offs in terms of quality of care, equity, and cost savings.

13

Equity and Costs

Mark V. Pauly

The task of determining who should or should not have access to a life-prolonging procedure would not be easy even if cost were no consideration. In an era in which the health industry has largely converted to the cost cutting religion, or at least the religion of budget limitation, a conversion for which health economics is partly responsible—the task becomes doubly difficult.

At one level, the Massachusetts Task Force on Organ Transplantation has dealt with this task simply by recommending that the final decision be postponed, and that a limited program of organ transplantation be introduced in an "Initial Social Assessment" phase. There is a faith that somehow this period will permit the gathering of data which, although unidentified, will "provide the basis for a decision." What sort of decision might that be? If the final version is anything like the recommended initial phase—a real possibility, given the general discussion in the Task Force Report—I would argue that a serious error would be made.

The Task Force obviously accepted most of the cost-cutting dogma, and the rituals—such as rate limitation and determination of need—which often accompany it. Indeed, the Task Force recommends that organ transplantation in Massachusetts, despite its already proven efficacy for patients with severe disease, take place only within a fixed total budget (for inpatient hospital care) and only to the extent that activities which have to be eliminated in order to free hospital resources for transplants can somehow be shown to have "lower priority." The implicit model is very much one in the spirit of a fully publicly controlled system with a fixed budget, in which individual choices and values have almost no role to play.

Economists are among the least likely to object to being concerned about resource costs in health care. Nevertheless, I am concerned that the Task Force, in accepting only the "cost" part of cost-benefit analysis (and its larger welfare economics framework), has been led to make recommendations which have some serious problems. These problems may well make the recommendations unacceptable, especially if viewed as the precursors of a more permanent solution. To put it bluntly, acceptance of the recommendations, even as an interim measure, would cause some people to die unnecessarily.

Reprinted with permission from *Law, Medicine & Health Care*, vol. 13, no. 1; © 1985, American Society of Law & Medicine, Boston, Massachusetts.

The major defect in the Task Force's analysis is its elevation of a political expedient—limitations on hospital spending—to the role of a moral postulate. Why are hospital costs limited in Massachusetts and in some other states? Given conventional forms of insurance and conventional ways in which information is transmitted to patients, it is believed that the current system would render care which is worth less than its cost. Although some politicians (and some budget directors) talk as if there were something intrinsically evil about having the health share of the Gross National Product exceed a certain percentage, this is only shorthand for the notion that we are not getting value for money. Even worse, it may be shorthand for the sentiment that publicly financed medical care costs cause problems for the public budget. Yet, if there should occur a medical innovation that is worth what it costs, the amount of resources available for this sector ought to be expanded by cutting inefficiency if that is possible; if it is not, we should reduce the amount we spend on other things—television, chocolate, books, bombs, and computers. That is, one ought require only that the resources used for the transplant have a lower priority in the economy as a whole, not that those resources be drawn necessarily (or even presumptively) from other health care services.

Suppose we then assume that there is no intrinsic merit to a fixed medical or hospital care budget. Suppose we also assume, as the Report itself suggests, that with feasible arrangements the supply of organs for transplantation will be adequate for all who desire transplants. Suppose that heart and liver transplants have passed the research stage, and are known to be effective, if expensive, ways of extending life, and that accurate information concerning the transplants is transmitted to patients and insurers. Finally, suppose that a financing method is developed in which someone who receives a transplant is charged the full resource costs of "producing" that transplant. The purchaser, in effect, causes no additional costs to be imposed on anyone except his household if he obtains a transplant. There could be insurance coverage of such expenses, but the premiums would apply only to those who had specifically elected transplant coverage; there would be no general spillover onto other insureds, either for the transplant surgery, or for the follow-up care. My understanding of the Task Force's recommendations is that they would prohibit a person who lives in Massachusetts from buying a transplant under such circumstances. In effect, the Task Force finds objectionable a family's decision that it is willing to sacrifice other things it might consume in order to prolong the life of one of its members.

Why would this be objectionable, even in the assessment phase? Ought it to be objectionable, so objectionable in principle that someone should die unnecessarily—that human life should be sacrificed? The consumption of this procedure in no way reduces the resources available to others, since the family is spending its own property, property which it would not make available to others in any case. Who gains from having such people die?

Another area where I have difficulty with the Task Force Report is the part that deals with the terrain most familiar to me: Section III's discussion of, and rationale for rejecting, cost-benefit analysis. The Task Force interprets cost-benefit analysis as based on this premise: "If, and only if, consumers are willing to pay more than the cost of producing what they consume, is it efficient to provide that output." The Task Force objects to the use of this method because "the views of the rich are given greater weight in the analysis;" such a procedure is inappropriate because "we do not believe that the only objective in allocating resources should be the satisfaction of current individual tastes and preferences.

Instead, we are persuaded that most citizens want to serve a variety of objectives, including fairness and freedom."

Technically speaking, the interpretation that cost-benefit analysis applies to "consumers" is incorrect; instead, it refers to the valuations that people (or citizens) place on activities for whatever reason, *whether they are direct consumers or not.* For example, if people place positive values on additional consumption of primary education by others, or negative values on the consumption of cigarettes, these valuations ought in principle to be incorporated into any cost-benefit analysis. In this sense, if "citizens" value additional consumption by an individual as a way of improving "fairness" in the distribution of a service, these valuations ought to be added to the individual's valuations as a consumer of that service.

In regard to transplants, the economic notion that seems most plausible to me is that a taste for "fairness" on the part of the citizenry could be represented as a psychic benefit that higher-income persons achieve from lower-income persons' receipt of medical care. I would regard a situation in which all poor people were unable to afford transplants, as unfair and unlovely; I would be willing to pay, via taxation, to subsidize their use of this undoubtedly life-saving measure. The number of such transplants for which I and others are willing to pay may unfortunately be smaller than the number at which there is no additional positive benefit, but it will surely be above the level which the poor— and the not-so-poor—could finance on their own.

In contrast, what does the Task Force mean by equity? Here we come to the critical part of the argument, in which the Task Force is vague. The report is replete with appeals to "equity" and "fairness," but there is no clear statement (except tautologically) of what fairness means, or how one determines how much of it one wants. The closest the Report comes to a definition is in the executive summary, where the conclusions of the President's Commission for the Study of Ethical Problems in Medicine and Biomedical and Behavioral Research are quoted with favor, and are alleged to support the Task Force's view. But how, in fact, does the President's Commission define "equitable access?" The Commission specifically rejects the notion that equity means a right either to "all care that others are receiving" or to unlimited care. In their place, the Commission proposes a standard of "an adequate level of care, which should be thought of as a floor below which no one ought to fall, not a ceiling above which no one may rise."[1] In contrast, as noted above, it is clear that the Task Force's recommendation, in prohibiting people from purchasing transplants they are willing to buy, does set a ceiling as well as (in fact, at the same level as) a floor.

I find myself more in agreement with the President's Commission than with the Task Force. Improving equity or equality of access to care in this country has always meant "bringing up the bottom" of the distribution [or use of health care]. Under the guise of an artificial budget constraint, the Task Force proposes a radical departure from this tradition—achieving equity by "cutting off the top" of the distribution.

What can be said in favor of this sort of distribution? In a society shot through with envy, such a view might make sense, but the Task Force offered no empirical evidence for such envy (or for that matter, for its assertion about citizens' beliefs about fairness). In the absence of such evidence, I have serious difficulties about raising envy as a moral principle equal to altruism. In any case, envy would call for at most an excise (sumptuary) tax on purchased transplants, not a total prohibition.

I would like to offer some brief comments on some other aspects of the Task Force Report. First, it is clear that it would not be *feasible* to achieve the Task Force's idea of equity, given the low cost of domestic travel; "the rich" would still travel to other states (or countries) for transplants. The net impact of the proposal could be to widen the gap between the rich and the non-rich.

Second, the Task Force seems to have the idea that it can pressure hospitals to squeeze out alleged inefficiency through the mechanism of allowing them to obtain resources for transplants only by limiting these hospitals' budgets. However, I would suggest that having people die is not the best way to get hospitals to run their laundries more efficiently; there must be incentives that are not as lethal.

Finally, I believe that the Task Force probably overstates the current marginal resource cost of transplants, and surely overstates the cost that could be achieved after additional research and after an increase in the volume of transplants. Most of the current "costs" are taken from teaching-research situations; if the costs (or the benefits) of such activities are as large as I think they are, the costs attributable to patient care as such are likely to be well below the minimum costs of $60,000 and $30,000 per life year for livers and hearts respectively.

As to what one might expect to happen to patient care costs with the passage of time and an increase in volume, the renal dialysis program is instructive. The payment level for outpatient dialysis for that program was not changed at all between 1972 (when the program began) and 1983, with no apparent reduction in supply. This occurred in a period when the general medical care input price index rose by 250 percent, implying a 72 percent fall in the real price.[2] In 1983 the price for dialysis was *reduced* in nominal terms, with still no evidence of reduction in supply. This evidence is consistent with massive declines in the real cost of dialysis. (I might add that the Task Force Report greatly overestimates the saving from home dialysis; recent calculations put the saving at less than $5,000 without adjusting for the better health of the home dialysis patient.)[3] In any case, "society" is today clearly willing to pay (or is at least unwilling to stop paying) $25,000 per life year for in-facility dialysis patients, which is about the same as what I suspect heart transplants would cost.

Conclusion

The Task Force wrote a report that was appropriately if not excessively cautious in its discussion of the phasing in of a new potentially life-saving technology. But its elevation of budget limitation to the level of a moral principle, and its full-scale transfer of the entire hospital budget to the public sector, with political directives replacing choice, are inappropriate.

Notes

1. President's Commission for the Study of Ethical Problems in Medicine and Biomedical and Behavioral Research, *Securing Access to Health Care* (U.S. Gov't Printing Office, Washington, D.C.) (vol. 1 1983) at 4.

2. These data are derived from Gibson, R., Waldo, D., Levit, K., "National Health Expenditures, 1982," *Health Care Financing Review* 5(1): 1–31 (Fall 1983).

3. Eggers, P., "Trends in Medicare Reimbursement for End Stage Renal Disease, 1974–79," *Health Care Financing Review* 6(1): 31–38 (Fall 1984).

14

Lessons Learned from the End-Stage Renal Disease Experience: Their Implications for Heart Transplantation

Roger W. Evans and Christopher R. Blagg

The most comprehensive analysis of the End-Stage Renal Disease (ESRD) Program of Medicare was completed by Rettig in 1980 (Rettig, 1980a; 1980b). Rettig's report is a detailed account of the first six years of the ESRD Program wherein he examines the implementation of the program and studies the mechanisms by which policy control is exercised within the federal bureaucracy. The report illustrates very nicely the complex manoeuvering that occurs when legislators, policymakers, physicians, and patient-consumers attempt to avoid what Calabresi and Bobbitt (1978) have described as "tragic choices." It is in this regard that Rettig (1980a:1) when answering the question "Why study the ESRD program?" notes that: "This program claims our attention because life-saving medical treatment is being provided to a very small number of beneficiaries at a very high cost to society, the result of public policy to affirm the value that life is beyond price even though such affirmation requires substantial public resources."

Without question, heart transplantation raises many of the same questions that were just posed in connection with the ESRD program. Questions about who will pay, how much will be paid, who will receive a transplant, and how many, if any, will be performed are all questions that have, at one time or another, been asked of dialysis and kidney transplantation. For this reason it is instructive to consider the legislative history of the ESRD Program, examine its budgetary impact, address the problems of changes in the patient population and what they have meant, and speculate on possible changes that are in store for the program based on an analysis of international policies. If one question was to capture the general intent of this chapter, it would be as follows: What lessons, if any, have been learned from the ESRD Program? The chapter concludes with a brief analysis of the implications that treatment of end-stage renal disease has for the treatment of end-stage cardiac disease.

Reprinted by permission from R. W. Evans et al., *The National Heart Transplantation Study: Final Report* (Seattle, WA: Battelle Human Affairs Research Centers, 1984), pp. 44-1–44-47.

The ESRD Legislation

By the mid-1960's dialysis and kidney transplantation had evolved to a point where both were considered to have therapeutic value. The problem, however, was that both transplantation and maintenance dialysis were beyond the economic means of most people. Two technologies were available to treat a chronic and eventually terminal disease, but people were simply unable to afford them. In response to this situation, Congress held several hearings in connection with legislation that included provision for payment for ESRD treatment services. Nonetheless, as noted by Rettig (1980a:27) "The policy authorizing the ESRD Program had lengthy antecedents . . . but a brief legislative history."

The bill containing the pertinent legislation was H.R. 1 which initially contained very little specifically concerning dialysis and transplantation. H.R. 1, introduced in the House of Representatives in early 1971 at the outset of the 92nd Congress, proposed a number of major amendments to the Social Security Act, ". . . including provisions for the consolidation of 54 federal-state programs for the needy aged, blind, and disabled; the establishment of more effective cost controls for Medicare and Medicaid; the provision of health care to Medicare and Medicaid recipients through health maintenance organizations; and various modifications of the Social Security benefit structure" (Rettig, 1980a:27–28). Also included were substantial modifications of the family welfare system. The latter proved to be the most controversial aspect of the bill and debates on welfare reform consumed so much time that passage of any bill appeared to be threatened. Nonetheless, given the upcoming election year, Congress was bent on getting legislation on the President's desk by election day, November 7, 1972 (Rettig, 1980a:28).

During the extensive hearings on H.R. 1, neither the House nor the Senate heard testimony on renal disease. In November, 1971, the House Ways and Means Committee, while hearing testimony on national health insurance, did gain exposure to end-stage renal disease as it was recommended that coverage for this be included as part of a national health insurance program. It was during these hearings that a patient was dialyzed in the hearing room before members of the Ways and Means Committee, and in December, Representative Wilbur Mills (D., Arkansas) introduced a bill to amend the Social Security Act and to provide financing for the treatment of patients with chronic renal failure.

The ESRD amendment was never considered by the Senate until the provisions of the entire bill were being debated. On September 30, 1972, Senator Vance Hartke (D., Indiana) proposed an amendment on chronic renal disease that was quickly adopted and the provision ultimately became "simply one part of an already complex bill," signed by President Nixon on October 30, 1972 (Rettig, 1980a:29).

As described by Rettig (1980a:30), the intent of Congress in passing the ESRD legislation was "relatively clear"—"the amendment was to provide *access* to life-saving therapy for all who needed it where the costs of treatment was beyond the means of practically all individuals." Rettig (1980a:30) further notes that: "In providing access, the underlying rationale was to resolve the 'tragic choice' between this allocation of scarce resources and the value of human life." Cited in Rettig (1980a:30–31) are quotes from several senators which capture the overall temperament of the times. Senator Hartke said:

In what must be the most tragic irony of the 20th century, people are dying because they cannot get access to proper medical care. We have learned how to treat or to cure some of the diseases which have plagued mankind for centuries, yet these treatments are not available to most Americans because of their cost. . . . Mr. President, we can begin to set our national priorities straight by undertaking a national effort to bring kidney disease treatment within the reach of all those in need.

Senator Henry Jackson (D., Washington) said:

> I think it is a great tragedy, in a nation as affluent as ours, that we have to consciously make a decision all over America as to the people who live and the people who will die. We had a committee in Seattle, when the first series of kidney machines were put in operation, who had to pass judgment on who would live and who would die. I believe we can do better than that. . . . So I would hope that we would make an effort here, at least a beginning, to approve the amendment, so that we can do better than we have done heretofore.

Senator Chiles (D., Florida) repeated a similar point when he said:

> . . . in this country with so much affluence, to think that there are people who will die this year merely because we do not have enough of these machines and do not have enough dollars, so that we do have to make the choice of who will live and who will die, when we already know we have a good treatment that can succeed and keep these people alive, while we are working out other improvements on transplants, finding cures, and everything else necessary. This should not happen in this country.

Only a lone voice in the Senate decried the amendment. Senator Wallace Bennett (R., Utah) argued that this amendment along with others represented "Christmas in September" and was ". . . an additional straw that will break the back of the social security system." He also opposed the fact that renal disease was being singled out for special treatment. Bennett argued that "a more reasonable way to handle this amendment would have been to delay action until it becomes part of a broader health insurance bill."

The inclusion of what was to become Section 2991 of the bill caught the Bureau of Health Insurance (BHI) of the Social Security Administration by surprise. Eventually BHI officials were able to secure a statement from Senator Long that, in Rettig's (1980a:33) words, ". . . established the basis for significant Medicare policy departures in the reimbursement of ESRD treatment and proved critical on several later occasions in the implementation of the (ESRD) program." Long stated that:

> With respect to the coverage of kidney dialysis and transplantation, the Secretary would have the authority to define reasonable charges in terms related to the reasonable costs of the treatment provided and comparable charges for physicians' time and skills, since obtaining customary and prevailing charges for new and complex procedures—many of which will be reimbursed in all instances by the program—would be quite difficult administratively.

Section 2991 was unique in extending Medicare benefits to nearly all persons with a single condition for which there were two established therapies— hemodialysis and transplantation. Medicare entitlement was established for individuals under 65 years of age who were "fully or currently insured" or "entitled to monthly insurance benefits" under the Social Security Act, or who were the spouses of dependent children of insured individuals, if the individual was "medically determined to have chronic renal disease" and required hemodialysis or renal transplantation to live. Eligibility was to begin "with the third month after the month in which a course of renal dialysis is initiated" and would end with the twelfth month after a transplant or after dialysis treatment had been terminated. Individuals meeting these criteria, the statute declared, "shall be deemed to be disabled for purposes of coverage under parts A and B of Medicare subject to the deductible, premium, and copayment provisions of Title XVIII."

In an attempt to control the number and distribution of providers of ESRD services, the statute also included provisions which imposed constraints on potential providers of ESRD services in the form of minimum utilization rates. The statute enabled the Secretary of Health, Education, and Welfare to exercise some discretion in order that it might "limit reimbursement under Medicare for kidney transplant and dialysis to kidney disease treatment centers which meet such requirements as he may by regulation prescribe." This delegation of authority to the Secretary also included a provision allowing for "a minimum utilization rate for covered procedures" and "a medical review board to screen the appropriateness of patients for the proposed treatment procedures" (Rettig, 1980a). This latter provision may have been an explicit statement of legislative concern for quality of care or alternatively it may have been an echo of the committee approach to decisions on selection for treatment.

To summarize, Rettig (1980a:34) notes that the goal structure for the ESRD program consisted of several objectives, namely:

- To provide access to ESRD medical services, both dialysis and transplantation, to all those individuals eligible to receive such services.
- To insure the high quality of delivered services.
- To contain total program costs.

Despite amendments to the statute authorizing the ESRD program, these overall objectives have remained unchanged (Iglehart, 1982), although the objective of containing costs has become the subject of increased attention since a large proportion of the Medicare, Part B budget is now devoted to ESRD patients who comprise a very small fraction of all beneficiaries. As a result there have been attempts to deal with the cost containment issue. For example, in 1978, P.L. 95-292 was enacted to provide incentives for: (1) the use of lower cost, medically appropriate self-dialysis, particularly home dialysis, as an alternative to high-cost institutional outpatient dialysis, (2) elimination of program disincentives to use of transplantation, and (3) implementation of incentive reimbursement methods to assure more cost-effective delivery of services to patients dialyzing at institutions and at home. Because overall program expenditures continued to increase each year further amendments were introduced in the Omnibus [Budget] Reconciliation Act of 1981 to limit program costs by reducing reimbursement rates generally and encouraging greater use of home dialysis by reimbursing at one level—the composite rate—for all dialysis, whether as an outpatient or at home.

The Cost of the End-Stage Renal Disease Program

In testimony before the Subcommittee on Health, Committee on Ways and Means of the United States House of Representatives, on February 9, 1984, Dr.

TABLE 14.1
End-Stage Renal Disease Program Costs by Selected Years

Year	Total Program Costs (dollars)
1965	NK[a]
1968	NK
1969	NK
1974	242 million
1976	450 million
1980	1.1 billion
1982	1.8 billion
1983	2.1 billion

[a]NK = Not known.

Sources: Office of Technology Assessment (OTA), 1982; HFCA, 1978, 1979, 1980, 1981, 1982.

Carolyne Davis, administrator of the Health Care Financing Administration (HCFA), made the following statement:

> Medicare costs for ESRD patients were about $2 billion in 1982. This was about four percent of total program expenditures and represents about 13 percent of Part B expenditures. These expenditures were for 70,000 beneficiaries, or one quarter of one percent of Medicare beneficiaries, and they have grown much faster than were originally projected when the law was passed.

Indeed, as Davis' testimony indicates, there has been a tremendous increase in total program (Medicare) expenditures as well as the total number of (Medicare) beneficiaries. Table 14.1 summarizes this growth while Table 14.2 reveals the increase in the number of dialysis and transplant patients by year. In 1965 there were approximately 300 patients undergoing chronic hemodialysis in the U.S. By January, 1968, this number had increased to more than 800, and by early 1969 more than 1,000 patients were receiving treatment at approximately 250 dialysis centers. In January, 1974, shortly after the Medicare ESRD Program began, there were 10,300 dialysis patients, and by the end of 1974 this number had increased to 18,875. In June, 1976, data reported by the Department of Health, Education, and Welfare indicated that there were approximately 24,500 dialysis patients (Evans et al., 1981), and by the end of that year, 30,100 patients were on maintenance dialysis. Today there are more than 70,000 patients on maintenance dialysis.

A similar increase occurred with respect to kidney transplantation, also shown in Table 14.2, and the largest increase in transplants immediately followed enactment of Section 2991. Since then the number of kidney transplants has continued to increase and during 1983 more than 6,000 kidney transplants were performed at 159 renal transplant centers. The current distribution of ESRD patients according to treatment modality is shown in Table 14.3.

Although the actual cost per patient per year for treatment of end-stage renal disease (when adjusted for the rate of inflation) has decreased, total program costs have increased tremendously (Lowrie and Hampers, 1981; 1982). Over the years the proportion of total Medicare funds allocated to the ESRD Program has continued to increase, largely as a function of the growth in the ESRD patient population (Rettig, 1980a; 1980b). In 1978, ESRD benefit payments constituted 1.3 percent of the Hospital Insurance Trust Fund (Part A), while

TABLE 14.2
Number of Patients on Dialysis or Receiving Kidney Transplants by Year

Year	Total Number of Patients on Kidney Dialysis at Year End	Total Number of Kidney Transplants Performed Each Year
1951–1962	NK[a]	75
1963	NK	163
1964	NK	239
1965	300	305
1966	NK	338
1967	NK	448
1968	800	676
1969	1,000	838
1970	2,456	1,091 (1,460)[b]
1971	3,482	1,616 (2,909)
1972	10,000	1,993 (2,852)
1973	11,000	3,017
1974	18,875	3,190
1975	22,000	3,730
1976	30,131	3,504
1977	32,435	3,973
1978	36,463	3,949
1979	45,565	4,271
1980	53,364	4,697
1981	58,770	4,883
1982	65,233	5,358
1983	72,028	6,112

[a]NK = Not Known.
[b]Numbers in parentheses reflect discrepancies in the literature.

Sources: OTA, 1982; HFCA, 1978, 1979, 1980, 1981, 1982.

TABLE 14.3
Distribution of ESRD Patients by Modality, 1983

	Number	Percent
Dialysis		
In-center hemodialysis	57,031	65.5
Home hemodialysis	4,323	5.0
CAPD[a]	8,532	9.8
Intermittent peritoneal dialysis	1,535	1.8
Dialysis training	607	0.7
Subtotal	72,028	82.9
Transplantation		
All functioning grafts[b]	15,000	17.1
Total	87,028	100.0

[a]Chronic ambulatory peritoneal dialysis.
[b]These figures are estimates (from Krakauer, 1983) derived from what is known about the survival of transplants and the number performed each year.

Source: Authors' calculations.

TABLE 14.4
Projected Medicare ESRD Patient Population, and Annual ESRD Benefit Payments

Year Ending September 30	Average Annual Enrollment (thousands)	Total Benefit Payments (millions of dollars)	Income Generated by Second Payer Regulations (millions of dollars)
1974	16.6	184	—
1975	25.3	327	—
1976	33.2	481	—
1977	40.3	654	—
1978	46.7	835	—
1979	53.9	1,037	—
1980	62.0	1,268	—
1981	68.2	1,532	—
1982	72.8	1,814	—
1983	76.8	2,056	—
1984	80.5	2,153	10
1985	83.7	2,337	25
1986	86.7	2,561	35
1987	89.4	2,782	45
1988	91.2	3,004	55
1989	92.2	3,220	55
1990	93.0	3,437	60
1991	93.6	3,671	65

Source: Susan Kunkel, Health Care Financing Administration, personal communication, May 5, 1984.

ESRD benefit payments for Supplementary Medical Insurance Trust Fund (Part B) amounted to 8.9 percent. By 1982, 13.0 percent of total Part B expenditures were allocated to ESRD patients, 4.0 percent higher than initially projected.

Since the ESRD patient population is not expected to stabilize in the near future (Eggers et al., 1983), it is expected that total payment costs will continue to increase. The estimated ESRD patient population and annual benefit payments, projected to 1991, are shown in Table 14.4.

In an attempt to better understand the continued actual and projected increases in the cost of the ESRD Program, questions are being asked about the selection of patients for dialysis and transplantation. Over the past decade, the ESRD patient population as a whole has become older and sicker, their rehabilitation potential is less, and the complexities associated with treating patients with multiple comorbidities may contribute to greater overall ESRD program costs.

Changes in the Composition of the ESRD Patient Population: The Relaxation and Elimination of Patient Selection Criteria

In a paper published in 1981, Evans and coworkers (1981) examined the ESRD patient population at two points in time in order to speculate on how the effect of changes in composition of the patient population would have important health policy implications. Their analysis began with a brief discussion of how patient selection played a key role in passage of the ESRD legislation, an analysis that is particularly relevant today. They noted that:

Until 1973 there was substantial patient selection by physicians or committees, and although all ESRD patients had a terminal condition, some had better prospects for treatment than others. Patients, if not treated on a first-come, first-served basis, were selected for treatment based on a number of criteria. These included, for example, age, medical suitability, mental acuity, family environment, criminal record, economic status (income, net worth), employment record, availability of transportation, willingness to cooperate in the treatment regimen, likelihood of vocational rehabilitation, psychiatric evaluation, marital status, educational background, occupation, and future potential (Fox and Swazey, 1974).

Clearly social class considerations and social worth often were more important in treatment decisions than other more equitable and less controversial criteria. In order to eliminate any access barrier, Medicare benefits were extended to all ESRD patients.

Comparing the ESRD patient population four years prior to passage of the ESRD legislation and five years after its enactment, Evans and coworkers (1981) found major changes in its composition. Table 14.5 . . . shows that prior to Medicare, only 25 percent of dialysis patients were female, but by 1978 this figure increased to 51 percent. In 1967, 91 percent of dialysis patients were white, compared with 64 percent in 1978; blacks increased from 7 to 35 percent of the population. In 1967, dialysis patients on the whole were well-educated and 25 percent had attained a college degree, while in 1978 only 7.5 percent had done so. The average age of patients also changed dramatically before and after Medicare; in 1967 only 7 percent of dialisys patients were aged 55 or over but by 1978, this had increased to 46 percent. In 1967, only 5.0 percent of dialysis patients were separated, divorced, or widowed, while by 1978, 25 percent were. Another very significant change was that in 1967, 64 percent of all dialysis patients were working but by 1978, only 13 percent were.

These changes were consistent with the intent of the ESRD legislation—equal access was created for patients in need of treatment for chronic renal failure. The problem, however, has been that these changes have tended to limit the utilization of the lower cost treatment modalities—home hemodialysis and kidney transplantation. Evans and coworkers (1981:490) made note of this:

> It is also evident, however, that the trend away from home dialysis as well as the higher cost of therapy are due in part to the changing composition of the hemodialysis patient population.

They also suggested that medical considerations as well as sociodemographic factors were creating both cost and utilization problems:

> There are also an increasing number of patients starting to receive dialysis who have diabetes mellitus or other serious medical problems (Manis and Freidman, 1979; Blagg, 1977). These factors, along with age, combine not only to produce patients who are unsatisfactory candidates for home dialysis, but patients who are high users of other medical care services. Such patients are chronically ill, often requiring frequent hospitalization and a disproportionate share of other medical resources.

Such patients are among those most likely to receive disability benefits. As noted by Evans and coworkers (1981:490–491):

> . . . considering that these patients are among the least likely to be rehabilitated, the disability benefits they receive also add greatly to the total cost of their care. Thus, the cost of dialysis per se is but only one component of the total health care and social welfare dollar expended for patients in this category.

TABLE 14.5
Social and Demographic Characteristics of the Hemodialysis Patient Population, 1967 and 1978

	Population (%)	
Characteristic	1967	1978
Sex		
Male	75.0	49.2
Female	25.0	50.8
Race		
White	91.0	63.7
Black	7.0	34.9
Other	2.0	1.4
Education		
Junior high school or less	10.0	28.7
Some high school	17.0	17.2
High school graduate	27.0	28.4
Some college	20.0	18.2
College graduate	12.0	5.7
Postgraduate school	13.0	1.8
Unknown	1.0	0.0
Age, yr		
25	8.0	3.4
25–34	24.0	10.0
35–44	32.0	14.6
45–54	27.0	25.8
55	7.0	45.7
Unknown	2.0	0.5
Marital status		
Single	16.0	13.0
Married	79.0	61.8
Separated, divorced, widowed	5.0	25.2[a]
Employment status		
Employed	41.7	18.4
Unemployed	38.3	17.7
Disabled, student, retired	13.2	63.8[b]
Other	0.0	0.1
Unknown	6.8	0.0

[a]In 1978, the percentages were as follows: separated, 6.3; divorced, 7.4; widowed, 11.5.
[b]In 1978, the percentages were as follows: disabled, 53.6; retired, 10.2. The student category was not coded in the 1978 figures.

Source: Roger Evans et al., *Journal of the American Medical Association* 245 (February 6, 1981): 488. Copyright 1981, American Medical Association. Reprinted by permission.

In 1980, Rettig (1980a:viii) estimated that ". . . fully one-third of the ESRD beneficiaries are eligible for Social Security monthly disability (income support) benefits." Based on 1976 data, Evans and coworkers (1981:490) estimated that 36 percent of dialysis patients had total household incomes below the poverty level, and 46 percent of patients had a household income lower than when they began dialysis. In a more recent analysis, based on results from the National Kidney Dialysis and Kidney Transplantation Study, Garrison and coworkers (1984) determined that nearly two-thirds of the ESRD population are receiving federal income support either through the Social Security Program or Supplementary Security Income (see Table 14.6). Results shown in Table 14.7 reveal that the incomes of ESRD patients are substantially below those of the general U.S. population. Even with federal income support, nearly one-third of ESRD

TABLE 14.6
Percent of ESRD Patients Receiving Income Support Through Federal Programs, by Treatment Modality

	Treatment Modality			
Type of Support	In-Center Hemodialysis	Kidney Transplant	Home Hemodialysis	Continuous Peritoneal Dialysis
Social Security benefits (disability or retirement only)	59.1	41.0	50.6	64.6
Supplementary Security Income only	8.6	3.8	6.7	2.5
Both SSB and SSI	8.9	0.7	2.5	0.0
Total percent receiving federal support	76.6	45.5	59.8	67.1
Sample size	325	132	273	79

Source: Garrison et al., 1984.

TABLE 14.7
1981 Family Income of ESRD Patients by Modality: Percentage Distribution and Comparison with All U.S. Households[a]

	Treatment Modality				
Income range (in dollars)	In-center Hemodialysis	Kidney Transplant	Home Hemodialysis	Continuous Peritoneal Dialysis	All U.S. Households[a]
0– 2,499	5.8	4.8	3.2	1.4	2.9
2,500– 4,999	24.7	10.4	11.9	12.9	7.6
5,000– 7,499	22.9	7.2	10.7	8.6	7.8
7,500– 9,999	8.2	5.6	7.1	7.1	7.1
10,000–14,999	9.3	14.4	17.5	18.6	14.4
15,000–19,999	10.3	11.2	11.9	11.4	12.3
20,000–24,999	5.5	10.4	7.1	10.0	11.4
25,000–29,999	4.8	10.4	7.5	4.3	9.7
30,000–39,999	4.5	11.2	9.9	12.9	13.1
40,000–74,999	3.4	12.0	10.7	12.9	12.0
75,000+	0.7	2.4	2.4	0.0	1.7
Percent below poverty line	41.7	23.2	21.4	15.7	—
Total respondents	292	125	252	70	—
Total nonrespondents	55	19	35	11	—

[a]This aggregate income measure includes any 1981 labor earnings (before tax) of all household members plus annualized imputations of any benefits (i.e., Social Security, pension, etc.) they are currently receiving. Other income from assets (dividends, interest, etc.) is not included in the sample estimates but is included in the U.S. household estimates.
[b]The number of U.S. households in 1981 was 83,527,000. This percentage distribution is from Table 3 in the U.S. Bureau of the Census (1983).

Source: Garrison et al., 1984.

TABLE 14.8
Percentage of ESRD Patients Below the Poverty Line Receiving Federal Income Support

	Treatment Modality			
Type of Support	In-Center Hemodialysis	Kidney Transplant	Home Hemodialysis	Continuous Peritoneal Dialysis
Percent receiving SSB and/or SSI	88.1	81.0	86.1	100.0
For those receiving benefits, benefit amount as percent of poverty line	52.3	48.0	54.9	58.7
Number below poverty line	99	21	36	8

Source: Garrison et al., 1984.

patients are living in households with an income below the poverty line (see Table 14.8).

Based on the foregoing, with the absence of patient selection criteria, the overall status, both medical and social, of the ESRD patient population has declined. Nonetheless, it is inappropriate to rule the ESRD program as unsuccessful—success it seems is a relative notion. Rettig (1980a:viii) comments on this as follows:

> In many ways the ESRD program is a success. Congress established it to pay for the treatment of individuals with kidney failure so that no one lacked access to life-saving treatment for financial reasons. Patients are receiving treatment, bills are being paid, and access to care is no longer an issue. Although program and individual treatment costs are high, the cost experience includes some encouraging aspects, and there is no reason to believe that quality of care has declined, even though more elderly and sicker patients are now being treated than before.

According to Iglehart (1982:493), Congress views the ESRD program similarly. In his words:

> Politically, Congress views the ESRD program with some ambivalence. Generally speaking, the program is deemed a success because it pays for the treatment of patients with kidney failure who otherwise might have been denied such care.

Despite these indications of success, the future of the ESRD program may not necessarily be the same as its past, although the nature of any changes are by no means clear, nor are they being openly discussed at this time. As the future of the Medicare program has become increasingly uncertain, so have the prospects of the ESRD program.

The Future of the ESRD Program

It is difficult to speculate on the future of the ESRD program. Perhaps the best one can hope for is to identify the signposts for the future (Blagg and Scribner, 1980a; 1980b; Blagg, 1983; Relman and Rennie, 1979). While at this time no overt attempt is being made to invoke a structured set of patient criteria with uniform application, there are serious efforts being made to increase economic efficiency and, thus, reduce the cost of the ESRD program. As alluded to above, twice in the ten-year history of the program Congress has enacted ESRD amendments to the Social Security Act (Iglehart, 1982).

The first set of ESRD amendments came in 1978. These were intended to accomplish five major objectives, according to a document published by the Senate Finance Committee (Committee on Finance, 1981; cited in Iglehart, 1982:493):

> . . . to provide incentives for the use of lower cost, medically appropriate self-dialysis, particularly home dialysis, as an alternate to high-cost institutional dialysis; eliminate program disincentives to the use of transplantation; provide for the implementation of incentive reimbursement methods to assure more cost-effective delivery of services to patients dialyzing in institutions and at home; develop a long-range objective, on the basis of the continuing review and judgment of professional peer review organizations, with respect to the most effective use of resources for treating renal disease; and provide for studies of alternative ways to improve the program and for regular reporting to the Congress on the renal disease program.

As a result of the 1978 amendments, several optional incentives intended to increase the use of home dialysis and transplantation were introduced. These included early entitlement without the 2- to 3-month waiting period for patients entering self-care dialysis training, 100% of the cost of purchasing home dialysis equipment, and the establishment of target rate reimbursement for home dialysis. This latter provided for a home dialysis treatment to be reimbursed at 70% (later set at 75%) of the adjusted regional rate for outpatient dialysis. Despite these changes, outpatient dialysis remained relatively profitable and an easier form of care to deliver; and so, with the exception of the development of continuous ambulatory peritoneal dialysis, there was little increase in the use of home dialysis as a result of these amendments. Even worse, from the cost-containment viewpoint, the number of outpatient dialysis facilities, chiefly hospital facilities, with exceptions to charge more than the standard rate continued to increase; and by 1982 about half of all hospital dialysis units had such exceptions.

The second set of ESRD amendments were approved by Congress as part of the Omnibus Budget Reconciliation Act of 1981 (Blagg et al., 1982a; 1982b). These amendments were intended to establish a dual-rate reimbursement system that differentiates between hospital-based and freestanding dialysis facilities, promote home dialysis and transplantation, and strive for other improvements in efficiency in the program. The new regulations were published in the *Federal Register* on February 12, 1982, as a Notice of Proposed Rulemaking. This resulted in a storm of responses from organizations, professionals and patients, related especially to the question of whether there should be a dual rate or one single rate for both hospital and freestanding units, and also the level of reimbursement set, as this was based on outdated audit data from three to five years before.

While the new regulations would continue to provide for exceptions, control of the process for granting exceptions would be much tighter. Also included in the package was a significant change in the method of physician reimbursement for care of ESRD patients. The overall goal remained the same—to reduce federal costs through the promotion of home dialysis. In a memorandum to then Secretary of DHHS Richard Schweiker, Dr. Carolyne K. Davis, Administrator of HCFA, noted the intent of modifying the current method of paying physicians:

In consideration of our goal to stimulate home dialysis, we do not believe it is sufficient to place our emphasis solely on facilities to generate the desirable shift to more home dialysis; it is likely that equal or greater incentive belongs with the physicians.

Despite the barrage of comments, the proposed regulations were published in final form on May 11, 1983. As a result, the National Association of Patients on Hemodialysis and Transplantation (NAPHT), the Renal Physicians Association (RPA), and a freestanding dialysis facility joined forces to sue the government to attempt to block implementation of the new regulations. As of June 1984 the judge ruled that HCFA had set the rates at a reasonable level, and the judge believed that HCFA would monitor quality of care and safety carefully. However, certain other changes related to physician reimbursement and coverage were decided in favor of NAPHT and the other organizations. Currently, the Justice Department is considering an appeal based on the question of whether the courts have jurisdiction over procedural issues related to the Part B Medicare program—a precedent of great significance to health care generally.

Meanwhile the intent of the government remains clear—to contain costs through creating greater efficiency in the ESRD program. However, there is a limit to the degree to which increased efficiency can be fostered, and more drastic solutions may be in the offing. Dr. Constantine Hampers (cited in Iglehart, 1982:295), commenting upon the 1981 amendments, speculated that:

> . . . the implications of the proposal will be devastating to beneficiaries. Even now, people are speculating that this is an attempt by HHS to emulate the English health care system, under which few patients over the age of 55 are accepted for treatment (dialysis).

The suggestion that some version of the British system may be adopted in the U.S. for the treatment of patients with ESRD, as well as other types of patients, is not completely unrealistic. Although such a suggestion is not being entertained either in Congress or by officials of the Health Care Financing Administration at this time, the suggestion that such a major overhaul of the health care system may be necessary is worthy of further comment (Iglehart, 1983; 1984).

An International Perspective

Aaron and Schwartz (1984) recently completed an extensive analysis of the British National Health Service (also see Schwartz and Aaron, 1984). In order to gain a better understanding of the resource rationing process, something Schwartz and Aaron clearly feel is inevitable in the U.S. due to ". . . resistance to the decades-long rise in the cost of hospital care," a careful study was undertaken to establish how the British allocate scarce funds among various technological approaches and patients. They conducted many interviews with officials of the National Health Service and with physicians and other providers. The technologies of interest included CT scanning, cancer chemotherapy, bone marrow transplantation, long-term dialysis, treatment of hemophilia, intensive care, coronary artery surgery, hip replacement, total parenteral nutrition, diagnostic X-ray examination, and radiotherapy.

Generally, Aaron and Schwartz (1984) found that the British are quite capable of living within limits. Of the therapies studied, only three were provided at the same levels as in the U.S. Hemophiliacs were provided medical care in the quantity and of the quality required, megavoltage radiotherapy was readily available and bone-marrow transplantation was provided at approximately the same rate as in the U.S.

Other technologies were rationed. For example, the overall rate of treatment for ESRD in Britain is less than half that in the U.S.; kidneys are transplanted at an equivalent rate, but dialysis is provided at a rate that is only one-third that in the U.S. Other technologies were similarly rationed. When compared with the U.S., the British perform half as many X-rays per capita, provide only one-quarter the amount of total parenteral nutrition, have only one-sixth the CT scan capability, one-fifth to one-tenth the number of intensive care beds relative to population, and perform one-tenth as many coronary bypass grafts as the U.S. However, there is some question as to whether the U.S. may be overproviding in some of these areas of care.

How is this accomplished in Britain? Schwartz and Aaron (1984) found that physicians serve as the gatekeepers and over time have ". . . developed standards of care that incorporate economic reality into medical judgments." Rationalization is frequent, and selection of patients for dialysis provides an example of the ease with which physicians are able to reconcile a set of difficult circumstances. Schwartz and Aaron (1984:101) describe the process as follows:

> Confronted by a person older than the prevailing unofficial age cutoff for dialysis, the British GP tells the victim of chronic renal failure or his family that nothing can be done except to make the patient as comfortable as possible in the time remaining. The British nephrologist tells the family of a patient who is difficult to handle that dialysis would be painful and burdensome and that the patient would be more comfortable with it; or he tells the resident alien from a poor country that he should return home, to be among family and friends who speak the same language—where, as it happens, the patient will die because dialysis is unavailable.

There is some freedom within the system to alter the explicit pattern of care, but the physician recognizes that this may well impact upon the quality and quantity of care that he is able to offer other patients. Nonetheless, occasions inevitably arise when the physician must say no—refusing to provide the older patient dialysis is a prime example. In this case, Schwartz and Aaron (1984:55) note that, "Often in such a case the local internist either does not raise the possibility of dialysis or simply states that the treatment does not seem to be indicated." Unlike patients in the U.S., the British are much more compliant and are likely to follow their doctor's orders with little complaint.

Commenting further on the denial of dialysis services to certain patients, Schwartz and Aaron (1984) note that:

> The local physician's role as gatekeeper explains why dialysis centers rarely have to turn away patients. Older patients are not usually referred because the local physician is well aware that they could not be accommodated. The general practitioner or internist thus spares the nephrologist from having to say no, spares the patient and family a painful rejection, and avoids having to face the patient and relatives after rejection.

While most patients are likely to comply with their local physician's recommendations, there are occasions when patients and their family may choose to "work the system." Some patients request, and get, a second opinion; others may choose to present themselves at an emergency room for treatment. In the case of dialysis, a patient refused dialysis may report directly to a clinic and, as one British nephrologist explained to Schwartz and Aaron (1984:56), ". . . a patient who sits down in the waiting room will probably be seen and a slot found for him or her in the dialysis program."

In other instances, patients may go from one geographic area to another to gain access to the care they want as budgets and priorities are established at the regional level. Such exploitation of geography, as Schwartz and Aaron refer to it, is relatively rare, but as Brahams (1984:386) so bluntly notes:

> The patient or his or her family may be able to persuade another health region to help or they may be able to afford the private sector, but for many the refusal to treat is the end of the road to the cemetery.

While the British system has effectively controlled health care costs and the growth of selected technologies such as kidney dialysis, transferability of the British approach to the U.S. is questionable (Laing, 1980). Schwartz and Aaron (1984) are cautious in this regard.

> Although there are differences between our two countries, one shared language and the common elements in our political and medical cultures make the British experience relevant to the United States. To be sure, the British experience cannot be taken as a literal forecast for the coming years in the United States. For example, it seems unlikely that Americans would accept rationing as willingly as have the British, who have a special affection for the National Health Service since its creation just after World War II. Nevertheless, the British experiment has yielded the best data we are likely to find on an intensive program to curb medical expenditures.

At the conclusion of their analysis Schwartz and Aaron (1984:56) underscore the unique ability of the British to live within limits and offer cautious optimism:

> It appears doubtful that the citizens of the United States would accept such limits— or even less severe ones—as readily. If limits are set, however, we believe that they will stimulate responses in physicians and patients that will be similar in many respects to those we observed in Britian.

Even in Britain, disaffection with the selection of patients for renal dialysis is increasing (Wing, 1983; Iglehart, 1984). There have been several recent papers in the *British Medical Journal* which reflect this trend, including a report on the successful treatment of kidney patients over 65 years of age, and a paper arguing why blind diabetics should be offered dialysis. Iglehart (1984) notes that even popular television has been attracted to the issue, but then concludes:

> Thus far, though, there is no general evidence of change in the restricted availability of dialysis treatment in Britain. The officials at the Department of Health and Social Security with whom I discussed this issue said that any appreciable increase for renal dialysis simply is not a priority at this time.

In the end, the winds of change may prevail, however. Diana Brahams, a British barrister, has examined the "doctor's duty and the patient's right" in the treatment of end-stage renal failure. The British Kidney Patient Association (BKPA) estimates that between 2,000 and 3,000 deaths occur each year in Britain from renal failure, many of which are unnecessary. The BKPA has decided to escalate their efforts to attain more dialysis services for those in need and recently announced that the next patient refused treatment by the National Health Service (NHS) and who is brought to their attention will be treated privately at the Association's expense. Bills for the patient's treatment subsequently will be presented to the NHS and if they are not paid, in Brahams' (1984:386) words, the BKPA ". . . is prepared, apparently, to take the Secretary of State to court—presumably for failing to provide necessary treatment as required under the National Health Service Act, the private hospital bills amounting in effect to damages."

In her analysis, Brahams notes that refusal to treat a patient can occur because: (1) the patient is too old and sick to be treated, or (2) there is a lack of facilities at which patients can be treated. To argue that a patient is untreatable because of a lack of facilities is clearly questionable:

> It seems to me that a doctor who tells a patient that he is untreatable when he is indeed treatable, but is simply not going to be treated because of the lack of facilities, is failing in his duty of care. Surely he should tell the patient that there would be a chance for him if he could receive the correct treatment and that he should seek it in a different health area which may have greater facilities.

She then goes on to concede that:

> After all, dialysis is nothing experimental and new: it is not an extraordinary way of keeping people alive only in one or two centres of the world; it is a treatment offered all over the UK and the industrialized world. On the other hand, the doctor may argue that if the patient is unlikely to find alternative treatment in a different region, then what is the point of upsetting both him and his family? Might it not be kinder and simpler to tell them that the condition is incurable and must be accepted? Yet, in so doing, the doctor is misinforming the patient and depriving him of the chance at least of receiving alternative care and any other legal options as yet untried that may be open.

Brahams (1984) makes it clear that in the future it may become increasingly difficult to deny ESRD patients dialysis or transplantation regardless of their social and medical characteristics. Perhaps the decision will ultimately rest with the courts. Her concluding remark is as follows: "As pleas for change by press and doctors and patients fail to elicit any positive response, the only alternative route seems to lie through either the criminal or the civil arm of the law—though such a course is dogged by expensive uncertainty."

Those close to the ESRD program in the U.S. have become fearful that a variation of the British system of rationing by simple exclusion ultimately may be adopted, perhaps on the basis of age and comorbidity. Thus, while there has been support for initiatives to reduce total program expenditures, there is also an implicit fear that there is a limit to such reductions without improving quality of care and/or access to treatment. Also, it is recognized that while technological developments may effectively reduce future program expenditures, no promising developments appear on the horizon at this time.

The U.S. stands out in stark contrast to many other countries with regard to treatment of ESRD patients. As shown in Table 14.9, the dialysis rate per million population in the U.S. greatly exceeds those of all countries represented in the European Dialysis and Transplant Association (Prottas et al., 1983; Eggers et al., 1983). Studies of cross-national policies for the treatment of ESRD patients

TABLE 14.9
Dialysis Prevalence Rates

Nation	Dialysis Prevalence (per million)
Austria	69
Belgium	123
Denmark	86
Finland	36
France	133
West Germany	117
Greece	61
Ireland	47
Israel	144
Italy	120
Luxembourg	80
Netherlands	92
Norway	31
Spain	78
Sweden	65
Switzerland	127
United Kingdom	53
United States	209

Source: Prottas et al., 1983.

have been completed recently by Evans, Blagg and coworkers (1984) and by Prottas and associates (1983), and both analyses illustrate how unusual the U.S. is in this regard.

Evans, Blagg and coworkers (1984) surveyed policies with regard to the treatment of ESRD in 30 countries. Twenty-two of the countries had a formal patient selection process, but in the majority the final decision was a medical one. Of the 22 countries with a formal patient selection process, in only 7 were all patients with ESRD treated, but, as in Britain, lack of formal referral of such patients to a major treatment center may act as a form of selection. In the other 15 countries some form of patient selection occurred.

Table 14.10 indicates the selection criteria used. As expected, patients are most freuently excluded from treatment on the basis of multisystem disorders and age. Social factors also play a significant role in the selection process, with psychological stability and availability of social supports being key factors, together with an estimate of the individual's "social worth" as evidenced by their social responsibility and contributions to the community. Ability to pay is a criterion of lesser importance, as are the various factors which would facilitate kidney transplantation as a treatment option. Other criteria, such as a poor prognosis and likelihood of early death, ability to comply with the treatment regimen, residential status, marital status, and occupaton, also may be considered in the decision process.

Evans, Blagg, and coworkers (1984) also documented both primary and secondary sources of payment for ESRD treatment–related expenses. As shown in Table 14.11, the government most frequently (26 out of 30 countries) serves as primary source of payment for such expenses, and in the remainder of the countries studied the government was listed as a secondary source of payment. Private insurance and patients themselves are the most important secondary sources of support. Only one country . . . indicated that the patient . . . [was and only one country, that] "other organizations" . . . [were] the primary source

TABLE 14.10
Patient Selection Criteria Followed in Countries with Formal Policies Regarding Treatment of End-Stage Renal Disease (N = 15)

Criterion	Percent Mentioned	Percent Not Mentioned
Multisystem disorders	80.0	20.0
	(12)[a]	(3)
Age	60.0	40.0
	(9)	(6)
Psychological stability	33.3	66.7
	(5)	(10)
Social supports	20.0	80.0
	(3)	(12)
Social responsibility, contribution	13.3	86.7
	(2)	(13)
Ability to pay	6.7	93.3
	(1)	(14)
Suitability for transplant	6.7	93.3
	(1)	(14)
Eligible living donor available	6.7	93.3
	(1)	(14)
Other	26.7	73.3
	(4)	(11)

[a]Number of countries is given in parentheses.
Source: Evans et al., 1984.

TABLE 14.11
Sources of Payment for Treatment Expenses in All Countries (N = 30)

	Type of Source	
Source of Payment	Percentage Primary Source	Percentage Secondary Source
Government	86.7	14.8
	(26)[a]	(4)
Private insurance	6.7	29.6
	(2)	(8)
Other organizations	3.3	14.8
	(1)	(4)
Private fund raising	0.0	14.8
	(0)	(4)
Patient	3.3	26.0
	(1)	(7)

[a]Number of countries is in parentheses.
Source: Evans et al., 1984.

of payment. Secondary sources of payment include, in rank order, private insurance and the patient, other organizations, the government, and public fund-raising efforts.

Ultimately, it is unclear what changes, if any, are likely to be made in the delivery of end-stage renal disease services in the United States. The U.S. is atypical when compared with other countries, but this is probably the result of several factors such as affluence that are not necessarily characteristic of many other countries. In this regard there is a clear relationship between the prevalence rate for ESRD treatment and gross national product (Jacobs et al., 1981). However, while other approaches to the ESRD problem have been applied successfully, in those countries where patient selection is common, there remains considerable uneasiness as characterized by the recent events in Britain. Further speculation on changes in the U.S. are beyond the scope of this report, but are likely to become increasingly focused in years to come. The general problem of resource scarcity, whether economic or otherwise, is, unfortunately, an issue legislators and policymakers will have to grapple with continually (Evans, 1983a; 1983b).

Conclusion: Implications for Heart Transplantation

Some important lessons with application to heart transplantation may be learned from the ESRD experience, but there are limits in the scope of application. For example, patients with ESRD have several treatment approaches or modalities available to them; transplantation and several types of dialysis are now used with varying degrees of success. Not all patients are equally well-suited to the available modalities, thus raising the question of what form of treatment is best suited to which subset of patients. Also, dialysis is a mechanical approach to treatment, and transplantation a biological approach. While patients with cardiac disease have several modalities of treatment available to them, only one of these is directly applicable to end-stage cardiac disease (ESCD)—transplantation. Percutaneous transluminal coronary angioplasty (PTCA) is now widely used for patients in the early stages of heart disease (Dotter et al., 1983; Council on Scientific Affairs, 1984) and coronary artery bypass grafting is available to those whose disease has progressed further. In addition, a wide array of drugs is now available for various heart problems, the benefits of which may not be reaped for several years (Braunwald and Colucci, 1984).

Treating end-stage cardiac disease is not directly analogous to treating end-stage renal disease for one major reason. The mechanical options available to ESCD patients are very limited, and no long-term clinically effective device is currently available to substitute for the heart. Pierce and coworkers and others (Pierce, 1983; Pennock et al., 1982; 1983; Norman, 1981; NHLBI, 1982; Pierce et al., 1982; Sturm, 1982) have reported on progress with a variety of left ventricular assist devices, and DeVries and coworkers (Jarvik, 1981; Devries et al., 1984) continue to make progress in the development of a totally implantable heart. Neither device, however, is likely to be available soon, although Pierce (cited in Simmons, 1984:700) predicts that clinical trials with an implantable assist device are expected to begin in 1988. He predicts that use of the device is "going to start off slowly," with at most 50 patients per year being involved.

Given the lack of availability of a long-term assist device or an implantable heart, speculation on the implications that the ESRD experience has for heart transplantation must be qualified appropriately. Nevertheless, relevant areas of concern include: (1) patient selection, (2) patient outcomes, and (3) treatment costs. Of these, patient selection is the primary consideration because both outcomes and costs will be profoundly affected by who is transplanted.

The legislative history of the ESRD program has revealed that it is very difficult to deny available lifesaving treatment to patients in need—despite relative medical and social contraindications. Thus, while a well-intended set of selection criteria can be derived, it is doubtful whether such criteria would remain unchanged with time. Poor candidates for a heart transplant today may be among the prime candidates tomorrow. Also, . . . patient selection criteria may be suspended due to legal and ethical considerations. Consequently, any attempt to estimate need must take into account the great potential for relaxation of patient selection criteria.

A second lesson learned from the ESRD experience concerns patient outcomes, not only survival, but quality of life and rehabilitation. Elsewhere Evans and coworkers (1984b) have examined the impact of different ESRD treatment modalities and patient characteristics on the outcomes of treatment. They confirmed that patient selection factors, as evidenced by the characteristics of patients on each of the available treatment modalities, had a substantial affect on patient outcomes. Also, as described above, as ESRD patient selection criteria have been relaxed, the outcomes experienced by patients have concomitantly declined. In other words, it does not appear that all patients treated today will have the same quality of life and longevity reported for the patient population of several years ago.

In this same regard, it is expected that more relaxed criteria for heart transplant recipients may greatly jeopardize their outcomes. As older and sicker patients are transplanted, the complication rate will increase and quality of life and rehabilitation will decline. Although a complex social, legal, and ethical dilemma, there is no means by which the quality of life of all heart transplant recipients, regardless of age and medical contraindications, can be guaranteed to be similar to that of younger patients with fewer complications.

Perhaps the most profound lesson from the ESRD experience is the importance of cost. Here cost is used in a generic sense to denote program expenditures, patient expenses, and social welfare payments. The cost of the ESRD program continues to increase at a rate that pales in comparison with earlier projections. A period of leveling-off is not yet in sight, and policymakers, legislators, and other observers are unsure what the future may hold (Caplan, 1981). Whether experience with heart transplantation will be directly comparable is debatable, but in all likelihood it will be similar. Again, program cost will mirror patient input to the system. If patient selection criteria become relaxed and the patient case-mix more medically complex, overall expenditures are likely to rise.

Patient expenses, although not substantial at this time, may increase as public and private insurers limit reimbursement for various treatment-related expenses, thus increasing the share that patients must bear out-of-pocket. If patients are unable to return to gainful employment, as has been the case for many dialysis patients, such a shift in "expense-sharing" may be particularly devastating.

Finally, experience with ESRD vividly shows that treatment-related costs are only one part of total expenditures. Many ESRD patients become dependent on various government income maintenance programs, but even with these income supports are in difficult financial straits. Again, it is uncertain whether the same would hold true for heart transplant patients. On the positive side, of all ESRD patients, successfully transplanted patients are among the best rehabilitated. Probably as a result of patient selection, 46.0 percent of kidney transplant patients as opposed to 77.0 percent of in-center hemodialysis patients receive income support through federal programs (see Table 14.6, above). Also, 23.2 percent of kidney transplant recipients studied by Garrison et al. (1984) had family incomes below the poverty level, as compared with 42.0 percent of in-center hemodialysis patients. Thus, there may be some reason for optimism.

In conclusion, experience has been gained and lessons have been learned from the ESRD program (Rettig, 1983; Caplan, 1981). Although this program is often criticized, it serves as a prototype of what a catastrophic health care program may entail, both administratively and operationally. It does have certain limitations for creating the kinds of analogies proposed here, and the extent to which these are recognized will greatly facilitate more general health planning efforts.

References

Aaron HJ, Schwartz WB. The Painful Prescription: Rationing Hospital Care. Washington, DC: The Brookings Institution, 1984.

Blagg CR. After ten years of the Medicare End-Stage Renal Disease Program. Am J Kidney Dis. 1983; 3:1–2.

Blagg CR, Scribner BH. Medicare End-Stage Renal Disease Program: more than a billion dollar question. Ann Intern Med. 1980a; 93:501–502.

Blagg CR, Scribner BH. Long-term dialysis: current problems and future prospects. Am J Med. 1980b; 68:633–635.

Blagg CR, Capelli JP, Diener M, Hull AR, Simmons DS. Position paper on the ESRD Program and the proposed regulations (first of two parts). Contem Dial. 1982a; 7:35–39.

Blagg CR, Capelli JP, Diener M, Hull AR, Simmons DS. Position paper on the ESRD Program and the proposed regulations (second of two parts). Contem Dial. 1982b; 9:18, 20, 22–23, 33.

Brahams D. End-stage renal failure: the doctor's duty and the patient's right. Lancet. 1984; 1(8373):386–387.

Braunwald E, Colucci WS. Vasodilator therapy for heart failure: has the promissory note been paid? N Engl J Med. 1984; 310:459–461.

Bureau of the Census. Current Population Reports. Series P-60, No. 137, Money Income of Households, Families, and Persons in the United States, 1981. Washington, DC: U.S. Government Printing Office, 1983.

Calabresi G, Bobbitt P. Tragic Choices. New York: Norton and Co., 1978.

Caplan AL. Kidneys, ethics, and politics: policy lessons of the ESRD experience. J Health Politics, Policy and Law. 1981; 6:488–503.

Committee on Finance. End-stage renal disease (ESRD) program under Medicare. Committee print No. 97-9. Washington, DC: U.S. Government Printing Office, 1981.

Council on Scientific Affairs. Percutaneous transluminal angioplasty. JAMA. 1984; 251:764–768.

Davis CK. Testimony before the Subcommittee on Health, Committee on Ways and Means, U.S. House of Representatives. February 9, 1984.

DeVries WC, Anderson JL, Joyce LD, Anderson FL, Hammond EH, Jarvik RH, Kolff WJ. Clinical use of the total artificial heart. N Engl J Med. 1984; 310:273–278.

Dotter CT, Gruntzig AR, Schoop W, Zeitter E (eds.) Percutaneous Transluminal Angioplasty: Technique, Early, and Late Results. New York: Springer-Verlag, 1983.

Eggers PW, Connerton R, McMullan M. The Medicare Experience with End-Stage Renal Disease: Trends in Incidence, Prevalence and Survival. A HCFA Working Paper. Baltimore, MD: Health Care Financing Administration, 1983.

Evans RW, Blagg CR, Bryan FA, Jr. Implications for health care policy: a social and demographic profile of hemodialysis patients in the United States. JAMA. 1981; 245:487–491.

Evans RW. Health care technology and the inevitability of resource allocation and rationing decisions. (First of two parts). JAMA. 1983a; 249:2047–2053.

Evans RW. Health care technology and the inevitability of resource allocation and rationing decisions. (Second of two parts). JAMA. 1983b; 249:2208–2219.

Evans RW, Blagg CR, Bowen L, Hart LG. National Policies for the Treatment of End-Stage Renal Disease. National Kidney Dialysis and Kidney Transplantation Study Update Report 33. Seattle, WA: Battelle Human Affairs Research Centers, 1984a.

Evans RW, Manninen DL, Garrison LP, Jr., Hart LG, Blagg CR, Gutman RA, Hull AR, Lowrie EG. A comparative assessment of the quality of life of end-stage renal disease patients on four treatment modalities. Seattle, WA: Battelle Human Affairs Research Centers, 1984b.

Fox RC, Swazey JP. The Courage to Fail. Chicago, IL: University of Chicago Press, 1974.

Garrison LP, Jr., Evans RW, Manninen DL, Hart LG. The Demographic Characteristics of the National Kidney Dialysis and Kidney Transplantation Study: A Comparison with the End-Stage Renal Disease Population. Update Report 21. Seattle, WA: Battelle Human Affairs Research Centers, 1983.

Garrison LP, Jr., Hart LG, Evans RW, Manninen DL. Income and Poverty Among End-Stage Renal Disease Patients: Results from the National Kidney Dialysis and Kidney Transplantation Study. Update Report 36. Seattle, WA: Battelle Human Affairs Research Centers, 1984.

Health Care Financing Administration. End-Stage Renal Disease. First Annual Report to Congress, FY1979. Baltimore, MD: Office of Special Programs, Health Care Financing Administration, 1980.

Health Care Financing Administration. End-Stage Renal Disease. Second Annual Report to Congress, FY1980. Baltimore, MD: Office of Special Programs, Health Care Financing Administration, 1981.

Health Care Financing Administration. 1981 End-Stage Renal Disease Annual Report to Congress. Washington, DC: U.S. Government Printing Office, 1982.

Health Care Financing Administration. 1982 End-Stage Renal Disease Annual Report to Congress. Washington, DC: U.S. Government Printing Office, 1983.

Health Care Financing Administration. 1983 End-Stage Renal Disease Annual Report to Congress. Washington, DC: U.S. Government Printing Office, in preparation [published, 1984].

Iglehart JK. Funding the End-Stage Renal Disease Program. N Engl J Med. 1982; 306:492–496.

Iglehart JK. The British National Health Service under the Conservatives. N Engl J Med. 1983; 309:1264–1268.

Iglehart JK. The British National Health Service under the Conservatives—Part II. N Engl J Med. 1984; 310–63–67.

Kraukauer H. Personal communication to Louis P. Garrison, Jr., Ph.D., 1983.

Jacobs C, Broyer M, Brunner FP, et al. Combined report on regular dialysis and transplantation in Europe, XI, 1980. Proc Europ Dial Transpl Assoc. 1981; 18:2–58.

Jarvik RK. The total artificial heart. Sci Am. 1981; 244:74–80.

Laing W. End-Stage Renal Failure. London: Office of Health Economics, 1980 (Briefing No. 11).

Lowrie EG, Hampers CL. The success of Medicare's End-Stage Renal Disease Program: the case for profits and the private marketplace. N Engl J Med. 1981; 305:434–438.

Lowrie EG, Hampers CL. Proprietary dialysis and the end-stage renal disease program. Dial Transplant. 1982; 11:191–204.

Manis T, Friedman EA. Dialytic therapy for irreversible uremia (first of two parts). N Engl J Med. 1979; 301:1260–1265.

National Heart, Lung, and Blood Institute Advisory Council. Report of the artificial heart working group. Artif Organs. 1982; 6:335–340.

Norman JC. Mechanical ventricular assistance: a review. Artif Organs. 1981. 5:103–117.

Office of Technology Assessment. Strategies for Medical Technology Assessment. Washington, DC: U.S. Government Printing Office, 1982.

Pennock JL, Pierce WS, Wisman CB, Bull AP, Waldhausen JA. Survival and complications following ventricular assist pumping for cardiogenic shock. Ann Surg. 1983; 198:469–478.

Pennock JL, Wisman CB, Pierce WS. Mechanical support of the circulation prior to cardiac transplantation. Heart Transplantation. 1982; 1:294–305.

Pierce WS. Artificial hearts and blood pumps in the treatment of profound heart failure. Circulation. 1983; 68:883–888.

Pierce WS, Pan GVS, Myers JL, Pae WE, Jr., Bull AP, Waldhausen JA. Ventricular assist pumping in patients with cardiogenic shock after cardiac operations. N Engl J Med. 1982; 305:1606–1610.

Prottas J, Segal M, Sapolsky HM. Cross-national differences in dialysis rates. Health Care Financing Review. 1983; 4(3):91–103.

Relman AS, Rennie D. Treatment of end-stage renal disease. N Engl J Med. 1979; 303:996–998.

Rettig RA. Lessons learned from the end-stage renal disease experience. In: Egdahl RH, Gertman PM (eds.), Technology and the Quality of Health Care. Germantown, MD: Aspen Systems Corp., 1983:153–173.

Rettig RA. Implementing the End-Stage Renal Disease Program of Medicare. Publication No. R-2505-HCFA/HEW. Santa Monica, CA: The Rand Corporation, 1980a.

Rettig RA. The politics of health cost containment: end-stage renal disease. Bull NY Acad Med. 1980b; 56:115–138.

Schwartz WB, Aaron HJ. Rationing hospital care: lessons from Britain. N Engl J Med. 1984; 310:52–56.

Simmons K. Implantable assist pump—final heart option? JAMA. 1984; 251:700–701.

Sturm JT. Left ventricular assist. N Engl J Med. 1982; 306:1236.

Wing AJ. Why don't the British treat more patients with kidney failure? Br Med J. 1983; 287:1157–1158.

15

Economic Issues in Organ Substitution Technology

Mary Ann Baily

As everyone knows, organ transplantation is a costly technology that benefits a relatively small number of people. The goal of this chapter is to spell out this fact in a little more detail and to explore its implications. In doing so, I will discuss the financing aspects of transplantation decisions and fit the technology into the larger picture of resource allocation in health care.

The first question is Just how big a demand on society's resources is at stake here? In other words, what does a transplant cost and how many are needed? These questions are extremely difficult to answer.

Need for Transplantation

Need is a slippery word in medicine. Contrary to naive opinion, there is no hard and fast definition of medical necessity. Estimates of need for transplants begin with the incidence of medical conditions for which transplantation is a "reasonable option," but this depends very much on the strictness of the medical criteria applied. Decisions about appropriate criteria are difficult value judgments, not mere technical decisions. The history of the use of kidney dialysis, for example, shows that people who were for many years considered to be medically unsuitable candidates for dialysis, such as diabetics and the very elderly, are now being dialyzed routinely.

Of particular significance in estimates of need are the age restrictions currently imposed. Patients may be considered either too old or too young to benefit from organ transplants. These age limitations are defended on medical grounds, but the lines between medically based age requirements and age discrimination is difficult to draw. If the age cut-offs are judged to be unfairly discriminatory—and either changed or eliminated—the pool of transplant candidates will increase dramatically.

Estimates of need for heart transplants range from a low of 2,000 per year to 75,000 per year (1 in 4 patients under 50 with heart disease).[1] The most detailed study to date, the National Heart Transplantation Study, estimated that about 14,000 people (60 per million population) die annually of conditions for which transplantation may be appropriate, assuming age restrictions of between 10 and 54 years old. Using current medical selection criteria (such as those employed at Stanford University), fewer than 2,000 would actually be accepted for transplant.[2]

Estimates of the need for liver transplants depend on the extent to which people with liver cancer and people whose livers have been damaged by alcoholism and drugs are considered suitable candidates. Using current selection criteria, which exclude these groups as well as those over 50 to 55 years old, estimated need is 5,000 (21 per million population); including them, the number rises to 9,500 (40 per million population).[3]

Because kidney transplantation is a well-established procedure and dialysis is available as a backup treatment, estimates of the need for kidneys might be expected to vary less. However, changes in medical opinion on who is a suitable transplant candidate and changes in patient preferences for transplantation over dialysis affect these numbers. There are 8,500 people on the waiting list for kidneys now, but it has been estimated that as many as 25,000 of the more than 80,000 people now on dialysis might be suitable for transplantation.[4]

Cost per Transplant

Figures on the cost of a transplant are very approximate. The number most frequently given is an estimate of average direct medical care costs in the year of transplant, per person receiving a transplant or per one-year survivor, based on current experience. For kidney transplants, the averages usually range from $25,000 to $50,000; for hearts, from $95,000 to $148,000; and for livers, from $130,000 to $320,000.[5] The cost of care for individual patients varies even more widely.

For several reasons it is difficult to be precise about these costs. First, an individual patient's medical course is complicated and unpredictable; it depends on the patient's initial condition, the skill of the transplant team and support staff, and pure chance. Second, reported cost figures are generally incomplete. Often they exclude surgeon's fees, organ procurement costs, capital costs, and the cost of screening patients not accepted as candidates. These costs may be omitted because they are not available, or more typically, because the focus of those compiling them is only on the budget of a particular institution or program (e.g., the transplant center, Medicare, or Medicaid), as opposed to complete medical care costs. Finally, the figures that are available, especially those for hospital care, generally reflect arbitrary accounting conventions rather than true economic cost.

Total first-year medical costs are only a portion of the medical care costs attributable to the procedure. Transplant recipients who survive the first year continue to require care for the rest of their lives: follow-up monitoring, immunosuppressive drug therapy, and treatment for later complications. These costs are generally estimated to be $5,000 or more per year.[6]

However, some transplant costs merely replace costs that would have been incurred during the patient's terminal illness, in the absence of a transplant. The case of kidney transplantation is unique in that there is an artificial substitute for kidney function, dialysis, which is routinely provided to patients with end-stage renal disease. Successful transplantation becomes cost saving after three years, it is estimated, compared to the alternative of long-term dialysis.[7] In the case of heart and liver transplant estimates, omissions of transplant-related costs probably more than offset omissions of cost savings in standard treatment. Nevertheless, it is important to remember that the marginal cost of transplantation does depend on assumptions about the level and cost of care that would be provided to the patient were a transplant not performed, assumptions that are in themselves subject to examination and evaluation.

Amounts paid to medical care providers for medical goods and services are not the only costs to society attributable to the procedures. There are also nonmedical costs, such as transportation to the transplant center and care provided to the patient at home by family members. These costs are even more difficult to estimate than medical care costs.

Additional uncertainty exists when costs are projected into the future. Some costs can be expected to decrease. If the procedures become routine, surgeons' fees may come down, and improvements in the ability to manage complications after transplants may reduce follow-up medical care costs. In contrast, other costs—such as medical care input costs—may rise. Medical selection criteria may be relaxed to include patients who are sicker and therefore more expensive to treat. Obviously, tremendous uncertainty exists about the cost of an organ transplant.

Organ Supply

Society's ability to respond to the need for organ transplantation is currently constrained by the availability of suitable organs. The strict medical requirements for donors of hearts, livers, and kidneys set a natural limit on supply. Estimates of the number of people dying annually who would meet these requirements are very approximate. The President's Commission for the Study of Ethical Problems in Medicine estimated 20,000.[8] The National Heart Transplantation Study estimated 16,000.[9] The Task Force on Organ Transplantation's review of available information led that group to conclude that the size of the potential donor pool was 17,000 to 26,000. The actual number of donors now is, of course, much lower (the task force estimates that there were 3,290 organs donated in 1984, for example), but it is believed that the number could be increased by public education and greater effort devoted to procurement.[10]

Moreover, advances in artificial organ technology may diminish the importance of the natural supply constraint. An artificial substitute for kidney function was developed along with kidney transplantation and is still the only treatment possible for many end-stage renal disease patients. As noted, dialysis costs are at least as great, on average, as those for successful transplantation.

Advocates of heart transplantation have argued that the natural supply constraint will always protect society from the commitment of a large share of medical resources to this procedure.[11] This, however, seems unrealistic. Development of an artificial heart is already well under way. The cost of implantation, follow-up medical care, and maintenance of the device is expected to parallel the cost of transplantation, follow-up medical care, and immunosuppressive drugs.[12] If heart transplantation is accepted as routine, it is difficult to see how access to artificial hearts can be denied on principle. Moreover, if the dialysis experience is any guide, medical and age criteria will become less restrictive as supply constraints are removed.[13] Thus, in the long run, the high estimates of need for heart replacement may be of policy importance.

Total Cost of Organ Substitution

With all the uncertainty inherent in the estimates of need, cost per transplant, and organ supply, estimates of the total cost of this technology can be little more than guesses. Nevertheless, it is instructive to examine the total cost figures that are implied by existing estimates.

Table 15.1 gives some very crude computations of total cost in the year of transplant. The costs of heart and liver transplantation procedures have been calculated by continuing estimates of need, first-year costs per precedure and costs of follow-up medical care. Because the need for heart transplants greatly exceeds the available donor pool, estimates of the need constrained by the donor pool are also relevant (here it is somewhat arbitrarily assumed that the donor pool is 16,000 and that all suitable organs are harvested). Similar restraints do not exist in the case of livers (where the demand for organs is substantially below the available donor pool) or kidneys (where an artificial organ is available to those who do not receive a transplant). Follow-up care costs are significant for any calculation of costs, because in any given year the true cost of transplantation is not only the cost of that year's transplants, but also the cost of caring for all previous transplant recipients who are still alive. For the calculations in Table 15.1, it is assumed that 85 percent of heart transplant recipients survive to the end of the first year and live an average of five years or more. The cost of follow-up care is assumed to be $6,261 in the first four years, and $8,911 in the fifth year (including the cost of dying).[14] A 70 percent first-year survival rate is assumed for liver transplant recipients; survivors are assumed to live an average of five years at an annual cost of $5,000 in follow-up medical costs.[15] The total cost figures combine procedure cost and follow-up cost, assuming that a transplant program has been operating at full strength for more than five years so there is a full cohort of patients receiving posttransplant care.

For kidneys, a slightly different procedure seemed in order because an artificial organ substitute is already available. The average annual cost of replacing kidney function under current societal arrangements is roughly the cost of the End-Stage Renal Disease Program under Medicare plus the offsetting payments collected from other third parties. An estimate of this cost in 1985 is $2,362 million for 83,800 enrollees.[16] Average life expectancy for dialysis recipients is eight years,[17] so the average annual need for kidney replacement (i.e., new patients with end-stage renal disease) is about 10,500.

Of course, this figure is only an approximation: Not all patients and costs are included, and some costs are overstated. For example, costs and numbers are overstated because transplant recipients become ineligible for the program three years after a successful transplant. However, total program costs would be lower if more enrollees received the cheaper forms of treatment, transplants or home dialysis. Nevertheless, the figure does permit a rough comparison between costs of kidney replacement and costs of heart and liver transplants.

Table 15.2 presents the total cost figures in a different form. The annual percent of the population whose lives would be saved by a transplant or dialysis (i.e., people who receive a transplant and survive at least a year and the average number of new dialysis recipients per year) is shown. Also included is the annual per capita cost of having a program to save those lives (i.e., the total annual cost of the procedures and follow-up care, divided by the total population). One way of thinking about these numbers is to think of the per capita amount as the size of the annual insurance premium each U.S. resident would have to pay to protect himself or herself against the risk of needing organ substitution, assuming the risk and the cost are spread evenly over the entire population. In other words, at the high estimate of need, everyone would have to pay $39

TABLE 15.1
Cost of Organ Substitution

	Number of Transplants Performed	First-Year Cost (millions of dollars)	Annual Cost, Follow-Up Care (millions of dollars)	Total Annual Cost (millions of dollars)
Heart				
High estimate of need	75,000	7,169–11,100	2,164.0	9,333–13,264
Need constrained by donor pool	16,000	1,530–2,368	462.0	1,992–2,830
Low estimate of need	2,000	191–296	57.8	249–354
Liver				
High estimate of need	9,500	1,235–3,040	166.0	1,401–3,206
Low estimate of need	5,000	650–1,600	87.5	738–1,688
Kidney[a]				2,362
Total annual cost: heart, liver, kidney				
High estimate of need				13,096–18,832
Need constrained by donor pool				5,755–8,398
Low estimate of need				3,349–4,404

[a]Includes costs of dialysis and transplants.

Source: Author's calculations.

TABLE 15.2
Organ Substitution: Percent Benefiting and Annual Per Capita Costs

	Number of Transplants Performed	Percent of Population Benefiting	Annual Per Capita Cost (dollars)
Heart			
High estimate of need	75,000	0.0267	39.00–55.00
Need constrained by donor pool	16,000	0.0057	8.33–11.84
Low estimate of need	2,000	0.0007	1.04– 1.48
Liver			
High estimate of need	9,500	0.0028	5.86–13.41
Low estimate of need	5,000	0.0015	3.09– 7.06
Kidney	10,500[a]	0.0044	9.88

[a]Annual number (average) of new entrants in end-stage renal disease program.

Source: Author's calculations.

to $55 a year for protection against a possibility of 2 in 10,000 that he or she would need and benefit from a heart transplant.

Are the numbers in the tables large or small? Of course, they are certainly large in some absolute sense. Even in our wealthy society, we have not reached the point where million-dollar figures are just pocket money. But that is not exactly the issue. In a household budget, a judgment about whether a particular expenditure is large or small is a relative one—relative to the total budget, relative to what one is getting for the money (How important is the item to the household, and is it good value for the money?) and relative to what one could buy if one did not buy this.

People in the United States consumed $30.8 billion worth of tobacco products in 1984.[18] If we cut down on smoking, we would have more than enough money to pay for organ transplants and would improve the nation's health at the same time. The 1988 defense budget is estimated at $298 billion;[19] surely a few percent could be shaved off and the money spent for transplantation instead of weapons.

In contrast, the total 1988 budget for health and human service–related research and development is only $6,300 million ($6.3 billion).[20] Even at the lowest need and cost estimate, the total cost of heart and liver transplantation is 16 percent of this budget. The estimated 1988 federal contribution to Medicaid is $28,225 million ($28.225 billion) (at current savings levels).[21] Medicaid coverage has been slowly eroding in recent years; currently only 45 percent of people below the poverty line are eligible for Medicaid benefits.[22] The high figures for organ substitution constitute half or even more of the total federal share of Medicaid and benefit less than 0.04 percent of the population. Moreover, political reality suggests that it is health and welfare expenditures that are marginal, not defense; the administration's 1988 budget proposes a $1,256 million ($1.256 billion) cut in Medicaid but leaves the total defense budget unchanged.[23]

In a society in which 13 percent or more of the population has no health insurance,[24] in which up to 30 percent lack enough insurance to protect themselves against financially catastrophic medical events of much higher probability than the need for an organ transplant,[25] in which the cost of a few heart or liver transplants can displace an entire program for patients with Alzheimer's disease or for crippled children in a state Medicaid budget—the cost of ensuring access to this expensive technology is significant.

Financing

As the cost figures suggest, the financing of these procedures is a serious problem. Moreover, it is a problem that society has been reluctant to face.

Organ transplantation holds intense fascination for the public. A great deal of media attention has been focused on the subject, especially on the availability of organs. It has often appeared that although financing is, of course, important, the supply of organs is the chief obstacle to the use of the technology. However, the current system of organ procurement is actually more effective than the public perceives and there are latent positive attitudes toward donation. As good a case can be made, I think, that the greatest obstacle to the development of an organ procurement network that maximizes donations has been the fact that the question of who is to pay the cost of transplants has remained unresolved.

By the same token, scientists are correct in asserting that the designation of "experimental" has remained on heart and liver transplants for much longer than it would have if the technology were cheaper or less visible. In fact, third-party payers have used the experimental designation to postpone the difficult decision of whether to cover these very expensive but lifesaving procedures.

The central question is What should be the role of ability to pay in obtaining a transplant? But this question can only be answered in the context of a larger question: What is a fair distribution of health care and of its cost? Many people would like to see organ transplantation as a special case and handle it as such. However it is *not* a special case. It is merely an extreme and highly visible example that highlights basic structural problems in the U.S. health care system.

Fair Distribution of Health Care

Many people in this country think of health care as special, as having particular importance to individual well-being, equality of opportunity, and a sense of community. So they believe that society has an obligation to ensure that health care is available to everyone. One can see evidence of this shared feeling of social responsibility in the numerous public and private programs devoted to increasing access to care. However, these programs also show a confusion about the extent of the obligation. Health care is important, but so are other social goods. To provide everyone with all possible beneficial medical care would be costly indeed and would require that other important needs go unmet. It seems that the societal obligation cannot be unlimited. But if this is the case, then how much care should a person expect to receive?

There are related questions: How much of the cost of their care ought individuals to bear themselves and how much should be shared with others? It is important that people be able to obtain health care, but surely they should not have to forgo everything else to pay for it. Again, there is agreement among many people that patients with large medical bills should be helped, but there also seems to be considerable confusion about how much to help, and how the cost of helping should be distributed.

The President's Commission for the Study of Ethical Problems in Medicine addressed these issues in a report entitled *Securing Access to Health Care.*[26] In the report the commission's goal was to provide a consistent ethical framework for thinking about the allocation of resources in health care, based on principles that seem to be widely held. The final report commanded the support of people holding a wide spectrum of political views and thus is a useful starting point for considering the issue of fair distribution.

A central concept in the commission's framework was that of an "adequate level" of health care—a level of care to which society is morally obligated to ensure access. The report derived the existence of this obligation from the special features of health care and health needs. It was argued that the obligation is not unlimited; the adequate level is not identical to everything of benefit; instead, its specific content is determined in relation to the resources and preferences of society and to those features of health care that make it special. The commission concluded that the cost of making this level of care available to all should be spread over the entire population, so that the healthy share the burden of the less healthy and the rich share the burden of the poor, on a national basis. Those who want more than this level of care should be free to have it, provided they use their own resources to purchase the care itself, or they obtain insurance guaranteeing them access to it in case of need.

Hence one way of thinking about transplantation (or any other expensive treatment) is to ask: Is it part of an adequate level of care? The question cannot be readily answered because there is no consensus on what an adequate level is. In fact, as a society we have been reluctant to face this issue squarely and decide how to limit care in an equitable manner. Instead, health programs are set up as unlimited entitlements and when the costs predictably become intolerable, arbitrary limits—on eligibility for care as well as on the kinds and amounts of care provided—are imposed without reference to relative benefits and costs. Priorities among competing health needs seem to be related to the degree to which a particular need is able to capture the public's attention (whether because of the nature of the need itself or the energy of those lobbying for it) rather than to a rational process of evaluation.

One possible response to the question of whether transplantation is part of an adequate level of health care is that the existence of the End-Stage Renal Disease Program under Medicare suggests that it is. The legislative history of the program shows that people were uncomfortable with the fact that lifesaving treatment for kidney disease was not available to all. They were especially uncomfortable with the prospect that only those who could pay would get it. The Task Force on Organ Transplantation reasons from the ESRD experience to the conclusion that organ transplants should be available to all without regard to ability to pay, with the cost borne by the federal government if necessary.[27] But the message is not so clear. The ESRD program proved to be very expensive, and Congress has been unexpectedly firm in refusing to extend the same treatment to other health conditions. The federal government has moved very slowly in extending coverage for heart and liver transplants in programs that normally extend coverage automatically to new procedures offering any prospect of benefit. There is no consensus, at least in the federal government, that organ transplants are part of an adequate level.

Of course, if they are not, it is not necessarily unfair to offer organ transplants, so long as the recipients pay the cost themselves (directly, or through insurance policies). Some argue that if lifesaving treatment is not available to all, it should not be available to any, but it is difficult to see why millionaires may spend money on jewels and fancy cars but not on their own health.

The trouble is, of course, that millionaires usually do not pay the full cost of the transplantation, but use publicly subsidized facilities and resources, diverting them from uses with perhaps greater social value. Much of the cost of the initial phases of development of transplantation has been paid out of public funds for medical research. Should a technology developed with public research funds be available only to the wealthy? Or should the past devotion of public funds to the development of this costly technology be considered a mistake that should not now be compounded by devoting more scarce public funds to ensuring access?

Scenarios for the Future

As these fundamental questions are so difficult, let us turn instead to what is actually going to happen. In considering the role that ability to pay is likely to play in gaining access to a transplant, it is useful to outline three possibilities, from least to most likely.

Ability to Pay Plays No Role

A situation in which the ability to pay plays no role could happen in either of two ways. The first and the more desirable would be in the context of a restructuring of the entire health care delivery system to guarantee an adequate level of care without excessive burdens to all. A serious weighing of societal priorities would occur, and the result would be the inclusion of organ transplants as part of the adequate level of health care offered to all. Contributions to the total cost of guaranteeing this to all would be scaled according to ability to pay, but ability to pay would not be a factor in getting a transplant (although other patient characteristics such as medical condition might be). This would be extremely expensive, but perhaps the restructuring of the system would save enough elsewhere so that it could be done.

The second way is less unlikely but more troubling ethically. In this case, federal funding would be provided for organ transplants in the form of a special program like the ESRD program, either for all patients getting these procedures or as a "last resort" program for those not covered by existing private and public insurance programs and unable to afford the cost of a transplant from their own resources. (The latter is the recommendation of the Task Force on Organ Transplantation.)[28]

This is troubling because it sets up a special category of illness and gives it preferential treatment. There are other conditions that impose similar burdens on sufferers and for which care could provide similar benefits at similar costs, yet these patients do not have the same automatic access to the care they need and may have to meet far more of the cost themselves if they do get it. Even worse, once the commitment is made to a particular category of illness like this, public funds may have to be diverted from other kinds of care as the dollar size of the commitment grows and grows. The current concern about the cost of entitlement programs in health care makes this outcome unlikely also.

Ability to Pay Is the Sole Determining Factor

In a situation in which ability to pay is the sole determining factor, no government program (including the ESRD program) covers transplantation. Private insurance covers it through special riders for which the subscriber pays the full actuarial cost. People receive transplants only if they have private insurance, personal resources, or private charitable support. As noted, an ethical case can be made for this on the grounds that this kind of care is not part of the adequate level guaranteed to all, but ought to be available to those who are able and willing to pay the full cost.

This outcome is also extremely unlikely because it would be a radical departure from past policy. For example, if kidney transplantation were ended, logic would suggest ending public support of kidney dialysis also because dialysis is a more expensive, less effective treatment for the same condition. Many would not accept such a policy as fair, especially given the identifiability of the victims and the degree of public sympathy with their plight that would be felt.

Ability to Pay Plays Some Role

The final possibility is a patchwork system, in which some have easy access to the necessary financing for transplantation and others do not. This is the traditional U.S. response to access to health care and is in fact happening now.

The costs of kidney transplants have for some time been met by private insurance, the Medicare End-Stage Renal Disease Program, and Medicaid. By 1985, membership surveys by industry associations showed that more than 80 percent of Blue Cross/Blue Shield and private health insurance companies offered some form of coverage for heart and liver transplants. The extent of coverage was variable. A few limited coverage for liver transplants to children with congenital liver disease, and as with health insurance generally, the comprehensiveness with which costs were covered differed greatly across policies. HMO (health maintenance organization) coverage was less extensive, although more comprehensive when present. Seventy-four percent of HMOs covered liver transplants for at least some enrollees and 30 percent covered heart transplants.[29]

CHAMPUS, the health benefit program for active military personnel, their dependents and for retired military personnel, covers kidney and liver transplants. The medical programs of the military services provide or pay for kidney and heart transplants.[30]

After a long delay, Medicare finally issued regulations in October 1986 on heart and liver transplants. Coverage was extended for heart transplants if done at specified centers and for liver transplants for Medicare-eligible children with certain specified medical conditions.[31] Because existing selection criteria for heart transplants exclude the elderly, and most younger patients die before the end of the twenty-nine-month waiting period for Medicare's disability program if they do not receive a transplant, the actual effect of this decision will be small, unless Medicare decides to eliminate the waiting period for transplant candidates.

Medicaid coverage varies across states, although it is expanding. The Task Force on Organ Transplantation reported that thirty-three states were covering liver transplants and twenty-four states were covering heart transplants. However, coverage was not always automatic, and in some states, decisions were being made on a case-by-case basis.[32] A later survey by the Intergovernmental Health Policy Project showed that the number had risen to forty states and the District of Columbia for liver transplants, and thirty-two states and the District for heart transplants. Forty-seven states provided coverage for outpatient immunosuppressive drugs. There was considerable variation in the comprehensiveness of coverage for other costs. Particularly bemusing, for instance, is Oklahoma's heart transplant policy. It does not cover heart transplants but will pay for diagnostic evaluations for them.[33] Presumably, if the patient is not a good candidate, he can die content that nothing could have saved him; if he is judged to be suitable, then he can mobilize a media appeal.

The trend seems to be in the direction of coverage. However, even if all existing public and private third-party payers eventually cover organ transplantation, the 31 to 37 million people who are completely uninsured will still be without coverage,[34] and millions more will be covered for only a fraction of the cost.

This patchwork outcome, the most likely, is also the worst. Although opinions differ about exactly which dimensions are relevant in deciding what distribution of health care is fair, there is agreement on one principle: People who are similar along all ethically relevant dimensions should be treated in a similar fashion. However, whatever dimensions one chooses, this principle is likely to be violated in dramatic ways. For example, a resident of a generous state may get a heart transplant under Medicaid, while a similar person who resides in a less generous state goes without. The child of a member of the armed forces may get a liver transplant, while the child of uninsured working parents does not. Private charity may fill in some gaps but is unlikely to eliminate them entirely.

Even when patients do obtain transplants, the share of the cost they bear directly will vary in arbitrary and inequitable ways, depending on the source and comprehensiveness of third-party coverage. To make matters worse, based on existing patterns of coverage, it is members of minority groups, the poor, and the unemployed who will have the greatest difficulty.

These problems of access to transplantation are not unique. They already exist for other forms of care, especially very expensive care, and have for years. Thus, the argument made by advocates of transplantation—that other expensive forms of treatment that are done routinely provide no more benefits than organ transplants, so it is arbitrary to single out organ transplantation—misses the point.[35]

First, questions are increasingly being raised about whether the benefits of other kinds of expensive medical care are worth the costs. For example, it is questioned whether it is worthwhile to pursue aggressive chemotherapy and radiation treatment for terminally ill cancer patients, when the expected benefit is a few more months of life in painful circumstances. The benefits of neonatal intensive care for severely defective or very low birth-weight infants also have been debated. In addition, there is increasing scrutiny of the value of intensive care for the adult patient with a very poor prognosis and, alternatively, for the patient being monitored for a serious complication that only rarely occurs. And the value of coronary artery bypass surgery for certain subgroups of patients is controversial.

Second, not everyone has ready access now to treatments that are already standard medical practice. Many people in the United States *do* have serious difficulty obtaining health care that is of significant, sometimes even lifesaving, importance. In fact, kidney dialysis and transplantation are the only expensive high-technology medical procedures to which access is virtually universally guaranteed.

Failure to receive a heart or liver transplant dramatically and directly results in death. Other consequences of our patchwork financing system are less visible, but no less real. They show up in anecdotal examples of people being refused care for economic reasons, in higher levels of mortality and morbidity from preventable conditions among the poor and the uninsured, in the difficulty of obtaining care reported in periodic health surveys, and in severe financial hardship and restricted opportunity resulting from catastrophic medical bills.

Conclusion

If public funds are to be used to guarantee access to highly beneficial care, it is not at all clear that one should begin with including organ transplantation technology. The right solution to the financing problem is not obvious, but it is difficult to see how it can be approached in an ethically acceptable way outside the context of an evaluation—and perhaps even a complete restructuring—of the entire financing system.

This is a painful conclusion and one for which the U.S. public has not seemed ready. The larger problem is the need for us as a society to reach a consensus on what an adequate level of care is and how the burden of guaranteeing it should be shared, and then to develop institutions to distribute the care and its costs in accord with this consensus.

Those who have raised questions about whether it is good public policy to fund organ transplantation have generally sought to use the public's fascination with this dramatic technology as a vehicle to educate the public about the larger problem. They have wanted to use this case as the first step toward a broader reevaluation of the benefits and costs of *all* forms of medical care. Advocates of transplantation, however, have generally sought to do the opposite. They have tried to slip transplantation into the standard of medical practice as other new technologies have been slipped in, without fundamental assessment of whether the benefits of the new technology were worth the costs. At this point in history, the second group—those who think we should proceed with a widespread dissemination of the technology regardless of the cost—seems to be on the winning side.

Notes

1. Ward Casscells, "Heart Transplantation: Recent Policy Developments," *New England Journal of Medicine* 315: 1365–1368, 1986.
2. Roger W. Evans et al., *The National Heart Transplantation Study: Final Report* (Seattle, WA: Battelle Human Affairs Research Centers, 1984), p. ES-29.
3. Task Force on Organ Transplantation, Health Resources and Services Administration, *Organ Transplantation: Issues and Recommendations* (Washington, D.C.: Government Printing Office, 1986), p. 226.
4. Don Colburn, "Organ Transplants: Who Lives? Who Decides?" *Washington Post Health*, January 10, 1987, p. 17.
5. The Task Force on Organ Transplantation reported the low figures for heart and liver transplants (Task Force, *Transplantation*, p. 99); Group Health Cooperative of Puget Sound used the higher figures (see Paul Menzel's Chapter 11 in this volume). Colburn ("Who Lives?") reported the lower figure for kidney transplants, and the higher figure was estimated by Philip Held of the Urban Institute in a personal communication.
6. Casscells, "Heart Transplantation," p. 1367; Roger W. Evans, "The Economics of Heart Transplantation," *Circulation* 75: 63–76, 1987.
7. Enrique Carter, National Center for Health Services Research, personal communication.
8. President's Commission for the Study of Ethical Problems in Medicine, *Securing Access to Health Care* (Washington, D.C.: Government Printing Office, 1983), Chapter 1.
9. Evans et al., *Heart Study*, p. ES-35.
10. Task Force, *Transplantation*, p. 35.
11. See, for example, Evans, "Economics," p. 66.
12. D. P. Lubeck, "The Artificial Heart: Costs, Risks and Benefits—An Update," *International Journal of Technology Assessment in Health Care* 2: 369–386, 1986.

13. Lubeck, "Artificial Heart," estimates the annual need for the artificial heart to be 32,000, counting only persons between the ages of 55 and 70 (on the assumption that those under 55 will obtain human heart transplants).

14. These numbers are from Evans, "Economics." The survival pattern is, of course, a distribution (over 50 percent of the recipients live more than five years, and 25 percent live more than ten years). However, five years is a reasonable approximation to this distribution.

15. Information on survival rates and the cost of follow-up care for liver recipients is very shaky, and the situation is changing rapidly. Five years probably *overestimates* current life expectancy, but $5,000 probably *underestimates* the cost of follow-up care.

16. Evans et al., *Heart Study*, p. ES-105.

17. Massachusetts Task Force, *Report*, p. 65.

18. *Statistical Abstract of the United States, 1986* (Washington, D.C.: USGPO), p. 435.

19. *The Budget for Fiscal Year 1988* (Washington, D.C.: USGPO, 1987), p. A-32.

20. *Budget*, p. J-21.

21. *Budget*, p. A-25.

22. Gail Wilensky, "Viable Strategies for Dealing with the Uninsured," *Health Affairs*, 33-46, 1987.

23. *Budget*, pp. A-25 and A-32.

24. Wilensky, "Strategies," p. 35.

25. Pamela Farley, "Who Are the Underinsured?" *Milbank Memorial Fund Quarterly* 63: 476-503, 1985.

26. President's Commission, *Securing Access*.

27. Task Force, *Transplantation*, pp. 102ff.

28. Task Force, *Transplantation*, p. 105.

29. Task Force, *Transplantation*, pp. 99ff.

30. Task Force, *Transplantation*, pp. 99ff.

31. Casscells, "Heart Transplantation," pp. 1367–1368.

32. Task Force, *Transplantation*, pp. 99ff.

33. S. Zachery, *Medicaid Coverage and Payment Policies for Organ Transplants: A Fifty State Review* (Washington, D.C.: Intergovernmental Health Policy Project, 1986).

34. Wilensky, "Strategies," p. 35.

35. See, for example, Task Force, *Transplantation*, p. 103.

16

Justice and the Dissemination of "Big-Ticket" Technologies

Norman Daniels

When we are concerned with technologies whose total costs may add up to several billion dollars a year, once they are deployed, it is reasonable to ask what else could be accomplished with the same investment. That is, we may ask about the *opportunity costs* of these technologies. Let us call the opportunity costs of a given technology problematic if the same investment would produce greater benefits were it spent on an alternative technology or service. Organ transplantation shares an important property with a number of other high-cost—or "big-ticket"—medical technologies: They all deliver a significant benefit to a small number of people at a high cost. This fact about big-ticket technologies opens them to serious objections, for it seems likely that their opportunity costs will be problematic.

Let us suppose that disseminating a big-ticket technology has highly problematic opportunity costs. Then we may object that it is an ineffective or inefficient way to use our resources. This is a powerful objection, but it may not be decisive. The urgency of the medical needs met by transplant or other big-ticket technologies may incline us to accept this sort of inefficiency. (Who can stand by and let this charming child die for lack of a liver transplant?)[1] Nevertheless, it may also be claimed that deploying the big-ticket technology rather than alternatives is unjust or unfair because there may be morally superior claims of other classes of patients to have their medical needs met.

In what follows I will show how such a complaint about injustice can be developed within a theory of justice for health care. Unfortunately, it is not completely clear where this complaint about injustice (or the complaint about inefficiency) leads us. There are important structural features of our health care system that prevent decision-makers from responding to either kind of complaint. These features explain why such decision-makers are insensitive to claims about problematic opportunity costs. If we want our system to be more just, we will have to change these structural features.

Before proceeding, I should clarify some of my assumptions about organ transplant technologies. First, I said that transplants can give a significant benefit to a relatively small number of patients, but at high cost. Of course, how large a benefit a transplant will produce for a patient depends on success rates for the type of transplant in question and on facts about the type of patient receiving the organ. On the average, the significance of the benefit will diminish, the less selectively the procedure is used. Second, in contrast to some other big-ticket technologies (e.g., neonatal intensive care units and artificial organs), total costs for transplant technologies will be limited by the availability of donor organs, not merely by the quantity of resources we are willing to devote to meeting these needs. Third, some technologies may not have the very high cost per use that transplant technologies have, in part because they can be more widely used, even when they yield small benefits, as they are not invasive (e.g., CT-scans). Such technologies may also count as big-ticket items because their cost per use is high when we count only the cases in which their use is likely to produce significant benefits. In what follows, I abstract from many important differences between organ transplant technologies and other big-ticket items in order to concentrate on the opportunity-cost argument.

I should also make it quite clear from the outset that the problem of justice I will be discussing does not involve the question of *micro* policy: Who should get the organ when there are not enough to go around? I am not concerned here with the important problem of how to make the use of this technology equitable. Rather, I am concerned with the *macro* allocation question: Should we be disseminating this technology? My concern is more directly relevant to the kind of question that faces federal or state legislators when they consider extending Medicare or Medicaid reimbursements to heart, liver, and pancreas transplants (kidneys are already covered). Similarly, my concern is more directly relevant to the question hospital or HMO directors ask: Should we add a transplant team to our institution? I will consider the relevance of arguments about opportunity cost to these kinds of decisions.

Justice and Opportunity Costs

Let us suppose that a particular organ transplant technology has highly problematic opportunity costs. That is, we would produce far greater aggregate benefits by investing our resources in an alternative service or technology. I would like to consider two ways of converting this complaint about the inefficacy and inefficiency of the investment into an objection based on claims about justice. The first way involves a straightforwardly utilitarian argument; the second will appeal to a more egalitarian account of just health cost.

To say that we could produce far greater aggregate medical benefits by investing our resources in an alternative technology carries us quite far toward a utilitarian objection to the big-ticket technology. If we can suppose that there are few other relevant benefits and costs we need consider when assessing the alternative technologies, then we can use the estimates of opportunity costs as approximations to aggregate utility. For example, we might suppose that the benefits and costs associated with treating patients with one technology—the benefits to families, to providers, to society—will tend to be proportional to the medical benefits and costs. This presumption may be rebuttable in particular cases, which will affect the overall utilitarian calculation. Similarly, we may suppose that there are no special entitlements or "right" claims, themselves justifiable on utilitarian grounds, that might obligate us or the relevant decision-makers to ignore estimates of the relative opportunity costs of each technology. Under these assumptions, the decision to deploy the big-ticket technology falls under the following utilitarian principle: The right act or policy is the one that produces at least as great a net benefit as any relevant alternative. Or we might think that decision-makers in public policy contexts are governed by the following rule, which itself could be given a utilitarian justification: Choose the alternative policy or action with the least problematic opportunity costs, unless there are special considerations or rules that exclude that alternative. In general, a utilitarian will believe that distributions of resources are just if they are made in accordance with such principles or rules. Thus, if a particular organ transplant technology had highly problematic opportunity costs, the utilitarian would infer that justice required deploying resources in another way.

In the next section, I shall argue that features of our health care institutions make it very difficult to utilize this argument in a straightforward way to guide decision-making about resource allocation. First, however, I want to sketch an alternative, nonutilitarian argument from justice, an argument that again appeals to the opportunity costs of alternative technologies. Because this argument, too, will prove ineffective in the context of our health care institutions, the problems I will point to in the next section should seem all the more serious. Our institutions will turn out to be insensitive to appeals to justice from quite different perspectives. The insensitivity cannot merely be dismissed as a reaction to controversial appeals to considerations of justice.

The nonutilitarian account is one I have developed in detail elsewhere, and here I can only provide its basic outlines.[2] We can begin with the question, Is health care special? Is it a social good that we should distinguish from other goods, say video recorders, because of its special importance? Does it have a special moral importance? And does that moral importance mean that there are social obligations to distribute it in ways that might not coincide with the results of market distribution? I believe the answer to all these questions is "yes."

Health care—I mean the term quite broadly—does many important things for people. Some health care extends lives, some reduces pain and suffering, some merely gives important information about one's condition, and much health care affects the quality of life in other ways. Yet, we do not think all things that improve quality of life are comparable in importance: The way quality is improved seems critical. I have argued elsewhere that a central, unifying function of health care is to maintain and restore functional organization, or "functioning," that is typical or normal for our species. This central function of health care derives its moral importance from the following fact: Normal functioning has a central effect on the opportunity open to an individual. This claim can be made more precise.

The *normal opportunity range* for a given society is the array of life plans reasonable people in it are likely to construct for themselves. The normal range is thus dependent on key features of the society, such as its stage of historical development, level of technological development and wealth, and other cultural facts. In this way, the notion of normal opportunity range is socially relative. Facts about social organization, including the conception of justice regulating its basic institutions, will also determine how the total normal range is distributed in the population. The share of the normal range open to an individual is also determined in a fundamental way by his talents and skills. Fair equality of opportunity does not require opportunity to be equal for all persons. It only requires that it be equal for persons with similar skills and talents. Thus individual shares of the normal range will not in general be *equal*, even when they are *fair* to an individual. This means that the general principle of fair equality of opportunity does not imply leveling individual differences.

I can now state a fact central to my approach: Impairment of normal functioning through disease and disability restricts an individual's opportunity relative to that portion of the normal range his skills and talents would have made available to him were he healthy. If an individual's fair share of the normal range is the array of life plans he or she may reasonably choose, given his or her talents and skills, then disease and disability shrinks that person's share from what is fair. Restoring normal functioning through health care has a particular and limited effect on the individual's share of the normal range. It lets him or her enjoy that portion of the normal range to which a full range of skills and talents would give him or her access, assuming these are not also impaired by special social disadvantages. Again, there is no presumption that we should eliminate or level individual differences, which act as a baseline constraint on the degree to which individuals enjoy the normal range. Only where differences in talents and skills are the results of disease and disability, not merely normal variation, is some effort required to correct for the effects of the natural lottery. The suggestion that emerges from this account is that we should use impairment of the normal opportunity range as a fairly crude measure of the relative moral importance of health care needs at the macro level.

Some general theories of justice, most notably Rawls's,[3] provide foundations for a principle protecting fair equality of opportunity. If such a principle is indeed a requirement of an acceptable general theory of justice, then I believe we have a natural way to extend such general theories to govern the distribution of health care. We should include health care institutions among those basic institutions of a society that are governed by the fair equality of opportunity principle.[4] If this approach to a theory of just health care is correct, it means that there are social obligations to provide health care services that protect and restore normal functioning. In short, the principle of justice that should govern the design of health care institutions is a principle that calls for guaranteeing fair equality of opportunity. Moreover, this principle can be refined so that it protects fair equality of opportunity at each stage of life and thus gives us an answer to the problem of the just distribution of health care among age groups.[5]

This principle of justice has implications for both access and resource allocation. It implies that there should be no financial, geographical, or discriminatory barriers to a level of care that promotes normal functioning. It also implies that resources be allocated in ways that are effective in promoting normal functioning. That is, because we can use the effect on normal opportunity range as a crude way of ranking the moral importance of health care services, we can guide hard public policy choices about which services are more important to provide. Thus the principle does not imply that any technology that might have a positive impact on normal functioning for some individuals should be introduced: We must weigh new technologies against alternatives to judge the overall impact of introducing them on fair equality of opportunity—this gives a slightly new sense to the term *opportunity cost*. The point is that social obligations to provide just health care must be met within the conditions of moderate scarcity that we face. This is not an approach that gives individuals a basic right to have all their health care needs met. There are social obligations to provide individuals only with those services that are part of the design of a system that, on the whole, protects equal opportunity.

A big-ticket technology, such as organ transplantation, could turn out to have highly problematic opportunity costs (in the new sense of opportunity costs). This would constitute a reason of justice for forgoing this technology in favor of other services or technologies that more effectively protect fair equality of opportunity. In a system that complied with the fair equality of opportunity account, decision-makers should allocate resources in favor of alternative services rather than the big-ticket technology. But this conclusion applies in an *ideal* context, one in which there is general compliance with the underlying account of just health care. We do not live in a health care system that complies with this account. Nevertheless, the conclusion may be relevant to what we ought to do now to make our system more just. It may serve as a critical guide to action. I turn now to consider why it is so difficult to respond to such appeals to what is ideally just in our health care system.

The Failure of Opportunity-Cost Arguments in the United States

My main concern in the remarks that follow is to show that certain features of health care institutions in the United States make it especially difficult for decision-makers to respond to opportunity-cost arguments, even those based on claims of justice. First, however, I would like to point to a more general difficulty, on which I have commented elsewhere.[6] When decision-makers in public policy contexts know that they are working within a system that does not comply with more general principles of distributive justice and when they cannot undertake very basic reforms of the institutions they encounter, then it is not always clear how they should be guided by claims that justice ideally requires a certain policy. This general difficulty requires some explanation.

Suppose we are told by our general theory of justice that the opportunity costs of certain big-ticket technologies are too high and that our system can better protect equality of opportunity if it deploys resources in other ways. (Alternatively, if we are utilitarians, we might believe we could produce greater net utility without compromising rules of justice if we avoided the big-ticket technologies.) For example, we might use the resources from new big-ticket technologies to close major gaps in access to health care; these gaps have serious effects on blacks and poor children. If decision-makers could effect changes of the basic design of the health care system, perhaps they might be able to move the system into greater compliance with the requirements of justice. But decision-makers rarely are in a position to effect such basic changes. Legislators and providers who make decisions about reimbursements and about the dissemination of technology generally work within nonbasic frameworks: Few of their decisions can really effect change at the very basic institutional level needed to make the system comply overall with requirements of justice.

Policymakers thus face a double difficulty. They may hope to receive guidance from an ideal theory of justice, but they work in a context in which there is at best partial compliance with that general theory. Basic institutions do not fully conform to the requirements of justice. Moreover, they are in a nonbasic framework: They do not have the power to effect basic institutional reforms. Instead they can only modify less basic features of institutions. In this context they may well wonder how to use ideal theory to guide their decisions. Such theory throws very little light on two critical issues: What is the most effective strategy for moving from noncompliance to compliance contexts? What deviations from ideal principles are permissible in the pursuit of compliance? Moreover, a general moral theory can throw light on principles that guide action in less basic frameworks only if we assume compliance with appropriate principles of justice for the more basic framework. Under such assumptions about compliance, the principles for less basic frameworks are constrained not to undermine more basic principles. In the absence of compliance we lack even this constraint.

How then do we evaluate the justice of proposals for less basic frameworks? We might aim for the principles that would be ideal were compliance with more basic principles already in effect. Such an approach might have its justification in its value for moral education. The principles would provide us with a living example of the ideal. An alternative approach might lead us to seek priorities for principles that have the effect of moving the whole distribution toward a more just one, that is, toward a distribution that would better comply with the requirements of the more basic principles. Each suggestion faces objections. The former seems insensitive to the deeper injustices that exist in the institution and risks degenerating into a somewhat hypocritical moral scrupulosity. The alternative approach risks using the occasion of isolated reform proposals to try to rectify far deeper injustices, which it may not have the leverage to do at all. The risk is that other inequities emerge. In particular circumstances, we would have to decide which objections are more serious.

Consider the decision a legislator or insurance administrator must make about reimbursements for a particular transplant technology. His or her framework is clearly a nonbasic one: He is not contemplating a fundamental revision of the system, say one that introduces a national health service or insurance scheme. He is aware that his framework is nonbasic even if he is worried about the precedent that financing transplants will set, that is, even if he sees that some of the implications of this macro decision may influence others. The point is that he or she may not end up responsible for such later decisions, nor need the precedent involved in the current policy actually end up serving as one. A renal dialysis financing scheme may or may not end up a precedent for financing heart transplants. Political pressures may change, new technologies may arise, and the more systematic ramifications of the current decision may never become actual. Unless it is very clear that the macro question is raised in a basic framework and is intended as part of a more fundamental reform of the system, as it might be if we were concerned with proposals to establish a national health service or insurance scheme, the question is best understood as arising in a nonbasic framework.

Direct appeal to our ideal theory of just health care may mislead us in a nonbasic framework in any of several ways. If we interpret the theory to say that we should not finance heart transplants, but we continue to finance renal dialysis and transplants through public funds, then we introduce an inequity: We fail to treat similarly cases of similar levels of need, for which we have roughly comparable treatments. More generally, we are appealing in this instance to a principle, say the fair equality of opportunity principle (it could be the utilitarian principle), which may be quite generally violated in the system as a whole. As a result, we may be unfair to the group of patients who are desperately in need of transplants, for we are suddenly scrupulous about applying a principle that we generally ignore! We are telling them that justice now requires that they forgo this service, though we have never much worried about the just distribution of resources before and may previously have treated them unfairly as a result. But we are not acting justly if we only occasionally or erratically apply a principle of justice. Rather, the effect is to make the public policy decision seem arbitrary and indefensible—ad hoc at best.

The problem arises at another level as well. If the system as a whole is not in compliance with the principles of justice that apply specifically to health care, it is also not likely to be in compliance with more general principles of justice. Decision-makers will then face the following anomaly: They are asked to refrain from putting resources to the *beneficial* use of supporting transplants, on the ground that ideal justice requires such rationing, while at the same time even greater resources are put to far more questionable uses elsewhere in the system. In nonbasic frameworks that are also nonideal, we get no reassurance that forgoing the chance to provide transplants to patients who need them will yield better uses of those resources either inside or outside the health care system. This anomaly thus undercuts the appeal to justice based on opportunity costs. Decision-makers may think their duty as providers to offer the patient the best care they can will count for more in their moral deliberations than the appeal to ideal justice. They may reason that it is better to deliver the benefit they can control than the potentially greater benefit whose realization depends on the workings of an unjust system. Thus, decision-makers in nonideal contexts and nonbasic frameworks may encounter moral considerations that conflict with opportunity-cost arguments and claims about ideal justice.

I would like to consider now a different obstacle facing such opportunity-cost arguments. This obstacle is largely the result of specific institutional features of the U.S. health care system. Consider the decisions that are made by hospital administrators deliberating whether to add a new transplant technology to their hospital. Imagine that in the context of this deliberation, someone objects that resources are scarce and that the opportunity costs of the transplant technology are highly problematic. Were the hospital to forgo adding transplant services, it could provide alternative services that would meet comparable medical needs for a larger group of patients. Suppose that the opportunity-cost argument is couched as a claim about the requirements of ideal justice. How would (how do) administrators respond to this argument?

One response that is often made is to deny the claim about resource scarcity. This is the suggestion that we need not really choose between the big-ticket item and other technologies or services that the hospital does or could provide. After all, resource allocation is not made within a fixed budget; no overall expenditure ceiling operates in the U.S. health care system. Even the hospital can add indeterminately many services if it can do so profitably within the reimbursement schemes that pay for its services. In such a context, the administrator can say: We need not forgo this beneficial service, even if it has high opportunity costs, because nothing is stopping others from adding the more effective or efficient alternative services or technologies. The administrator could in good conscience add that complaints about resource scarcity come from employers or legislators who are worried about profits or taxes and not about high-quality health care. The medical provider may even know that those who want to contain costs would prefer forgoing the big-ticket technology in order to spend the resources on socially less-worthwhile projects. This reply says not only that the scarcity is unnecessary, but also that the *real* opportunity costs for the big-ticket technology are not problematic. The resources could be spent on more effective services, but they will not be; instead they will be spent on projects with even more highly problematic opportunity costs.

The skepticism about resource scarcity has some merit. Other health care systems, for example in Sweden, spend significantly more than the 11 percent of the gross national product (GNP) that we in the United States spend on health care. Of course, some other systems, such as the British, also spend less, with generally comparable health care outcomes. Some claim that eliminating unnecessary services would free resources for all beneficial technologies we could really introduce. Others claim that we will soon, if we do not now, face decisions about which technologies to disseminate widely and which we must ration, for it is technology that is driving health care costs up at such an alarming rate. I cannot resolve this dispute about the level of actual scarcity here; what is in general clear, however, is that justice will require us to make decisions about which technologies and services it is more important to disseminate under conditions of moderate scarcity.

Two other points about scarcity should be noted. First, it is a matter of political reality that pressure exists to restrict health care expenditures and that this pressure imposes an actual scarcity. We might complain that in an ideally just world this pressure would not exist; but it does, and then we have to consider how we should expend our health care resources under such nonideal constraints. This means we must face the full force of the opportunity-cost argument, which is the second point. The big-ticket item may not be the most effective way to expend resources, and introducing it in a context of nonideal resource constraints may thus make things worse than they need be. That is the point of saying the opportunity costs are highly problematic. The point is that even if in an ideally just arrangement we would not have to forgo the less-effective technology, this does not forgive our failure to do so when we know the facts about actual scarcity.

The temptation of the decision-maker to reject assumptions about resource scarcity is understandable, especially in a system in which there is no centralized budgeting for health care. And the temptation does explain why some will try to avoid the force of the opportunity-cost argument. But the real force of the argument cannot be avoided in this way.

A more serious problem for the opportunity-cost argument arises as a result of other features of our health care institutions. Most of our health care decision-making is not regionally or nationally coordinated. Different providers often compete directly with each other, which gives them some different, merely agent-relative, rather than common, goals. Even where there is no direct competition, there is still no coordination and cooperation. When the providers pursue these goals—that is, when they successfully pursue these goals—they may still produce outcomes that are collectively worse for them. It is important to see how this problem arises.

Suppose that we agree that in an ideally just arrangement, the health care system would invest resources in services other than the big-ticket item it is considering. We agree that it would be better if no one introduced this technology. On the one hand, if we forgo introducing this item, some other providers may do so anyway. Then those providers would be seen as the technologically most advanced hospitals and medical centers. They would attract physicians who seek the glamour and profit involved in offering such services; they would attract patients. They would thus be in a superior competitive situation to us. So if other providers introduce the new technology, we are better off if we do too. On the other hand, if other providers refrain from introducing the technology while we add it, then we would enhance our competitive situation relative to them. Of course, each provider will reason this way. In the absence of political constraints that compel us to do otherwise, each will add the technology. But when we all introduce the big-ticket items, then the health care system clearly fails to work as well as we would like it to; moreover, we end up in a competitive situation that is no better than if we all had refrained from disseminating the inappropriate technologies.

It may seem that only bad motives could drive us to reason in this way, but this is not the case. Good motives can produce the same bad results. For example, we may be motivated to do the best we can for our patients; we may think that we have a special obligation to deliver all medically feasible benefits to our own patients. We may then reason that if we add the big-ticket item and others refrain from doing so, we can best achieve our goal of delivering medically feasible benefits to our patients. Not only will our patients benefit because other institutions are adding more cost-effective services, but out patients will in addition be able to get the benefits of the big-ticket technology. However, if others add the big-ticket item while we refrain from doing so, then we will not be an institution that is competitive with other institutions, and therefore we will not be able to deliver the best health care we can to our patients. We can thus best achieve our goal of being the deliverer of the best care we can only by adding the big-ticket technology. This may be true even if we agree from the start that patients would be better off in a just system that allocated resources differently.[7] Because we can reason in these ways, we seem compelled to ignore the opportunity-cost argument, even when it is based on considerations of justice.

Two important features of the U.S. health care system create this problem. We allow health care institutions to operate competitively instead of requiring them to act cooperatively and collectively. And we do not force each institution to pay the price for introducing technologies with highly problematic opportunity costs. (Indeed, research, development, and reimbursement are all heavily subsized by public funds.) Together, these features create a context in which appeals to opportunity costs on grounds of justice fail to obtain a grip on allocation decisions. These features of our institutions clearly have an impact at all levels at which macro allocation decisions are made, not just at the level of particular hospitals or HMOs. State and federal decision-makers can make no macro decisions that do not take these institutional arrangements into account—which is why some earlier attempts at the regulation of capital investment, through certificates of need, for example, had little real effect. My argument suggests that macro decisions at the federal and state levels will have to establish specific priorities for technology dissemination and will have to provide the regulative and legislative muscle needed to produce cooperative and not merely competitive decision-making.

Eliminating these features of our institutions will have to be an explicit priority for those who wish to make our system conform to acceptable ideals of just health care. In pointing out the institutional obstacles that stand in the way of making our system more just, I do not intend to build skepticism about the relevance of ideal theory to practical decisions. It is important to know, however, that even if people understand what would be just, institutional arrangements may make it impossible for them to make the appropriate decisions. Even when we know we cannot fully achieve the ideal, it is still important to know just what stands in our way. What stands in our way in this case is not sacred or immutable, but only institutions that we have constructed and can alter.

Notes

1. We should not accept the view that we are here paying the price for encountering an identified victim rather than a merely statistical victim. We can quite specifically identify the victims of forgoing disseminating alternative technologies as well.

2. See N. Daniels, *Just Health Care* (New York: Cambridge University Press, 1985).

3. See J. Rawls, *A Theory of Justice,* (Cambridge, MA: Harvard University Press, 1971), chapters 2 and 3.

4. This requires modifications of Rawls's equal opportunity principle, however. Cf. Daniels, *Just Health Care,* Chap. 3.

5. This account is developed in my *Am I My Parents' Keeper? An Essay on Justice Between the Young and the Old* (New York: Oxford University Press, 1988).

6. See Daniels, *Just Health Care,* Chap. 9, on which I base the next few paragraphs.

7. This case is analogous to the Parents' Dilemmas, which Derek Parfit discusses in *Reasons and Persons* (Oxford: Clarendon Press, 1984:96). Ours is a many-person Providers Dilemma. By our refraining from adding the big-ticket item, we can give your patients a greater benefit (the opportunity costs fund it); if we add the technology and you do not, our patients will be best off, and yours worst off (because you will not be competitive); if we add the technology and you do too, then our patients will be better off than they would be if we do not add it and thus fail to be competitive.

17

Allocating Scarce Medical Resources and the Availability of Organ Transplantation: Some Moral Presuppositions

H. Tristram Engelhardt, Jr.

The Problem

Some controversies have a staying power because they spring from unavoidable moral and conceptual puzzles. The debates concerning transplantation are a good example. To begin with, they are not a single controversy. Rather, they are examples of the scientific debates with heavy political and ethical overlays that characterize a large area of public-policy discussions.[1] The determination of whether or not heart or liver transplantation is an experimental or nonexperimental procedure for which it is reasonable and necessary to provide reimbursement is not simply a determination on the basis of facts regarding survival rates or the frequency with which the procedure is employed. Nor is it a purely moral issue.[2]

It is an issue similar to that raised regarding the amount of pollutants that ought to be considered safe in the work place. The question cannot be answered simply in terms of scientific data, unless one presumes that there will be a sudden inflection in the curve expressing the relationship of decreasing parts per billion of the pollutant and the incidence of disease or death, after which very low concentrations do not contribute at all to an excess incidence of disability or death. If one assumes that there is always some increase in death and disability due to the pollutant, one is not looking for an absolutely safe level but rather a level at which the costs in lives and health do not outbalance the costs in jobs and societal vexation that most more stringent criteria would involve. Such is not a purely factual judgment but requires a balancing of values. Determinations of whether a pollutant is safe at a particular level, of whether a procedure is reasonable and necessary, of whether a drug is safe, of whether heart and liver transplantations should be regarded as nonexperimental procedures

Paper presented at the Annual Meeting of the Massachusetts Medical Society, May 12, 1984, and published under the title "Shattuck Lecture—Allocating Scarce Medical Resources and Availability of Organ Transplantation," by H. Engelhardt, in the *New England Journal of Medicine* 311: 66–71, July 5, 1984. Copyright 1984, Massachusetts Medical Society. Reprinted by permission.

are not simply factual determinations. In the background of those determinations is a set of moral judgments regarding equity, decency, and fairness, cost-benefit trade-offs, individual rights, and the limits of state authority.

Since such debates are structured by the intertwining of scientific, ethical, and political issues, participants appeal to different sets of data and rules of interference, which leads to a number of opportunities for confusion. The questions that cluster around the issue of providing for the transplantation of organs have this distracting heterogeneity. There are a number of questions with heavy factual components, such as, "Is the provision of liver transplants an efficient use of health-care resources?" and "Will the cost of care in the absence of a transplant approximate the costs involved in the transplant?" To answer such questions, one will need to continue to acquire data concerning the long-term survival rates of those receiving transplants.[3-8] There are, as well, questions with major moral and political components, which give public-policy direction to the factual issues. "Does liver or heart transplantation offer a proper way of using our resources, given other available areas of investment?" "Is there moral authority to use state force to redistribute financial resources so as to provide transplantations for all who would benefit from the procedure?" "How ought one fairly to resolve controversies in this area when there is important moral disagreement?"

These serious questions have been engaged in a context marked by passion, pathos, and publicity. George Deukmejian, governor of California, ordered the state to pay for liver transplantation for Koren Crosland, and over $265,000 was raised through contributions from friends and strangers to support the liver transplantation of Amy Hardin of Cahokia, Illinois.[9] Charles and Marilyn Fiske's testimony to the Subcommittee on Investigations and Oversight of the House Committee on Science and Technology provided an example of how fortuitous publicity can lead to treatment[10]—in this case, to their daughter Jamie's receiving payment through Blue Cross of Massachusetts by agreement on October 1, 1982,[11] along with contingency authorization for coverage for liver-transplantation expenses through the Commonwealth of Massachusetts on October 29, 1982.[12] The proclamation by President Reagan of a National Organ Donation Awareness Week, which ran from April 22 through 28, further underscored the public nature of the issues raised.[13] In short, several serious and difficult moral and political dilemmas have been confronted under the spotlight of media coverage and political pressures.[14-17] What is needed is an examination of the moral and conceptual assumptions that shape the debate, so that one can have a sense of where reasonable answers can be sought.

Why Debates About Allocating Resources Go On and On

The debates concerning the allocation of resources to the provision of expensive, life-saving treatment such as transplantation have recurred repeatedly over the past two decades and show no promise of abating.[18-21] To understand why that is the case, one must recall the nature of the social and moral context within which such debates are carried on. Peaceable, secular, pluralist societies are by definition ones that renounce the use of force to impose a particular ideology or view of the good life, though they include numerous communities with particular, often divergent, views of the ways in which men and women should live and use their resources. Such peaceable, secular societies require at a minimum a commitment to the resolution of disputes in ways that are not fundamentally based on force.[22] There will thus be greater clarity regarding how peaceably to discuss the allocation of resources for transplantation than there will be regarding the importance of the allocation of resources itself.[23] The latter requires a more concrete view of what is important to pursue through the use of our resources than can be decisively established in general secular terms. As a consequence, it is clearer that the public has a right to determine particular expenditures of common resources than that any particular use of resources, as for the provision of transplantation, should be embraced.

This is a recurring situation in large-scale, secular, pluralist states. The state as such provides a relatively neutral bureaucracy that transcends the particular ideological and religious commitments of the communities it embraces, so that its state-funded health-care service (or its postal service) should not be a Catholic, Jewish, or even Judeo-Christian service. This ideal of a neutral bureaucracy is obviously never reached. However, the aspiration to this goal defines peaceable, secular, pluralist societies and distinguishes them from the political vision that we inherited from Aristotle and which has guided us and misguided us over the past two millennia. Aristotle took as his ethical and political ideal the city-state with no more than 100,000 citizens, who could then know each other, know well whom they should elect, and create a public consensus.[24,25] It is ironic that Aristotle fashioned this image as he participated in the fashioning of the first large-scale Greek state.

We do not approach the problems of the proper allocations of scarce resources within the context of a city-state, with a relatively clear consensus of the ways in which scarce resources ought to be used. Since the Reformation and the Renaissance, the hope for a common consensus has dwindled, and with good cause. In addition, the Enlightenment failed to provide a fully satisfactory secular surrogate. It failed to offer clearly convincing moral arguments that would have established a particular view of the good life and of the ways in which resources ought to be invested. One is left only with a general commitment to peaceable negotiation as the cardinal moral canon of large-scale peaceable, secular, pluralist states.[26]

As a result, understandings about the proper use of scarce resources tend to occur on two levels in such societies. They occur within particular religious bodies, political and ideological communities, and interest groups, including insurance groups. They take place as well within the more procedurally oriented vehicles and structures that hold particular communities within a state. The more one addresses issues such as the allocation of scarce resources in the context of a general secular, pluralist society, the more one will be pressed to create an answer in some procedurally fair fashion, rather than hope to discover a proper pattern for the distribution of resources to meet medical needs. However, our past has left us with the haunting and misguided hope that the answer can be discovered.

There are difficulties as well that stem from a tension within morality itself: a conflict between respecting freedom and pursuing the good. Morality as an alternative to force as the basis for the resolution of disputes focuses on the mutual respect of persons. This element of morality, which is autonomy-directed, can be summarized in the maxim, Do not do unto others what they would not have done unto themselves. In the context of secular pluralist ethics, this element has priority, in that it can more clearly be specified and justified. As a result, it sets limits to the moral authority of others to act and thus conflicts with that dimension of morality that focuses on beneficence, on achieving the good for others. This second element of morality may be summarized in the maxim, Do to others their good. The difficulty is that the achievement of the good will require the cooperation of others who may claim a right to be respected in their nonparticipation. It will require as well deciding what goods are to be achieved and how they are to be ranked. One might think here of the conflict between investing communal resources in liver and heart transplantations and providing adequate general medical care to the indigent and near indigent. The more one respects freedom, the more difficult it will be for a society to pursue a common view of the good. Members will protest that societal programs restrict their freedom of choice, either through restricting access to programs or through taxing away their disposable income.

The problem of determining whether and to what extent resources should be invested in transplantation is thus considerable. The debate must be carried on in a context in which the moral guidelines are more procedural than supplied with content. Moreover, the debate will be characterized by conflicting views of what is proper to do, as well as by difficulties in showing that there is state authority to force the participation of unwilling citizens. Within these vexing constraints societies approach the problem of allocating scarce medical resources and in particular of determining the amount of resources to be diverted to transplantation. This can be seen as a choice among possible societal insurance mechanisms. As with the difficulty of determining a safe level of pollutants, the answer with respect to the correct level of insurance will be as much created as discovered.

Insurance Against the Natural and Social Lotteries

Individuals are at a disadvantage or an advantage as a result of the outcomes of two major sets of forces that can be termed the natural and social lotteries.[27,28] By the natural lottery I mean those forces of nature that lead some persons to be healthy and others to be ill and disabled through no intention or design of their own or of others. Those who win the natural lottery do not need transplantations. They live long and healthy lives and die peacefully. By the social lottery I mean the various interventions, compacts, and activities of persons that, with luck, lead to making some rich and others poor. The natural lottery surely influences the social lottery. However, the natural lottery need not conclusively determine one's social and economic power, prestige, and advantage. Thus, those who lose at the natural lottery and who are in need of heart and liver transplantation may still have won at the social lottery by having either inherited or earned sufficient funds to pay for a transplantation. Or they may have such a social advantage because their case receives sufficient publicity so that others contribute to help shoulder the costs of care.

An interest in social insurance mechanisms directed against losses at the natural and social lotteries is usually understood as an element of beneficence-directed justice. The goal is to provide the amount of coverage that is due to all persons. The problem in such societal insurance programs is to determine what coverage is due. Insofar as societies provide all citizens with a minimal protection against losses at the natural and the social lotteries, they give a concrete understanding of what is due through public funds. At issue here is whether coverage must include transplantation for those who cannot pay.

However, there are moral as well as financial limits to a society's protection of its members against such losses. First and foremost, those limits derive from the duty to respect individual choices and to recognize the limits of plausible state authority in a secular, pluralist society. If claims by society to the ownership of the resources and services of persons have limits, then there will always be private property that individuals will have at their disposal to trade for the services of others, which will create a second tier of health care for the affluent. Which is to say, the more it appears reasonable that property is owned neither totally societally nor only privately, and insofar as one recognizes limits on society's right to constrain its members, two tiers of health-care services will by right exist: those provided as a part of the minimal social guarantee to all and those provided in addition through the funds of those with an advantage in the social lottery who are interested in investing those resources in health care.

In providing a particular set of protections against losses at the social and natural lotteries, societies draw one of the most important societal distinctions— namely, between outcomes that will be socially recognized as unfortunate and unfair and those that will not be socially recognized as unfair, no matter how unfortunate they may be. The Department of Health and Human Services, for instance, in not recognizing heart transplantation as a nonexperimental procedure, removed the provision of such treatment from the social insurance policy. The plight of persons without private funds for heart transplantation, should they need heart transplantation, would be recognized as unfortunate but not unfair.[29-31] Similarly, proposals to recognize liver transplantation for children and adults as nonexperimental are proposals to alter the socially recognized boundary between losses at the natural and social lotteries that will be understood to be unfortunate and unfair and those that will simply be lamented as unfortunate but not seen as entitling the suffering person to a claim against societal resources.[32]

The need to draw this painful line between unfortunate and unfair outcomes exists in great measure because the concerns for beneficence do not exhaust ethics. Ethics is concerned as well with respecting the freedom of individuals. Rendering to each his or her due also involves allowing individuals the freedom to determine the use of their private energies and resources. In addition, since secular pluralist arguments for the authority of peaceable states most clearly establish those societies as means for individuals peaceably to negotiate the disposition of their communally owned resources, difficulties may arise in the allocation of scarce resources to health care in general and to transplantation in particular. Societies may decide to allocate the communal resources that would have been available for liver and heart transplantation to national defense or the building of art museums and the expansion of the national park system. The general moral requirement to respect individual choice and procedurally fair societal decisions will mean that there will be a general secular, moral right for individuals to dispose of private resources, and for societies to dispose of communal resources, in ways that will be wrong from a number of moral perspectives. As a result, the line between outcomes that will count as unfortunate and those that will count as unfair will often be at variance with the moral beliefs and aspirations of particular ideological and moral communities encompassed by any large-scale secular society.

Just as one must create a standard of safety for pollutants in the work place by negotiations between management and labor and through discussions in public forums one will also need to create a particular policy for social insurance to cover losses at the natural and social lotteries. This will mean that one will not be able to discover that any particular investment in providing health care for those who cannot pay is morally obligatory. One will not be able to show that societies such as that of the United Kingdom, which do not provide America's level of access to renal dialysis for end-stage renal disease, have made a moral mistake.[33,34] Moral criticism will succeed best in examining the openness of such decisions to public discussion and control.

It is difficulties such as these that led the President's Commission for the Study of Ethical Problems in Medicine and Biomedical and Behavioral Research to construe equity in health care neither as equality in health care nor as access to whatever would benefit patients or meet their needs. The goal of equality in health care runs aground on both conceptual and moral difficulties. There is the difficulty of understanding whether equality would embrace equal amounts of health care or equal amounts of funds for health care. Since individual health needs differ widely, such interpretations of equality are fruitless. Attempting to understand equality as providing health care only from a predetermined list of services to which all would have access conflicts with the personal liberty to use private resources in the acquisition of additional care not on the list. Construing equity as providing all with any health care that would benefit them would threaten inordinately to divert resources to health care. It would conflict as well with choices to invest resources in alternative areas. Substituting "need" for "benefit" leads to similar difficulties unless one can discover, among other things, a notion of need that would not include the need to have one's life extended, albeit at considerable cost.

The commission, as a result, construed equity in health care as the provision of an "adequate level of health care." The commission defined adequate care as "enough care to achieve suffficient welfare, opportunity, information, and evidence of interpersonal concern to facilitate a reasonably full and satisfying life."[35] However, this definition runs aground on the case of children needing liver transplants and other such expensive health-care interventions required to secure any chance of achieving "a reasonably full and satisfying life." There is a tension in the commission's report between an acknowledgment that a great proportion of one's meaning of "adequate health care" must be created and a view that the lineaments of that meaning can be discovered. Thus, the commission states that "[i]n a democracy, the appropriate values to be assigned to the consequences of policies must ultimately be determined by people expressing their values through social and political processes as well as in the marketplace."[36] On the other hand, the commission states that "adequacy does require that everyone receive care that meets standards of sound medical practice."[37] The latter statement may suggest that one could discover what would constitute sound medical practice. In addition, an appeal to a notion of "excessive burdens" will not straightforwardly determine the amount of care due to individuals, since a notion of "excessiveness" requires choosing a particular hierarchy of costs and benefits.[38] Neither will an appeal to excessive burdens determine the amount of the tax burden that others should bear,[39] since there will be morally determined upper limits to taxation set by that element of property that is not communal. People, insofar as they have private property in that sense, have the secular moral right, no matter how unfeeling and uncharitable such actions may appear to others, not to aid those with excessive burdens, even if the financial burdens of those who could be taxed would not be excessive.

Rather, it would appear, following other suggestions from the commission, that "adequate care" will need to be defined by considering, among other things, professional judgments of physicians, average current use, lists of services that health-maintenance organizations and others take to be a part of decent care, as well as more general perceptions of fairness.[40] Such factors influence what is accepted generally in a society as a decent minimal or adequate level of health care. As reports considering the effects of introducing expensive new technology suggest, there is a danger that treatments may be accepted as part of "sound medical practice" before the full financial and social consequences of that acceptance are clearly understood. Much of the caution that has surrounded the development of liver and heart transplantation has been engendered by the experience with renal dialysis, which was introduced with overly optimistic judgments regarding the future costs that would be involved.

Even if, as I have argued, the concrete character of "rights to health care" is more created as an element of societal insurance programs than discovered and if the creation is properly the result of the free choice of citizens, professional and scientific bodies will need to aid in the assessment of the likely balance of costs and benefits to be embraced with the acceptance of any new form of treatment as standard treatment, such as heart and liver transplantation. A premature acceptance may lead to cost pressures on services that people will see under mature consideration to be more important. At that point it may be very difficult to withdraw the label of "standard treatment" from a technologic approach that subsequent experience shows to be too costly, given competing opportunities for the investment of resources. On the other hand, new technologic developments may offer benefits worth the cost they will entail, such as the replacement by computerized tomography of pneumoencephalography. But in any event, there is not reason to suppose that there is something intrinsically wrong with spending more than 10.5 per cent of the gross national product on health care.

Is Transplantation Special?

All investments in expensive life-saving treatment raise a question of prudence: Could the funds have been better applied elsewhere? Will the investment in expensive life-saving treatment secure an equal if not greater decrease in morbidity and mortality than an investment in improving the health care of the millions who lack health-care insurance or have only marginal coverage? If the same funds were invested in prenatal health care or the treatment of hypertension, would they secure a greater extension of life and diminution of morbidity for more people? When planning for the rational use of communal funds, it is sensible to seek to maximize access and contribution to the greatest number of people as a reasonable test of what it means to use communal resources for the common good. However, not everything done out of the common purse need be cost effective. It is unclear how one could determine the cost effectiveness of symphony orchestras or art museums. Societies have a proclivity to save the lives of identifiable individuals while failing to come to the aid of unidentified, statistical lives that could have been saved with the same or fewer resources. Any decision to provide expensive life-saving treatment out of communal funds must at least frankly acknowledge when it is not a cost-effective choice but instead a choice made because of special sympathies for those who are suffering or because of special fears that are engendered by particular diseases.

The moral framework of secular, pluralist societies in which rights to health care are more created than discovered will allow such choices as morally acceptable, even if they are less than prudent uses of resources. It will also be morally acceptable for a society, if it pursues expensive life-saving treatment, to exclude persons who through their own choices increase the cost of care. One might think here of the question whether active alcoholics should be provided with liver transplants. There is no invidious discrimination against persons in setting a limit to coverage or in precluding coverage if the costs are increased through free choice. However, societies may decide to provide care even when the costs are incurred by free decision.

Though none of the foregoing is unique to transplantation, the issue of transplantation has the peculiarity of involving the problem not only of the allocation of monetary resources and of services but of that of organs as well. In a criticism of John Rawls' *Theory of Justice*, which theory attempts to provide a justification for a patterned distribution of resources that would redound to the benefit of the least-well-off class, Robert Nozick tests his readers' intuitions by asking whether societal rights to distribute resources would include the right to distribute organs as well.[41] He probably chose this as a test case because our bodies offer primordial examples of private property. The example is also forceful, given the traditional Western reluctance, often expressed in religious regulations, to use corpses for dissection. There is a cultural reluctance to consider parts of the body as objects for the use of persons. No less a figure than Immanuel Kant argued for a position that would appear to preclude the sale or gift of a body part to another.[42] This view of Kant's, one should note, is very close to the traditional Roman Catholic notion that one has a duty to God regarding one's self not to alter one's body except to preserve health.[43]

The concern to have a sufficient supply of organs for transplantation has expressed itself in recent political proposals and counterproposals regarding the rights of individuals to sell their organs, the provision of federal funds for the support of organ procurement, the study of the medical and legal issues that procurement may raise, and even the taking of organs from cadavers by society with the presumption of consent unless individuals have indicated the contrary.[44-49] It will be easier to show that persons have a right to determine what ought to be done with their bodies, even to the point of making donor consent decisive independently of the wishes of the family, than to show that society may presume consent. A clarification of policy, to make donor decisions definitive, would be in accord with the original intentions of the Uniform Act of Donation of Organs and would ease access to needed organs. It would not impose on people the burden of having to announce to others that they do not want their organs used for transplantation. The more one presumes that organs are not societal property, the more difficult it is to justify shifting the burden to individuals to show that they do not want their organs used. If sufficient numbers of organs are not available, it will be unfortunate, but from the point of view of general secular morality, not unfair. Free individuals will have valued other goals (e.g., having an intact body for burial) more highly than the support of transplantation. One will have encountered again one of the recurring limitations on establishing and effecting a general consensus regarding the ways in which society ought to respond to the unfortunate deliverances of nature.

Living with the Unfortunate, Which Is Not Unfair

Proposals for the general support of transplantation are thus restricted by various elements of the human condition. There is not simply a limitation due to finite resources, making it impossible to do all that is conceivably possible for all who might marginally benefit. There are restrictions as well that are due to the free decisions of both individuals and societies. Individuals will often decide in ways unsympathetic to transplantation programs that would involve the use of their private resources, including their organs. Insofar as one takes seriously respect for persons, one must live with the restrictions that result from numerous free choices. One may endeavor to educate, entice, and persuade people to participate. However, free societies are characterized by the commitment to live with the tragedies that result from the decisions of free individuals not to participate in the beneficent endeavors of others. There are then also the restrictions due to the inability to give a plausible account of state authority that would allow the imposition of a concrete view of the good life. Secular, pluralist societies are more neutral moral frameworks for negotiation and creation of ways to use their common resources than modes for discovering the proper purpose for those resources. If societies freely decide to give a low priority to transplantation and invest instead in generally improving health care for the indigent in the hope of doing greater good, there will be an important sense in which they have acted within their right, even if from particular moral perspectives that may seem wrongheaded.

These reflections on the human condition suggest that we will need in the future to learn to live with the fact that some may receive expensive life-saving treatment while others do not, because some have the luck of access to the media, the attention of a political leader, or sufficient funds to purchase care in their own right. The differences in need, both medical and financial, must be recognized as unfortunate. They are properly the objects of charitable response. However, it must be understood that though unfortunate circumstances are always grounds for praiseworthy charity, they do not always provide grounds, by that fact, for redrawing the line between the circumstances we will count as unfortunate but not unfair and those we will count as unfortunate and unfair. To live with circumstances we must acknowledge as unfortunate but not unfair is the destiny of finite men and women who have neither the financial nor moral resources of gods and goddesses. We must also recognize the role of these important conceptual and moral issues in the fashioning of what will count as reasonable and necessary care, safe and efficacious procedures, non-experimental treatment, or standard medical care. Though we are not gods and goddesses, we do participate in creating the fabric of these "facts."

Notes

1. Engelhardt HT Jr, Caplan AL, eds. Scientific controversies. London: Cambridge University Press. (in press). [published, 1985].

2. Newman H. Medicare program: solicitation of hospitals and medical centers to participate in a study of heart transplants. Fed Regist. January 22, 1981; 46:7072-5.

3. Copeland JG, Mammana RB, Fuller JK, Campbell DW, McAleer MJ, Sailer JA. Heart transplantation: four years' experience with conventional immunosuppression. JAMA 1984; 251:1563-6.

4. DeVries WC, Anderson JL, Joyce LD, et al. Clinical use of the total artificial heart, N Engl J Med 1984; 310:273-8.

5. Dummer JS, Hardy A, Poorsattar A, Ho M. Early infections in kidney, heart, and liver transplant recipients on cyclosporine. Transplantation 1983; 36:259-67.

6. Shunzaburo I, Byers WS, Starzl TE. Current status of hepatic transplantation. Semin Liver Dis 1983; 3:173-80.

7. Starzl TE, Iwatsuki S, Van Thiel DH, et al. Evolution of liver transplantation. Hepatology 1982; 2:614–36.

8. Van Thiel DH, Schade RR, Starzl TE, et al. Liver transplantation in adults. Hepatology 1982; 2:637–40.

9. Wessel D. Transplants increase, and so do disputes over who pays bills. Wall Street Journal. April 12, 1984; 73:1, 12.

10. Spirito TH. Letter of October 29, 1982. In: Organ transplants: hearings before the subcommittee on investigations and oversight. 98th Congress, 1st Session. Washington, D.C.: Government Printing Office, 1983:226.

11. Litos PA. Letter of October 1, 1982. In: Organ transplants: hearings before the subcommittee on investigations and oversight. 98th Congress, 1st Session. Washington, D.C.: Government Printing Office, 1983:227.

12. Fiske C, Fiske M. Statements of Charles and Marilyn Fiske, and daughter Jamie, liver transplant patient. In: Organ transplants: hearings before the subcommittee on investigations and oversight. 98th Congress, 1st Session. Washington, D.C.: Government Printing Office, 1983:212–8.

13. Gunby P. Organ transplant improvements, demands draw increasing attention. JAMA 1984; 251:1521–3, 1527.

14. Idem. Media-abetted liver transplants raise questions of 'equity and decency.' JAMA 1983; 249:1973–4, 1980–2.

15. Iglehart JK. Transplantation: the problem of limited resources. N Engl J Med 1983; 309:123–8.

16. Idem. The politics of transplantation. N Engl J Med 1984; 310:864–8.

17. Strauss MJ. The political history of the artificial heart. N Engl J Med 1984; 310:332–6.

18. Ad Hoc Task Force on Cardiac Replacement. Cardiac replacement: medical ethical psychological and economic implications. Washington, D.C.: Government Printing Office, 1969.

19. Artificial Heart Assessment Panel. The totally implantable artificial heart. Bethesda, Md.: National Institutes of Health, 1973. (DHEW publication no. (NIH)74-191).

20. Leaf A. The MGH trustees say no to heart transplants. N Engl J Med 1980; 302:1087–8.

21. Barnes BA, Dunphy ME, Koff RS, et al. Final report of the task force on liver transplantation in Massachusetts. Boston: Blue Cross and Blue Shield, 1983.

22. Engelhardt HT Jr. Bioethics in pluralist societies. Perspect Biol Med 1982; 26:64–78.

23. Idem. The physician-patient relationship in a secular, pluralist society. In: Shelp EE, ed. The clinical encounter. Dordrecht, Holland: D Reidel, 1983:253–66.

24. Aristotle. Nicomachaean ethics. ix 10.1170b.

25. Idem. Politics. vii 4.1326b.

26. Engelhardt HT. Bioethics: an introduction and critique. New York: Oxford University Press. (in press). [published, 1986, as The Foundations of Bioethics].

27. Rawls J. A theory of justice. Cambridge, Mass.: Belknap Press, 1971.

28. Nozick R. Anarchy, state, and utopia. New York: Basic Books, 1974.

29. Newman H. Exclusion of heart transplantation procedures from Medicare coverage. Fed Regist 1980; 45:52296.

30. Knox RA. Heart transplants: to pay or not to pay. Science 1980; 209:570–2,574–5.

31. Evans RW, Anderson A, Perry B. The national heart transplantation study: an overview. Heart Transplant 1982; 2(1):85–7.

32. Consensus Conference. Liver transplantation. JAMA 1983; 250:2961–4.

33. Who shall be dialysed? Lancet 1984; 1:717.

34. Aaron HJ, Schwartz WB. The painful prescription: rationing hospital care. Washington, D.C.: Brookings Institution, 1984.

35. President's Commission for the Study of Ethical Problems in Medicine and Biomedical and Behavioral Research. Securing access to health care. Vol. 1. Washington, D.C.: Government Printing Office, 1983:20.

36. President's Commission, p. 37.
37. President's Commission, p. 37.
38. President's Commission, p. 42–3.
39. President's Commission, p. 43–6.
40. President's Commission, p. 37–47.
41. Nozick R. Anarchy, state, and utopia. New York: Basic Books, 1974:206–7.
42. Kant I. Kants werke: akademie textausgabe. Vol. 6. Berlin: Walter de Gruyter, 1968:423.
43. Kelly G. Medico-moral problems. St. Louis: Catholic Hospital Association. 1958:245–52.
44. Caplan AL. Organ transplants: the costs of success. Hastings Cent Rep 1983; 13(6):23–32.
45. Kolata G. Organ shortage clouds new transplant era. Science 1983; 221:32–3.
46. Overcast TD, Evans RW, Bowen LE, Hoe MM, Livak CL. Problems in the identification of potential organ donors: misconceptions and fallacies associated with donor cards. JAMA 1984; 251:1559–62.
47. Prottas JM. Encouraging altruism: public attitudes and the marketing of organ donation. Milbank Mem Fund Q 1983; 61:278–306.
48. U.S. Congress, House. To amend the public health service act to authorize financial assistance for organ procurement organizations, and for other purposes. By: Gore A. 98th Congress, 1st Session. H. Rept. 4080. 1983.
49. U.S. Congress, Senate. To provide for the establishment of a task force on organ procurement and transplantation and an organ procurement and transplantation registry, and for other purposes. By: Hatch O. 98th Congress, 1st Session. S. Rept. 2048. 1983.

PART FOUR

Decisions at the Experimental Stage: The Case of the Artificial Heart

18

Introduction

Deborah Mathieu

The chapters in this part address major ethical, legal, and public policy problems of research using human subjects. Although the device on which they focus is the artificial heart, the issues they discuss are applicable to most experimental situations with human subjects.

The precursor of the artificial heart was the heart-lung machine, which offered a boon to medicine because it permitted cardiac surgery. Although it is still utilized today, the heart-lung machine suffers from the same serious shortcomings that existed when it was first tested on human patients in the early 1950s: It is unwieldy and it destroys blood cells, so it cannot be used on a long-term basis. Hence it was imperative that other artificial devices be developed to assist patient recovery. Today, there are two types of artificial heart available: assist devices and total artificial hearts. The assist devices (such as the intra-aortic balloon pump and the left ventricular assist) were designed primarily to serve as temporary aids to recovery.[1] In contrast, the total artificial hearts (such as the Jarvik-7 and the Penn State heart) were designed to be implanted as permanent replacements for the human heart. Some of these devices—the left ventricular assist, for example, and the Jarvik-7—can be used for both purposes.

The Total Artificial Heart as a Permanent Implant

From the beginning, the total artificial heart had been conceived of as a *permanent* replacement for a failed human heart, and attention was first focused on it as a completely implantable device. In 1964, the National Heart Institute (NHI) of the National Institutes of Health (NIH) launched a program to encourage research on the completely implantable total artificial heart, anticipating that a device would be ready by early 1970. The most obvious choice for the power source was a battery, but that was rejected because of anticipated problems of battery replacement. Biologic fuel cells also were considered and rejected when it became clear that no one had the technology to develop them. Hence the decision was made to pursue atomic power, and the controversy over the totally implantable nuclear-powered artificial heart was born.

Most of the concerns voiced about that heart are heard again with regard to the artificial hearts used today: the tremendous cost of the program, the questionable quality of life of the recipient, the relatively small number of beneficiaries, the priority of other forms of health care, the difficulty of getting the truly informed consent of the recipient. Some of the concerns, though, focused on the radioactive material the nuclear-powered heart required, thus were unique to that device. Environmental risks associated with nuclear technology were one cause of anxiety, for instance, as were the possible negative effects of the radioactive material on individuals other than the owner of the heart.[2] It was estimated, for instance, that radiation emitting from the artificial heart would cause between 3,000 to 15,000 cancer deaths annually.[3] It became clear before too long that the problems with the nuclear-powered artificial heart outweighed its potential benefits, so the NHI abolished the program and turned its attention and its funds to supporting the development of assist devices—in particular the left ventricular assist device—which could be used as temporary replacements for the human heart.

The Jarvik-7

The artificial heart that has received the most public attention, however, was not developed with the support of the NHI. The Jarvik-7—a plastic and titanium device attached by hoses to a pneumatically powered drive unit—was designed by researchers at the University of Utah, who had found funding sources outside the federal government. The artificial device is now controlled by Symbion, Inc., a for-profit corporation.

The researchers at Utah tested the Jarvik-7 on sheep and calves, and the results were decidedly mixed. It kept several of the animals alive for five months or longer, but never for more than 268 days, and the causes of death were varied: infection, malfunctioning valves and/or connections between parts, respiratory failure, acidosis, hypotension, and pneumothorax.[4] Despite the obvious limitations of the artificial heart, the Utah team decided to seek permission from the Food and Drug Administration (FDA) to test it in human patients. Some commentators have seen this decision as a result, at least in part, of the "ritualized optimism," of the researchers, "in which hopes for success rest on more than scientifically based assumptions."[5] These other factors, the commentators suggest, included: the belief that successful implants of the device into human subjects would encourage the federal government to continue its support of research on the artificial heart; the "conviction and drive" of a member of the team, Dr. William DeVries; and the hope that complications would not be as devastating to the human subjects as they were to the animals.

That the Jarvik-7 was utilized according to FDA rules and not NIH rules is significant, as the latter are considerably more demanding than the former. The NIH has very strict rules regarding the testing of experimental artificial hearts on human subjects, and researchers sponsored by the NIH must demonstrate that the device passes three important tests: (1) it is reliable; (2) it offers the patient more benefit than harm; and (3) it offers as much benefit as other available treatment modalities.[6] But because the Jarvik-7 was not developed under the aegis of the NIH, it was not required to pass these difficult tests. It did, however, fall under the jurisdiction of the Food and Drug Administration and thus had to conform to those rules. In keeping with the FDA's regulations, researchers did not have to demonstrate that the device would benefit the human subject, for instance, but rather that the device would generate new knowledge whose import was great enough to outweigh the risks to the human subject.[7]

The Food and Drug Administration accepted the arguments of the Utah researchers and the Utah Institutional Review Board that the Jarvik-7 was ready to be used on humans, at least on a carefully controlled basis, and in September 1982 it gave permission for the artificial device to be tested as a permanent replacement for a human heart. On December 2, 1982, a Jarvik-7 was implanted into sixty-one-year-old Barney Clark.

After 112 days on the artificial heart—and a series of complications including seizures, heart failure, kidney failure, and infection—Dr. Clark died of circulatory collapse. The next patient to receive the Jarvik-7 as a permanent implant was fifty-two-year-old William Schroeder, who survived for 620 days with the device and who also suffered serious side effects, including strokes, infections, and excessive bleeding.

Much of the other experience with the Jarvik-7 as a permanent replacement for the human heart has been equally unsuccessful. Most patients have suffered devastating complications, many of which can be traced to the artificial device itself. An evaluation has concluded that "the major complications, which in various ways seem to be at least partly device-related, include: 1) a mysterious initial severe suppression of the immune system, which increases susceptibility to 2) infections; 3) hemolytic anemia; 4) renal insufficiency and in one patient renal failure due to acute tubular necrosis; 5) respiratory insufficiency; 6) bleeding; and 7) blood clotting."[8] Because of these negative side effects, a significant number of critics have contended that the artificial heart is not ready for implantation into human subjects as a permanent replacement for the human heart. Indeed, Dr. DeVries has experienced considerable difficulty finding subjects for his experiments with the Jarvik-7 because physicians have become reluctant to recommend that their patients have artificial hearts permanently implanted.[9]

Criticisms that the artificial heart was prematurely used on human subjects have been taken seriously by the federal government, and in December 1985 the FDA decided to reconsider its approval of the Jarvik-7. Many people expected the FDA to call a moratorium on the use of the artificial heart as a permanent replacement for the human heart and were surprised when the FDA decided instead to monitor the situation more closely. In principle, the artificial heart may still be used as a permanent implant on an experimental basis, but in practice the FDA itself will decide if, when, and where it may be done.

The situation raises three important questions with regard to use of the artificial heart in human subjects. The first pertains to the original decision to allow the device to be tested on human patients: Given the knowledge of the limitations of the device prior to its use on humans, was it justifiable to implant it into human patients? The second focuses on the continuation of the use of the artificial device: Given the negative experiences with the first two implant patients, were the subsequent implantations of the artificial device justifiable? The third question concerns the wisdom of choosing to pursue the development of this extremely costly technology, which is expected to benefit only a relatively few patients.

The Artificial Heart as a Bridge
to Transplant

So far, we have addressed issues regarding the use of the artificial heart as a permanent replacement for a human heart. But there is another use for it and that is as a temporary measure, a "bridge to transplant" of a human donor heart. Indeed, because of the difficulties experienced by patients who have received the Jarvik-7, many people contend that (at least in its present forms) it is not yet ready to be used as a permanent replacement but instead is best utilized as a temporary bridge to transplant.

Although the implantation of a Jarvik-7 into Barney Clark in 1982 was the first time that an artificial heart had been implanted into a human being as a *permanent* device, it had been used before as a *temporary* device. In 1969 and again in 1981, Dr. Denton Cooley implanted a plastic heart into a patient—using a different type of artificial device each time—as a means of keeping the patient alive until a suitable donor heart could be located.[10] The artificial heart has been used in this way on several occasions since then. Perhaps the clearest success story is that of Michael Drummond, who survived for nine days in 1985 on the Jarvik-7 until he received a successful heart transplant, and whose life today seems to be fairly comfortable.

But use of the artificial heart as a temporary device is problematic because it creates difficulties for the already chaotic allocation of human donor hearts. As George Annas and Dale Jamieson point out in chapters 20 and 21 respectively, this use of the artificial heart will not save any additional lives because the number of heart transplants that can be performed is limited by the number of human donor organs available. All the artificial heart does is change the *identity* of the lives saved. A patient with a temporary artificial heart is usually put at the front of the line for the next available donor heart. He or she is given priority over other patients, even though these patients may have been waiting longer, they may be in better physical condition to benefit from the transplant, and even though they may die because no other heart is available.

The use of the artificial heart as a temporary measure also raises a different sort of problem: There is no certainty that the "temporary" device will not become permanent. If a suitable donor heart cannot be found or if the patient suffers severe strokes while attached to the artificial heart, the device will not be removed. Michael Drummond was very lucky—he could have found himself permanently attached to a vibrating, unwieldy, dangerous machine.

Another failing is that so far no consistent and reasonable rules for when to stop have been followed. Bernadette Chayrez, for example, remained tethered to her "temporary" mini-Jarvik-7 for 240 consecutive days in 1986, undergoing in the meantime a series of operations to counteract multiple system failure. At one point, she was on dialysis and a respirator, her ruptured spleen was removed, she suffered from massive internal bleeding, and she contracted pneumonia. Although she eventually recovered from most of these life-threatening conditions, she still suffered from the awesome combination of a hyperactive immune system (which precluded transplantation of a human donor heart) and serious viral infections (which precluded her remaining on the artificial device).

Responsible Decision-Making

Although each of the chapters in this section focuses on a different type of dilemma posed by the use of the artificial heart, all of them ultimately address one crucial background issue: the *process* of decision-making. One basic problem with the current situation is that no one seems to be in control. As we shall see from the following chapters, it is not inaccurate to describe the current artificial heart program—if we can call it a program—as proceeding in a scientifically unsound and ethically inappropriate fashion. In a sense, artificial heart implants have been largely uncontrolled experiments.

This has been the case from the beginning. For instance, neither of the artificial hearts implanted by Dr. Cooley had been approved by the FDA or the NIH for use in human subjects. There were many critics of Dr. Cooley's actions who argued that his use of these experimental devices on human subjects was premature and unwarranted. The issue of using untested and unapproved devices on human beings was raised again in 1985, when Dr. Jack Copeland implanted the "Phoenix heart" into Thomas Creighton in an extraordinary but ultimately futile attempt to keep him alive.

One objection to the use of the Phoenix heart in the Creighton case was that neither the surgeon who performed the operation nor the artificial device had received approval from the Food and Drug Administration. In fact, the Phoenix heart was still in its early experimental stages and was designed to be transplanted into a calf, not a human. Much to the surprise of many people, though, the FDA itself softened the criticism of the unauthorized use of an experimental device by an unauthorized physician because, the FDA stated, the artificial heart had been used in "a very unique emergency situation." Hence no sanctions were taken against the surgeons involved or the medical facility in which the implantation took place.

But important ethical, legal, and public policy questions regarding the legitimacy of circumventing federal regulations in these types of case remains, which Leslie Francis examines in Chapter 19. She first looks at three examples of lawbreaking by researchers—beginning research without Institutional Review Board (IRB) approval, ignoring IRB guidelines during experimentation, and avoiding the U.S. government's strict regulations on research by performing it abroad—and then compares them with cases of lawbreaking often considered to be justifiable, such as certain acts of civil disobedience. They are, she concludes, not analogous. Instead, she argues, if scientific lawbreaking is ever justifiable, it is only when the act is similar to legally acceptable means of proceeding in emergency situations.

Francis then turns her attention to the Creighton case, and focuses on the response by the FDA to the unapproved use of an unapproved device. The federal government recognizes that there may be life-threatening emergencies in which use of an experimental medical is warranted, even without prior approval, and the FDA allows a loosening of its rules under certain circumstances. The question Francis examines is whether the implantation of the Phoenix heart into Thomas Creighton was a legitimate exception to the FDA regulations governing experimentation with human subjects. She also addresses the impact of the FDA's updated guidelines for the emergency use of unapproved medical devices (published in October 1985) and its new regulations governing use of experimental drugs (announced in May 1987) on emergency situations.

George Annas addresses the Thomas Creighton case as well, but for a different reason. It appears that the implantation of an artificial heart was not one of the treatment options discussed with Mr. Creighton prior to his operation, and that the decision to implant the device was made only after the donor heart had failed, when Mr. Creighton was no longer competent to accept or refuse the offer. Annas is concerned with the fact that Mr. Creighton had not consented to receive an artificial heart and he had not even known that it was a possibility.

This is a very important criticism indeed, for it is a basic tenet of good medical practice that a competent patient must give his or her informed,·voluntary consent to all medical procedures. This holds especially true for risky, experimental procedures, such as implantation of an artificial heart. Indeed, an important element of all codes of ethics governing research with human subjects—including the Nuremberg Code, the World Medical Association's Declaration of Helsinki, the American Medical Association Ethical Guidelines for Clinical Investigation, and the regulations of the Department of Health and Human Services—is the requirement that the researcher obtain the voluntary, informed consent of the competent subject before proceeding with the experiment. This includes informing the potential subject of a variety of aspects of the study: its aims, methods, anticipated benefits, potential hazards, and discomforts to the subject.

The objection that Mr. Creighton had not consented to receive the artificial heart was perhaps mitigated somewhat by the fact that his parents gave their approval for the implantation while their son was incompetent to do so. But it is still important to note that Mr. Creighton *himself*, who was not a minor, should have been the one to decide whether to resort to that extreme and experimental method of sustaining life. One wonders what Mr. Creighton was led to expect from the original heart transplant—whether he had realized that the transplant might not work. And one wonders what steps he had agreed to should something go wrong. Unfortunately Mr. Creighton never regained consciousness, but one also has to wonder how he would have reacted had he awakened to find himself attached to an artificial heart and how he would have felt had the device become a permanent part of him—which was a good possibility, given the propensity of patients with artificial hearts to suffer severe strokes and infections, which often preclude transplantation of another heart.

Hence the complaint is not simply that Mr. Creighton was not able to give his informed consent to the implantation of the artificial heart but also that he had not been given the opportunity to *refuse* the procedure—and thus that he had to live with the imposing consequences of someone else's decision. Annas's point is that it is not always the case that death should be avoided at all costs and it is not always the case that a patient would choose any extension of life over death. It is, after all, the patient's choice, and he or she should be given the option. Speaking of heart transplantations more than fifteen years ago, Paul Ramsey raised a similar concern:

> Unless the hopes of the surgeon-investigator and the desperation of patients are to conspire to push them onward, a renewal of the notion that death may be electable, fostered and held in common by surgeons and patients alike, would seem to be the only way to sustain a covenant of free men between them. This requires a frank discussion of the possible acceptability of death over the chances of life, or the kind of life the surgeons can realistically promise. Unless this alternative procedure is fully explored and weighed, then the desperation of patients and the interest of surgeons rightly have in performing remedies, however radical, and in pushing back the frontiers of transplantation therapy must always prove overriding—certainly not against the wills of their patients but still without their choices being fully free and fully human. This, I confess, should require a sea-change in the attitude toward death in our culture, and the adoption by physicians of a rather more priestly and therefore more human relation to their patients, and of a less triumphalist attitude toward death.[11]

As Annas's chapter clearly demonstrates, this "sea-change" has not yet occurred.

All of the chapters in this section argue that there should be more control over the decision-making process—at every stage—and that the locus of decision-making power should be changed. In Chapter 21 Dale Jamieson addresses another level of decision-making and in doing so provides additional support for this conclusion. Jamieson's main point is that we need a responsible and rational institutional mechanism for the reevaluation of large-scale social investments in experimental technologies.

In tracing the history of the total artificial heart, Jamieson demonstrates that its development was led largely by a scientific elite that consistently ignored the important ethical and social issues at stake. Thus factors that *should* have played a pivotal role in the decision whether to proceed with the development of this costly technology were overlooked. It is not surprising that a scientific elite would neglect such issues as the impact of widespread use of the artificial heart on the availability of other health care services, its effect on government programs like Medicaid and Medicare, and the difficulty of providing fair access to the technology. Had the decision-makers themselves been more broadly based, Jamieson argues, it is more likely that these issues would have been addressed. And had the ethical and social issues been given proper consideration, he contends, it is likely that the total artificial heart would have met with significantly more opposition than it did.

Thus Jamieson illustrates, as do Francis and Annas, the influence that the nature of the decision-maker has on the nature of the decision. This point cannot be stressed too much, for a great many people will be affected by the decisions made by a few unrepresentative individuals. As Thomas Preston, one of the staunchest critics of the artificial heart, has explained:

> The central issue is whether our utilization of the artificial heart shall be directed by a small group of medical investigators and their entrepreneurial backers, or by representatives of the society that has developed the technology and will have to live with its consequences. It is a classic conflict between the economic independence of individuals, and the determination of the public good in an increasingly interdependent society.[12]

This is not to suggest that the development of the artificial heart confronted no hostility or that no constraints were placed on it. On the contrary, the total artificial heart has met with a considerable degree of opposition and regulation from a variety of quarters, especially the federal government.[13] Some commentators even have concluded from this that those who favor unfettered technological development may have cause for dismay, while "those who favor greater restraints on the development and use of new health care technologies may find that the current system serves their purposes better than they anticipated."[14] The point of the chapters in this section, however, is that the constraints placed on the development and use of the technology need, at every level, to be more rational and more responsible.

It is crucial that comprehensive and impartial evaluation be brought to bear on the initial decision to make a large-scale investment in a technology, instead of waiting until the momentum of the program has exceeded its promise and the special interests that feed upon it have become all but irresistible. It is crucial, also, that investigators act on the basis of realistic assessments of the efficacy of the technology they are testing, rather than on the basis of unrealistic hopes regarding its benefits. Finally, it should be clear by now that any experimental device, drug, or technique requires continuous monitoring and periodic reassessment and that this process of evaluation should include attention to ethical, legal, and public policy issues. Hence it must be kept in mind that the task is to make a series of assessments and decisions, not a once-and-for-all commitment.

Notes

1. The balloon pump was the first cardiac assist device developed, and it is still the most widely used. Its main shortcoming is that it works only if the left ventricle of the patient's own heart works—hence the need for the development of a left ventricular assist device.

2. Artificial Heart Assessment Panel, National Heart and Lung Institute, "The Totally Implantable Artificial Heart: Economic, Ethical, Legal, Medical, Psychiatric, and Social Implications," in *Ethics and Health Policy*, Robert M. Veatch and Roy Branson, eds. (Cambridge, MA: Ballinger, 1976), pp. 219–246.

3. The range depends on the assumptions made in the calculation. Cf. D. P. Lubeck and J. P. Bunker, *The Implications of Cost-Effective Analysis of Medical Technology. Background Paper No. 1: Case Studies of Medical Technology: Case Study 9: The Artificial Heart* (Washington, D.C.: Government Printing Office, 1982).

4. W. L. Hastings, J. L. Aaron, J. Deneris, et al. "A Retrospective Study of Nine Calves Surviving Five Months on the Pneumatic Total Artificial Heart," *Transactions of the American Society of Artificial Internal Organs* 27: 71–76, 1981. For more on this preliminary testing, see Judith P. Swazey, Judith C. Watkins, Renee C. Fox, "Assessing the Artificial Heart: The Clinical Moratorium Revisited," *International Journal of Technology Assessment in Health Care* 2: 387–410, 1986.

5. Swazey et al., "Artificial Heart," pp. 392–393.

6. National Institutes of Health Guide for Grants and Contracts, *Criteria for Clinical Investigative Use for Therapeutic Devices Under Contract to the National Heart and Lung Institute*, August 7, 1974.

7. James H. Maxwell, David Blumenthal, and Harvey M. Sapolsky, "Obstacles to Developing and Using Technology: The Case of the Artificial Heart," *International Journal of Technology Assessment in Health Care* 2: 411–424, 1986.

8. Swazey et al., "Artificial Heart," pp. 393–397.

9. Swazey et al., "Artificial Heart," p. 406.

10. The first patient, Haskell Karp, survived for sixty-four hours on the artificial heart; he died thirty-two hours after transplantation of a human donor heart. The second patient, Willebrordus Meuffels, survived for fifty-four hours on his artificial heart and died approximately eight hours after transplantation of a human donor heart.

11. Paul Ramsey, *The Patient as Person* (New Haven: Yale University Press, 1970), pp. 220–221.

12. Thomas Preston, "Who Benefits From the Artificial Heart?" *Hastings Center Report* 15: 5–7, 1985.

13. This is well documented by Maxwell et al., "Obstacles."

14. Maxwell et al., "Obstacles," p. 421.

19

Legitimate Emergencies, Experimentation, and Scientific Civil Disobedience

Leslie P. Francis

Creation of the current regulatory system governing research with human subjects was impelled by shock over reports of scientific experimentation conducted with little regard for human autonomy, dignity, or even the minimization of pain.[1] Yet there remains periodic grumbling about the need for extensive review processes. Regulation of research is cumbersome and time consuming for both regulators and the regulated. It slows the development of lifesaving therapeutic procedures. Some of the complaints have been channeled into ordinary political activity, such as efforts to encourage the Food and Drug Administration to exempt additional classes of research from the major regulatory mechanism or scrutiny by Institutional Review Boards (IRBs) at the investigator's research setting.[2] Spurred by advocacy groups, especially pharmaceutical companies and AIDS patients, the FDA made major changes in the regulations governing therapeutic use of experimental drugs, effective June 22, 1987. The changes are aimed to make promising drugs available during clinical trials to patients with serious or life-threatening conditions, but without therapeutic alternatives.[3]

There is also, however, talk about researchers who circumvent, or believe they would be justified in circumventing, regulations governing research with human subjects. Some of these concerns were aired more publicly in the wake of the spring 1985 events in Arizona relating to artificial heart implantation.[4] If the regulations have indeed curtailed excesses of experimental enthusiasm, lawbreaking in the interests of science stands in need of justification.[5]

In this discussion, I consider whether some of the allegedly more common examples of circumvention of the federal regulatory process can be justified as lawbreaking in the interests of science. I begin with three types of violations involving human subjects research. I then argue that none can be defended as analogous to more classic forms of justified lawbreaking such as conscientious refusal and civil disobedience. Finally, I suggest that where scientific lawbreaking seems appropriate, it does so because of analogies to entirely legal ways of proceeding in emergency situations.

243

Three Examples of Scientific Lawbreaking

1. *Beginning experiments prematurely.* Even at a relatively efficient institution, the process of IRB review can take several months. IRB approval is likely to be delayed if members of the board wish additional information from investigators or if there is disagreement about the permissibility of the research. Investigators who believe that their research will be of therapeutic value to patients—or who are simply excited about what they are doing—have understandable incentives to start research without IRB approval. These incentives are augmented for investigators who do not believe that IRBs contribute anything of value to the scientific enterprise or who find them confusing or useless red tape. There are controls: federal funding of much of the research involving human subjects is contingent on IRB approval, and companies seeking market approval for drugs or devices should not provide them to unapproved investigators.[6] Episodes such as the use of an unapproved artificial heart by an unauthorized surgeon in Arizona trigger FDA investigation. These controls have somewhat more force for investigational drugs than for investigational devices, because sponsors and investigators may be disqualified for use of investigational drugs in violation of the regulations, but not for disobedience in the clinical investigation of medical devices.[7] Nonetheless, it is probable that some research is undertaken without legally required IRB approval, especially where state or local regulations extend human subjects protection beyond the federal requirements.

2. *Ignoring requirements of protocols.* Experimenters seeking IRB approval must submit research proposals, together with informed consent documents. Once proposals are approved, they may not be modified without persmission from the IRB. The informed consent process must be performed and documented as stipulated by the IRB. Untoward incidents must be reported to the IRB and if appropriate, to the FDA or the Office for Protection from Research Risks within HHS.[8] Projects must be reviewed at least once a year.[9] Researchers often find these and other requirements annoying, particularly if initial IRB approval was contingent on modifications in the research design or the consent process as originally submitted. It is tempting to alter research design unilaterally if problems become apparent midstream, or to foreshorten the informed consent process if it seems to frighten off patients who in the judgment of the investigator would benefit by participation in the research. Nobody really knows how frequently these sorts of disobedience occur, but there has been growing advocacy lately of IRBs playing more active roles in the continuing surveillance of research.

3. *Going abroad.* Despite international efforts to protect human subjects through the World Medical Association's Declaration of Helsinki,[10] some nations do not regulate research to the extent that the United States does.[11] The United States probably has the strictest regulatory standards in the world, and estimates are that it now takes about ten years for drugs to go through the U.S. testing and approval process.[12] Research might therefore be expected to move abroad to avoid the costs of regulation, especially in cases where large economic interests in product development are at stake.[13] Some federal regulations do apply to research conducted by U.S. nationals abroad. For example, an investigational medical device may not be exported without FDA approval, based, among other factors, on a showing that the device is consistent with the laws of the country to which it is being exported and has been approved for import by the appropriate agency of that country.[14] Data submitted in support of an application to market new drugs must have been obtained in compliance with the Declaration of

Helsinki or the laws of the country in which the research was conducted, whichever is stronger.[15] In addition, many institutions require IRB approval of all sponsored research, wherever conducted. Nevertheless, some research may go abroad in violation of these regulations.[16]

Conscientious Refusal, Civil Disobedience, and Scientific Lawbreaking

Dramatic they may not be, but jumping the gun, changing research proposals without authorization, and going abroad without approval are all clear violations of the federal regulations. One way to try to justify them is by analogy to other forms of social protest.[17] I argue that the examples of lawbreaking in the interests of science given here cannot be compared either to conscientious refusal or to justified civil disobedience—but I should emphasize that I do not thereby mean to suggest that the present federal regulations are optimal.

The models of conscientious refusal and civil disobedience that I use are drawn from John Rawls.[18] Conscientious refusal is deliberate noncompliance with an applicable legal order. It may be overt or covert; in the latter case Rawls suggested that it is more appropriately described as "conscientious evasion." It is not aimed to appeal to the sense of justice of the majority or to bring about legal change. Rather, it is a statement by the actor that he or she, on ground of conscience, must refuse to do what the law requires. Classic examples are Thoreau's refusal to pay taxes or the draft resister's refusal to participate in war.

The scientist confronting restrictions on research would be hard put to argue that to participate in the review process is itself to act immorally. That process involves only such activities as submitting protocol information and describing a process for obtaining informed consent from patients. In contrast, some health professionals do refuse to perform abortions or to carry out directives of living wills, from conscientious disapproval of the activities themselves. Legal structures may be designed to accommodate these dissenting moral views, by allowing the professional to opt out of care, if he or she makes sure that alternatives are arranged for the patient.[19]

Instead, if the scientist objecting to regulation is to be viewed as a conscientious refuser, it is on the model of Thoreau's claim that paying taxes would make him the agent of immorality to others. The scientist might argue that if participation in the review process delays research and its therapeutic applications to a significant extent, he or she becomes an agent of immorality to potential beneficiaries. In this claim, the scientist might compare himself to a physician-member of a health maintenance organization who contemplates disobeying cost controls that prevent him from delivering beneficial care to patients.

This view of the scientist, however, confuses the roles of researcher and therapist. One important difference is that the therapist, by beginning treatment, may have implicitly or explicitly promised to pursue the patient's best interests. Bowing to external cost constraints on therapy might violate these promissory obligations. The researcher, qua researcher, has not promised implicitly or explicitly to utilize techniques as yet not fully verified. Individuals do, of course, simultaneously play roles of researcher and therapist; the role confusion inherent in this situation is one of the difficulties with randomized clinical trials.[20] But it is important to analyze the roles separately.

Another important difference between researcher and therapist, the difference I develop here, is that the researcher who violates regulations in the interests of patients is relying on layered private judgments. At base is a judgment that the therapy under study will be of sufficient benefit to patients that it is immoral not to deliver it to them as quickly as possible. Overlying this judgment is the researcher's self-confidence that he or she is so likely to be right about the research's potential value that it is better to enter subjects into the study than to delay to allow external review to take place.[21] By contrast, the therapist who conscientiously refuses to adhere to cost controls on medically beneficial therapy is not making a private judgment about the efficacy of therapy. His or her judgment is instead that loyalty to patients outweighs decisions about the allocation of resources, a judgment that may itself be problematic.[22]

Both of the researcher's private judgments are dangerous. Although researchers may have good reasons to believe a procedure will prove beneficial, the aim of research is to determine whether or not it will be so. Researchers who assume the results are so likely to be favorable that it is wrong not to enter subjects into a study as quickly as possible are abandoning the role of researcher, just when they are most likely to be overoptimistic. The research review and informed consent process protects patients from overeager misjudgments of therapeutic benefit. Conscientiously refusing researchers bypass this process in reliance on their own judgment. They do so without public scrutiny. They enlist subjects who by reason of ignorance, disease, poverty, or, most importantly, the stress of illness, may be poorly equipped to protect themselves. This is not to compare the conscientious refuser with the self-interested investigator who engages in research fraud to enhance his or her professional reputation, but it is to question the role of private judgment in the research process. Cumbersome though they may be, the federal regulations reflect the conclusion that decisions about whether subjects may be entered into research are best made after impartial assessment.

Civil disobedience, in contrast to conscientious refusal, is not a private judgment that following the law would be immoral. It is aimed to bring about legal change. In Rawls's words, civil disobedience is "a public, nonviolent, conscientious yet political act contrary to law usually done with the aim of bringing about a change in the law or policies of the government. By acting in this way one addresses the sense of justice of the majority of the community and declares that in one's considered opinion the principles of social cooperation among free and equal men are not being respected."[23] Because it may undermine support for otherwise just institutions and ignore reciprocity to fellow citizens, civil disobedience in Rawls's view can only be justified under limited circumstances. It must be aimed to correct substantial injustice, especially structural injustice that blocks removal of other injustices. Normal appeals to the political process must have been tried without success, and further attempts must reasonably seem fruitless. Finally, it must be unlikely that the disobedience will raise the level of disorder to an extent that risks breakdown of just institutions overall.

Lawbreaking in the interests of science fails several of these tests. It is doubtful that researchers have tried ordinary political channels and failed to change the manner in which research is regulated. Most importantly, the lawbreaking scientist's immediate actions are directed at getting on with research, not at remedying an unjust federal scheme. Indeed, it is difficult to isolate what underlying injustices in the regulation of research the lawbreaking scientist might be seeking to change. There are some possibilities: the cumbersome nature of the review process, bureaucratic misjudgment of a particular project, or the substitution of a public review process more generally for individual researchers' decisions. These are not, however, systematic injustices of the type generally thought to warrant civil disobedience. Neither groups of researchers nor groups of patients are excluded from the research process—as they would be, for example, if a particularly promising research protocol were opened only to whites or only to the wealthy. Even if individual scientists are sometimes right that the federal regulations stand in the way of lifesaving research, it does not follow that the system is significantly unjust. The fact that review might be improved to minimize mistakes or delay does not show that we should abandon public scrutiny of research with human subjects.

A utilitarian analysis of scientific civil disobedience would reach similar conclusions. The act-utilitarian lawbreaker would need to show that the good to be achieved by violating the regulation to further a particular research protocol, most likely health benefits or lives saved, outweighs the potential risks of individual judgment. Our regulatory scheme is the result of a social determination that we will do better if the assessment of these risk/benefit ratios is not left up to individual investigators. The days of inoculating experimental subjects with cancer, or allowing syphilis patients to remain untreated so that the course of their disease might be studied, are not far behind us. Moreover, the utilitarian must consider the consequences that violations of the regulations might have for our regulatory scheme. There are concerns that deregulation of research would gradually weaken what have been developing norms of subject protection among researchers,[24] and these concerns might equally apply to a growing practice of disobedience.

Thus lawbreaking in the interests of science should not be compared to conscientious refusal or civil disobedience. The dangers of private judgment are too great. Nonetheless, there are some very tough cases that appear to support the scientific lawbreaker's position. For example, consider the situation of researchers engaged in important work on species preservation at a university that has lost its permission to use animal subjects in research. The researchers' work will be lost if they cannot continue to use their animal subjects. The researchers were not themselves at fault for the loss of permission; it occurred because other researchers, in a different department and supervised by a different animal subjects committee, persistently mistreated their animals.[25] In this case, worthy research may be lost because of the scientific misdeeds of others. Perhaps the case reveals an important flaw in the structure of institutional sanctions. But there are some potential good consequences from the sanctions that may be sufficient to outweigh even the loss of the research. That university, and researchers within it, had tolerated a structure of review of animal research that allowed substantial mistreatment of animals to continue unchecked. Loss of permission to engage in animal research may generate needed institutional change more effectively than any other course of action. A situation like this is complex; perhaps the best resolution is to continue with an announced policy of prohibition and sanctions and to consider exemptions from sanctions in worthy individual cases.

The rush of artificial hearts to Arizona illustrates another possible type of hard case. A heart transplant patient suffered an acute rejection episode and the only chance to keep him alive until a second transplant could be performed appeared to be the implantation of an artificial heart. The patient had no connection to any artificial heart research program.[26] Surgeons in Arizona were not approved investigators for an artificial heart, and the device actually used was not approved for testing in human subjects. What gives this situation its appeal as a case where action was warranted is that it was an immediately life-threatening emergency in which a patient would die without use of an unapproved device. I shall argue in the next section that there is flexibility in the federal review scheme to allow reasonable therapeutic responses to emergencies that are genuine and that this was not a case of justified lawbreaking to advance research.

The Federal Regulations
and the Emergency Situation

At common law, it is a battery to impose medical treatment without consent. Consent to treatment is not required in a life-threatening emergency, when the patient cannot consent and no appropriate proxy is available. The justification—and potential constraint—is hypothetical consent: The patient would have agreed to the therapy had consultation been possible. Of course, the consent is not actual, and there may be patients who for religious or other reasons would have declined the proffered therapy. The justification for the departure from autonomy rests on the generalization that most patients would prefer lifesaving therapy to death, and it is therefore better to err on the side of preserving life.

The federal regulations governing human subjects research apply to three types of research: federally funded research, research with new medical devices such as the artificial heart, and research with new drugs. As the regulations have developed, policymakers have struggled to achieve uniformity to the extent warranted by differences in the research contexts. Like the common law, the regulations reflect accommodation of the values of preserving autonomy and preserving life, with the additional complexity of protecting subjects against inappropriately risky research. Regulations of the Department of Health and Human Services, covering federally funded research, remain closest to the ordinary treatment situation because they do not involve appeals for the use of otherwise unavailable drugs or devices. The HHS regulations require IRB approval of research protocols and informed consent from participating subjects. They specify, however, that they are not intended to alter the ordinary availability of medical care without consent, to the extent permitted under federal, state, or local law.[27] In addition, they allow IRBs to waive informed consent in some research involving government benefit programs and in other research when experimental subjects are not exposed to more than minimal risk and the research could not be carried out without the waiver.[28] It should be emphasized, however, that the background to the waiver is IRB scrutiny of the experimental process. Researchers are not authorized to decide on their own that risks are minimal or that an emergency necessitates entering subjects into a study without informed consent.

Regulations issued by the FDA governing research with new medical devices and new drugs must confront the additional incentives of eager marketers and eager purchasers of new medical products. In order to conduct the clinical trials needed for ultimate FDA marketing approval, developers of new medical devices must seek an investigational device exemption (IDE) authorizing use of an otherwise unapproved device; developers of a new drug must work under an investigational new drug (IND) application. FDA requirements for IRB approval and informed consent in clinical trials now parallel the HHS requirements. They contain in addition specific provisions governing the use of experimental products in two types of emergency situations.

The first type of situation involves research protocols that propose to test experimental drugs or devices in emergency situations, such as tests of anticoagulants on patients suffering heart attacks. IRBs may approve these protocols despite the obvious vulnerability of their proposed subjects. Here, IRB scrutiny provides an independent assessment of the risks and benefits of the research for participating subjects and, one hopes, screens out experimental products with unfavorable risk/benefit ratios for patients.

Unanticipated emergency situations, however, may not wait for the deliberations of IRBs. To handle such crises, the FDA regulations allow a second possibility: use of an experimental article without an approved protocol on a one-time emergency basis. This use must be reported to the IRB within five days. No further use of the experimental article is permitted at the institution in question until the investigation undergoes IRB review. At this point, the investigator is aware that the experimental article may be needed for emergency use again; therefore he or she should seek IRB approval beforehand.[29]

In both types of emergency situations contemplated by the federal regulations, informed consent is required in a sense much stronger than the consent required for ordinary medical treatment.[30] Even so, there is an exemption from the informed consent requirements for research under approved protocols if the requirements are not feasible because a human subject confronts a life-threatening situation necessitating use of the test article, he or she cannot give consent, the subject's legal representative cannot be reached quickly enough, and there is no available alternative therapy with an equal or greater chance of saving his or her life. These conditions must be attested to by the investigator and evaluated by an independent physician if possible before the article is used and otherwise within five days. Documentation of the emergency conditions must be provided to the IRB within five days.[31] Thus the FDA regulations do allow one-time emergency use when research has not been submitted for IRB approval and exemption from informed consent when it is not feasible. It is difficult to transfer the doctrine of imputed consent into the research process because the generalization that most people would prefer to receive the procedure at issue is so much more problematic.[32] These exceptions incorporate the doctrine of imputed consent into the research process to a limited extent, with constraints provided by external review of both the use of the experimental article and the feasibility of consent.

The "Phoenix heart" story unfolded rapidly and illustrates the pressures on the FDA regulations for emergency situations.[33] The patient, suffering end-stage heart disease, had been accepted as a heart transplant candidate at University Medical Center in Tucson, Arizona. On March 4, a donor heart became available, and although there were some questions about its quality, Dr. Copeland performed the transplant operation. When the operation was completed, early in the morning of March 5, the donor heart did not respond to reperfusion and quickly failed. Whether this occurred because of initial damage or acute rejection is unclear. Dr. Copeland immediately began efforts to find a second donor heart, but by early March 6, the patient was placed on heart-lung bypass. Because the patient could not remain on bypass for very long and because efforts to locate a second natural heart had apparently failed, Dr. Copeland called possible sources for an artificial heart. The Phoenix heart was the most readily available and while it was en route to Tucson, Dr. Copeland alerted the patient's mother and sister about the possibility of using an artificial heart as a temporary device. Before the artificial heart was used, Dr. Copeland got consent from the patient's mother and sister, notified the hospital chief of surgery, and called the IRB chair's office. Other than examination by the physician bringing the artificial heart, no additional or independent assessment of the patient's condition was performed. Because a second natural heart became available from Stanford rapidly after implantation of the artificial pump, the Phoenix heart was actually left in place for only eleven hours. The second donor heart transplant took place on the night of March 6–7, but the patient's condition never really stabilized, apparently because of the extended period on heart-lung bypass, and he died on March 8, 1985.

On March 8, the FDA wrote the University of Arizona hospital about the use of the artificial heart.[34] The FDA's letter reminded the hospital that in order to protect patients, artificial heart research must ordinarily be part of an approved clinical trial. If Arizona anticipated further use of an artificial heart, it should apply for an investigational device exemption from the FDA. The FDA letter also notified Arizona that it would investigate the Phoenix heart implantation to decide whether it was a justified emergency use.

The FDA's investigation recommended taking no action against Dr. Copeland or the University of Arizona Medical Center. The recommendation was based on findings that the emergency was genuine and unique and that Dr. Copeland had followed basic FDA procedures for unanticipated emergency use by notifying the IRB, consulting other clinicians, and obtaining consent from the patient's mother and sister. Of particular importance to the investigatory findings was that "there was no evidence that the use of the artificial heart was premeditated."[35] Also noted in the report were efforts at the University of Arizona Medical Center to establish a Bioethics Committee and formulate guidelines for use of the artificial heart in subsequent emergencies. Based on this report, the FDA decided to withhold regulatory action against those involved in the Phoenix heart case.[36] The FDA's decision, however, cautioned the University of Arizona hospital that the FDA has procedures for the approval of protocols allowing experimentation in emergency situations and that any further use by the institution of an artificial heart must be under such an approved protocol.

The conclusion of the FDA investigation was simplistic at best. The report contains no explanation of why the emergency was "unique." Although there is no doubt that the emergency was genuine, it is not so clear that it was surprising. Dr. Copeland is a surgeon who acquires deep feelings of personal responsibility for the continued survival of his patients and is motivated to try any option. As the investigative report portrays his self-description:

> He had transplanted a heart that failed, and he was a party to that failure. He feels responsibility for providing the most appropriate care for any patient in such dire stress, but particularly in this patient who had decided to accept transplantation by Dr. Copeland. . . . He knew he could have backed out at that point, and it would have been said he did all he could, but he decided he couldn't do that. He had to try, and that set off . . . the ensuing chain of events.[37]

The death of an earlier transplant patient from acute rejection had prompted Dr. Copeland to vow to take action the next time such an emergency arose.[38] Dr. Copeland's view as expressed to the FDA investigators is that decisions in emergencies should be left to the doctor, institution, and patient.[39] There is evidence of earlier inquiries by Dr. Copeland about cardiac assist devices, including artificial hearts. Dr. Copeland reported, however, that "there had been no real thinking in advance because nothing was really available."[40] No independent consultation on the patient's condition was obtained. Finally, the investigation raises some questions about the informed consent process. Although the patient's mother and sister had discussions with Dr. Copeland before and after the arrival in Tucson of the Phoenix heart, the actual consent form signed for the implant was a standard hospital surgical consent form. It was supplemented on March 8, possibly after the patient's death, by a consent form based on that of the University of Utah's artificial heart program.[41] It seems fair to conclude that although the use of the particular artificial device was not planned or premeditated in any precise sense, the type of emergency and likely response to it from Dr. Copeland were surely predictable before the Phoenix heart crisis occurred.

The FDA investigative report ends with an appeal: "We need to consider the same 'what if' as the surgeons who are faced with these extraordinary circumstances in the future. . . . 'What if' this happens again at Arizona? Will they use the Phoenix heart or some other unproven device to save a life? What really *should* we do about bona fide emergency uses of unapproved devices?"[42]

In October 1985, from concern about the Phoenix heart incident, the FDA published additional regulatory guidance for the emergency use of unapproved medical devices, use of them in unapproved ways, or use by unapproved investigators. The guidance document clarifies the existing FDA regulations governing emergency use of medical devices, the regulations that were in place at the time of the Phoenix heart implant. The document defines an emergency as a situation that is immediately life threatening for the patient, without acceptable treatment alternatives, and too imminent to allow FDA approval of use of the device. Physicians are cautioned to use "reasonable foresight with respect to potential emergencies" and to make arrangements to use the regular FDA approval process whenever possible. Patient protection is mandated, including informed consent, review by an independent physician, institutional approval and concurrence by the IRB chair, and sponsor authorization. Under these conditions, unapproved devices may be shipped—as was the artificial heart in Arizona—without FDA objection, provided the FDA is immediately notified. Emergency use of devices the FDA has disapproved for investigation is prohibited entirely.[43]

This guidance document warrants a different result in the next Phoenix heart case. Reasonable foresight suggests the possibility of acute patient failure in any heart transplant program and thus the need to engage the FDA review process for emergency use of currently unapproved assistance devices. The guidance document's provisions for informed consent and institutional approval were followed informally or unsystematically in the Phoenix heart case. Moreover, the decision to use the Phoenix heart was taken without independent physician review, for the only review of the patient came from the surgeon who brought the Phoenix heart to Tucson.

As the Phoenix heart and the guidance document illustrate, regulation is a trade-off between costs of forgone therapy and risks to patients from overeager researchers or their own desperation.[44] With this balance in view, the FDA has taken several further steps concerning the emergency situation since publication of the guidance document. In 1986, the FDA announced review of regulation of investigational medical devices and sought specific information about costs of regulation and benefits in risks avoided.[45] As of July 1, 1987, this review had not resulted in proposed changes in the medical device regulations.

In May 1987, the FDA announced a major addition to the regulations governing use of investigational drugs. The new regulations develop the mechanism of a "treatment protocol," or "treatment IND," under which drugs may be used for treatment while they are still being tested clinically.[46] Because treatment INDs are aimed to make drugs more readily available to extremely ill patients, they provide an important new means for responding to patient distress. Treatment protocols are limited to drugs intended to treat patients suffering from either immediately life-threatening or serious diseases. "Life-threatening" diseases are defined as diseases from which death will occur within months or that are likely to cause premature death. Examples of conditions in which death is likely within roughly six months include advanced AIDS, metastatic refractory cancer, recurrent sustained ventricular tachycardia, and Class IV congestive heart failure. The only example given by the FDA of a disease likely to cause premature death if left untreated is AIDS-related complex.

Serious diseases are left undefined in the regulations, but examples given suggest severe compromise of function and likely death over the longer term: Alzheimer's disease, advanced multiple sclerosis, and transient ischemic attacks.[47] The difference is important because the FDA has more stringent criteria for approval of treatment protocols involving patients with serious diseases. Drugs intended for patients with immediately life-threatening conditions may not be used under a treatment IND if there is insufficient evidence that the drugs may be effective or do not expose patients to unreasonable and significant risks.[48] For drugs used in treatment of serious disease, treatment INDs may be denied if evidence of safety and effectiveness does not justify the treatment use.[49] Except in unusual situations, drugs for serious conditions will not be given treatment INDs before clinical trials have been completed or widespread (Phase 3) clinical trials have begun. Drugs for life-threatening diseases, however, may be available even at Phase 1 of clinical trials, therefore, when it is possible that less evidence is available of risks and benefits in human use.[50]

Other restrictions apply to all treatment protocols. No protocols may be approved if comparable or satisfactory alternative therapy is available for the intended patient population, although the FDA has indicated plans to interpret this restriction flexibly to cover, for example, patients who are unsatisfactory candidates for existing therapies.[51] Protocols are limited to situations in which controlled clinical trials are ongoing or have been completed and in which the sponsor of the clinical trial is actively pursuing FDA approval. Thus treatment protocols are not available unless the drug has been used in clinical trials subject to IRB and FDA approvals. Treatment protocols must conform to safeguards of the regular IND process, including informed consent and IRB review. The sponsor of the protocol is responsible for ensuring that all participating investigators comply with the FDA's informed consent requirements.[52] Finally, under a treatment protocol, the sponsor may charge patients for costs of the drug's manufacture, research, development, and handling.[53]

The provisions for IRB review and ongoing FDA surveillance are especially important. The FDA's original regulatory proposals had waived IRB review for treatment protocols, in reliance on informed consent for patient protection. The FDA, in making the decision to require IRB review, was persuaded most by the ability of local IRBs to judge the adequacy of informed consent and the qualifications of practitioners.[54] Ongoing FDA surveillance includes the sponsor's responsibilities to report safety information to the FDA[55] and the possibility of placing a treatment IND on hold. An ongoing treatment IND may be placed on hold if satisfactory therapeutic alternatives become available, if ongoing clinical trials are placed on hold, if the sponsor fails to pursue marketing approval diligently, or if the scientific evidence apparently warranting the initial treatment authorization no longer does so.[56]

These regulations go as far as—if not further than—it would seem wise to go in the pressure to make new drugs available. They safeguard patients by impartial review by IRBs and the FDA both of the risks and benefits of the treatment protocol and of the informed consent process. Nevertheless, there are risks. Perhaps the greatest risk is that of premature widespread use of a drug that proves harmful. This is most likely to occur in patients with life-threatening conditions, especially those whose conditions might cause premature rather than immediate death, who may receive investigational treatment at very early stages of clinical trials. To limit this risk, it is important for reviewers to stress showings of potential efficacy and risk before approving treatment INDs. Another risk of the treatment IND process is reliance on sponsors and investigators for safety reports, particularly in light of the fact that there is no requirement for systematic information gathering under a treatment protocol. The regulations stress sponsor responsibility and IRB knowledge of local conditions, but realistically these are less likely to be effective in a treatment protocol with widely scattered participating practitioners than in a limited clinical trial. Similar risks attend the informed consent process, already difficult given the desperation of seriously ill patients. The FDA does not list failure to obtain informed consent as a ground for placing a therapeutic protocol on hold; perhaps this omission can be justified by the interests of other participating patients, but it leaves enforcement to the sanctions of the IND process generally. Finally, it remains to be seen whether the availability of treatment INDs will undermine ongoing controlled clinical trials, especially those in which some subjects will be randomized to a no-treatment group.

Admittedly, under both the FDA and the HHS regulations some patients will still lose out in emergencies despite all the current flexibility. FDA regulations prohibit a second appeal to the emergency exception as a justification for unapproved implantation. If a second emergency case arises during the period in which approval is being sought but has not yet been given, a patient who might have benefited will die. In addition, the regulations governing HHS-funded research do not allow waiver of informed consent by the patient or his proxy when a protocol involves more than minimal risk, even when the procedure being tested could be lifesaving, although the investigator could step out of the research and offer innovative therapy as allowed under state law.

However, it is important to recognize that the federal regulations do allow considerable scope for treatment in emergency situations. The FDA regulations allow use of a test article in the first most genuinely unanticipated emergency. It is only in later situations, which are life threatening to the patient but foreseeable by researchers, that emergency use is prohibited. The importance of external review of research involving human subjects justifies this prohibition. Moreover, the independent judgment provided by review of research should not be overridden easily by investigators' private decisions that procedures are in the vital interests of their patients.

Notes

1. President's Commission for the Study of Ethical Problems in Medicine and Biomedical and Behavioral Research, *Protecting Human Subjects* (Washington, D.C.: Government Printing Office, 1981), p. 22 and n. 12.

2. Survey research, for example, is exempt from IRB review unless it identifies subjects, deals with sensitive aspects of behavior, and places subjects at risk of civil or criminal liability. 45 C.F.R. § 46.101(b)(3) (1986). The American Society for Artificial Internal Organs has recently submitted a citizens' petition to the FDA to modify the Investigational Device Exemption regulations to allow limited feasibility investigations of new devices under IRB supervision, 51 Fed. Reg. 11266 (April 1, 1986), and the investigational device exemption regulations are under more general FDA review. 51 Fed. Reg. 26830 (July 25, 1986).

3. 52 Fed. Reg. 19455 (May 22, 1987).

4. Lawrence Altman, "Strong Curbs Urged in Wake of Unsanctioned Heart Implant," *New York Times*, sec. 1, p. 30, col. 1, March 10, 1985; Eric Eckholm, "A Dedicated Heart Surgeon: Jack Green Copeland 3d," *New York Times*, sec. 1, p. 18, col. 5, March 8, 1985; George Annas, "The Phoenix Heart: What We Have to Lose," *Hastings Center Report* 15: 15–16, June 1985.

5. There is little recent data on either the extent to which the regulations have constrained experimental abuse or the frequency with which they are disobeyed. From 1975 to 1977, the National Commission for the Protection of Human Subjects conducted a study of the federal scheme for regulating research. The commission concluded that IRBs were not adequately involved in continuing review of research projects. Four years later, the President's Commission for the Study of Ethical Problems in Medicine and Biomedical and Behavioral Research concluded that the federal government does not adequately supervise IRB monitoring of ongoing research and made a number of recommendations for improvement. See President's Commission for the Study of Ethical Problems in Medicine and Biomedical and Behavioral Research, *Protecting Research Subjects* (Washignton D.C.: Government Printing Office, 1981), pp. 35, 48 [hereinafter, *Protecting Research Subjects*]. In its second biennial report, the president's commission reported that responses to its recommendations had been disappointing and suggested a program of site visits to IRBs. President's Commission for the Study of Ethical Problems in Medicine and Biomedical and Behavioral Research, *Implementing Human Research Regulations: The Adequacy and Uniformity of Federal Rules and of Their Implementation* (Washington D.C.: Government Printing Office, 1983).

6. 21 C.F.R. § 312.1(a)(2) (1986) (new drugs for investigational use), 21 C.F.R. § 812.43(b) (1986) (investigational device exemptions); 45 C.F.R. § 46.101 (1986) (HHS funded research).

7. 21 C.F.R. § 312.1(c)(1), (2) (1986); 51 Fed. Reg. 26830 (July 25, 1986).

8. 21 C.F.R. § 312.1(a)(6) (1986) (new drugs); 21 C.F.R. § 812.150(a)(1) (1986) (investigational devices); 45 C.F.R. § 46.108 (1986) (HHS funded research).

9. 21 C.F.R. § 56.109(e) (1986) (FDA); 45 C.F.R. § 46.109(e) (1986) (HHS).

10. Reprinted in Warren T. Reich, ed., *Encyclopedia of Bioethics*, vol. 2 (New York: Free Press, 1978), pp. 1770–1773.

11. The United States was the first to develop a system of ethics committees to review research with human subjects. Britain and Sweden followed suit relatively quickly, although in neither case do such committees play so comprehensive or so legally sanctioned a role as in the United States. Western European countries generally have made efforts to regulate research along the lines of the Helsinki declaration. Research in third world countries, by contrast, is especially unlikely to receive careful review, and concern has been expressed about exploitation of poorly informed and economically disadvantaged subjects. N. Howard-Jones and Z. Bankowski, eds., *Medical Experimentation and the Protection of Human Rights*, XIIth Round Table Conference of the Council for International Organizations of Medical Sciences (Cascias, Portugal: Council for International Organizations, 1979).

12. "Pharmaceuticals," *The Economist*, pp. 4–14, Feb. 7, 1987.

13. For example, there is some suggestive evidence that research was shifted from Britain after the initiation of regulation. D. W. Vere, "Basis for Initiating Clinical Trials," in Public Health Service, *Issues in Research with Human Subjects* (Washington, D.C.: Government Printing Office, 1980), pp. 23–39.

14. 21 C.F.R. § 812.18(b) (1986); Bureau of Medical Devices, *Regulatory Requirements for Marketing a Device* VI-95 (Washington, D.C.: Government Printing Office, 1982).

15. 21 C.F.R. § 312.20(b)(1)(iv) (1986). The requirement that individual case records be obtained, id. § 312.20(b)(1)(iii), is a significant deterrent to the use of drug studies conducted abroad.

16. There seem to have been no recent systematic efforts to measure how frequently this occurs, although examples are periodically reported. The University of California, Los Angeles (UCLA) requires review of all sponsored research, and probably the most notorious case of "going abroad" involved a UCLA investigator who conducted bone marrow transplants in Italy and Israel without the required UCLA IRB review. The materials used in the transplants were prepared at UCLA as part of NIH-funded research, and the investigator was sanctioned by NIH, *Protecting Research Subjects*, pp. 181–185.

17. One disadvantage of the comparison for the protesting investigator is the argument that the civil disobedient has a duty to pay the penalty for his disobedience. Daniel Callahan has suggested that disobedient investigators should consider their willingness to pay the penalty. See Altman, "Unsanctioned Heart Implant." For a critique of the view, see Daniel Farrell, "Paying the Penalty: Justifiable Civil Disobedience and the Problem of Punishment," *Philosophy and Public Affairs* 6: 164–184, 1977. Investigators or institutions that engage in serious noncompliance with the federal regulations may be debarred from HHS funding. 45 C.F.R. § 76.10 (1986). The regulations specifically state, however, that the purpose of debarment is to protect subjects, not to punish. 45 C.F.R. § 76.1(a) (1986). Investigators who engage in misconduct may lose their entitlements to receive investigational drugs, 21 C.F.R. § 312.1(c)(2) (1986). There is no provision for debarment of investigators of devices, although sponsors of investigational devices who discover noncompliance must either secure correction or end the investigator's participation in the study, 21 C.F.R. § 812.46(a) (1986).

18. John Rawls, *A Theory of Justice* (Cambridge, MA: Harvard University Press, 1971), pp. 363–391.

19. Uniform Rights of the Terminally Ill Act § 7, 9A Uniform Laws Ann. (Supp. 1986).

20. Don Marquis, "Leaving Therapy to Chance," *Hastings Center Report* 13: 40–47, August 1983.

21. In *On Liberty*, John Stuart Mill criticized a similar structure of layered judgments as grounds for censorship: that the censor's moral views are the right ones and that the censor's judgment about their rightness is so likely to be right that censorship is justified. J. S. Mill, *On Liberty* (New York: Penguin, 1982).

22. Although I don't explore them here, there are very interesting questions about whether it would be permissible or obligatory for a therapist to disobey regulations in the interests of patient care. On one side of the balance are the therapist's fiduciary obligations to patients; on the other side are social judgments about the allocation of resources. There may, of course, be situations when the efficacy of the therapy is in dispute, in which case the therapist's dilemma is more like that of the researcher. We might expect such moral conflicts to arise with more frequency if we move toward the kinds of cost constraints found in the British National Health Service. See H. J. Aaron and W. B. Schwartz, *The Painful Prescription* (Washington, D.C.: The Brookings Institution, 1984). For discussion of the possibility of conscientious objection to treatment practices in neonatal intensive care units, see Robert F. Weir, *Selective Nontreatment of Handicapped Newborns: Moral Dilemmas in Neonatal Medicine* (New York: Oxford University Press, 1984).

23. Rawls, *Justice*, p. 364.

24. Robert S. Broadhead, "Human Rights and Human Subjects: Ethics and Strategies in Social Science Research," *Sociological Inquiry* 54: 107–123, 1984.

25. I owe this example to Anita Silvers.

26. In the lawsuit that followed the first implantation of an artificial heart some fifteen years ago, the allegation was made that Dr. Cooley had selected the patient for initial surgery (a wedge resection) because of his desire to test the artificial device. *Karp v. Cooley*, 493 F.2d 408 (5th Cir. 1974), *cert. denied*, 419 U.S. 845 (1974).

27. 45 C.F.R. § 46.116(f) (1986).

28. 45 C.F.R. § 46.116(c), (d) (1986).

29. 21 C.F.R. § 56.104(c) (1986). A third possibility is FDA allowance of "compassionate use" of an unapproved drug or device for treatment of individual patients. This is not

an emergency situation, however, but authorization of a last-ditch alternative for patients before widespread clinical trials have been approved.

30. For example, the research subject must be informed of any reasonably foreseeable risks and benefits, of available alternative forms of therapy, of costs or payments, and of the extent to which his or her privacy will be protected. 21 C.F.R. § 50.25 (1986). In some states, by contrast, written consent of a competent patient creates a rebuttable presumption that consent was informed. See, for example, Idaho Code Ann. § 39-4305 (1985).

31. 21 C.F.R. § 50.23 (1986).

32. Annas, for example, emphasized the possibility that an individual would prefer death to experimental prolongation of a life of limited quality. Sec supra note 4.

33. This narrative is based on the FDA's investigation into the Phoenix heart implant. Memorandum from Tucson Resident Consumer Safety Officer, HFR-9540, and Regional Medical Officer, HFR-018 to District Director, HFR-9200, "Investigation Into Circumstances Leading to An Unapproved Use of an Experimental Total Artificial Heart at the University of Arizona Medical Center—March 6, 1985," April 3, 1985. [hereinafter, Memorandum].

34. Letter from John C. Villforth, director, Center for Devices and Radiological Health, Food and Drug Administration, to Alethea Caldwell, administrator, University Medical Center, Tucson, Arizona, March 8, 1985.

35. Memorandum, p. 2.

36. Letter from John C. Villforth, director, Center for Devices and Radiological Health, FDA, to Alethea Caldwell, administrator, University Medical Center, Tucson, Arizona, May 10, 1985.

37. Memorandum, pp. 8–9.

38. Annas, "The Phoenix Heart" pp. 15–16.

39. Memorandum, p. 20.

40. Memorandum, p. 21.

41. Memorandum, p. 26.

42. Memorandum, p. 27.

43. 50 Fed. Reg. 42866 (Oct. 22, 1985).

44. For an argument urging tough safeguards against overeager use of patients as research subjects in emergencies, see Ellen J. Flannery, "Should It be Easier or Harder to Use Unapproved Drugs and Devices?" *Hastings Center Report* 16: 17–23, February 1986.

45. 51 Fed. Reg. 26830 (July 25, 1986).

46. 21 C.F.R. § 312.35 (1987).

47. 52 Fed. Reg. 19467 (May 22, 1987).

48. 21 C.F.R. § 312.34(3)(a), (b) (1987).

49. 21 C.F.R. § 312.34(2) (1987).

50. 21 C.F.R. § 312.34(a) (1987).

51. 52 Fed. Reg. 19468 (May 22, 1987).

52. 21 C.F.R. § 312.35(a)(2)(vii) (1987).

53. Indeed, one of the most troubling features of the new regulations is that sponsors of clinical trials may likewise charge patients, provided the clinical trial is not undermined. 21 C.F.R. § 312.7 (1987). A discussion of the problems of pricing, equity, access, and financing that this change forebodes is beyond the scope of this paper.

54. 52 Fed. Reg. 19470 (May 22, 1987).

55. 21 C.F.R. §§ 312.32, 312.35(b)(1)(vii) (1987).

56. 21 C.F.R. § 312.42(b)(3)(ii) (1987).

20

Death and the Magic Machine: Informed Consent to the Artificial Heart

George J. Annas

Introduction

Jay Katz introduces his remarkable and insightful book, *The Silent World of Doctor and Patient*,[1] by recounting a portion of Solzhenitsyn's *Cancer Ward*.[2] He describes an encounter between a patient, Oleg Kostoglotov, and his doctor, Dr. Ludmilla Afanasyevna. The doctor wanted to use experimental hormone treatment, but the patient refused. Katz argues that what made conversation impossible between them was the patient's undisclosed intention of leaving the hospital to treat himself with "a secret medicine, a mandrake root from Issyk Kul." He could not trust the doctor with this information because the doctor would make the decision for the patient in any event, because the doctor believed, "doctors *are* entitled to that right . . . without that right there's be no such thing as medicine."[3]

Katz objects to this notion, pointing out that "if doctors are 'entitled to that right,' then patients must continue to trust them silently." But he also chastises "proponents of informed consent and patient self-determination" (among whom I number myself),[4] who "have insufficiently appreciated that trusting oneself and others to become aware of the certainties and uncertainties that surround the practice of medicine, and to integrate them with one's hopes, fears, and realistic expectations, are inordinately difficult tasks" (p. xv). His purpose in this book, he tells us, is not to explore informed consent in great depth, but to "identify as many issues as possible and to pursue them for some distance" (p. xx).

My own purpose is to explore one of the many "leads" Professor Katz offers in a bit more depth: the application of informed consent to artificial heart experimentation. Using this extreme example, I will argue that Katz is certainly correct in proposing more in-depth, informed and trusting conversation between doctor-researcher and patient-subject. But much more than conversation is required to promote and protect the rights *and* welfare of individual subjects.

Solzhenitsyn's fictional patient, Oleg, *knows* about his folk remedy, and so satisfies the informational requirements of informed consent:

> When I get back to Ush-Terek I'll use the issyk-kul root to keep the tumor from producing metastases. There is something noble in curing with strong poison. Poison doesn't pretend to be innocent medicine. *It says plainly: I am poison. Watch out! Or else. And we know what risk we're taking.*[5]

Suppose that it was not Oleg, but Dr. Afanasyevna who was proposing to use the issyk-kul root; and suppose doctor and patient had discussed this "experimental treatment" at length, and that Oleg understood the risks perfectly. Under these conditions would we or should we conclude that it is perfectly acceptable for the issyk-kul root to be administered to Oleg? This commentary argues that while such informed consent is a necessary precondition to lawful human·experimentation, it is not a sufficient one. Prior to the conversation and offer of an experimental intervention, an *independent judgment* must be made that the proposed therapy, be it surgery, radiation, or an issyk-kul root, is a reasonable medical experiment from both a scientific and public policy perspective. This is necessary to protect the patient's *welfare;* to prevent patients from being demeaned and dehumanized by accepting offers they are in no position to refuse.

Medical ethicist John Fletcher of the National Institutes of Health (NIH), for example, correctly argues that "the major ethical question in research is whether the experiment ought to be done at all."[6] The law, as embodied in the Nuremberg Code[7] and current NIH regulations,[8] is consistent with this view. The Nuremberg Code, formulated on the basis of international criminal law by American judges sitting in the Nazi War Crimes Trials, sets forth ten prerequisites for *legal* human experimentation. The first principle deals with the informed consent of the research subject, or what may be termed the subject's rights. The other nine principles have primarily to do with protecting the subject's welfare: they set forth actions that must be taken *prior to* seeking subject enrollment in the experiment. These actions include a determination that the experiment is designed properly to yield fruitful results "unprocurable by other methods"; that its "anticipated results" will justify performance of the experiment; that all "unnecessary physical and mental suffering and injury" is avoided; that there is no "*a priori* reason to believe that death or disabling injury will occur"; that the project has "humanitarian importance" that outweighs the degree of risk; that "adequate preparation" is taken to "protect the experimental subject against even the remote possibilities of injury, disability, or death"; that only "scientifically qualified" persons conduct the experiment; that the subject can terminate participation at any time; and that the experimenter is prepared to terminate the experiment if "continuation is likely to result in injury, disability, or death to the experimental subject."[9]

NIH and FDA [Food and Drug Administration] have codified these general preconditions in their regulations, and local committees, called Institutional Review Boards (IRBs) are mandated to review research protocols prior to subject recruitment to see to it that these preconditions have been observed.[10] Our initial experience with heart transplantation, and our current experience with the artificial heart, illustrate how informed consent can be used improperly as an excuse to justify massive assaults on the welfare of human subjects, even though the quality of the consent is highly questionable, and the quality of the experiment itself does not meet the welfare requirements of the Nuremberg Code.

Informed Consent to Heart Transplantation

Professor Katz's casebook *Experimentation with Human Beings*,[11] has had a profound impact on my own thinking, and I used it as a text in more than a dozen courses during the 1970s. It is the finest collection of materials ever assembled on this subject. One of my favorite readings from the casebook is the excerpt from Philip Blaiberg's *Looking at My Heart*,[12] portions of which Jay Katz also reproduces in his powerful chapter VI, "Respecting Autonomy: The Obligation for Conversation" in *The Silent World of Doctor and Patient* (pp. 130–39). In this chapter, Katz persuasively demonstrates that Philip Blaiberg, the recipient of the world's second human-to-human heart transplant, regressed when in the presence of Dr. Christiaan Barnard. He saw him as an "omnipotent parent and hero . . . Barnard became General Smuts, under whom Blaiberg had served and admired greatly . . . Barnard also became Christ, the powerful protector" (p. 132). But in identifying Barnard as Christ, Blaiberg may have "confused his own identity with that of the surgeon" (pp. 132–33). He actually said he wanted to go through with the operation "not only for my sake but for you [Barnard] and your team who put so much into your effort to save Louis Washkansky" (p. 132). Barnard himself seemed unaware of this confusion on the part of his patient, and of his own conflict of interest between wanting to perform the world's second human heart transplant for himself, and attempting to convince Blaiberg that the operation was in Blaiberg's best interests. Indeed, Barnard even began talking about the operation as fulfilling not his own goals, but "Washkansky's dream." This, as Professor Katz notes, "is startling and suggests that he was as confused about his identity as Blaiberg was about his own" (pp. 139–40).

Louis Washkansky, the recipient of the world's *first* human-to-human heart transplant, it turned out, also was not particularly interested in discussing the details of heart transplantation. Barnard did not press the issue, deciding "no words were needed." But were they? Katz argues that more words (conversation) may not have changed the ultimate decision, but could have improved "the nature and quality of Barnard's and Washkansky's thinking about available choices" (p. 137).

> Both, at best, had reflected on the forthcoming operation in isolation, and neither had any idea what had transpired in the other's mind. At the least, respect for Washkansky's psychological autonomy required Barnard to challenge his patient's silent acquiescence. . . . *If Washkansky wanted a new heart, he also had to have the heart to learn more about the operation* (pp. 140–41).[13]

Katz continues by noting that since the first heart transplant operations were "extraordinary" procedures, candidates should be *required* to learn about them, and not permitted to give disclosure and consent. "Barnard should have insisted they talk for a while" (p. 141). Katz concludes his discussion of this case by noting the common clinical controversy over whether to respect the patient's "rights" or "needs" (p. 141). I shall restate this "conflict" by attempting to construct a system that protects both the "rights" and "welfare" of subjects of "extraordinary" human experimentation.

Katz presents a psychoanalytic explanation of the dynamics of the doctor-patient relationship in the dramatic human experimentation context, and suggests conversation to help elucidate issues of transference and countertransference. He argues powerfully that "[m]agical and hopeful expectations exist side by side with expectations of cruel disappointment" (p. 144). And later, he notes that when medical knowledge and skill prove impotent against the claims of nature, "all kinds of senseless interventions are tried in an unconscious effort to cure the incurable magically through a 'wonder drug,' a novel surgical procedure, or a penetrating psychological interpretation" (p. 151). He hopes that through education,

[a]t least medical students can learn to appreciate that *it may be their magical hopes that cause them to intervene,* rather than believing that they are responding to the *magical expectations of their patients.* Thus doctors' heroic attempts to try anything may not necessarily be responsive to patients' needs but may turn out to be a *projection of their own needs onto patients* (p. 151).[14]

This powerful insight is descriptive not only of the behavior of human heart transplant pioneers, but also seems to have set the standard for the behavior of surgeons involved in artificial heart experimentation. In his autobiography, *One Life,*[15] Christiaan Barnard has a conversation with himself in which he tries to explain why he did not have further discussions with Louis Washkansky about the risks and likely outcomes of the first human-to-human heart transplant:

I offered a chance, and he grabbed it, without asking any questions. *At the South Pole, the wind can blow in one direction only—north. At the point of death, any promise of help can go in one direction only—toward hope.* So I offered him hope, believing this was my duty. To have refused it would be a betrayal of myself and my profession. In a way, *we share the same hope.* We're in this together.[16]

This rationalization, of course, is consistent with Katz's notion that Barnard had confused himself with his patient. It also is consistent with Dr. Afanasyevna's view that "doctors *are* entitled." It takes this view even further, however, by arguing that doctors have a *duty:* "to have refused it would be a betrayal of myself *and my profession.*" But it also indicates that Dr. Barnard believed that for Washkansky *there really is no choice;* that since he was dying he *must* accept a heart transplant. It was his only hope, and some hope is always better than none. Later, Dr. Barnard refined the analogy, and the rationale for action in the absence of full discussion, by arguing that for Washkansky the alternatives were so obvious that the choice was trivial:

For a dying man, it is not a difficult because he knows he is at the end. If a lion chases you to the bank of a river filled with crocodiles, you will leap into the water convinced you have a chance to swim to the other side. But you would never accept such odds if there were no lion.[17]

This "lion and the crocodiles" analogy has become the standard by which artificial heart experimenters discuss the decisions of their patient-subjects to this day. For example, when Dr. Denton Cooley implanted the world's first total *artificial* heart into the chest of Haskell Harp, in 1969, he initially argued that his own skill and the patient's consent were the only justification needed:

I have done more heart surgery than anyone else in the world. . . . Based on this experience, I believe I am qualified to judge what is right and proper for my patients. *The permission I receive to do what I do, I receive from my patients.* It is not received from a government agency or from one of my seniors.[18]

Later, however, he restated the issue of the patient's consent in "lion and crocodile" terms: "He was a drowning man. *A drowning man can't be too particular what he's going to use as a possible life preserver.* It was a desperate thing, and he knew it."[19]

More recently we have witnessed the advent of "permanent" artificial hearts, and renewed interest in using artificial hearts on a temporary basis as a "bridge" (or "tollgate") to a human heart transplant. The informed consent issues explicated by Katz remain relegated to matters of secondary concern and unaddressed in any but crude and primitive manners.

Permanent Artificial Hearts and Informed Consent

Prior to performing the world's first *permanent* artificial heart implant, Dr. William DeVries, like Dr. Cooley, underlined his view of the importance of informed consent as the primary justification for performing the procedure. One major problem was that the only power source available was an approximately 400 pound drive cart, which had to be attached to both a power source and a source of compressed air, that made ambulation almost impossible. Many, including one of the device's designers, Dr. Robert Jarvik, believed the device shouldn't be used on humans until it was easily portable or entirely implantable. Dr. DeVries disagreed:

Many people have asked us the question as to—it's not fully implantable, why then would you do it? Why don't you wait ten years, when it's implantable, and then do it? *But the key is informed consent. Why should I let people die,* when I can give them a chance to live—if they're willing to accept the limitations of the external pumping system?[20]

Dr. DeVries is certainly correct insofar as he asserts that the informed consent of his subject is a *necessary* prerequisite to acceptable human experimentation: if the subject's competent, voluntary, informed and understanding consent cannot be obtained, the experiment cannot be performed lawfully or ethically.[21] Even in this regard, however, it can be argued persuasively that although the consent form and process used by Dr. DeVries in the Barney Clark case is a *vast* improvement over the consent process used by Dr. Christiaan Barnard, and a considerable improvement over the consent form and process used by Dr. Denton Cooley, it was still seriously deficient.

Specifically, Dr. Clark signed an eleven page consent form that is more notable for its length than its content. It was incomplete, internally inconsistent, and confusing. It assumed, as his physicians then believed, that Dr. Clark would either die on the table, or go home in about ten days and continue to be mentally competent for the rest of his life. It took no account at all of a "halfway success"; survival coupled with severe confusion, mental incompetence, or coma. The consent form made no provisions for proxy consent to additional procedures or experiments in the event of incompetence, for a mechanism to terminate the experiment, or for how Dr. Clark would die. These and other shortcomings are serious and evidence a lack of clear thinking and planning on the part of Dr. DeVries and the Utah IRB.[22] But one can argue that it is easy to be critical of *any* initial attempt, and that no local IRB could have done better. As Professor Al Jonsen has put it, the Utah IRB, in devising a consent form and process with Dr. DeVries, was asked "to build a Boeing 747 with Wright Brothers parts."[23] What about changes that have been made over the past four years in the consent form and process?

Disturbingly, there have been very few changes, and most have been for the worse. Since Dr. DeVries moved to Humana Audubon in Louisville, Kentucky, to conduct his permanent artificial heart implants, he has done three more as of December, 1986. In May, 1985, after completing all four of his implants, he discussed the issue of informed consent to the artificial heart with *New York Times* medical writer, Dr. Lawrence K. Altman. Dr. Altman reports:

> Dr. DeVries has repeatedly said that the four men in whom he has implanted artificial hearts were so coerced by their diseases that they felt that death was their only alternative. In signing the 17-page consent form, each recipient, Dr. DrVries has said, "told me in their own way that they didn't care" if they read it or not, and had signed it primarily because they had to [in order] to get the device.[24]

This is a devastating admission from a surgeon who uses informed consent as *the* primary justification for permanent artificial heart implants in humans. Was it the patients or Dr. DeVries who believed in every case that "death was their only alternative?" And what would it take to persuade Dr. DeVries either that there were other alternatives, or that death could be preferable to the "magic machine?"[25] Professor Katz's concern with requiring conversation, and exploring what myths or beliefs the surgeons and their patients are harboring that permit them to accept silence seems especially critical when dealing with the most highly publicized experiment in the history of the world.

The primary rationale for accepting silence seems to be the same one that comforted Drs. Barnard and Cooley: the patient was dying and so had no choice. In Dr. DeVries' words concerning Dr. Barney Clark: "He was too old for a transplant, there were no drugs that would help; the only thing that he could look forward to was dying."[26]

These experiences raise the question as to whether we can ever justify experimentation on very sick, terminally ill patients. Doesn't their disease, Solzhenitsyn's story of Oleg notwithstanding, inevitably coerce them into "volunteering" for something they necessarily will see as hopeful? And won't parents inevitably volunteer their children for even bizarre and unprecedented experiments, like xenografts, if they are led to believe the experiment might prevent death?[27] Here Katz helps us again, by insisting on explicit recognition of the limits of interventions at the end of life. Of course, we can justify experimentation on such individuals *only* if we can obtain their voluntary and informed consent.

But informed consent *alone* is an insufficient justification for radical human experimentation. Proper attention to the other nine precepts of the Nuremberg Code, for example, would have required us to address the question of whether there isn't an "*a priori*" reason to believe that "death or disabling injury" will necessarily follow from this experiment; whether such a "halfway success" of continued life in a severely compromised state doesn't amount to "unnecessary physical and mental suffering and injury"; and whether the "anticipated results" justify the performance of this experiment. The welfare of the subject of this experiment does not seem to have been addressed adequately, and until it was, consent for the experiment should not have been sought.

Dr. DeVries sometimes seemed to justify this experimental shortcoming by acting as if he believed he was engaged in therapy, not experimentation at all. At times, for example, he suggested that his goal was to get his patient to go home, or to "play a round of golf." In fact, this scenario never seems to have been realistic. Dr. Clark realized, shortly before his death, that although he also had hoped for some therapeutic gain, he had become involved in "pure nontherapeutic experimentation" for others. Asked by Dr. DeVries in his only publicly shown videotaped interview if the experience had been hard, Dr. Clark replied, "[y]es, it's been hard, but the heart itself has pumped right all along and *I think it's doing well.*"[28] Clark, it seems, fully realized what DeVries could not admit openly: the subject, who at the outset was a patient seen as an end with the artificial heart used as a means to sustain him, had become simply a means to the end of sustaining the artificial heart. Dr. Clark nonetheless might have agreed to this experiment in advance even if he had known that he would spend most of his 112 remaining days on earth in an intensive care unit, extremely debilitated and depressed, and mentally incompetent at most times. But if this had been known, the IRB should not have approved the experiment since it would have violated most of the basic precepts of subject protection set forth in the Nuremberg Code.

Consent, even informed consent, cannot convert an otherwise unacceptable experiment into an acceptable one. *Before* patients are asked to consent to experimental procedures, the procedure itself must be judged *independently* to be a reasonable one to perform on a human being. Using informed consent in a vacuum without such independent review, makes desperate, dying patients targets for quackery, because an offer of "life" from a physician (whom patients are likely to mistake and misidentify as Christ or God) is an offer dying patients are in no reasonable position to refuse. Use of informed consent in this context converts it from a shield designed to protect the patient into a sword designed to attack the patient's vulnerability. There is an element of paternalism in this suggestion, of course, but no more than that involved in licensing physicians, including these experimenters, and regulating prescription drugs. But we are unlikely to succeed at protecting subject welfare unless we provide terminally ill patients with more procedural protections than we provide healthy volunteers. Much more imaginative work needs to be done on informed consent to permanent implants (and more experimentation with animal models as well) before additional implants can be justified. IRBs have been unable to contribute much to protecting patients in this setting, and although their prior review is legally and ethically required, it has been superficial to date and remains insufficient to protect potential subjects adequately.[29]

Artificial Hearts for "Temporary" Use

Dr. Denton Cooley implanted the world's first two mechanical hearts for temporary use in 1969 and 1981.[30] After these two implants, Dr. DeVries performed four permanent implants and Dr. Bjarne Semb performed one in Sweden. After these seven implants, "temporary" mechanical implants, used to sustain the patient until a human heart for transplant becomes available, have dominated the field. This use is controversial for many reasons, not the least of which is that as long as there is a shortage of human hearts for transplant, temporary artificial hearts are unlikely to save any net lives; they will only change the identity of those who actually obtain the human hearts.[31] Moreover, the way these devices change the recipient's identity is an inherently unfair one, by permitting those with artificial hearts to "jump the queue" and become first in line for the next available matching human heart.[32]

But my quarry here is informed consent. Initially, note that temporary artificial hearts *always* have the possibility of becoming *de facto* permanent (*e.g.*, if the patient suffers a complication, such as a stroke, that makes him or her ineligible for a human heart transplant). Since this risk is real,[33] we should require informed consent procedures to be at least as rigorous as those for permanent implantation.

But the historical record to date is one of almost indifference to informed consent. This highly experimental intervention has been justified consistently primarily on the basis that it is a therapeutic modality in an *emergency* setting. The third use of such a temporary device (after Dr. Denton Cooley's two) was perhaps the most clumsy and embarrassing since it involved a device that was not even designed or approved for use in human beings.[34] I describe the case in some detail because it has set the tone for a rash of "me-too" experiments similar to those that followed Christiaan Barnard's first human-to-human heart transplant,[35] and has directly caused the FDA to take a *laissez faire* attitude toward "temporary" implants that seems to be an abdication of the agency's responsibility to protect the public from unproven and untested medical devices.

The Case of the Phoenix Heart

On Tuesday morning, March 5, 1985, Dr. Jack Copeland, Chief of University Medical Center's Heart Transplant Team in Tucson, Arizona, performed a human heart transplant on Thomas Creighton, a thirty-three year old, divorced father of two. The procedure was not a success, as Mr. Creighton's body rejected the heart. At 3:00 a.m. Wednesday morning a search for another human heart began, and Dr. Copeland placed Mr. Creighton on a heart-lung machine. At 5:30 a.m. the medical team placed a call to Dr. Cecil Vaughn of Phoenix, asking if he had an artificial heart ready for human use. Dr. Vaughn was scheduled to implant an experimental model developed by dentist Kevin Cheng into a calf later that day, and had never considered use of the device in a human. Nonetheless, he called Dr. Cheng. Dr. Cheng told him, "It's designed for a calf and not ready for a human yet." Asked to think about it for ten minutes, Dr. Cheng recalls, "I knelt and prayed." When Vaughn called him back he said, "The pump is sterile, ready to go."[36] The two helicoptered from the hospital to the airport, chartered a jet to Tucson, and then took another helicopter to the Tucson hospital. They arrived at 9:30 a.m. Wednesday morning. The implant procedure began at noon. Designed for a calf, it was too large, and surgeons could not close the chest around the device. The implant maintained circulation until 11:00 p.m. that night when, in preparation for a second heart transplant, doctors turned it off and put Mr. Creighton back on the heart-lung machine. By 3:00 a.m. Thursday, Dr. Copeland completed a second human heart transplant. The next day Mr. Creighton died.

The press treated the story like a modern American melodrama. *USA Today* called the implantation of Dr. Chen's heart "the fulfillment of an American dream."[37] *The New York Times* editorialized that "the artificial heart has at last proved it has a useful role. . . ."[38] *Time* headlined the event as a "bold gamble";[39] and *Newsweek* faulted the FDA, noting, "[i]t's hardly fair to doctors, or their patients, to make them break the law to save a life."[40] The FDA initially termed the unauthorized experiment a violation of the law, but by week's end had done an about face and was flailing itself as "part of the problem."[41]

Dr. Copeland relied upon the same two basic excuses his predecessors had used to justify the implant in the absence of the patient's consent: (1) the "only other option was just to let him die" so "we had nothing to lose"; and (2) in an emergency, a physician can do anything to save the patient's life.[42] Neither of these assertions can stand scrutiny. The physician may have "nothing to lose," but the patient certainly does. The choice is *not*, as the five permanent implant patients have all demonstrated, simply one between "life and death." The much more likely scenario is life in a severely disabled and debilitated state; a risk to which *only the patient himself or herself* should be able to consent. The rationale that for a dying patient anything is justified, is an illustration of what Professor Katz has termed the "magical thinking"; that the doctor actually has the power to conquer death, and that prolonged life (or prolonging the dying process) is *always* a reasonable medical goal.[43]

Likewise, the emergency argument is misplaced. *All* heart-diseased patients will encounter such an "emergency" before they die, and to use this as an excuse to experiment dehumanizes them, making them "fair game" for any experiment no matter how bizarre or extreme. This, of course, is not the law. "Emergencies" like this are anticipatable[44] and must be planned for, with the patient's consent, if risky and extreme experimental interventions are to be offered.[45]

The FDA collapsed when Dr. Copeland asserted he was only trying to "save a life" and did not notify the agency of his plans because he did "not want to make the government his [Mr. Creighton's] executioner."[46] Professor Katz would probably see this assertion as another example of identity confusion on the part of the surgeon: Dr. Copeland seems to be projecting the role of "executioner" upon himself, and took objectively useless steps to try to prevent the death of his patient which he had (albeit in an attempt to save him), directly caused by his own interventions. Conversations with the patient might clarify this confusion, but more than conversation is required to prevent a recurrence of such well-intentioned but pointless "experimentation."

Instead of attempting to curtail and contain experimental temporary use, the FDA actually took steps that served to encourage and spread it, and did so in a way that almost guarantees that nothing scientifically useful will be learned from temporary implants. In October, 1985, the FDA released proposed guidelines that permit *any* surgeon to use any artificial heart in an "emergency" like the one just described.[47] By February, 1986, the FDA had also given four centers approval to do ten such implants each and by the end of 1986, surgeons had performed at least fifteen additional "temporary" implants.[48] There was no master protocol, no uniform patient selection criteria, and, as the reader should be able to guess by now, we have seen no advancements in the area of informed consent.

Indeed, the informed consent forms and processes devised by the first four centers to use the artificial heart as a planned temporary measure are all different and all significantly inadequate, suffering from all or almost all of the shortcomings involved in obtaining consent for permanent use. It seems likely that the reason doctors have not taken consent seriously at all in the "temporary" setting is because the primary argument given for use of the temporary artificial heart is its alleged "emergency" nature. In fact, in at least two of the first five such implants, the patients themselves did not personally participate in any meaningful way in the consent process.[49] And in Europe's first "temporary" use, doctors did not even tell the patient of the planned procedure "because we wanted to prevent him from being disturbed."[50] This is unacceptable. The medical community should never view a patient who does not personally consent to its implantation as an appropriate subject for experimentation with the artificial heart since this is a profoundly radical experiment that can have predictable, devastating effects on the subject.

Indeed, Dr. Copeland's third "bridge" patient (his second was a spectacular success),[51] endured perhaps the most brutal course of any of the permanent or temporary recipients to date, and it is impossible to argue reasonably that her personal consent should not have been required for each step of her experimental course. Mrs. Bernadette Chayrez became the second woman in the world to receive an artificial heart on February 3, 1986. Four days later Dr. Copeland removed it, and replaced it with a human heart. The transplant was unsuccessful. Subsequently, without the patient's consent, but with that of her family, she became the first person to receive a second artificial heart on February 9. The implant turned out to be permanent, and Mrs. Chayrez spent the rest of her life, 212 days, in the hospital on her "temporary" artificial heart. She died on October 11, 1986, shortly after an attempt to transplant another human heart into her body.[52]

In commenting on the experience, Dr. Copeland has been unable to recognize the ethical issues, or properly separate his own identity from that of his patient. He has said, for example, "It was almost like we were married to her, we all felt so close to her after all these months."[53] In this spousal role, he could not envision terminating the experiment even when it was a clear failure. In his words, "[i]f you cannot transplant a patient, *the only option* is to maintain them the best you can on a total artificial heart."[54] He could not face the patient's death, and suggests that perhaps "a committee of bioethicists and critics who want to save a few bucks could turn the pump off . . . let them turn the *damned thing* off."[55] The "damned thing" Dr. Copeland was referring to was, of course, the artificial heart; but he may just as well have been describing his patient. As for ethical problems, Dr. Copeland is clear, "I don't see any ethical problems at all in what happened with Bernadette . . . I see the work that we are doing here in the same light as . . . sending up the spacecraft into outer space. Now what possible benefit can we derive from that? A tremendous benefit. *Our endeavors are the same.*"[56]

With such a fantasyland view of one's activities, it should probably not be surprising that informed consent is a relatively trivial matter to the heart implanters. They should, however, recall that even at the height of our competition with the Soviet Union to put the first man on the moon, the United States rejected a proposal to send a manned flight before we could insure its safe return. Even though volunteers could be obtained, it was thought to be *a priori* wrong to send a man to his death even for something clearly seen as in the national interest. Informed consent was simply an inadequate justification for the taking of a human life. It is also an inadequate justification for artificial heart experimentation.

Even if it were sufficient, however, we are not taking it seriously at all in the temporary setting. And informed consent must be taken seriously, at least seriously enough to establish *uniform minimal standards* that all American centers using "temporary" artificial hearts must meet regarding informed consent. Of course, these should be developed in conjunction with a uniform master protocol and patient selection criteria, so that some useful scientific information can be obtained from multicenter use.[57] The consent forms and processes from the four primary American centers currently doing temporary implants demonstrate major variations on significant issues that should be clarified and agreed upon before further implants are permitted.[58]

Conclusion

Artificial hearts did not create all the problems they have exposed in our informed consent procedures and IRB review. Nonetheless, these problems are real, and the advent of the artificial heart provides us with an opportunity to take meaningful action. This action should not only protect the rights and welfare of potential recipients of the artificial heart, but also should help set high standards for other controversial human experiments and develop fair and equitable allocation schemes for human organs. Work on informed consent is *necessary,* but not alone sufficient to permit artificial heart experimentation.

Because the issues of patient consent and quality medical research in the area of the artificial heart have not received sufficient attention and concern to adequately protect subjects of these experiments, there should be a moratorium on further artificial heart research with humans. This moratorium should continue until a joint review and oversight committee of the FDA and NIH[59] has developed and approved the scientific reasonableness, proper use, clear patient selection criteria, adequate informed consent procedures, and clear rules on stopping individual experiments. Permanent artificial heart implants should be suspended at least temporarily because of the devastating results they have had on subjects and their families, because their original justifications are no longer valid, and because the consent process used is too primitive to protect human subjects. Temporary artificial heart implants should be suspended for the same reasons, and additionally because there are no multicenter protocols, and the United States has yet to develop a fair and equitable method for allocating scarce human hearts.

Human experimentation is a public enterprise, and the use to which humans are put, as well as the mandatory minimum procedures used to protect their rights and welfare, are matters of serious public concern. As illustrated by the most public experiments in the history of the world, these issues are taking a back seat to the hype and glitz of what currently passes for "scientific medicine." It is imperative that we reassert the importance of human values implicit in the Nuremberg Code before the Code is quietly rewritten by well-meaning inventors and researchers.

I hope Professor Katz will find the following thoughts of another patient in the *Cancer Ward* a fitting conclusion to a discussion of "death-defying" magical heart implants and informed consent.

Of course he knew that since all people are mortal, some day he too would have to turn in his check. But *some day,* not now! It was not frightening to die right now. Why? Because: How would it be? Afterwards, what? And how would it be not to exist, how would it be without me? . . . *[H]e could not even think about it, he could not decide or say anything.*[60]

Notes

1. J. Katz, The Silent World of Doctor and Patient (1984) [hereinafter Katz].
2. A. I. Solzhenitsyn, The Cancer Ward (1968).
3. *Id., quoted in* Katz, *supra* note 1, at xv.
4. G. J. Annas, The Rights of Hospital Patients 57–91 (1975).
5. A. I. Solzhenitsyn, *supra* note 2, at 347 (emphasis added).
6. Fletcher, *The Evolution of the Ethics of Informed Consent,* in Research Ethics 211 (K. Berg & K. Teanoy eds. 1983).
7. *Reprinted in* J. Katz, Experimentation with Human Beings 305–06 (1972) [hereinafter Experimentation with Human Beings]. The Declaration of Helsinki is similar, but has been described as "less legalistic." *E.g.,* Refshauge, *The Place for International Standards in Conducting Research on Humans,* 55 Bull. World Health Org. 135 (1977).
8. Protection of Human Subjects, FDA, HHS, 46 Fed. Reg. 8942 (1981). *See also* Proposed Model Federal Policy for Protection of Human Subjects, Office of Science and Technology, 51 Fed. Reg. 20,204 (1986).
9. *See* Experimentation with Human Beings, *supra* note 7, at 305–06.
10. R. Levine, Ethics and Regulation of Clinical Research (2d ed. 1986).
11. Experimentation with Human Beings, *supra* note 7.
12. *Id.* at 640–42.
13. (emphasis added).
14. (emphasis added).
15. C. Barnard, One Life (1969).
16. *Id.* at 293 (emphasis added).
17. *Id.* (emphasis added). Recently, Dr. Barnard has moved to the United States, "discovered" Glycosphingolipids, a compound he believes rejuvenates the skin, and has begun arguing that physicians should be legally granted "the right of active euthanasia. . . . [Because] [t]here is no point in using medical technology to prolong a painful death or an empty life." In discussing his own past heart transplant work he says individuals inevitably and wrongly asked him "how long" his patients had survived. "They should have asked whether surgery had improved the patient's life. If so, it was a success, even if he survived only a few months. If not, it had failed, no matter how long he lived. . . ." He argues that "patients usually understand this better than the rest of us": "They are seldom obsessed with surviving at all costs, and they grow less so in proportion to their illness. *In contrast, it is the healthy who need to cling even to the bitterest life."* Barnard, First Word, Omni, Mar. 1986, at 6 (emphasis added). These words, of course, have direct application to Dr. Barnard's conversations with both Washkansky and Blaiberg. They also indicate how radically his own thinking about death has changed over the past twenty years.
18. T. Thompson, Hearts 216 (1971) (emphasis added).
19. J. Thorwald, The Patients 402 (1971) (emphasis added). The Karp implant led to a lawsuit by his widow against Dr. Cooley primarily alleging lack of informed consent. Both the trial court and the appeals court summarily dismissed the notion that more than the patient's consent was needed to justify this experiment. They concluded that the implant was therapy for a dying man: "[T]he record contains no evidence that Mr. Karp's treatment was other than therapeutic and we agree that in this context an action for experimentation must be measured by traditional evidentiary malpractice standards." Karp v. Cooley, 493 F.2d 408, 423–24 (5th Cir. 1974), *aff'g* Karp v. Cooley, 349 F. Supp. 827 (S.D. Tex. 1972). This conclusion is untenable. Either the judge was not presented with sufficient evidence at trial about the nature of this first-of-its-kind human experiment, or the judge viewed the risks involved as irrelevant. For a fuller discussion of this case, see G. J. Annas, L. H. Glantz & B. F. Katz, Informed Consent to Human Experimentation: The Subject's Dilemma 11–14 (1977).
20. *Nova, Artificial Heart* (Time-Life Video 1984) at 3 (transcript). The other major problem was and remains the incompatibility of human blood and the device's surface that leads to clotting.
21. *See* G. J. Annas, L. H. Glantz & B. F. Katz, *supra* note 19, at 27–61.

22. For a fuller discussion of this form, see Annas, *Consent to the Artificial Heart: The Lion and the Crocodiles,* Hastings Center Rep., Apr. 1983, at 20–22. For arguments that the form and process was reasonable, see After Barney Clark 22–24 (M. Shaw ed. 1983) ("I believe that Barney Clark's consent was autonomous, voluntary, and fully informed.") [hereinafter After Barney Clark]; Galetti, *Replacement of the Heart with a Mechanical Device: The Case of Dr. Barney Clark,* 310 New Eng. J. Med. 312 (1984); Levine, *Total Artificial Heart Implantation—Eligibility Criteria,* 252 J. A.M.A. 1458 (1984) ("Considering the alternatives . . . I think he made an easily understandable choice . . . ."). For a discussion of Dr. Clark's psychiatric history before and during the experiment, see Berenson & Grosser, *Total Artificial Heart Implantation,* 41 Arch. Gen. Psychiatry 910 (1984).

23. On the role of the IRB, see Eichwald, Woolley, Cole & Beamer, *Insertion of the Total Artificial Heart,* IRB, Aug./Sept., 1981 at 6; Woolley, *Ethical Issues in the Implantation of the Total Artificial Heart,* 310 New Eng. J. Med. 292 (1984).

24. Altman, *The Ordeal of a "Human Experiment,"* N.Y. Times, May 14, 1985, at C3, col. 2.

25. After performing his second implant, on William Schroeder, Dr. DeVries had this to say when he might consider calling a halt to the experiment: "[I]t's impractical on the basis of two patients to determine whether or not these questions [whether society can afford artificial heart implants] can be answered. The third patient may have a stroke, the fourth patient may have a stroke, the fifth patient may have a stroke. In that case the question is not going to be can society pay for it. The question will be: *is it proper to even do this? Should it even be done anymore?" Q&A: Dr. William C. DeVries,* Louisville Courier J., Feb. 3, 1985, at 13, col. 2 (emphasis added).

And after the first four permanent artificial heart implants, the director of the Humana Heart Institute was asked how Humana could argue that any progress was being made given the severe problems suffered by the recipients. Dr. Lansing replied: "Yes, there is progress. [William] Schroeder is improving and showing signs of recovery; [Murray] Haydon will soon be off the respirator and beginning to make a recovery; and yes, [Jack] Burcham has required dialysis for a pre-op condition, but we hope it is temporary. All the patients are living, and at this time *none of the three has a condition that is either irreversible or immediately life-threatening."* Am. Med. News, May 10, 1985, at 58 (emphasis added). This statement, made on April 24, 1985, unfortunately turned out to be wishful thinking. Within hours, Mr. Burcham was dead. Also, prior to their deaths, Mr. Schroeder suffered subsequent devastating strokes, and Mr. Haydon was not able to leave his intensive care room for more than brief periods. The only other patient in the world to receive the Jarvik-7 as a permanent implant, Leif Stenberg, suffered a stroke and died, and the Swedish surgeon who did the implant, Bjarne Semb, has said publicly that he will not do any more implants because the device is simply too crude and causes such terrible effects in its recipients. Of Mr. Stenberg, Dr. Semb said, "[h]e might as well have died." Kolata, *Surgeons Disagree on Artificial Heart,* 230 Science 786 (1985).

It is possible to make an argument that the initial implant in Barney Clark was justifiable in that it was not known *"a priori"* that it would cause such devastating results. It is no longer possible reasonably to make this argument. Recipients have died and/or suffered devastating problems. It would seem that there is simply not enough known about anticoagulation therapy to prevent either bleeding or strokes, for this device to be used in humans at this time. More animal and laboratory research is required before human experimentation can ethically recommence.

It should also be emphasized that while the inventor and researcher may believe in the Jarvik-7, almost no one else does. The NIH Working Group, for example, while endorsing research on fully implantable electrical artificial hearts, noted that "pneumatically actuated . . . systems that do not permit substantial levels of ambulation and relatively normal activity are *importantly suboptimal."* Working Group on Mechanical Circulatory Support of the National Heart, Lung, and Blood Institute, Artificial Heart and Assist Devices: Directions, Needs, Costs, Societal and Ethical Issues 33 (1985) (emphasis added).

26. Clark, *An Incredible Affair of the Heart,* Newsweek, Dec. 13, 1982, at 71–72. *See also supra* note 17.

27. Perhaps the example of the most "magical thinking" in recent history is provided by Dr. Leonard Bailey and his transplant of a baboon's heart into a dying infant known as "Baby Fae." Of course this infant herself could not consent to this first-of-its-kind human experiment, and since one of the primary hypotheses being tested (the effectiveness of cyclosporin on xenografts) could have been tested on an adult, I believe this experiment should not have been tried first on a child who could not agree to it. The case was made even worse because the infant's parents were separated, and the family impoverished. But Dr. Bailey's belief in himself and his procedure is remarkable. Within ten days after the transplant he said, "[i]n the best scenario, Baby Fae will celebrate her 21st birthday without the need of further surgery. That possibility exists." Breo, *Interview with "Baby Fae's" Surgeon: Therapeutic Intent was Topmost*, Am. Med. News, Nov. 16, 1984, at 1.

In fact, this was never a realistic or reasonable expectation, and it raises serious questions both about Dr. Bailey's ability to separate science from emotion (or to distinguish medicine from magic), and what exactly he led the parents of Baby Fae to expect. I have said flatly that this transplant was an "inadequately reviewed, inappropiately consented to, premature experiment on an impoverished, terminally ill newborn that cannot be justified"; and that "therapy was never a realistic goal." Annas, *Baby Fae: The "Anything Goes" School of Human Experimentation*, Hastings Center Rep., Feb. 1985, at 15–17. Others have been somewhat kinder, but consistent with Katz's "magical thinking" hypothesis. The experiment, for example, has been described as a "leap of faith." Dr. Jack Provonsha, Director of Loma Linda's Center for Christian Bioethics, has even asserted that such "leaps of faith" are more likely to occur at religious institutions like Loma Linda (predominately Seventh Day Adventists): "The person who is part of a supportive, communal religion can 'become more secure' in the atmosphere, and then may be willing to take chances that a less secure, less religiously committed individual is willing to take." Colen, *Ethics and Baby Fae*, Newsday, Nov. 2 1984, Part II, at 2, col. 1. This seems more "faith healing" than science. Cf. Fox, *It's the Same, but Different: A Sociological Perspective on the Case of the Utah Artificial Heart*, in After Barney Clark, supra note 22, at 68–90 (discussion of the role for Mormonism in the Barney Clark case).

Medical-scientific commentators on Dr. Bailey's published paper on Baby Fae, Bailey, Nehlsen-Cannarella, Concepcion & Jolley, *Baboon-to-Human Cardiac Xenotransplantation in a Neonate*, 254 J. A.M.A. 3321 (1985), used words like "essentially irrelevant" to describe the tissue typing done on the baboon, and "wishful thinking" to describe the "belief that the infant's immune system was immature and thus more readily immunosuppressed . . . ." Jonasson & Hardy, *The Case of Baby Fae*, 254 J. A.M.A. 3358, 3359 (1985). Bailey later accused these authorities of "representing dated, historical thinking . . . ." Breo, *Precise Cause of Death Eludes "Baby Fae" Team*, Am. Med. News, Dec. 20, 1985, at 18. On the other hand, his immunologist, Dr. Nehlsen-Cannarella, admitted that with "dying babies . . . it's difficult to separate strong desires and wishes from scientific truth . . . ." *Id.* at 16. See also Caplan, *Ethical Issues Raised by Research Involving Xenografts*, 254 J. A.M.A. 3339 (1985).

28. Altman, *Recipient of Artificial Heart Calls the Ordeal Worthwhile*, N.Y. Times, Mar. 3, 1983, at A1, col. 2 (emphasis added).

29. See Williams, *Why IRB's Falter in Reviewing Risks and Benefits*, IRB, May/June 1984, at 1–5. On December 20, 1985 the FDA held a hearing to determine if Dr. DrVries should be permitted to complete his "series of seven" permanent implants that had originally been approved, or whether such research should be suspended in view of the devastating effects it had had on the first four recipients. The FDA decided to permit Dr. DeVries to continue, but only if additional information was supplied to the FDA, and future implants were reviewed on a case-by-case basis. *See* Clark, *Stiffer Rules for the Heart*, Newsweek, Dec. 30, 1985, at 68; Boffey, *More Implants of Artificial Hearts Are Urged by U.S. Health Panel*, N.Y. Times, Dec. 22, 1985, at 34, col. 1. No major problems were seen by the agency in the consent form or process, although Dr. DeVries reported to a U.S. Congressional committee on February 5, 1986, that modifications were planned for both.

Following a three day visit to Dr. DeVries in August, 1985, I suggested further exploration of a number of problem areas in informed consent:

[L]et me outline some of the major areas of concern I have about the protocol review and consent process, and suggestions that might help to improve it in the event further implants are done.

1. *Correspondence between the protocol and the consent form.* . . . As we discussed, a review of the protocol indicates that the lack of correspondence between the studies you are conducting and those actually consented to is substantial and serious and should be corrected. Specifically: (a) The assertion in the protocol that the primary goal is therapy cannot stand scrutiny, the protocol itself needs to be amended to place experimental goals first, and therapeutic goals (if any) in a clearly secondary position. (b) As to the experimental studies, *none* of the ones that are so clearly described in the protocol are detailed at all in the consent form, and this is, of course, the primary purpose of the consent form, i.e., to spell out what experimental things will be done, including their risks to the patient. Specifically, you need to at least describe the non-invasive studies (*e.g.*, circulatory response studies; nutritional studies; and exercise studies); and to both describe in detail, and list the risks of the invasive studies (*e.g.*, the hemodynamics studies; the pharmacological studies, including Isoproterenol, Do-pamine, Sodium Nitroprusside, Nitroglycerin, and, unless it has been deleted, Ephedrine; and the studies with the Heimes driver). Since many of these studies are designed to take place at three different times (at the time of the implant; one week after the implant; and 6–8 weeks after the implant), each occasion should have a separate consent form (the original master consent form should describe those studies that will be done at the time of the implant, and indicate what followup studies are planned and that a separate consent form and process will be employed for the followup studies).

2. *Defining the role of the Subject's "Advocate" and that of the IRB "monitor."* The role of each of these separate individuals is unclear and needs clarification if they are to contribute to making the consent process a meaningful one for the subject and his family. . . .

3. *The Role of the IRB.* My own impression is that the Humana IRB has done both you and your subjects a disservice by permitting use of the current consent form (for the reasons outlined both above, and *infra*), and by failing to either understand or support the basic functions of an IRB. Specifically, the three members of the IRB I met with argued vigorously for such propositions as: (1) the implant procedure was not experimental at all, but "the whole thing is primarily therapeutic" and we should treat these research subjects "like any other patient"; (2) informed consent is "just a parade of horribles" to the patient and so serves only to scare them; and (3) withdrawal from the experiment by the research subject would be "murder" if the researcher permitted it and turned off the artificial heart. . . . If the Humana IRB actually believes the propositions these possibly non-representative members put to me on August 27, 1985, it should come as no surprise to anyone that they found their task so simple that they were able to adopt the Utah form almost verbatim, changing primarily only the identity of the hospital in the submitted consent form. . . .

4. *The Publicity Clause.* As I discussed with you, members of the IRB, and your attorneys, this clause is unprecedented and unacceptable. Subjects have never before in the history of human experimentation had to sign away all rights to privacy regarding every possible mode of communication, and should not have to in their case. It should be separated from the "master form" and rewritten in a manner which more closely mirrors a reasonable attempt to protect privacy. [*Humana's publicity clause provides:* "I am fully aware of the considerable public interest anticipated in my story as a recipient of a Total Artificial Heart. I am also aware that Humana Hospital Audubon has an obligation to disseminate medical information concerning my hospital course as deemed appropriate in the judgment of my physician. In addition to those materials identified in paragraph 13 [regarding medical professionals and the FDA] Humana Hospital Audubon, as approved by my physician, is authorized to make, or permit to be made, photographs, slides, films, video tapes, recordings and other means of recording and/ or communicating hereinafter referred to as "material(s)," that may be used in news-papers, magazine articles, television, radio broadcasts, movies or any other media or

means of dissemination. I consent to the use of my name, likeness, or voice for such purposes. I agree that Humana Hospital-Audubon or Humana, Inc. will be the sole and exclusive owner of such materials, and I release the Humana Heart Institute, International, Humana, Inc., Humana Hospital Audubon, their officers, agents and employees from all claims of liability with respect to the showing, use or dissemination of such material(s). I understand that the materials which are made public, as described in this paragraph, will protect my modesty and be within generally accepted bounds of good taste.]

5. *Deletion of the Right to Withdraw Clause.* (a) This is, as we discussed at length, a profound and serious omission, since it seems to indicate that all involved have adopted the view of the IRB Chairman that terminating the experiment by turning off the artificial heart, even at the express demand of the patient, is a crime of some sort, perhaps murder. This conclusion indicates that very little thought has gone into this. I can understand the reasons for not overly dramatizing this issue with the promise of a "key" to turn off the driver; but to swing entirely the other way and imply that under no circumstances can the patient or his doctor turn off or disconnect the artificial heart is to transform the subject entirely into a means of preserving the "life" of the artificial heart, instead of a willing volunteer in an experiment that concludes when he decides he has had enough. If this really is what is intended, at the very least subjects should be informed in advance that the artificial heart will be kept in place and running as long as possible no matter what the patient, his family and doctor wants, and no matter what his physical condition. Even if the artificial heart was therapeutic (which I think we agree it is not) a patient would still have the right to order its use disconnected, as patients can now discontinue kidney dialysis or mechanical ventilator support, or even artificial feeding, although all are necessary to maintain their lives. When the artificial heart becomes totally implantable and reliable enough to be therapeutic, we may have debating issues here; but at the current time arguments that turning off the Utah drive with the patient's consent is "murder" is simply uninformed hysteria, that has the result of making the patient a servant of the artificial heart itself. (b) Related to this is the problem of what to do if the patient is incompetent to make a decision. This eventuality should be planned for in advance (since it is very predictable) and the prospective subject asked to (1) spell out as best he can the circumstances under which he wants the heart turned off if he cannot communicate; and (2) designate a proxy with the authority to make the decision for him under the criteria he outlines. . . .

6. *The Consent Process.* We all believe that consent is a process, not a form, and that the form is merely evidence that the process actually took place. . . . I think it would be useful to devise a question or two to ask the subject regarding every major point made in the consent form. The question should not, of course, be one that can simply be answered "yes" even if "yes" does not reflect the patient's actual understanding, *e.g.,* "Do you understand all of the risks?" Instead, the question should demand use of specific information about the experiment that you believe it is critical that they understand in order to give their "informed consent" to it. (*e.g.,* Can you describe the types of studies I am going to perform on you and the artificial heart shortly after it is implanted?; What happened to the last five individuals who had permanent artificial hearts implanted in them?, etc.). If the subject cannot adequately answer the questions, he is incapable of giving informed consent, and cannot be accepted as a suitable candidate until the information needed to answer the questions is mastered. Such a procedure may help both the researcher and the subject to take the informed consent process more seriously.

Realistic answers probably will not be found in simply trying to apply rules and regulations developed primarily for routine drug studies. What is involved in the artificial heart experiment is nothing short of transforming a life, and with it all previous interrelationships with the environment and with one's family. Indeed, your experiments will probably teach us much about these transformations and interactions . . . [as] about the interaction of the artificial heart with the human body. Accordingly, what is needed is much more relevant (as opposed to simply more detailed) information about the impact of the artificial heart on one's lifestyle, mobility, psychology, and relationships to one's family. Indeed, if as now appears to be the case, the artificial heart utterly transforms not only the patient, but also the patient's family (at least the entire life of the patient's spouse) a good deal more attention needs to be given to this aspect of the experiment. Much, if not all, of this information should be supplied to prospective subjects *before* they even come to Louisville to be formally screened for the program. Consent forms themselves are clearly inadequate. What is needed is a book-length treatment on the program and the experiences of the first subjects, together with appropriate illustrations. This could probably be usefully supplemented by videotapes of past and current recipients, as well as telephone conversations with their family members. These should be mastered *before* a potential recipient is on site since the trip to Louisville itself represents a decision to seek the artificial heart and individuals are likely to arrive at Louisville with misperceptions of what is likely to occur if the artificial heart is implanted in them. It is, of course, much harder to dispel misperceptions that have been acted on than it is to present information to an uncommitted individual. Accordingly, as I think your own experience to date illustrates, by the time the subject is actually given the consent form to read (or reads it himself) it is too late for them to care about the consents or to "change their minds" and turn back from the course they seem to have inevitably embarked on. . . . (Letter from George J. Annas to Dr. William DeVries [Sept. 26, 1985].)

30. Cooley, Liotta & Hallman, *Orthotopic Cardiac Prosthesis for Two-staged Cardiac Replacement,* 24 Am. J. Cardiology 723 (1969); Cooley, *Staged Cardiac Transplantation: Report of Three Cases,* 1 Heart Transplantation 145 (1982).

31. Annas, *No Cheers for Temporary Artificial Hearts,* Hastings Center Rep., Oct. 1985, at 27–28 [hereinafter *No Cheers for Temporary Artificial Hearts*]. *Contra,* Hill, Farrar, Hershon, Compton, Avery, Levin & Brent, *Use of a Prosthetic Ventricle as a Bridge to Cardiac Transplantation for Postinfarction Cardiogenic Shock,* 314 New Eng. J. Med. 626 (1986).

32. *See No Cheers for Temporary Artidicial Hearts, supra* note 31. *See also,* Annas, *The Prostitute, the Playboy, and the Poet: Rationing Schemes for Organ Transplantation,* 75 Am. J. Pub. Health 187 (1985).

33. For example see the cases of Mary Lund, who waited more than 40 days on a "temporary" artificial heart before obtaining a human heart replacement; and Bernadette Chayrez, who has received *two* "temporary" artificial hearts and lived on her second one for more than 200 days before dying during her second human heart transplant. *See infra* notes 58–62 and accompanying text.

34. For a detailed description of the case of Thomas Creighton, see Annas, *The Phoenix Heart: What We Have to Lose,* Hastings Center Rep., June 1985, at 15–16 [hereinafter *The Phoenix Heart*]; Copeland, Levinson, Smith, Icenogle, Vaughn, Cheng, Ott & Emery, *The Total Artificial Heart as a Bridge to Transplantation: A Report of Two Cases,* 256 J. A.M.A. 2991 (1986).

35. Following Dr. Barnard's initial human-to-human heart transplant, about 150 human heart transplants were done at 60 places around the world in the next two years. There were almost no long-term survivors in the unseemly rush to join the "me-too" club of heart transplant surgeons, and this episode stands as one of the blackest marks in the history of surgery. B. Jennett, High Technology Medicine 84–85 (1984).

36. Altman, *Anguish, Hope, a Moment of Fame: A Heart's Story is Told,* N.Y. Times, Mar. 19, 1985, at C1–2, col. 1; *See also,* Blakeslee, *Arizona Surgeon Defends Heart Implant,* N.Y. Times, Mar. 12, 1985, at C2, col. 1; Hubert & Ring, *Tucsonian Gets Mechanical Heart at UMC: New Device Doesn't Have FDA Sanction,* Arizona Daily Star, Mar. 7, 1985, at 2, col. 1.

37. Kuhn & Pesce, *Heartmaker: A Dentist with a Dream,* USA Today, Mar. 8, 1985, at 1A, col. 3.

38. *The Man with the Illegal Heart,* N.Y. Times, Mar. 9, 1985, at A22, col. 1. Even after having the benefit of another nine months to rethink the issue, and after concluding that the permanent artificial heart "in its present form . . . cannot be described as a

success"; the *Times* continued to describe temporary implants as "useful." Editorial, *The Heart that Fizzled*, N.Y. Times, Jan. 10, 1986 at A26, col. 1.

39. Wallis, *A Bold Gamble in Tucson*, Time, Mar. 18, 1985, at 63.

40. Adler, *When Life is on the Line*, Newsweek, Mar. 18, 1985, at 88.

41. Altman, *Learning to Live with the Artificial Heart*, N.Y. Times, Mar. 17, 1985, § 4, at 7, col. 3.

42. Hubert & Rothenberg, *Patient has a "long shot,"* Arizona Daily Star, Mar. 8, 1985, at 3, col. 2.

43. Nor is it appropriate to permit physicians *even to offer* certain interventions to patients on the sole justification that the patients are "dying anyway." Taken to its logical extreme, this rationale can justify *any* intervention. This, of course, undercuts the entire rationale for an FDA or any other rules or regulations about human experimentation. Nor is it the law. As the U.S. Supreme Court noted in upholding the FDA's authority to forbid the use of Laetrile, even on terminally ill cancer patients: "the terminally ill deserve protection . . . from the vast range of self-styled panaceas that inventive minds can devise." U.S. v. Rutherford, 442 U.S. 544 (1979).

44. Mr. Creighton was actually Dr. Copeland's third patient to experience immediate rejection of a heart transplant. Since rejection is a "reasonable foreseeable risk," it should be planned for, not treated as an ad hoc "emergency." *See The Phoenix Heart, supra* note 34.

45. The use of proxy consent to "emergency" experimentation, when allowed at all, is generally permitted only for alternative therapies that pose little or no additional risk to the subject, and even then only after a careful research protocol has been developed and independently approved by an institutional review board. *See, eg.,* Brain Resuscitation Clinical Trial I Study Group, *Randomized Clinical Study of Thiopental Loading in Comatose Survivors of Cardiac Arrest*, 314 New Eng. J. Med. 397 (1986).

46. Copeland, *We Can't Sacrifice Lives to Risks*, USA Today, Mar. 11, 1985, at 10A, col. 2.

47. FDA, HHS, "Guidance for Emergency Use of Unapproved Medical Devices; Availability," 50 Fed Reg. 42,866 (1985).

48. The original four hospitals to obtain FDA approval are: U. of Arizona at Tucson; Pennsylvania State U. at Hershey; Abbott-Northwestern Hospital, Minneapolis; and Presbyterian-University Hospital, Pittsburgh. The FDA (remarkably) has indicated it may approve up to ten or eleven more sites. Cole, *Four Years of Replacing Ailing Hearts: Surgeons Assess Data, Questions Remain*, 256 J. A.M.A. 2921, 2930 (1986).

49. Thomas Creighton at Tucson, and Mary Lund in Minneapolis. Michael Drummond's consent is also of questionable quality. *See The Phoenix Heart, supra* note 34.

50. The implant was done at the West Berlin Charlottenburg University Clinic by Dr. Emil Buecherl. *German Not Informed He Has Artificial Heart*, N.Y. Times, Mar. 10, 1986, at A17, col. 4. The case is reminiscent of another one collected by Professor Katz in his casebook, Experimentation with Human Beings, *supra* note 7, which concerned a twenty-three year old Brazilian cowboy who was the recipient of the first human-to-human heart transplant in South America. He was not told about the proposed transplant, and learned of it only when he heard a news broadcast about it in his hospital room a week later. He lived about three weeks: "[T]he Brazilian surgeons point out at the same time that no ethical questions are raised by da Cunha's [the patient] lack of informed consent. If a man is incapable of understanding an operation he vitally needs, they say, there is no choice but to proceed. . . . Besides, add the surgeons, da Cunha was psychologically better off not knowing and worrying about his risks." Med. World News, July 12, 1968, at 9–10, *quoted in* Experimentation with Human Beings, *supra* note 7, 1098.

51. *See supra* note 34.

52. Hubert, *Chayrez Dies*, Arizona Daily Star, Oct. 12, 1986, at 1, col. 1.

53. Epstein, *Heart Patient's Death: Sorrow, Lessons Endure*, Am. Med. News, Nov. 7, 1986, at 3.

54. *Id.* at 45 (emphasis added).

55. *Id.* (emphasis added).

56. *Id.* (emphasis added).

57. *See also* Relman, *Artificial Hearts—Permanent and Temporary,* 314 New Eng. J. Med. 644 (1986).

58. Three of the four centers used the Jarvik-7 (a smaller model was used for Mary Lund at Abbott-Northwestern, where she became the first woman recipient), and at Hershey a substantially similar device, called the "Penn State Heart," was used. The specific areas of disagreement or significant divergence in the consent forms include:

1. *The description of the nature of the experiment as contrasted with the artificial heart's past use.* One consent form, for example, describes it as having been "successfully implanted in five patients"; one says it "has supported life in growing calves for up to 260 days"; another that it has been subject to "extensive testing in experimental laboratory animals and humans"; and the fourth is silent on its past uses and results.

2. *The description of the risk/benefit ratio.* None mention two of the complications that all four of Dr. DeVries' patients have suffered: hemolytic anemia and immunosuppression; and only one mentions pulmonary insufficiency as a possible complication. One form says that all reasonable alternatives have been discussed, the other three allege that use of the artificial heart is the "only alternative" available to maintain life. But even among these three there are variations; one hedges with the phrase that it is "quite unlikely" that I will survive long enough to obtain a heart transplant without it, while another asserts there isn't "any possibility" of survival without use of the device.

3. *The ability to withdraw.* One form doesn't mention this issue at all; two others use boilerplate language common to most consent forms involving drug studies, and one uses somewhat reasonable language on the right to withdraw, "recognizing that such a decision after the total artificial heart is implanted will result in my death."

4. *Proxy consent.* None of the forms provide any mechanism for proxy consent; and one actually attempts to do away with the consent requirement altogether by providing: "If I am too sick to be consulted, I authorize such procedures as are *in the professional judgment of the medical staff necessary* and desirable for my life, safety or comfort." (emphasis added).

5. *Waivers.* Two forms have no waivers and three guarantee that confidentiality will be respected. One form, however, adopts the unacceptable publicity language of the Humana form (*see supra* note 25) (Abbott-Northwestern), and another uses boilerplate products liability waiver language: "I expressly understand that no warranties are made with respect to the implant and use of the temporary artificial heart, and all express or implied warranties are disclaimed, including without limitation any warranty of merchantability or warranty of fitness for a particular purpose."

6. *If a human heart transplant is not done.* Only one form discusses what will be done in this case, and says simply, "you will be supported by the artificial heart as long as possible."

All of these issues, as well as the issue of payment for the device and the procedure, are important enough and common enough to be dealt with in a uniform manner. It now seems apparent that neither the manufacturer nor the hospitals will voluntarily form a multicenter review panel to develop uniform standards related to the protocol, uniform patient selection criteria, and minimal standards for informed consent forms and processes.

59. I presented a proposal to this effect to the Subcommittee on Investigations and Oversight of the Committee on Science and Technology, U.S. House of Representatives on February 5, 1986, *Status of the Artificial Heart Program: Hearing Before the Subcomm. on Investigations and Oversight of the House Comm. on Science and Technology,* 99th Cong., 2nd Sess. 144–277 (1986) (testimony of Annas, G. J.). The two committee members present were not supportive, nor was the FDA. The hearing itself took place one week after the explosion of the space shuttle Challenger, and this disaster was commented on by almost all of the witnesses. Their point was that we should not let the disaster stop the space program. Of course no one had suggested that it should, any more than anyone would seriously suggest the disasters suffered by Barney Clark, William Schroeder, Murray Haydon, and Jack Burcham should end the quest for an effective, efficient and totally implantable artificial heart. But just as reality has caught up with the private hope and public hype of the space program, so it has caught up with the hype of the artificial heart. Our reactions to disappointment should be basically the same in both programs.

To reassess, move forward with more knowledge and more caution, "to liberate the space program, [artificial hearts] and technology in general from the mystique that we have placed on it. . . . Our technology is imperfect, because we are imperfect, so either worshipping or despising our technological age is just a neat shifting of blame." Walter McDougal (quoted by Wilford, *After the Challenger: America's Future in Space,* N.Y. Times, Mar. 16, 1986, (Magazine) at 38, 106).

    60. A. I. Solzhenitsyn, *supra* note 2, at 301 (emphasis in original).

21

The Artificial Heart: Reevaluating the Investment

Dale Jamieson

On December 1, 1982, at the University of Utah Hospital, Dr. William DeVries implanted a Jarvik-7 artificial heart into the chest of Barney Clark. Clark survived 112 days on the artificial heart. During that time he underwent two major operations in addition to the implantation and suffered from a number of other difficulties. An artificial heart ventricle broke on the operating table, bubbles appeared in his lungs, and a heart valve broke. Clark had seizures and serious nosebleeds. He contracted pneumonia, suffered from kidney failure, and experienced prolonged episodes of psychological disorientation.

Although many artificial heart experiments had been conducted on animals, Clark was only the third human subject of such experiments.[1] After Clark's death a number of troubling questions were asked.[2]

First, people asked whether the artificial heart implant was really in Clark's best interests. Several members of the hospital review board complained that the patient selection committee had not recognized that Clark suffered from severe emphysema, probably caused by smoking two packs of cigarettes a day for twenty-five years. Moreover, eight months before the Clark operation, a Florida firefighter who also suffered from cardiomyopathy and was regarded as near death had sought to be the first human recipient of a Jarvik heart. Although he was turned down for the operation, he outlived Barney Clark by about a year.

Second, questions were asked about the consent form signed by Clark and about whether his desires were fully respected. According to one critic, the consent form was "incomplete, internally inconsistent, and confusing."[3] When Clark first saw the experimental animals tethered to the power source, he declined to have the operation. He only changed his mind when his condition worsened. During his time on the artificial heart, Clark repeatedly expressed the desire to die and confessed to having tried to figure out how to kill himself. At least once he asked his medical attendants to kill him.[4]

Third, questions were raised about whether the animal studies provided sufficient justification for undertaking an experiment on a human. None of the more than one hundred experimental animals had lived longer than nine months on the artificial heart. In the animal experiments, parts had been transferred from one artificial heart to another without adequate records having been kept, and there was thus little information regarding the reliability of the valves. Although Clark suffered from multiple strokes while on the artificial heart, this problem had been totally unanticipated. Later, DeVries attributed this to the fact that the human circulatory system is radically different from that of calves, sheep, and goats, the animals on which the artificial heart was tested.[5]

Finally, questions were asked about the financial interests of those involved with the Clark implant. The Jarvik-7 implanted in Clark was manufactured by Kolff Medical Incorporated. Shortly after the Clark implant Kolff Medical succeeded in raising $20 million in a stock offering. Jarvik and Kolff were suddenly worth more than $6 million each, and DeVries's stock was worth about $350,000.

Since the death of Barney Clark, DeVries has implanted the Jarvik-7 in three other patients. All suffered from multiple strokes and had poor quality of life. William Schroeder lived 620 days, the longest of the four. During the first two weeks he joked with nurses, spoke with the president on the telephone, and was photographed drinking a beer. Shortly thereafter he suffered several strokes, which left him partially paralyzed and impaired both his speech and memory. After several periods of recovery and decline, he had another stroke, which left him semiconscious and unable to speak. For the last seven months of his life he was unable to recognize consistently members of his family. Finally a massive stroke destroyed most of his brain, and a chronic infection worsened around the site where the power lines to the artificial heart entered his body. William DeVries, together with Schroeder's wife, Margaret, and the six Schroeder children, turned the key that shut off the heart.

Although DeVries has FDA approval for three more implants and has said that he intends to do them, he has not implanted an artificial heart since April 15, 1985. He has said that this is because he has been unable to find a suitable candidate, due to the bad publicity surrounding the artificial heart program and the increasing success and availability of human heart transplants.[6] At the end of 1985 the FDA instituted tough new reporting requirements, which have had the effect of discouraging permanent artificial heart implants. It has also been reported that officials of Humana Hospital Corporation, which had hired DeVries to perform a minimum of one hundred implants, have told him not to do any more permanent implants.[7]

Increasingly, however, the artificial heart is being used as a "bridge" to keep terminal heart patients alive until they can receive human heart transplants. By May 1987, there had been more than eighty temporary artificial heart implants, and more than fifty of these patients had survived long enough to undergo successful human heart transplants.[8] Most of these patients were on artificial hearts less than three weeks, thus avoiding the most serious complications.

Although the artificial heart has clearly benefited those who have received it as a temporary bridge, there are objections even to this use of the heart.[9] First, there is an objection from fairness. As long as there is a shortage of transplantable human hearts, stacking people up on temporary artificial hearts will not save more lives. It will only change the identities of those who live. Placing a patient on a temporary artificial heart creates an emergency life-threatening situation and thereby moves the recipient to the top of the list for human heart transplants. This "queue jumping" results in some people not receiving heart transplants who otherwise would have.

Second, the temporary use of the artificial heart may result in fewer lives being saved. The survival prospects of those who have already undergone one major heart operation and spent time on the artificial heart are significantly less good than those of other transplant recipients. The four-year survival rate for people who received only human heart transplants and who were treated with cyclosporine is 76.4 percent.[10] Dr. Bartley P. Griffith, who has performed more temporary implants with the Jarvik-7 than anyone else in the United States, was recently quoted as saying that he "would be thrilled" to achieve a 65 percent one-year survival rate for patients who first received artificial heart bridges.[11]

Despite these objections to the temporary use of the artificial heart and the experiences of Barney Clark, William Schroeder, and other permanent recipients, the promoters of the artificial heart remain enthusiastic. Dr. Robert Jarvik began his recent testimony to a congressional oversight committee by declaring that "we have in this country a belief in science and technology as a foundation of our heritage." He then went on to compare Barney Clark and Bill Schroeder to Christa McAuliffe: Each demonstrated a "selfless willingness to enter the unknown."[12]

The members of Congress seemed honored to be in the presence of Jarvik and DeVries, and they expressed their sympathy for Dr. Jack Copeland, who had performed an unauthorized artificial heart implant but whose concern for his patients prevented him from traveling to Washington to answer questions about it. Some members of the committee worried that artificial heart research might be hampered by excessive government regulation. One congressman dismissed the idea of a temporary moratorium on artificial heart implants with the following remark: "The worst decision in experimentation . . . is to stop the experiment when you see failure or when you see problems."[13] One would hardly have guessed that the "failure" and "problems" he was alluding to were the experiences of Barney Clark, Bill Schroeder, and the others.

Thus far we have little to show for nearly thirty years of artificial heart research. Those who have received permanent implants have not significantly benefited from them, and those who have received temporary implants have benefited only at the expense of others. Perhaps one day the medical and technical problems of the artificial heart will be solved, and it will become a viable clinical option. On that day we will have to confront important questions about the cost of the artificial heart and about its allocation. Such questions have been implicit since the beginning of the program, but they have largely been ignored or treated as only of marginal interest.

Before we explore these questions of cost and allocation, there is another question that merits consideration: How did we come to have an artificial heart program in the first place? This question is important, I believe, because the story of the artificial heart program is all too typical of the development of new medical technologies. A small group of influential researchers who were pursuing a high-tech solution to a major multidimensional health problem succeeded in making their agenda a national priority. Once the development of the technology was under way, it developed a life of its own. At crucial stages in the decision process, little thought was given to the societal consequences of the widespread use of the technology or to alternative approaches to the problem it was intended to address. As long as we make important decisions in such an unreflective way, we will continue to confront difficult unanticipated problems concerning the social impacts of new technologies.[14]

The Origins of the Artificial Heart Program

After the Second World War biomedical research blossomed in the United States. During the 1950s the heart-lung bypass machine, artificial blood vessels, and various improved blood products were all brought into clinical practice. Great progress also was made in developing an artificial kidney. These developments made the idea of an artificial heart seem promising to many researchers.

In 1957, at the third annual meeting of the newly formed American Society for Artificial Internal Organs, Dr. Peter Salisbury devoted his presidential address to a plea for artificial heart research. At the next annual meeting Willem Kolff and Tetsuzo Akutsu were able to report that they had developed an artificial heart on which a dog had lived for ninety minutes.[15]

Dr. Willem Kolff had a great deal of credibility in the medical research community. In the early 1940s in Holland, he had used spare parts from an automobile foundry and an old bathtub to construct the first artificial kidney that could be used on a human.[16] After the war Kolff emigrated to the United States and joined the Cleveland Clinic Foundation's newly formed Department of Artificial Organs.

During the late 1950s artificial heart research was conducted at several locations around the United States, including Miner's Memorial Hospital in Kentucky, Interscience Research Corporation in Illinois, and Yale University. At about this time Dr. Michael DeBakey became interested in artificial heart research. Debakey was the influential chairman of the Department of Surgery at Baylor University, former member of the National Advisory Heart Council, and future president of the Baylor Medical School. By 1963 he had succeeded in keeping a dog alive on an artificial heart for thirty-six hours.

Much of this early work was privately funded. Proposals for artificial heart research were entertained by the National Heart Institute (NHI), but they had to compete with other projects for support.[17] The small community of artificial heart researchers was convinced that an artificial heart was feasible, but that large-scale government support was needed in order to develop it. In the early 1960s these people began a campaign to make the artificial heart a national priority.

In 1963 the *Journal of the American Medical Association* published a long optimistic article on artificial heart research.[18] Kolff was quoted as predicting that within three years there would be a workable artificial heart. Dr. C. Walton Lillehei of the University of Minnesota was more cautious: He thought that it might take as long as ten years, but he was reported as saying that he "admits that his estimate is 'conservative.'" Also in 1963 DeBakey raised the possibility of an artificial heart before the Senate Appropriations Subcommittee. After being introduced as "an old friend" of the committee, DeBakey testified: "Experimentally, it is possible to completely replace the heart with an artificial heart. . . . This idea, I am sure, could be reached to full fruition if we had more funds to support more work."[19]

The kind of program that DeBakey had in mind was an expensive one. Dr. William C. Hall, who was program director of the Baylor-Rice Artificial Heart Program, has told the following story about the program's first grant proposal. Having never before written a proposal, Hall presented DeBakey with several proposals with a total budget of $25,000. According to Hall, "he almost threw it at me. In fact, I think he actually did. . . . When Dr. DeBakey got finished with the grant proposal, it totaled $4.5 million, which was awarded."[20]

By October 1963, the planning committee of the National Advisory Heart Council, the primary policy advisory body to NHI, had recommended that development of an artificial heart should be given the highest priority. In November 1963, the full council endorsed this recommendation. In February 1964, NHI convened an ad hoc advisory group of seven artificial heart researchers, including DeBakey and Kolff. Not surprisingly, the group recommended that NHI create a special artificial heart program and pursue the project "with a sense of urgency."[21] In March 1964, the National Advisory Heart Council endorsed the recommendations, and in July 1964, Congress authorized the establishment of an Artificial Heart Program Office with its own budget line. The search for the artificial heart was off and running.

By spring 1965, a four-phase master plan was in place.[22] The first phase was to assess the state of the art and was supposed to take about a year. The second phase was devoted to the conceptual design of various alternative artificial heart systems and was also supposed to take about a year. In the third phase, lasting two years, prototypes of the best artificial heart systems were to be built and tested. In the final phase of the project, scheduled for a year, specifications were to be developed for the mass production and installation of artificial hearts. By 1970 the artificial heart would be ready for clinical use.

These initial decisions, which established the artificial heart program, were made by small elites in the medical research community and in Congress. Prominent researchers made exaggerated claims about the prospects for an artificial heart and successfully lobbied NHI and Congress to adopt their agenda.[23] NHI did not want to be seen as dragging its feet on a program that might win the support of powerful members of Congress and would certainly increase its budget. The congressional appropriations committees were generally strong supporters of medical research, and they had been assured by distinguished scientists that an artificial heart was feasible.[24]

With the public frozen out of the decision process and no attempt made to assess the possible societal impacts of the artificial heart or to subject the claims of DeBakey, Kolff, and the others to serious scrutiny, the closest approximation to a critic was Dr. James Shannon, director of NIH. Shannon represented the interests of the broader medical research community, which was unhappy that the artificial heart program was channeling research money away from peer-reviewed medical research proposals, toward contracts with engineers, systems analysts, and biomaterials experts. Shannon himself thought that the basic science needed for an artificial heart was lacking. Still, he publicly supported the program. Later he said that he had done so because he was trying to establish NIH as a world center for medical research and he needed the support of DeBakey and the other influential proponents of the artificial heart.[25]

Since the establishment of the artificial heart program there have been several program reviews. Unfortunately, the review panels either have been narrowly constituted or their charges have been limited.

In 1968, in the wake of an international epidemic of unsuccessful cardiac transplants, NHI assembled an ad hoc task force that was instructed to review the medical, ethical, psychological, and economic implications of cardiac replacement.[26] The task force's focus mainly was on cardiac transplantation, but it also considered the artificial heart. Although its charge was very broad, the task force was too narrowly constituted to fulfill it. Seven of its ten members were physicians. Of the other three members, one was an employee of NHI and another was executive vice president of the Texas Medical Center, whose surgeon-in-chief was Denton Cooley, who would soon perform the unauthorized first human artificial heart transplant. The third nonphysician member and only woman was Gladys Kammerer, a professor of public administration.

In 1972 the National Heart and Lung Institute (NHLI) convened the Artificial Heart Assessment Panel. This was the most broadly based of any of the program review panels, with ten members: three physicians (including one psychiatrist), two lawyers, two economists, a sociologist, a political scientist, and a medical ethicist. Their charge was to detail "the economic, ethical, legal, medical, psychiatric and social implications of clinical application of a totally implantable artificial heart."[27] The panel did its work admirably well. It succeeded in scuttling the ludicrous notion, on which millions had already been spent, that the artificial heart should be powered by 53 grams of plutonium surgically implanted in the recipient's chest. The panel also raised a wide range of social, economic, and ethical concerns. Unfortunately, however, the panel members were required to do their work on the basis of very optimistic and unrealistic assumptions about the ultimate success of the program. Moreover, they were not permitted to make any recommendations regarding program continuance.

The most recent National Heart, Lung, and Blood Institute (NHLBI) panel to review the artificial heart program was the 1985 Working Group on Mechanical Circulatory Support. Their charge was to examine "the broad medical, societal, ethical and economic aspects" of the "investigational and anticipated therapeutic use" of the artificial heart.[28] This panel recommended spending an additional $130 million for research over the next thirteen years and called for clinical trials to begin in 1991.

This report has been accused of being an in-house document in the guise of an independent review. What has been alleged is that the deputy directory of NHLBI wrote crucial sections of the final report and that the director of the Devices and Technology Branch, which oversees the artificial heart program, wrote some of the early drafts. Acting Assistant Secretary of Health Mason was reported to have said that the report was unduly optimistic and did not answer the major questions. One member of the panel challenged, in an appendix, the report's optimistic assumptions and complained that alternative projects, such as antismoking campaigns, should also have been considered.[29] Another member of the panel has said that he agreed with the report's conclusions but still regarded the artificial heart as a "distinct and direct threat to the health of others" because of its costs and potential impact on the system of health care financing.[30]

Whatever the merit of these criticisms, it is clear that NHLBI has returned to its earlier practice of appointing narrow review panels. Of the thirteen members of the 1985 working group, eight were physicians and almost all of the members were drawn from the biomedical establishment.

Recently Harold P. Green, who chaired the 1972 review panel, wrote:

NIH has not implemented one of the panel's most important recommendations: the establishment of a permanent, broadly interdisciplinary, and representative group of public members to monitor further steps, and to participate in the formulation of guidelines and policies for the artificial heart. Review of artificial heart developments today is in the hands of an essentially expert committee with only token participation by the kinds of "soft" disciplines that comprised the Artificial Heart Assessment Panel in 1972 and 1973. This probably reflects a judgment that the technological imperative should not be thwarted by the musings of those who are concerned with the broader social, ethical, and policy considerations.[31]

The artificial heart program began with unbridled optimism. The only problems taken seriously were technical ones, and they were thought to be soluble with enough money. Discussion of the social, economic, and ethical problems that would be entailed by the clinical use of the artificial heart was neglected in favor of prognostications about technical matters by medical researchers. If societal considerations had been taken seriously, there might never have been an artificial heart program. For even if the artificial heart is a technical success, it may still be a human failure. If the artificial heart becomes a clinical option, it will raise difficult problems about cost and allocation. These are the problems that will be addressed in the next two sections.

The Problem of Cost

Any attempt to estimate the probable cost of the artificial heart program must take two sorts of costs into account: the costs of research and development and those entailed by the clinical use of the artificial heart. Research and development costs have been underestimated throughout the history of the program. It remains to be seen whether estimates of the costs associated with the clinical use of the artificial heart will prove to be more accurate.

In the mid-1960s NHI predicted that total research and development costs would be about $40 million.[32] Well over $200 million has been spent on artificial heart research to date, and as we have seen, the 1985 review panel recommended spending $130 million more.

Although this spending might produce some indirect benefits, ultimately the case for artificial heart research must rest on the research program's achieving its goal: the development of a clinically acceptable artificial heart.[33] Our questions then are: How many lives can we expect the artificial heart to save and at what cost?

It is of course difficult to answer these questions. We cannot be certain that the research program will succeed. If it does succeed, we cannot be sure what the artificial heart's contribution to longevity will be or what quality of life its recipients will enjoy. Nor can we say with confidence how many people will benefit from the heart and what the costs of implantation and maintenance will be. The implants that have occurred thus far have been very expensive. Barney Clark's medical bills were more than a quarter-million dollars and Bill Schroeder's were well over a half-million—this despite the fact that many of the usual fees were waived. Still, these were experimental procedures that involved a great many complications. If the artificial heart becomes an acceptable clinical option, the costs will almost certainly decline.

A number of studies have tried to estimate the potential costs of the clinical use of the artificial heart. In 1965 NHI commissioned a series of six parallel studies on the costs, benefits, and feasibility of an artificial heart. A seventh firm was hired to analyze, evaluate, and summarize these studies. That firm's conclusion was that the artificial heart would extend the lives of many people, guarantee high quality of life, and be cost beneficial for the nation as a whole. At the outset it was assumed that no one would die on the operating table, that all artificial heart recipients would return to normal lives, and that on average they would live longer and be healthier than other people. The report estimated that there would be 60,000 implants per year at a cost of $10,000 each. The total cost of the program would be about $600 million per year, but during the first decade of the program the benefits would be about $19 billion, and in the second decade they would be about $41 billion.[34]

The 1968 ad hoc task force on cardiac replacement estimated that at most there would be 32,000 implants per year, at a cost ranging from $10,000 to $20,000 each. The total cost of the program would range between $320 million and $640 million. This study did not address the benefits of the artificial heart program, but it did recommend that the program go forward.[35]

As was noted, the 1972 NHLI panel was required to do its work on the basis of very optimistic assumptions. It was assumed that all implants would be successful and that for ten years thereafter artificial heart recipients would suffer no cardiac-related deaths. The ten-year mortality rate of artificial heart recipients was thus expected to be lower than that of the general population of the same age. The number of potential recipients was estimated at between 16,750 and 50,300 per year, and the average cost per implant was projected at $15,000 to $25,000. The annual cost to society was predicted to be $250 million to $1.25 billion per year. No attempt was made to quantify the wide range of social costs that the panel noted would be entailed by the clinical use of the artificial heart. Nor was any attempt made to quantify the artificial heart's potential benefits.[36]

In 1982 a background paper on the artificial heart was commissioned by the Office of Technology Assessment (OTA). It estimated the number of potential artificial heart recipients at between 16,000 and 66,000 per year. The cost of each implant was predicted to range from $23,000 to $75,000, with annual maintenance costs of $1,800 to $8,800 per heart. The authors stated that the total cost of the program "could easily reach $3 billion annually," but their own figures suggest the possibility of costs in excess of $5 billion per year. The authors also noted some additional social costs associated with the clinical use of the artificial heart, but they made no attempt to quantify them. As for the benefits of the program, the authors concluded that under "worst-case" assumptions someone who would otherwise die of ischemic heart disease would gain, on average, less than two months of additional life. Under "best-case" assumptions, such a person would gain a little over seven months of life.[37]

The 1985 NHLBI report predicted that between 17,000 and 35,000 persons annually would be candidates for the artificial heart. Average survival was projected at 3.5 years, at an average lifetime cost, including implantation and maintenance, of $150,000. The total cost of the program was estimated at between $2.5 billion and $5 billion per year.[38]

What are we to do with all these numbers? First, we should note how radically different these estimates are. Depending on which study we employ, the number of artificial heart recipients varies from 16,000 to 66,000 per year. Estimates of increased longevity vary from two months to ten years or more. Cost projections range from $10,000 to $150,000 per implant. This diversity of opinion should lead us, I think, to be skeptical of the results of any single study. What is clear, however, is that the artificial heart will be a very expensive clinical option.

Second, we should see that clinical use of the artificial heart will involve enormous social costs, certain of which are noted in some of the studies. These include: the impact of widespread use of the artificial heart on the availability of other health care services; its effect on government programs like Medicaid, Medicare, and Social Security; its impact on employers and employer-provided benefits such as health insurance; and its consequences for family and friends who care for patients once they leave the hospital. Because none of the studies attempted to quantify these concerns, the real cost of the artificial heart program was seriously understated in all of the projections.

Third, we should understand that the costs of the artificial heart program are additional costs that must be borne by the health care system. The artificial heart would not replace any other treatment that could then be dropped once the artificial heart is developed. Thus widespread use of the artificial heart would require several billion dollars of additional spending on health care or equivalent cutbacks in other health programs.[39]

These considerations taken together suggest that widespread use of the artificial heart would be extremely expensive. There is, however, a further problem. It is not clear what we would be getting in return for our investment.

We know very little about the artificial heart's potential benefits. The studies commissioned by NHI and its successors made unrealistic assumptions about the heart's contribution to longevity and about the recipients' quality of life. The 1985 report was a partial exception. It assumed a 10 percent mortality rate during implantation and later deaths from blood clots, infection, and mechanical failure. Still this report assumed that the technical problems that currently plague the program would be overcome and that a totally implantable artificial heart would be developed. The authors of the 1982 OTA background paper also employed what they took to be realistic assumptions, but their conclusions were very different. They thought that the artificial heart would make only minor contributions to longevity, and they expressed concern about the recipients' quality of life. Certainly quality of life on the artificial heart thus far has not been very good. Moreover, recent studies have suggested that depression and suicidal tendencies among those dependent on medical technology might be greater than had previously been thought.[40]

Our inability to say very precisely what the benefits of the artificial heart would be is important. If an artificial heart is developed, whether or not it is worth the enormous costs that clinical use would entail will depend crucially on the benefits it delivers. For ultimately, the costs and benefits of the artificial heart must be compared to those of other programs.

The evidence that we have thus far suggests that clinical use of the artificial heart would not fare well when compared to other programs. Even the optimistic 1985 report states: "The Working Group suspects that . . . [a cost-effectiveness study] would reveal the existence of more efficient activities and would indicate that a reallocation of health resources, involving not only the artificial heart, could improve the health of our population."[41]

It might be objected, however, that considerations of cost-effectiveness only have force when the programs that are being compared are genuine alternatives. Clearly the artificial heart fares poorly if we compare it to feeding programs for third world children, but not many people would consider these programs to be genuine alternatives. It is also clear, however, that the artificial heart program fares poorly when compared to many other government-financed or government-mandated health and safety programs. If we think in terms of life-years saved rather than lives saved, highway safety programs are dramatically more cost-effective than the artificial heart program would be.[42] The artificial heart does not look promising even when compared to other high-technology medical programs. More research money has been spent on the artificial heart at its current stage of development than was spent on hemodialysis at a comparable stage. Moreover the clinical costs associated with the artificial heart could well be as high as those associated with the hemodialysis program.[43]

Perhaps the most plausible alternatives to the artificial heart program are other programs designed to prevent cardiac-related deaths. The question is, given a fixed sum of money, could we prevent more cardiac-related deaths by investing in these alternative programs or by investing in the artificial heart? In the thirty years since Kolff and Akutsu kept a dog alive for ninety minutes on an artificial heart, the death rate from cardiac disease has declined 30 percent. Although there is little hard evidence, it is plausible to suppose that this reduction is primarily due to life-style changes and secondarily due to our increased capacity for rapid medical response to cardiac events. Good data are difficult to come by, but it appears that prevention and rapid response programs are much more cost-effective than the artificial heart program could ever hope to be. Studies suggest that mobile coronary care units involve costs of about $15,000 per life saved, or $1,800 per life-year saved; and that diet programs involve costs of about $102,000 per life saved, or $6,500 per life-year saved. Perhaps the most dramatic figure can be obtained from the 1982 OTA background paper, which also reviewed the Stanford Heart Disease Prevention Program. Although data were preliminary and incomplete, a comparative study of three communities showed that community education programs increased the life expectancy of an average person by about 1.5 years, at a cost of about $19 per person.[44]

It is difficult to assess the costs and benefits of the artificial heart program or to compare them with other programs. The cost of the program has been radically understated from the beginning, and there is disagreement about the costs that would be entailed by the clinical use of the artificial heart. The potential benefits are difficult to estimate, as the artificial heart may never become a viable clinical option.

Still, two things seem clear. First, the decision to develop the artificial heart was an extremely high-risk decision. No one really knew what it would cost then, and no one really knows what it will cost now. Second, the data that are available suggest that there is no serious question about whether or not the artificial heart will be cost-effective: It will not be. What this means is that our investment in the artificial heart will result in more lives being lost than if we were to invest in other lifesaving programs instead. This may not be a conclusive objection to the artificial heart program, but it is a very serious one. If this objection is to be overcome, there must be some very important value that is protected by the artificial heart program.

The Problem of Allocation

If the artificial heart program is successful, some people will benefit and others will not. Some of those who would otherwise die of heart disease will be the beneficiaries. They are disproportionately male, smokers; they eat high-fat diets and live sedentary lives. The losers will be those who would have benefited from an alternative allocation of resources.

Most of us know that different amounts are spent for lifesaving in different contexts and circumstances, but we probably do not know just how great these disparities are. One (rough) way of getting at them is to look at how different government agencies value life when evaluating policy options. On the low end, the policies of the National Highway Traffic Safety Administration (NHTSA) express a value of about $64,000 per life saved, Health and Human Services at about $102,000, and the Consumer Products Safety Commission at about $50,000. On the high end is the Environmental Protection Agency, whose regulations express a value of about $2.6 million per life saved, and the Occupational Safety and Health Administration (OSHA), whose policies value life at about $12.1 million. If we switch from lives saved to life-years saved, the disparities become even greater. The least expensive OSHA program is 7 times more expensive than the most expensive NHTSA program, and the median OSHA program is more than 400 times more expensive than the most expensive NHTSA program.[45]

When faced with these disparities, we might reasonably wonder whether it is fair to spend so much to prevent workplace deaths, for example, and so little to prevent highway deaths. There are different conceptions of what constitutes a fair allocation of lifesaving resources. Some would say that the fairest allocation is the one that is most efficient in saving life. There are complications, however. It is not clear which of two policies is more efficient: the one that saves the most lives or the one that saves the most life-years. If we are concerned with saving the most lives, then keeping an eighty-year-old cancer patient alive for a year would presumably count as much as saving a child from leukemia. If it is life-years that we are concerned with, then a good policy might be to ignore the elderly in favor of the young. It might be objected that neither of these approaches is fair, for both single out some people for special treatment. Those who can be saved cheaply benefit at the expense of those who can only be saved at great expense.

This objection suggests a second conception of fairness in allocation. Some would say that it is equality that matters. But just as the conception that appeals to efficiency needs to make clear what it is that we should be aiming to maximize, so the conception that appeals to equality needs to make clear what it is that we should be trying to equalize. Consider two possibilities: Our goal could be to equalize spending on lifesaving across contexts and circumstances, or it could be to equalize life expectancies across individuals or social groups.[46] These goals can come into conflict. A recent report to the secretary of Health and Human Services indicated that mortality rates are much higher for blacks and other minorities than they are for whites. If mortality rates were equalized at the level enjoyed by whites, more than 60,000 lives per year would be saved.[47] But in order to equalize mortality rates between whites and blacks we might have to spend different amounts on different people in different contexts.

Another approach would reject the very idea that fairness of allocation involves an appeal to some abstract principle, such as a principle of efficiency or equality. This view would urge us to focus on concrete contextual factors that affect the way that we think about risks. People are more reluctant to bear some risks than others even when the probability of death is the same. When risks involve the potential for large-scale catastrophe, when they are involuntary, uncontrollable, unknown, or inequitably distributed, we often fear them more than other risks.[48] It may be these characteristics of risks that motivate people to pay more to prevent a cancer death, for example, than a highway death. Moreover some people think that not only the character of the risk matters, but also who is at risk. On this view it may be important to spend disproportionate amounts to save certain people as a sign of national unity, as a gesture toward social justice, or as a demonstration of the high value we place on life.[49] People who think that it is reasonable to distinguish among potential victims, or among risks on grounds other than their probability of causing death, may support unequal or inefficient allocations of lifesaving resources. They may even defend our present system.

My aim here is not to develop or defend a particular account of how lifesaving resources should be allocated. Rather my point is that the initial decision to pursue the artificial heart was a decision to use public resources to benefit some people rather than others. Thus it was a decision that should have involved a systematic assessment of how such allocations ought to be made and of how artificial heart research was likely to fare with respect to such an assessment. If the artificial heart becomes a viable clinical option, the need for such an assessment will become even more acute.

One simple way to approach the problem of allocation would be to say that anyone can have an artificial heart who wants one, as long as he or she can pay for it. There are several problems with this approach, however. First, it might result in very few people benefiting from a technology that could benefit a great many more. Insurance companies have been reluctant to pick up the costs of expensive new procedures such as transplants and artificial implants. If they decline to pay for artificial heart implants, only the very rich will be able to afford them. If insurance companies do decide to cover artificial heart implants, many people will still be denied access to them. One-quarter of the population is currently uninsured or underinsured, and this percentage is expected to rise throughout the 1990s.[50]

There is a more fundamental objection to the free market approach. If a successful artificial heart is produced, it will be due to massive public investment in its research and development. Turning the artificial heart over to the free market once it becomes a clinical option would privatize its benefits after the public has already borne its costs. This is not defensible from the point of view of any reasonable moral or political theory, and the public should not be asked to stand for it. This suggests that if an acceptable artificial heart is developed, some system of public financing will be required in order to protect the public's legitimate claim to the benefits of the heart.

A second simple approach would protect this claim. Following the example of the End-Stage Renal Disease Program, we could establish a program, financed through Medicare, that would pay for artificial heart implants in all those who need them. This approach too has its problems. The End-Stage Renal Disease Program is under growing attack because it is expensive and difficult to justify on economic grounds.[51] A similar program for financing artificial heart implants would be subject to the same objections. Moreover, it is doubtful that a government trying to divest itself of one expensive open-ended program would willingly take on another.

A second problem with this approach is that it is difficult to justify massive federal spending on end-stage renal and cardiac patients when we do not make similar commitments to cancer patients or those who are dying from other causes. Universal provision of artificial hearts seems especially indefensible in view of the fact that we do not adequately fund a wide range of screening programs and basic health services that are clearly cheaper and more efficacious. The following example is especially appropriate in the present context. In 1983 California eliminated MediCal coverage for 270,000 medically indigent adults. During the next six months, among chronically hypertensive patients who had been eliminated from the program, the risk of cardiovascular-related death increased 40 percent.[52]

Programs can be designed that steer between the two simple extremes. For example we could establish a fixed budget for artificial heart implants and develop rigorous criteria for who would get them. Any such middle-course program will embody the defects of the more extreme programs, though perhaps to a lesser extent. The fixed-budget program would probably result in unequal access to the artificial heart. How could we deny the heart to someone who would die without it and was willing and able to pay for it, even if he or she did not satisfy the selection criteria? Moreover, the disparity between what we are willing to spend on artificial hearts as opposed to providing basic health services would remain. Finally, I doubt that a permanent system of rationing the artificial heart would be politically acceptable in our society. We have a great deal of resistance to rationing programs in general (except perhaps those that ration on the basis of price). We tend to see rationing as a temporary solution; in this case, perhaps, as a way station on the road to universal provision.

Questions about allocation were implicit in the very decision to undertake the development of an artificial heart. If the artificial heart becomes a clinical option, these questions will only become more urgent. The approaches to allocation and financing that we have discussed are all problematical. The question of fairness in allocation will loom very large if the artificial heart program eventually becomes a viable clinical option.

Conclusion

Investing in a new technology, by its very nature, is a risky undertaking. At the moment of investment we cannot be certain that the technology will be successfully developed or that it will win widespread social acceptance if it is developed. Technologies such as the artificial heart are doubly risky, for they involve these uncertainties as well as additional ones. If the artificial heart is successfully developed and deployed, it will forever change the way that we live and die. The effects of such profound changes are difficult even to imagine. Because of the risks associated with such technologies, it is imperative that we get as clear a picture as possible of their potential impacts before we set out to develop them. Because the chances of failure are great and the probability of unforeseen problems almost certain, we must continually reassess these technologies in the light of new information and changing circumstances.

Such assessments must take into account potential social impacts as well as the prospects for technical and scientific success. It may be within our power to produce technologies that would so disrupt the fabric of our social life that we ought not to develop them. Thus in assessing these new technologies, considerations regarding their social impacts are as relevant as considerations regarding their scientific and technical feasibility. For this reason experts from such disciplines as law, economics, philosophy, sociology, and psychology must be included in the assessment process.[53]

Experts involved in assessing new technologies should think of themselves as serving the general public. They should strive to do what people would want done if they were well informed and thinking clearly, while at the same time being sensitive to the diversity of values and interests that exists in our society. Neither the strongest advocates of a new technology nor those who would be its major beneficiaries can be allowed to dominate the assessment process. Enthusiasm about the possibilities afforded by new technologies is important, but so is sage and tempered skepticism.

The story of the artificial heart program is a case study in how not to make policy about medical technology. If we are to create a society in which we use our medical resources to provide the best possible lives for as many people as possible, we are going to have to get our runaway technologies under control. Our decisions must be more broadly based. We must no longer assume away difficult scientific and technical questions and ignore the hard ethical and social choices entailed by new technologies. If we fail to do this, we will continue to purchase very expensive life extensions for some highly visible people, at the cost of letting many "invisible" people die for lack of resources. This is not the way it should be, and this is not what we would want, were we to take an impartial point of view.

Notes

Thanks are due to Nancy Davis for stimulating me to write this chapter and for working overtime to help along the way; she has influenced the final result in more ways than I can detail here. Thanks also go to John A. Fisher who saved me from a major error and to Jacqueline L. Colby and Toby Jacober for their helpful suggestions.

1. The first artificial heart experiment on a human was conducted by Dr. Denton Cooley under extremely dubious circumstances. It eventually led to a suit for malpractice, negligence, and fraudulent misrepresentation against Cooley and an associate. For an account see Renee C. Fox and Judith P. Swazey, *The Courage to Fail*, 2d ed. (Chicago: The University of Chicago Press, 1978), pp. 135–197.

2. The issues raised by the Clark implant have been discussed in some detail by Barton J. Bernstein in "The Misguided Quest for the Artificial Heart," *Technology Review* 87, 8 (November/December 1984), pp. 13 ff.; and in "The Pursuit of the Artificial Heart," *Medical Heritage* 2, 2 (March/April 1986), pp. 80–100. I have greatly benefited from these articles.

3. George Annas, "Consent to the Artificial Heart: The Lion and the Crocodiles," *Hastings Center Report* 13, 2 (April 1983), p. 20.

4. See Claudia K. Berenson and Bernard I. Grosser, "Total Artificial Heart Implantation," *Archives of General Psychiatry* 41 (September 1984), pp. 910–916.

5. See DeVries' testimony in *Status of the Artificial Heart Program: Hearings Before the Subcommittee on Investigations and Oversight of the Committee on Science and Technology, Ninety-Ninth Congress, Second Session, February 5, 1986* (Washington: U.S. Government Printing Office, 1986), pp. 242–243. For further discussion of difficulties involved in extrapolating the results of animal experimentation to humans, see Dale Jamieson and Tom Regan, "On the Ethics of Using Animals in Science," in T. Regan and D. VanDeVeer (eds.), *And Justice For All: New Introductory Essays in Ethics and Public Policy* (Totowa: Rowman and Littlefield, 1982), pp. 169–196.

6. *Status of the Artificial Heart Program* (1986), p. 271.

7. *New York Times*, April 28, 1987.

8. *New York Times*, April 28, 1987.

9. These objections have been forcefully made by Barton J. Bernstein in "The Pursuit of the Artificial Heart" (1986), and by George Annas in "No Cheers for Temporary Artificial Hearts," *Hastings Center Report* 15, 5 (October 1985), pp. 27–28.

10. Bartley P. Griffith et al., "Temporary Use of the Jarvik-7 Artificial Heart Before Transplantation," *New England Journal of Medicine* 316 (January 15, 1987), pp. 130–134.

11. *New York Times*, April 28, 1987.

12. *Status of the Artificial Heart Program* (1986), p. 32.

13. *Status of the Artificial Heart Program* (1986), p. 265.

14. An account of the formation of U.S. medical research policy that is generally in keeping with my account of the artificial heart program is S. P. Strickland, *Politics, Science and Dread Diseases* (Cambridge: Harvard University Press, 1972). Strickland emphasized the interaction among interest groups, congressional committees, and federal agencies in the creation of our multibillion-dollar medical research establishment.

15. "Permanent Substitutes for Valves and Hearts," *Transactions of American Society of Artificial Internal Organs* 4 (1958), pp. 230–232.

16. Fox and Swazey, *The Courage to Fail* (1978), p. 201.

17. NHI is short for National Heart Institute. Throughout its history NHI has gone through a number of changes of name and provenance. In the 1970s it became the National Heart and Lung Institute (NHLI), and more recently, the National Heart, Lung, and Blood Institute (NHLBI). NHI and its successors are or have been constituents of the National Institutes of Health (NIH).

18. "Surgeons Prepare to Implant Mechanical Heart in Humans," *Journal of the American Medical Association* 185, 13 (September 28, 1963), pp. 24–31.

19. *Hearings Before the Subcommittee of the Committee on Appropriations, United States Senate, First Session, on H.R. 5888 Making Appropriations for the Departments of Labor and Health, Education, and Welfare, and Related Agencies, for the Fiscal Year Ending June 30, 1964, and for Other Purposes,* Part II (Washington: U.S. Government Printing Office, 1963), p. 1402.

20. Fox and Swazey, *The Courage to Fail* (1978), p. 143.

21. See the account of their report in *Hearings Before a Subcommittee of the Committee on Appropriations, House of Representatives, Eighty-Ninth Congress, First Session, Department of Health, Education, and Welfare, Part 3, National Institutes of Health* (Washington: U.S. Government Printing Office, 1965), p. 502.

22. For an account of the master plan see *Hearings* (1965), pp. 505–506.

23. There is at least one case in which data appear to have been falsified. See the discussion in Fox and Swazey, *The Courage to Fail* (1978), pp. 145 ff.

24. The congressional committees were dominated by powerful chairmen. The father of Lister Hill, chairman of the Senate committee, was a surgeon. The elder Hill named his son after Joseph Lister, the founder of modern antiseptic surgery. John Fogarty, the chairman of the House committee, suffered from heart disease. For him the artificial heart did not come soon enough. In early 1967 he died of a heart attack.

25. See Bernstein, "The Pursuit of the Artificial Heart." The best account of the politics of the establishment of the artificial heart program is in Michael J. Strauss, "The Political History of the Artificial Heart," *New England Journal of Medicine* 310, 5 (February 2, 1984), pp. 332–336.

26. Ad Hoc Task Force on Cardiac Replacement, *Cardiac Replacement: Medical, Ethical, Psychological, and Economic Implications* (Washington: U.S. Government Printing Office, 1969).

27. Artificial Heart Assessment Panel, National Heart and Lung Institute, *The Totally Implantable Artificial Heart: Legal, Social, Ethical, Medical, Economic, Psychological Implications* (Bethesda: DHEW Publication No. (NIH) 74-191, 1973), p. 1.

28. This account of the working group's charge is taken from a letter by Claude Lenfant, the director of NHLBI, to the *Hastings Center Report* 16, 6 (December 1986), p. 27. The citation for the working group's report is National Heart, Lung and Blood Institute Working Group on Mechanical Circulatory Support, *Artificial Heart and Assist Devices: Directions, Needs, Costs, Societal and Ethical Issues* (Bethesda: NIH Publication No. 85-2723, 1985). For accounts of this report I have mainly relied on Lenfant's testimony in *Status of the Artificial Heart Program* (1986); Albert R. Jonsen, "The Artificial Heart's Threat to Others," *Hastings Center Report* 16, 1 (February 1986), pp. 9–11; and Bernstein, "The Pursuit of the Artificial Heart" (1986).

29. See Bernstein, "The Pursuit of the Artificial Heart" (1986).

30. See Jonsen, "The Artificial Heart's Threat to Others" (1986).

31. Harold P. Green, "An NIH Panel's Early Warnings," *Hastings Center Report* 14, 5 (October 1984), pp. 13–15. Compare Green's sentiments with those of DeVries: "Who actually speaks for the public in its concern about experimentation? Is it the press? Bioethicists? Once again, the scientific community bears the ultimate responsibility for medical advances, because it is uniquely competent to conduct experiments as well as comment on them." (*Status of the Artificial Heart Program* (1986), p. 254.)

32. See *Hearings* (1965), p. 506.

33. DeVries has claimed that artificial heart research has important indirect benefits in educating the public about heart disease and in producing spin-off advances in other areas of medicine. See *Status of the Artificial Heart Program* (1986), p. 241. This may be

true, but it is plausible to suppose that these benefits could have been realized, at least as efficiently, by directly funding these other areas rather than investing in the artificial heart.

34. Hittman Associates, *Final Summary Report on Six Studies Basic to the Consideration of the Artificial Heart Program* (Baltimore: Hittman Associates, 1966). For accounts of this report I have relied on *Hearings Before a Subcommittee of the Committee on Appropriations, House of Representatives, Eighty-Ninth Congress, Second Session, Part 4: Department of Health, Education, and Welfare, National Institutes of Health* (Washington: U.S. Government Printing Office, 1966); Deborah P. Lubeck and John P. Bunker, *The Implications of Cost-Effectiveness Analysis of Medical Technology, Background Paper #2: Case Studies of Medical Technologies, Case Study 9: The Artificial Heart: Costs, Risks, and Benefits* (Washington: U.S. Government Printing Office, 1982); and the two articles by Bernstein previously cited.

35. Ad Hoc Task Force, *Cardiac Replacement* (1969).

36. Artificial Heart Assessment Panel, *The Totally Implantable Artificial Heart* (1973). Harold Green later commented that "the device implanted in Barney Clark bears little resemblance to the one that was the subject of our panel's deliberations." See Green, "An NIH Panel's Early Warnings" (1984), p. 13.

37. Lubeck and Bunker, *The Artificial Heart: Costs, Risks, and Benefits* (1982).

38. Working Group, *Artificial Heart and Assist Devices* (1985).

39. This point is made in Jonsen, "The Artificial Heart's Threat to Others" (1986).

40. See Berenson and Grosser, "Total Artificial Heart Implantation" (1984). See also Laurence R. Tancredi, "Social and Ethical Implications in Technology Assessment," in Barbara J. McNeil and Ernest G. Cravalho (eds.), *Critical Issues in Medical Technology* (Boston: Auburn House Publishing Co., 1982), pp. 95–96.

41. As quoted in Jonsen, "The Artificial Heart's Threat to Others" (1986), p. 11.

42. If we accept the conclusions of the 1985 NHLBI study, an artificial heart would extend the life of an average recipient 3.5 years at a cost of $150,000. This works out to a cost of about $40,000 per life-year saved. Almost any traffic safety program is more cost-effective than this. The estimates of the costs of requiring air bags in automobiles range from $78,000 to $117,000 per life saved. As victims of automobile accidents tend to be young, requiring air bags would save additional life-years at a cost of $1,900 to $2,300 per year. Other studies show that vigorous enforcement of the 55-mile-per-hour speed limit would save life-years at a cost of about $2,500 per life-year saved. These figures are reported in John D. Graham and James W. Vaupel, "Value of a Life: What Difference Does It Make?" *Risk Analysis* 1, 1 (1981), pp. 89–95.

43. The annual cost of hemodialysis is greater than the expected annual cost of artificial heart maintenance, but hemodialysis does not involve initial costs comparable to those of implantation.

44. Figures relating to the Stanford study are my own calculations based on data taken from the OTA background paper. The studies concerning mobile coronary care units and diet programs are taken from R. Zeckhauser and D. Shepard, "Where Now for Saving Lives?" *Law and Contemporary Problems* 40, 4 (Autumn 1976), pp. 5–45. It has been claimed recently that preventive measures rarely reduce medical expenditures. The debate around this claim seems to me to be largely confused. But even if this claim is true, not much follows from it without some additional premises regarding the benefits of prevention or some comparisons between preventive measures and their alternatives. At any rate this claim does not threaten my view that the artificial heart is unlikely to be cost-effective relative to cardiac disease prevention programs. See Louise B. Russell, *Is Prevention Better Than Cure?* (Washington: The Brookings Institution, 1986); and the exchange between Russell and Roy Shephard: R. J. Shephard, "The Economics of Prevention: A Critique," *Health Policy* 7:49–56 (1987), and L. B. Russell, "The Economics of Prevention," *Health Policy* 7:57–59 (1987).

45. Graham and Vaupel, "Value of a Life: What Difference Does It Make?" (1981).

46. This distinction is related to Ronald Dworkin's distinction between equality of resources and equality of welfare. See his two-part article, "What is Equality?" *Philosophy and Public Affairs* 10, 3–4, (Summer-Fall 1981), pp. 185–246, 283–345.

47. *New York Times*, October 26, 1985.

48. Baruch Fischoff et al., "How Safe Is Safe Enough? A Psychometric Study of Attitudes Towards Technological Risks and Benefits," *Policy Studies* 8 (1978), pp. 127–152.

49. Such views are discussed in Paul T. Menzel, *Medical Costs, Moral Choices* (New Haven: Yale University Press, 1983), Chap. 7.

50. See Robert J. Blendon, "Health Policy Choices for the 1990s," *Issues in Science and Technology* 2, 4 (Summer 1986), pp. 65–73.

51. For an argument that this program cannot be justified on economic grounds, see J. L. Anderton et al., *Living With Renal Failure* (Baltimore: University Park Press, 1978).

52. See Nicole Lure et al., "Termination from MediCal—Does It Affect Health?" *New England Journal of Medicine* 311, 7 (August 16, 1984), pp. 480–484.

53. For an explanation and defense of the view that philosophers are moral experts, see my "Is Applied Ethics Worth Doing?" forthcoming in David Rosenthal and Fadlou Shehadi (eds.), *Applied Ethics and Ethical Theory* (Salt Lake City: University of Utah Press).

PART FIVE

Appendixes

Appendix A:
Organ Transplantation—
Issues and Recommendations

Report of the Task Force
on Organ Transplantation, April 1986

EXECUTIVE SUMMARY

In response to widespread public interest and involvement in the field of organ transplantation, the Congress enacted the National Organ Transplant Act of 1984 (PL 98-507). In addition to prohibiting the purchase of organs, the act provided for the establishment of grants to organ procurement agencies (OPAs) and a national organ-sharing system. This act also established a twenty-five member Task Force on Organ Transplantation representing medicine, law, theology, ethics, allied health, the health insurance industry, and the general public. The Office of the Surgeon General of the Public Health Service, the National Institutes of Health (NIH), the Food and Drug Administration (FDA), and the Health Care Financing Administration (HCFA) were also represented.

The mandate given to the Task Force was to conduct comprehensive examinations of the medical, legal, ethical, economic, and social issues presented by human organ procurement and transplantation and to report on these issues within one year. In addition, we were asked to assess immunosuppressive medications used to prevent rejection and to report on our findings within seven months; this report also was to include a series of recommendations, including recommending a means of assuring that individuals who need such medications can obtain them.

During the twelve months following its organizational meeting on February 11, 1985, the Task Force met in public session on eight occasions and held two public hearings. We were supported by staff from the Office of Organ Transplantation and by consultants from HCFA and other agencies and organizations. Data were obtained through surveys, literature reviews, commissioned studies, consultations, and public testimony. Five workgroups were established within the Task Force to address each of the mandated issues identified by Congress and to prepare presentations and recommendations for consideration by the full membership.

As required by the act, the Task Force completed an assessment of immunosuppressive medications and the costs of these therapies, and submitted its report and recommendations to the Secretary and the Congress on October 21, 1985. Briefly, we found that the new immunosuppressive regimens, although expensive, proved to be cost-saving due to im-

Reprinted from *Report of the Task Force on Organ Transplantation*, April 1986, U.S. Department of Health & Human Services.

provement in outcome; for this reason, and in order to ensure equitable access, the Task Force recommended that the federal government establish a mechanism to provide immunosuppressive drugs to recipients otherwise unable to pay for these drugs, when Medicare paid for the transplantation procedure.

In this final report, the Task Force summarizes its arguments on the issues identified as major concerns by the Congress, and presents a series of recommendations for consideration of federal and state legislators, public health officials, the organ and tissue transplantation community, organized medicine, nursing, and the federal government.

Organ and Tissue Donation and Procurement

The serious gap between the *need* for organs and tissues and the *supply* of donors is common to all programs in organ transplantation, as well as to tissue banking and transplantation. The Task Force believes that substantial improvements in organ donation would ensue through new, innovative, and expanded programs in public and professional education and the coordination of efforts of the many organizations and agencies that engage in these activities. In particular, we support both the enactment of legislation in states that have not clarified determination of death based on irreversible cessation of brain function (the Uniform Determination of Death Act), and the enactment of legislation requiring implementation of routine hospital policies and procedures to provide the next-of-kin with the opportunity of donating organs and tissues. In addition, we found both a serious lack of uniform standards of accountability and quality assurance in organ and tissue procurement and a spectrum of effectiveness of procurement activities. Therefore, the Task Force supports the development both of minimum performance and certification standards, and of monitoring mechanisms.

Recommendations

1. To facilitate organ donation the Task Force recommends:

- The Uniform Determination of Death Act be enacted by the legislatures of states that have not adopted this or a similar act.
- Each state medical association develop and adopt model hospital policies and protocols for the determination of death based upon irreversible cessation of brain function that will be available to guide hospitals in developing and implementing institutional policies and protocols concerning brain death.
- States enact legislation requiring coroners and medical examiners to give permission for organ and tissue procurement when families consent unless the surgical procedure would compromise medicolegal evidence. Further, the legislation should (1) require coroners and medical examiners to develop policies that facilitate the evaluation of all non-heart-beating cadavers under their jurisdiction for organ and tissue donation, and (2) provide the next-of-kin with the opportunity to consider postmortem tissue donation. The Task Force further recommends that coroners develop agreements with local tissue banks to help implement these policies.

2. To facilitate the identification of potential donors and to provide the next-of-kin with appropriate opportunities to donate organs and tissues, the Task Force recommends that:

- All health professionals involved in caring for potential organ and tissue donors voluntarily accept the responsibility for identifying these donors and for referring such donors to appropriate organ procurement organizations.
- Hospitals adopt routine inquiry/required request policies and procedures for identifying potential organ and tissue donors and for providing next-of-kin with appropriate opportunities for donation.
- The Joint Commission on the Accreditation of Hospitals develop a standard that requires all acute care hospitals to both have an affiliation with an organ procurement

agency and have formal policies and procedures for identifying potential organ and tissue donors and for providing next-of-kin with appropriate opportunities for donation.
- The Department of Defense and the Veterans Administration require their hospitals to have routine inquiry policies.
- The Health Care Financing Administration incorporate into the Medicare conditions of participation for hospitals certified under subpart U of the Code of Federal Regulations, a condition that requires hospitals to have routine inquiry policies.
- All state legislatures formulate, introduce, and enact routine inquiry legislation.
- The Commission for Uniform State Laws develop model legislation that requires acute care hospitals to develop an affiliation with an organ procurement agency and to adopt routine inquiry policies and procedures.

3. In regard to living donors and the donor pool, the Task Force recommends that:

- A study of the potential donor pool be conducted using data available through the National Hospital Discharge Survey, supplemented by regional retrospective hospital record reviews.
- Living donors be fully informed about the risks of kidney donation. Health care professionals must guarantee that the decision to donate is entirely voluntary. In the case of all living donors, special emphasis should be placed on histocompatibility.
- A national registry of human organ donors not be established.

4. To improve public education in organ and tissue donation, the Task Force recommends that:

- Educational efforts aimed at increasing organ donation among minority populations be developed and implemented, so that the donor population will come to more closely resemble the ethnic profile of the pool of potential recipients in order to gain the advantage of improved donor and recipient immunologic matching.
- At the regional level, single consortia, composed of public, private, and voluntary groups that have an interest in education on organ and tissue donation should develop, coordinate, and implement public and professional education to supplement, but not replace, activities undertaken by local programs.
- A single organization, such as the American Council on Transplantation, composed of public, private, and voluntary groups that are national in scope and have an interest in education for organ and tissue donation, should develop and coordinate broad scale public and professional educational programs and materials on the national level. This umbrella organization would both develop and distribute model educational materials for use by national and local organizations and plan, coordinate, and develop national efforts using nationwide electronic and print media.
- A national educational program should be established, similar to the High Blood Pressure Education Program of National Institutes of Health's National Heart, Lung, and Blood Institute, aimed at increasing organ donation. This program should include development both of curricula and instructional materials for use in primary and secondary schools throughout the nation, and of programs directed to special target populations, e.g., minority groups, family units, and churches.

5. To improve professional education in organ and tissue donation the Task Force recommends that:

- Medical and nursing schools incorporate organ and tissue procurement and transplantation in the curriculum.
- The Accreditation Council of Graduate Medical Education, the body responsible for accrediting residency programs, include requirements for exposure to organ and tissue donation and transplantation in relevant programs in graduate medical education, such as emergency and critical care medicine and the neurological sciences.

- Each appropriate medical and nursing specialty require demonstration of knowledge of organ and tissue donation and transplantation for certification.
- All professional associations of physicians and nurses involved in caring for potential organ and tissue donors (especially neurosurgeons; trauma surgeons; emergency physicians; and critical care, emergency room, and trauma team nurses), establish programs to educate and encourage their members both to participate in the referral of donors and to cooperate in the organ donation process.
- Organizations of physician specialists who frequently come in contact with organ and tissue donors should establish mechanisms, such as a committee on transplantation, to facilitate communication and cooperation with physicians in the transplantation specialties.

6. The Task Force recommends that organ procurement agencies and procurement specialists be certified:

- Professional peer group organizations, e.g., the North American Transplant Coordinators Organization, should establish mechanisms for certification of nonphysician organ and tissue procurement specialists and standards for evaluation of performance at regular intervals.
- The Department of Health and Human Services should certify no more than one Organ Procurement Agency in any standard metropolitan statistical area or existing organ donor referral area, whichever is larger.
- The Department of Health and Human Services should use the criteria developed by the Association of Independent Organ Procurement Agencies as a guideline to develop consistent certification standards for Independent Organ Procurement Agencies and Hospital-Based Organ Procurement Agencies.
- The Department of Health and Human Services should establish minimal performance productivity standards as part of a recertification process that could be conducted at regular intervals. Such standards should address procurement activity, organizational structure and programs, staff training and competence, and fiscal accountability.
- Appropriate peer organizations should develop standards for certifying tissue banks and for conducting performance evaluations at regular intervals. Such standards should include assessment of quality and quantity of performance, organizational structure and programs, staff training and competency, and fiscal responsibility.

7. The Task Force recommends that the Department of Health and Human Services collect uniform data on organ procurement activities of all Organ Procurement Agencies, including, at a minimum, the number of kidneys procured, kidneys transplanted, kidneys procured but not transplanted, kidneys exported abroad, and relevant cost data. (The data could be collected through the Organ Procurement and Transplantation Network or from each Organ Procurement Agency.)

- The Department of Health and Human Services require all Organ Procurement Agencies to have, as a minimum, a form of governance that would be similar to that described for the national Organ Procurement and Transplantation Network, i.e., it should include adequate representation from each of the following categories: transplant surgeons from participating transplant centers, transplant physicians from participating transplant centers, histocompatibility experts from the affiliated histocompatibility laboratories, representatives of the Organ Procurement Agencies, and members of the general public. Representatives of the general public should have no direct or indirect professional affiliation with the transplant centers or the Organ Procurement Agency. Not more than 50 percent of the Board of Directors may be surgeons or physicians directly involved in transplantation, and at least 20 percent should be members of the general public. Where the governing boards of existing Organ Procurement Agencies differ from this composition, it is desirable that those boards be modified over a maximum of two years to achieve this distribution. The

Task Force believes that all Organ Procurement Agency boards should consider immediate steps to include public representatives.

8. To facilitate more effective collaboration between organ and tissue banks, the Task Force recommends that formal cooperative agreements be established among eye, skin, and bone banks.

- All Organ Procurement Agencies evaluate all potential donors for multiple organ and tissue donation.
- Organ procurement agencies and tissue banks enter into formal agreements for collaborative programs to educate the public and health professionals and to coordinate donor identifications, discussions with next-of-kin, and the procurement process.

Organ Sharing

The Task Force believes that establishment of a unified national system of organ sharing that encompasses a patient registry and coordinates organ allocation and distribution will go far in assuring equity and fairness in the allocation of organs. In addition, a national network organization, through adoption of agreed upon standards and policies, may serve as the vehicle both for improving matching of donors and recipients and for improving access of groups at special disadvantage (the sensitized and small pediatric recipients); thus, the outcome of organ transplantation in this country will surely improve. The development of a national network will permit the gathering and analysis of comprehensive data and, through the establishment of a scientific registry, will facilitate the exchange of new information vital to progress in the field. We assisted the Office of Organ Transplantation in developing specifications for a model network, and urge that the National Organ Procurement and Transplantation Network be established promptly; in addition, we urge Congress to appropriate the funds necessary to initiate the development of the scientific registry.

Recommendations

1. The Task Force recommends that a single national system for organ sharing be established; that its participants agree on and adopt uniform policies and standards by which all will abide; and that its governance include a broad range of viewpoints, interests, and expertise, including the public.

- The national network establish a method to systematically collect and analyze data related to both kidney and extrarenal organ procurement and transplantation. Further, to provide an ongoing evaluation of the scientific and clinical status of organ transplantation, a scientific registry of the recipients of kidney and extrarenal organ transplants should be developed and administered through the national network, and the Task Force urges the Congress to appropriate funds to initiate this activity.
- Organ sharing be mandated for perfectly matched (HLA A, B, and DR) donor-recipient pairs and for donors and recipients with zero antigen mismatches (assuming that at least one antigen has been identified at each locus for both donor and recipient).
- A system of serum sharing and/or allocation of organs based on computer-determined prediction of a negative crossmatch be developed to increase the rate of transplantation in the highly sensitized patient group by increasing the effective size of the donor pool.
Blood group O organs be transplanted only into blood group O recipients.
- Because of the limited local and regional donor pools available to small pediatric patients, the national organ-sharing system should be designed to provide pediatric extrarenal transplant patients access to a national pool of pediatric donors.

- The national organ-sharing network, when established, should conduct ongoing reviews of organ procurement activities, particularly organ discard rates, and develop mechanisms to assist those agencies and programs with high discard rates. In the meantime, we recommend that the Department of Health and Human Services conduct a study to identify why procured kidneys are not transplanted and why the discard rates vary widely from one organ procurement program to another.

2. The Task Force recommends regional centralization of histocompatibility testing where it is geographically feasible, and standardization of key typing reagents and crossmatching techniques.

3. The Task Force recommends that the Congress appropriate funds to establish a national ESRD registry that would combine a renal transplant registry with a dialysis registry. The Task Force further recommends that the national organ-sharing network be represented on any committee responsible for management and data analysis of a national ESRD registry.

Equitable Access to Organ Transplantation

The process of selecting patients for transplantation, both in the formation of the waiting list and in the final selection for allocation of the organ, is generally fair and for the most part has succeeded in achieving equitable distribution of organs. However, the Task Force believes that these processes must be defined by each center and by the system as a whole, and that the standards for patient selection and organ allocation must be based solely on objective medical criteria that are applied fairly and are open to public examination. Moreover, as vital participants in the process, the public must be included in developing these standards and in implementing the policies. We recognized the complex conflict between need for an organ (medical urgency) and the probability of success of the transplant, and did not presume to make recommendations in this sphere; rather we believe that a thoughtful process of development of policies for organ allocation, which takes into account both medical utility and good stewardship, must take place within a broadly representative group.

The Task Force condemns commercialization of organ transplantation and the exploitation of living unrelated donors. The Task Force also addressed the difficult problem of offering organ transplantation to non-immigrant aliens. Because transplantable organs are scarce, we have recommended that no more than 10 percent of all cadaveric kidney transplants in any center be performed in non-immigrant aliens and that extrarenal transplants be offered only when no suitable recipient who is a resident of this country can be found.[1] The Task Force also concluded that equitable access of patients to extrarenal organ transplantation is impeded unfairly by financial barriers, and recommends that all transplant procedures that are efficacious and cost effective be made available to patients, regardless of their ability to pay, through existing public and private health insurance or, as a last resort, through a publicly funded program for patients who are without insurance, Medicare, or Medicaid who could not otherwise afford to obtain the organ transplant.

Recommendations

1. The Task Force recommends that each donated organ be considered a national resource to be used for the public good; the public must participate in the decisions of how this resource can be used to best serve the public interest.

2. In order that patients and their physicians be fully informed, the Task Force recommends that:

- Health professionals provide unbiased, timely, and accurate information to all patients who could possibly benefit from organ transplantation so that they can make informed choices about whether they want to be evaluated and placed on a waiting list.

- Information be published annually for patients and physicians on the graft and patient survival data by transplant center. A clear explanation of what the data represent should preface the presentation of data. A strong recommendation should be made in the publication that each patient discuss with his or her attending physician the circumstances of medical suitability for transplantation and where that patient may best be served.

3. The Task Force recommends that selection of patients both for waiting lists and for allocation of organs be based on medical criteria that are publicly stated and fairly applied.

- The criteria for prioritization be developed by a broadly representative group that will take into account both need and probability of success. Selection of patients otherwise equally medically qualified should be based on length of time on the waiting list.
- Selection of patients for transplants not be subject to favoritism, discrimination on the basis of race or sex, or ability to pay.
- Organ-sharing programs that are designed to improve the probability of success be implemented in the interests of justice and the effective and efficient use of organs, and that the effect of mandated organ sharing be constantly assessed to identify and rectify imbalances that might reduce access of any group.

4. The Task Force recommends that non-immigrant aliens not comprise more than 10 percent of the total number of kidney transplant recipients at each transplant center, until the Organ Procurement and Transplantation Network has had an opportunity to review the issue. In addition, extrarenal organs should not be offered for transplantation to a non-immigrant alien unless it has been determined that no other suitable recipient can be found.

5. The Task Force emphatically rejects the commercialization of organ transplantation and recommends that:

- Exportation and importation of donor organs be prohibited except when distribution is arranged or coordinated by the Organ Procurement and Transplantation Network and the organs are to be sent to recognized national networks. Even then, when an organ is to be exported from the United States, documentation must be available to demonstrate that all appropriate efforts have been made to locate a recipient in the United States and/or Canada. The Task Force has every expectation that these international organ-sharing programs will be reciprocal.
- The practice of soliciting or advertising for non-immigrant aliens and performing a transplant for such patients, without regard to the waiting list, cease.
- Transplanting kidneys from living unrelated donors should be prohibited when financial gain rather than altriusm is the motivating factor.
- To the extent federal law does not prohibit the intrastate sale of organs, states should prohibit the sale of organs from cadavers or living donors within their boundaries.
- As a condition of membership in the Organ Procurement Transplantation Network (OPTN), each transplant center be required to report every transplant or organ procurement procedure to the OPTN. Moreover, transplantation procedures should not be reimbursed under Medicare, Medicaid, CHAMPUS, and other public payers, unless the transplant center meets payment, organ-sharing, reporting, and other guidelines to be established by the OPTN or another agency administratively responsible for the development of such guidelines. Failure to comply with these guidelines will require that the center show cause why it should not be excluded from further organ sharing through the OPTN.
- In order to insure that patients in need of an extrarenal organ transplant can obtain procedures regardless of ability to pay, the Task Force recommends that private and public health benefit programs, including Medicare and Medicaid, should cover heart

and liver transplants, including outpatient immunosuppressive therapy that is an essential part of post-transplant care.

- A public program should be set up to cover the costs of people who are medically eligible for organ transplants but who are not covered by private insurance, Medicare, or Medicaid and who are unable to obtain an organ transplant due to lack of funds.

Diffusion of Organ Transplantation Technology

The number of organ transplant centers in this country is rapidly increasing. As the technical aspects of the procedures have been mastered and patient management has become better understood and standardized, it is not surprising that diffusion of this technology has taken place. The issue of designating centers for reimbursement purposes requires careful consideration of many factors, including cost, criteria for facilities, resources, staffing, and the training and experience of personnel. After lengthy debate, the majority of the Task Force agreed with the widely accepted principle within surgery that the volume of surgical procedures performed is positively associated with outcomes and inversely related to cost and believe that this principle applies to organ transplantation procedures as well. Therefore, we recommend that a minimum volume criterion be enforced, together with other criteria defining the minimal requirements for both institutional and professional support and outcome of transplantation procedures.[2] In the context of scarcity of donor organs, we strongly support regulating diffusion of transplantation technology.

Recommendations

1. The Task Force recommends that transplant centers be designated by an explicit, formal process using well-defined, published criteria.
2. The Task Force recommends that the Department of Health and Human Services designate centers to perform kidney, heart, and liver transplants, and that the centers be evaluated against explicit criteria to ensure that only those institutions with requisite capabilities are allowed to perform the procedures.
3. The Task Force recommends that the Department of Health and Human Services adopt minimum criteria for kidney, heart, and liver transplant centers that address facility requirements, staff experience, training requirements, volume of transplants to be performed each year, and minimum patient and graft survival rates.

Research in Organ Transplantation

Organ transplantation continues to evolve and improve at a fast pace. Strong research programs in basic and applied clinical sciences have been vital to this fortunate development. As is clearly evident in the concerns of the public that resulted in the enactment of the National Organ Transplant Act, research also is needed in the social, ethical, economic, and legal aspects of organ donation and transplantation. The Task Force acknowledges the important role played by the NIH in transplantation research, and encourages the NIH to coordinate the free flow of information regarding transplant-related research through an interinstitutional council on transplantation. Moreover, we strongly urge that research on all aspects of transplantation be fostered and encouraged and that funding for this vital effort be increased. Therein lies the future of transplantation.

Recommendations

1. The Task Force recommends that basic research continue to receive high priority.
2. The Task Force recommends that both laboratory and clinical research of an applied nature directly related to transplantation also be fostered, encouraged, and increasingly funded. For the immediate benefit of patients, the Task Force further recommends that research be aggressively pursued in organ preservation and optimal immu-

nosuppression techniques. The Task Force also wishes to emphasize the importance of sponsoring prospective clinical trials, involving multiple institutions, to solve certain problems in patient management.

3. The Task Force recommends that continuing attention be devoted to collecting complete information on the status and efficacy of transplantation treatments.

4. The Task Force recognizes that the interaction and exchange of information between the agencies involved in transplantation research and its funding must be encouraged. Therefore, we recommend that the National Institutes of Health be provided with resources to establish an interagency and interinstitute Council on Transplantation that will serve as a focus for this activity.

Establishment of an Advisory Board on Organ Transplantation

At the final meeting of the Task Force, where this report was adopted, a recommendation was made to establish a National Organ Transplantation Advisory Board. The Task Force agreed in concept that a national group to advise the Secretary of Health and Human Services would continue to be needed to monitor implementation of the Task Force's findings and serve in an advisory capacity on organ procurement and transplantation issues. Therefore we adopted the following recommendation:

The Task Force recommends that a National Organ Transplantation Advisory Board be authorized and funded to review, evaluate, and advise with regard to the implementation of the recommendations of the Task Force on Organ Transplantation, to serve in an advisory capacity to the Office of Organ Transplantation and to other transplant-related activities of the Department of Health and Human Services, and that this board be established in the Office of the Secretary.

Notes

1. See page 137 [of the report] for a minority opinion and statement of exception from this recommendation.

2. See page 139 [of the report] for a minority opinion and statement of exception from this recommendation.

Appendix B:
The Pros and Cons of Cyclosporine

Nancy L. Ascher

I am Nancy L. Ascher, M.D., a transplant surgeon at the University of Minnesota Hospitals. I have been asked to comment on the use of cyclosporine in organ transplantation. Our transplant experience is substantial with approximately 190 kidney recipients/year, 25 pancreas recipients/year, 20 liver recipients/year and 20 heart recipients/year. We have used cyclosporine since 1980. Our group has conducted a randomized prospective trial with cyclosporine. We have documented a number of shortcomings with its use. Nonetheless, in spite of its limitations, cyclosporine has been a major advancement in the field of organ transplantation particularly in the areas of extrarenal transplantation.

Introduction

The purpose of any immunosuppressive regimen is to prevent graft rejection with a minimum of side effects. The ideal in transplantation would be to render the recipient tolerant specifically to donor tissue without altering the immune response to other foreign antigens such as viruses, bacteria or fungi which may lead to infections and to the development of tumors. Although there is substantial experimental and clinical research in this field such as Dr. Monaco's animal model of tolerance and Dr. Salvatierra's use of donor specific blood transfusions, we have not reached this goal.

Therefore, current therapy in organ transplantation is based on some type of global immunosuppression. Azathioprine and prednisone have been the mainstay of immunosuppression, but these agents diminish white blood cell count and profoundly inhibit the immune response nonspecifically. The patients become susceptible to a variety of opportunistic infections and the development of lymphoproliferative neoplasias. Because of these major drawbacks in the use of standard immunosuppressive drugs, newer agents or methods with fewer side effects have been sought. These efforts have largely failed either because of lack of efficacy or because of a new set of side effects. Our own results using conventional immunotherapy with antilymphoblast globulin in kidney transplant patients have yielded 1 year graft function of 85% in cadaveric graft recipients and even better results in recipients of living related grafts. Although these results are excellent, our patients have a substantial incidence of infectious complications and a number of patients have developed lymphomas. . . .

Reprinted from Hearings Before the Committee on Labor and Human Resources, U.S. Senate, October 20, 1983.

Summary

1. Cyclosporine is as effective in prolonging renal allograft survival as any other immunosuppressive protocol to date. The European Multicenter Trial compared cyclosporine and prednisone with conventional immunotherapy and demonstrated 73% - 1 year graft function in the cyclosporine group and 53% in the conventional group. Our own randomized study includes over 200 patients and has yielded 88% - 1 year graft function in the cyclosporine group and 80% in the conventional group. Kahan, Starzl and Stiller have all independently demonstrated its efficacy in kidney transplantation.

2. Cyclosporine with low dose prednisone has drastically reduced the incidence of infectious complications in these patients and in addition has significantly shortened the hospital stay, (close to 40%) resulting in significant reduction in hospital costs to these patients.

3. There are three major drawbacks to the use of cyclosporine. The first is its expense. Current cost estimates are that cyclosporine will cost between $4,000-6,000.00/year. It is unlikely that patients will be able to discontinue its use after time as there is no evidence that it induces a state of tolerance. The savings incurred in reduction in hospital stay, which we can attribute to cyclosporine, offset this expense.

Second, cyclosporine has a toxic effect on the kidney which is more pronounced in kidney transplant recipients than in recipients of extrarenal organs. The pathogenesis of this nephrotoxicity is not understood. As yet there is no useful animal model in which we can study it but its understanding is an important area for research.

Third, we do not know the long term side effects of its use, particularly in the area of neoplasia. Kidney transplant recipients receiving conventional immunosuppression have 20 x's the incidence of lymphoma than the central population. There have been a few cases of lymphoma reported with the use of cyclosporine but the incidence of its development is not known.

4. Cyclosporine with low dose prednisone has revolutionized the results in liver and cardiac transplantation. One year patient survival among liver transplant recipients has increased from 25% up to 50-75% and in the case of heart transplantation from 58% to 80%. Current studies are under way to determine the optimal immunosuppressive protocol for pancreas transplantation.

The effect of widespread improvements in renal as well as extrarenal transplant results means that there is potential for increased transplant activity. This means there will be an even greater demand for efficient organ procurement and fair and efficient methods of organ distribution. We strongly support the formation of a Nationalized Computerized Network to carry out these tasks.

5. I want to address a final point regarding organ preservation. We can preserve kidneys for 48 hours and even longer using a pulsatile perfusion apparatus. Livers and hearts can only be stored in the cold; liver preservation is limited to 8-10 hours and heart preservation is limited to 3-4 hours. We badly need research in the field of preservation of these organs. We need to extend the time of preservation so we can effectively distribute the needed organs.

Appendix C:
Contraindications to Heart Transplantation

Special Advisory Group,
National Heart, Lung, and Blood Institute

1. Advancing age—e.g., beyond the age (normally about 50) at which the individual begins to have diminished capacity to withstand postoperative complications;

2. Severe pulmonary hypertension as reflected, for example, by a pulmonary artery systolic pressure over 65–70mm Hg and exceeding pulmonary artery wedge pressure by about 40 or more mm Hg, or a calculated pulmonary vascular resistance above approximately 6 Wood units (applicable to orthotopic cardiac transplantation because of the limited work capacity of a normal donor right ventricle);

3. Irreversible and severe hepatic or renal dysfunction (because of the likelihood of exacerbation early postoperatively and because of interference with immunosuppressive regimens);

4. Active systemic infection (because of the likelihood of exacerbation with initiation of immunosuppression);

5. Any other systemic disease considered likely to limit or preclude survival and rehabilitation after transplantation;

6. A history of behavior pattern or psychiatric illness likely to interfere significantly with compliance with a disciplined medical regimen (because a lifelong medical regimen is necessary, requiring multiple drugs several times a day with serious consequences in the event of their interruption or excessive consumption);

7. Recent and unresolved pulmonary infarction or pulmonary roentgenographic evidence of abnormalities of unclear etiology (because of the likelihood of pulmonary infection or its exacerbation with initiation of immunosuppression under such circumstances);

8. Insulin-requiring diabetes mellitus (because of exacerbation by chronic corticosteroid therapy);

9. Symptomatic or documented severe asymptomatic peripheral or cerebrovascular disease (because of observed accelerated progression in some patients after cardiac transplantation and on chronic corticosteroid treatment);

10. Acute peptic ulcer disease (because of the likelihood of early postoperative exacerbation);

11. The absence of adequate external psychosocial supports for either short or long-term bases (because such support is generally necessary during the inevitable waxing and waning of the clinical status of the patient and for adherence to the lifelong medical regimen).

Reprinted from *Federal Register,* 46(14): 7072–7074, January 22, 1981.

Appendix D:
Public Law 98-507,
National Organ Transplant Act

Public Law 98-507, Oct. 19, 1984
98th Congress

An Act

To provide for the establishment of the Task Force on Organ Transplantation and the Organ Procurement and Transplantation Network, to authorize financial assistance for organ procurement organizations, and for other purposes.

Be it enacted by the Senate and House of Representatives of the United States of America in Congress assembled, That this Act may be cited as the "National Organ Transplant Act".

TITLE I—TASK FORCE ON ORGAN PROCUREMENT AND TRANSPLANTATION

Establishment and Duties of Task Force

SEC. 101. (a) Not later than ninety days after the date of the enactment of this Act, the Secretary of Health and Human Services (hereinafter in this title referred to as the "Secretary") shall establish a Task Force on Organ Transplantation (hereinafter in this title referred to as the "Task Force").

(b)(1) The Task Force shall—

(A) conduct comprehensive examinations of the medical, legal, ethical, economic, and social issues presented by human organ procurement and transplantation,

(B) prepare the assessment described in paragraph (2) and the report described in paragraph (3), and

(C) advise the Secretary with respect to the development of regulations for grants under section 371 of the Public Health Service Act.

(2) The Task Force shall make an assessment of immunosuppressive medications used to prevent organ rejection in transplant patients, including—

(A) an analysis of the safety, effectiveness, and costs (including cost-savings from improved success rates of transplantation) of different modalities of treatment;

(B) an analysis of the extent of insurance reimbursement for long-term immunosuppressive drug therapy for organ transplant patients by private insurers and the public sector;

(C) an identification of problems that patients encounter in obtaining immunosuppressive medications; and

(D) an analysis of the comparative advantages of grants, coverage under existing Federal programs, or other means to assure that individuals who need such medications can obtain them.

(3) The Task Force shall prepare a report which shall include—

(A) an assessment of public and private efforts to procure human organs for transplantation and an identification of factors that diminish the number of organs available for transplantation;

(B) an assessment of problems in coordinating the procurement of viable human organs including skin and bone;

(C) recommendations for the education and training of health professionals, including physicians, nurses, and hospital and emergency care personnel, with respect to organ procurement;

(D) recommendations for the education of the general public, the clergy, law enforcement officers, members of local fire departments, and other agencies and individuals that may be instrumental in effecting organ procurement;

(E) recommendations for assuring equitable access by patients to organ transplantation and for assuring the equitable allocation of donated organs among transplant centers and among patients medically qualified for an organ transplant;

(F) an identification of barriers to the donation of organs to patients (with special emphasis upon pediatric patients), including an assessment of—

(i) barriers to the improved identification of organ donors and their families and organ recipients;

(ii) the number of potential organ donors and their geographical distribution;

(iii) current health care services provided for patients who need organ transplantation and organ procurement procedures, systems, and programs which affect such patients;

(iv) cultural factors affecting the family with respect to the donation of the organs; and

(v) ethical and economic issues relating to organ transplantation needed by chronically ill patients;

(G) recommendations for the conduct and coordination of continuing research concerning all aspects of the transplantation of organs;

(H) an analysis of the factors involved in insurance reimbursement for transplant procedures by private insurers and the public sector;

(I) an analysis of the manner in which organ transplantation technology is diffused among and adopted by qualified medical centers, including a specification of the number and geographical distribution of qualified medical centers using such technology and an assessment of whether the number of centers using such technology is sufficient or excessive and of whether the public has sufficient access to medical procedures using such technology; and

(J) an assessment of the feasibility of establishing, and of the likely effectiveness of, a national registry of human organ donors.

Membership

SEC. 102. (a) The Task Force shall be composed of twenty-five members as follows:

(1) Twenty-one members shall be appointed by the Secretary of which:

(A) nine members shall be physicians or scientists who are eminent in the various medical and scientific specialties related to human organ transplantation;

(B) three members shall be individuals who are not physicians and who represent the field of human organ procurement;

(C) four members shall be individuals who are not physicians and who as a group have expertise in the fields of law, theology, ethics, health care financing, and the social and behavioral sciences;

(D) three members shall be individuals who are not physicians or scientists and who are members of the general public; and

(E) two members shall be individuals who represent private health insurers or self-insurers.

(2) The Surgeon General of the United States, the Director of the National Institutes of Health, the Commissioner of the Food and Drug Administration, and the Administrator of the Health Care Financing Administration shall be ex officio members.

(b) No individual who is a full-time officer or employee of the United States may be appointed under subsection (a)(1) to the Task Force. A vacancy in the Task Force shall be filled in the manner in which the original appointment was made. A vacancy in the Task Force shall not affect its powers.

(c) Members shall be appointed for the life of the Task Force.

(d) The Task Force shall select a Chairman from among its members who are appointed under subsection (a)(1).

(e) Thirteen members of the Task Force shall constitute a quorum, but a lesser number may hold hearings.

(f) The Task Force shall hold its first meeting on a date specified by the Secretary which is not later than thirty days after the date on which the Secretary establishes the Task Force under section 101. Thereafter, the Task Force shall meet at the call of the Chairman or a majority of its members, but shall meet at least three times during the life of the Task Force.

(g)(1) Each member of the Task Force who is not an officer or employee of the United States shall be compensated at a rate equal to the daily equivalent of the annual rate of basic pay in effect for grade GS-18 of the General Schedule under section 5332 of title 5, United States Code, for each day (including traveltime) during which such member is engaged in the actual performance of duties as a member of the Task Force. Each member of the Task Force who is an officer or employee of the United States shall receive no additional compensation.

(2) While away from their homes or regular places of business in the performance of duties for the Task Force, all members of the Task Force shall be allowed travel expenses, including per diem in lieu of subsistence, at rates authorized for employees of agencies under sections 5702 and 5703 of title 5, United States Code.

Support for the Task Force

SEC. 103. (a) Upon request of the Task Force, the head of any Federal agency is authorized to detail, on a reimbursable basis, any of the personnel of such agency to the Task Force to assist the Task Force in carrying out its duties under this Act.

(b) The Secretary shall provide the Task Force with such administrative and support services as the Task Force may require to carry out its duties.

Report

SEC. 104. (a) The Task Force may transmit to the Secretary, the Committee on Labor and Human Resources of the Senate, and the Committee on Energy and Commerce of the House of Representatives such interim reports as the Task Force considers appropriate.

(b) Not later than 7 months after the date on which the Task Force is established by the Secretary under section 101, the Task Force shall transmit a report to the Secretary, the Committee on Labor and Human Resources of the Senate, and the Committee on Energy and Commerce of the House of Representatives on its assessment under section 101(b)(2) of immunosuppressive medications used to prevent organ rejection.

(c) Not later than twelve months after the date on which the Task Force is established by the Secretary under section 101, the Task Force shall transmit a final report to the Secretary, the Committee on Labor and Human Resources of the Senate, and the Committee on Energy and Commerce of the House of Representatives. The final report of the Task Force shall include—

(1) a description of any findings and conclusions of the Task Force made pursuant to any examination conducted under section 101(b)(1)(A),

(2) the matters specified in section 101(b)(3), and

(3) such recommendations as the Task Force considers appropriate.

Termination

SEC. 105. The Task Force shall terminate three months after the date on which the Task Force transmits the report required by section 104(c).

TITLE II—ORGAN PROCUREMENT ACTIVITIES

SEC. 201. Part H of title III of the Public Health Service Act is amended to read as follows:

"Part H—Organ Transplants

"Assistance for Organ Procurement Organizations

"SEC. 371. (a)(1) The Secretary may make grants for the planning of qualified organ procurement organizations described in subsection (b).

"(2) The Secretary may make grants for the establishment, initial operation, and expansion of qualified organ procurement organizations described in subsection (b).

"(3) In making grants under paragraphs (1) and (2), the Secretary shall—

"(A) take into consideration any recommendations made by the Task Force on Organ Transplantation established under section 101 of the National Organ Transplant Act, and

"(B) give special consideration to applications which cover geographical areas which are not adequately served by organ procurement organizations.

"(b)(1) A qualified organ procurement organization for which grants may be made under subsection (a) is an organization which, as determined by the Secretary, will carry out the functions described in paragraph (2) and—

"(A) is a nonprofit entity,

"(B) has accounting and other fiscal procedures (as specified by the Secretary) necessary to assure the fiscal stability of the organization,

"(C) has an agreement with the Secretary to be reimbursed under title XVIII of the Social Security Act for the procurement of kidneys,

"(D) has procedures to obtain payment for non-renal organs provided to transplant centers,

"(E) has a defined service area which is a geographical area of sufficient size which (unless the service area comprises an entire State) will include at least fifty potential organ donors each year and which either includes an entire standard metropolitan statistical area (as specified by the Office of Management and Budget) or does not include any part of such an area,

"(F) has a director and such other staff, including the organ donation coordinators and organ procurement specialists necessary to effectively obtain organs from donors in its service area, and

"(G) has a board of directors or an advisory board which—

"(i) is composed of—

"(I) members who represent hospital administrators, intensive care or emergency room personnel, tissue banks, and voluntary health associations in its service area,

"(II) members who represent the public residing in such area,

"(III) a physician with knowledge, experience, or skill in the field of histocompatability,

"(IV) a physician with knowledge or skill in the field of neurology, and

"(V) from each transplant center in its service area which has arrangements described in paragraph (2)(G) with the organization, a member who is a surgeon who has practicing privileges in such center and who performs organ transplant surgery,

"(ii) has the authority to recommend policies for the procurement of organs and the other functions described in paragraph (2), and

"(iii) has no authority over any other activity of the organization.

"(2) An organ procurement organization shall—

"(A) have effective agreements, to identify potential organ donors, with a substantial majority of the hospitals and other health care entities in its service area which have facilities for organ donations,

"(B) conduct and participate in systematic efforts, including professional education, to acquire all useable organs from potential donors,

"(C) arrange for the acquisition and preservation of donated organs and provide quality standards for the acquisition of organs which are consistent with the standards adopted by the Organ Procurement and Transplantation Network under section 372(b)(2)(D),

"(D) arrange for the appropriate tissue typing of donated organs,

"(E) have a system to allocate donated organs among transplant centers and patients according to established medical criteria,

"(F) provide or arrange for the transportation of donated organs to transplant centers,

"(G) have arrangements to coordinate its activities with transplant centers in its service area,

"(H) participate in the Organ Procurement Transplantation Network established under section 372,

"(I) have arrangements to cooperate with tissue banks for the retrieval, processing, preservation, storage, and distribution of tissues as may be appropriate to assure that all useable tissues are obtained from potential donors, and

"(J) evaluate annually the effectiveness of the organization in acquiring potentially available organs.

"(c) For grants under subsection (a) there are authorized to be appropriated $5,000,000 for fiscal year 1985, $8,000,000 for fiscal year 1986, and $12,000,000 for fiscal year 1987.

"Organ Procurement and Transplantation Network

"SEC. 372. (a) The Secretary shall by contract provide for the establishment and operation of an Organ Procurement and Transplantation Network which meets the requirements of subsection (b). The amount provided under such contract in any fiscal year may not exceed $2,000,000. Funds for such contracts shall be made available from funds available to the Public Health Service from appropriations for fiscal years beginning after fiscal year 1984.

"(b)(1) The Organ Procurement and Transplantation Network shall carry out the functions described in paragraph (2) and shall—

"(A) be a private nonprofit entity which is not engaged in any activity unrelated to organ procurement, and

"(B) have a board of directors which includes representatives of organ procurement organizations (including organizations which have received grants under section 371), transplant centers, voluntary health associations, and the general public.

"(2) The Organ Procurement and Transplantation Network shall—

"(A) establish in one location or through regional centers—

"(i) a national list of individuals who need organs, and

"(ii) a national system, through the use of computers and in accordance with established medical criteria, to match organs and individuals included in the list, especially individuals whose immune system makes it difficult for them to receive organs,

"(B) maintain a twenty-four-hour telephone service to facilitate matching organs with individuals included in the list,

"(C) assist organ procurement organizations in the distribution of organs which cannot be placed within the service areas of the organizations,

"(D) adopt and use standards of quality for the acquisition and transportation of donated organs,

"(E) prepare and distribute, on a regionalized basis, samples of blood sera from individuals who are included on the list and whose immune system makes it difficult for them to receive organs, in order to facilitate matching the compatability of such individuals with organ donors,

"(F) coordinate, as appropriate, the transportation of organs from organ procurement organizations to transplant centers,

"(G) provide information to physicians and other health professionals regarding organ donation, and

"(H) collect, analyze, and publish data concerning organ donation and transplants.

"Scientific Registry

"SEC. 373. The Secretary shall, by grant or contract, develop and maintain a scientific registry of the recipients of organ transplants. The registry shall include such information respecting patients and transplant procedures as the Secretary deems necessary to an ongoing evaluation of the scientific and clinical status of organ transplantation. The Secretary shall prepare for inclusion in the report under section 376 an analysis of information derived from the registry.

"General Provisions Respecting Grants and Contracts

"SEC. 374. (a) No grant may be made under section 371 or 373 or contract entered into under section 372 or 373 unless an application therefor has been submitted to, and approved by, the Secretary. Such an application shall be in such form and shall be submitted in such manner as the Secretary shall by regulation prescribe.

"(b)(1) In considering applications for grants under section 371—

"(A) the Secretary shall give priority to any applicant which has a formal agreement of cooperation with all transplant centers in its proposed service area,

"(B) the Secretary shall give special consideration to organizations which met the requirements of section 371(b) before the date of the enactment of this section, and

"(C) the Secretary shall not discriminate against an applicant solely because it provides health care services other than those related to organ procurement.
The Secretary may not make a grant for more than one organ procurement organization which serve the same service area.

"(2) A grant for planning under section 371 may be made for one year with respect to any organ procurement organization and may not exceed $100,000.

"(3) Grants under section 371 for the establishment, initial operation, or expansion of organ procurement organizations may be made for two years. No such grant may exceed $500,000 for any year and no organ procurement organization may receive more than $800,000 for initial operation or expansion.

"(c)(1) The Secretary shall determine the amount of a grant made under section 371 or 373. Payments under such grants may be made in advance on the basis of estimates or by the way of reimbursement, with necessary adjustments on account of underpayments or overpayments, and in such installments and on such terms and conditions as the Secretary finds necessary to carry out the purposes of such grants.

"(2)(A) Each recipient of a grant under section 371 or 373 shall keep such records as the Secretary shall prescribe, including records which fully disclose the amount and disposition by such recipient of the proceeds of such grant, the total cost of the undertaking in connection with which such grant was made, and the amount of that portion of the cost of the undertaking supplied by other sources, and such other records as will facilitate an effective audit.

"(B) The Secretary and the Comptroller General of the United States, or any of their duly authorized representatives, shall have access for the purpose of audit and examination to any books, documents, papers, and records of the recipient of a grant under section 371 or 373 that are pertinent to such grant.

"(d) For purposes of this part:

"(1) The term 'transplant center' means a health care facility in which transplants of organs are performed.

"(2) The term 'organ' means the human kidney, liver, heart, lung, pancreas, and any other human organ (other than corneas and eyes) specified by the Secretary by regulation and for purposes of section 373, such term includes bone marrow.

"Administration

"SEC. 375. The Secretary shall, during fiscal years 1985, 1986, 1987, and 1988, designate and maintain an identifiable administrative unit in the Public Health Service to—

"(1) administer this part and coordinate with the organ procurement activities under title XVIII of the Social Security Act,

"(2) conduct a program of public information to inform the public of the need for organ donations,

"(3) provide technical assistance to organ procurement organizations receiving funds under section 371, the Organ Procurement and Transplantation Network established under section 372, and other entities in the health care system involved in organ donations, procurement, and transplants, and

"(4) one year after the date on which the Task Force on Organ Transplantation transmits its final report under section 104(c) of the National Organ Transplant Act, and annually thereafter through fiscal year 1988, submit to Congress an annual report on the status of organ donation and coordination services and include in the report an analysis of the efficiency and effectiveness of the procurement and allocation of organs and a description of problems encountered in the procurement and allocation of organs.

"Report

"SEC. 376. The Secretary shall annually publish a report on the scientific and clinical status of organ transplantation. The Secretary shall consult with the Director of the National Institutes of Health and the Commissioner of the Food and Drug Administration in the preparation of the report."

TITLE III—PROHIBITION OF ORGAN PURCHASES

SEC. 301. (a) It shall be unlawful for any person to knowingly acquire, receive, or otherwise transfer any human organ for valuable consideration for use in human transplantation if the transfer affects interstate commerce.

(b) Any person who violates subsection (a) shall be fined not more than $50,000 or imprisoned not more than five years, or both.

(c) For purposes of subsection (a):

(1) The term "human organ" means the human kidney, liver, heart, lung, pancreas, bone marrow, cornea, eye, bone, and skin, and any other human organ specified by the Secretary of Health and Human Services by regulation.

(2) The term "valuable consideration" does not include the reasonable payments associated with the removal, transportation, implantation, processing, preservation, quality control, and storage of a human organ or the expenses of travel, housing, and lost wages incurred by the donor of a human organ in connection with the donation of the organ.

(3) The term "interstate commerce" has the meaning prescribed for it by section 201(b) of the Federal Food, Drug and Cosmetic Act.

TITLE IV—MISCELLANEOUS

Bone Marrow Registry Demonstration and Study

Sec. 401. (a) Not later than nine months after the date of enactment of this Act, the Secretary of Health and Human Services shall hold a conference on the feasibility of establishing and the effectiveness of a national registry of voluntary bone marrow donors.

(b) If the conference held under subsection (a) finds that it is feasible to establish a national registry of voluntary donors of bone marrow and that such a registry is likely to be effective in matching donors with recipients, the Secretary of Health and Human Services, acting through the Assistant Secretary for Health, shall, for purposes of the study under subsection (c), establish a registry of voluntary donors of bone marrow. The Secretary shall assure that—

(1) donors of bone marrow listed in the registry have given an informed consent to the donation of the bone marrow; and

(2) the names of the donors in the registry are kept confidential and access to the names and any other information in the registry is restricted to personnel who need the information to maintain and implement the registry, except that access to such other information shall be provided for purposes of the study under subsection (c).

If the conference held under subsection (a) makes the finding described in this subsection, the Secretary shall establish the registry not later than six months after the completion of the conference.

(c) The Secretary of Health and Human Services, acting through the Assistant Secretary for Health, shall study the establishment and implementation of the registry under subsection (b) to identify the issues presented by the establishment of such a registry, to evaluate participation of bone marrow donors, to assess the implementation of the informed consent and confidentiality requirements, and to determine if the establishment of a permanent bone marrow registry is needed and appropriate. The Secretary shall report the results of the study to the Committee on Energy and Commerce of the House of Representatives and the Committee on Labor and Human Resources of the Senate not later than two years after the date the registry is established under subsection (b).

Approved October 19, 1984.

Appendix E:
Certification of Death Based on
Irreversible Cessation of All Brain Function
Including that of the Brain Stem

Presbyterian-University Hospital
Policy Manual

DATE: February, 1983

Policy

It is the policy of Presbyterian-University Hospital while assuring optimal medical care to all patients to recognize that under certain circumstances, all medical therapy and life support shall be withdrawn after certification of patient death, including those patients in whom total and irreversible cessation of brain function can be clearly demonstrated according to the criteria listed below.

Criteria

The patient must be observed for an appropriate period of time in the hospital ICU during treatment of potentially correctable abnormalities which may contribute to deteriorated brain function, e.g. hypovolemia, hypoxemia, hypotension, hypothermia and presence of CNS depressant drugs including alcohol.

The cause of coma must be established and be sufficient to explain irreversible cessation of all brain function.

A check list of criteria is attached for the diagnosis of brain death (originally approved by the Executive Committee of Presbyterian-University Hospital in April, 1969, PUH: form number 900) and must be utilized in the brain death evaluation and certification process.

In those cases where a donor is transferred to PUH following Certification of Brain Death at another hospital, the Death Certificate must accompany the body and this must be documented by a PUH staff physician.

Reprinted from Hearings Before the Subcommittee on Investigations and Oversight of the Committee on Science and Technology, U.S. House of Representatives, April 13, 14, 27, 1983.

Only when organs are donated for transplantation purposes will cardiopulmonary and other essential organ support continue after death until donated organs have been removed.

Procedure

A. When drugs may be implicated by the history of physical examination as a possible etiology of depressed brain function or in patients with coma of unknown etiology, toxicological screening and/or analysis for specific drugs are indicated. If, in addition, alcohol has been ingested, the synergistic effect between alcohol and such drugs must be considered and blood alcohol levels obtained. Recent general anesthesia, metabolic encephalopathies, encephalomeningitides, hypothermia and shock may also influence the brain injured patient's response during evaluation for potential brain death. Drugs known to be associated with an isoelectric EEG include barbiturates, methaqualone, diazepam, mecloqualone, meprobamate and trichlorethylene (JAMA 236:1123, 1976). Blood levels of all such agents must be absent or below therapeutic levels before brain death can be certified. Similarly, if neuromuscular blocking agents have been used, absence of the effects of these muscle relaxants must be secured by use of a nerve stimulator, before the examination can proceed.

Two separate clinical evaluations must be completed as prescribed in the stated criteria. The second may be conducted no sooner than two hours after the first. If any evidence of brain function is elicited during either examination, the patient does not fulfill the criteria and cannot be certified dead. Specific details relevant to the examination process include:

B. True decorticate or decerebrate posturing indicates brain stem function and excludes the diagnosis of brain death. However, complex muscle movements resembling decerebrate posturing but emanating from high spinal cord reflexes have been reported. Simple and complex spinal cord reflexes are often preserved in brain death and, being irrelevant to its diagnosis, are therefore not tested. Shivering indicates function of the temperature regulating center of the hypothalamus and also rules out the diagnosis of brain death.

C. 1. The pupils need not be equal or dilated but must be non-reactive to light stimulation. The pupillary reflex may be unreliable after the use of scopolamine, opiates, neuromuscular blocking agents, atropine, mydriatic eye drops, glutethemide and in the presence of eye trauma or disease, e.g. lens cataracts. The cilio-spinal reflex is not included in this testing.

   2. The corneal reflex may be absent due to pre-existing severe facial weakness.

   3. Painful stimuli are administered over the areas of cranial nerve distribution and not peripherally where spinal cord reflexes may be active.

   4. Function of the glossopharyngeal and vagus nerves and their brainstem nuclei is tested through insertion of a pharyngeal and endotracheal suction catheter. Any gagging or coughing indicates remaining brainstem function.

   5. The dolls eye phenomenon is tested through rapid head turning from side to side. If resulting in eye movement, this indicates remaining brainstem function.

   6. The volume of ice cold water used for caloric stimulation should be 50 ml given with the patient's head at 30 degrees elevation slowly into each external ear canal free of cerumen. This stimulus must be followed by several minutes of observation for any movement of the eyes. Pre-existing labyrinthine disease may abolish this reflex as might sedatives, anticholinergics, anticonvulsives, tricyclic antidepressants and ototoxic effect of certain antibiotics.

D. The apnea test is most important. The absence of spontaneous breathing tested during disconnection from the ventilator in the absence of muscle relaxants, necessitates documented $PaCO_2$ above 60 torr and arterial pH below 7.30. If a history suggestive of dependence on a hypoxic stimulus for ventilation (e.g. a COPD patient) is present, the PaO_2 at the end of the test must be less than 50 torr. Otherwise, an endotracheal catheter with a 3–4 1/min O2 flow may be used to avoid cardiac arrest due to hypoxemia, of particular importance in patients considered candidates for organ donation.

E. A single isoelectric electroencephalogram (EEG) is required. This EEG is usually obtained after the first complete clinical examination without identified brain activity. Technical guidelines for recording the EEG to insure maximal machine sensitivity have been established by and are the responsibility of the Department of Neurology. The interpretation of the EEG as isoelectric must be made by an attending staff neurologist or Neurology Resident who has completed the EEG Rotation and made available in writing before death certification can be completed. If the EEG is not isoelectric, the patient does not fulfill the necessary criteria and cannot be certified dead. If recorded activity is suspected to be of muscular rather than cortical origin, a muscle relaxant may be used for clarification. However, the effect of utilized muscle relaxants must be worn off or reversed prior to the second clinical evaluation of brain function.

F. Inactivity of the vagus nerve nuclei is inferred from unresponsiveness of the heart rate to an intravenous atropine bolus.

G. The abnormalities observed during the performed brain death evaluation should be noted on the check list. For instance, bizarre, complex arm movements are occasionally observed and may necessitate vertebral arteriography to rule out sustained function of the brain stem.

Certification

After the above diagnostic criteria have been completed, showing no evidence of continuing brain activity, the patient shall be certified dead. Such certification must be made by two physicians, licensed by the State of Pennsylvania. Members of the transplantation team may not be involved in death certification of a brain dead organ donor.

Brain death certification is equivalent to the pronouncement of death and the time documented for this certification is considered the time of death to be used for all legal matters including the Death Certificate issued by the hospital.

The pronouncement of death is by law a medical act. Therefore, consent is not required nor is it to be requested from the next-of-kin. However, the patient's family must have full information concerning this certification process.

In those cases wherein the Coroner has jurisdiction, his permission is not required for the death certification process or termination of medical therapy. However, the Coroner's consent must be obtained for removal of organs for transplantation.

When a brain dead donor of organs is transferred to PUH and Certification of brain death is made at the referring hospital, the referring institution will send a copy of the Death Certificate. This document will be made part of the donor record.

When organs are to be removed from a brain dead donor for the purposes of transplantations, death certification must be completed prior to removal. Removal of organs for transplantation must be preceded by consent from the next-of-kin (PUH Form No 874 or transferring hospital's equivalent form) unless the deceased has legally certified such donation. When transferred from another hospital, the donor body shall be placed in the ICU unless taken directly to the Operating Room and the Admitting Department will be notified.

A donor number will be assigned by the Admitting Department to each donor body received by this hospital. The donor acceptance process will not involve admission to the hospital. The donor number will be utilized for the coordination of medical documentation relating to the donor body and appropriate expense charges.

Those hospital policies and procedures concerning matters relevant to any deceased patient (i.e., death, autopsy and coroner cases, Policy #4001, etc.) apply equally to these patients after completion of the certification process and removal of all medical therapy or life support devices.

Members of the Critical Care Medicine Program are available at all times for the interpretation of this policy and the completion of the certification form.

Appendix F:
Minority Perspective Fact Sheet

Clive O. Callender

1. Transplants are 10–20% less successful in Blacks than Whites.
2. 10% Blacks opt for transplantation—20% Whites opt for transplantation.
3. 95% Whites are knowledgeable about organ transplantation, only 84% Blacks are knowledgeable about organ transplantation.
4. 27% Whites are willing to donate their own organs after death; 10% Blacks are willing to donate their own organs after death.
5. Kidneys from Black donors survive less well in Blacks or Whites than kidneys from White donors.
6. Transplantation histocompatibility antigens are less well known in Blacks than Whites.
7. 70% patients on dialysis in Southeastern part of the U.S. are black.
8. 20% of organs donated for transplantation after death are from Blacks.
9. Blacks have hypertension four times as frequently as Whites in the U.S.A. and end-stage renal disease four times as frequently as Whites.
10. Risk of end-stage renal disease for Blacks with hypertension is 17 times more frequent than for Whites.
11. Blacks have significantly less access to medical care than Whites.
12. Blacks live 4–5 years shorter than Whites.
13. Blacks weigh less at birth and have two times the infant mortality of White Americans.
14. Blacks have more deaths/100,000 of all causes of death except suicide and motor vehicle accidents.
15. Blacks are victims of homicide seven times more frequently than Whites.
16. 41 of 47 cadaver organs used for transplantation at Howard University were donated by non-Blacks.
17. Blacks donate less often than Whites because: a) lack of knowledge, b) religion, c) fear of complications, d) lack of communication between lay persons and health care providers.
18. 76% of the American population is aware of organ donor cards and 18% of them have signed organ donor cards, whereas only 65% of Blacks are aware of them and only 5% of Blacks have signed them.

Reprinted from Hearing Before the Committee on Labor and Human Resources, U.S. Senate, October 20, 1983.

19. The District of Columbia has the highest incidence of renal disease in the United States (299 cases per million population) and its incidence is 2–3 times that of Northern Virginia and Maryland (85–103 cases/million). Its prevalence (1,041.9) is 3–4 times the prevalence of Maryland and Northern Virginia based on 1980 census.
20. Black females are transplanted less than any other group except Orientals or Hispanics in D.C.: Black males—34%; White males—33%; White females—20%; Black females—8%.

Bibliography

Transplantation and Implantation—General

Abram, Harry S. "Psychological Dilemmas of Medical Progress." *Psychiatric Medicine* 3: 51–58, 1972.

Abram, Harry S.; Moore, Gordon L.; Westervelt, Frederic B. "Suicidal Behavior in Chronic Dialysis Patients." *American Journal of Psychiatry* 127: 1199–1204, 1971.

American Red Cross Scientific Symposium. *Advances in Immunobiology.* New York: A. R. Liss, 1984.

Austen, W. G., and Cosimi, A. B. "Heart Transplantation After Sixteen Years." *New England Journal of Medicine* 311: 1436–1438, 1984.

Blagg, Christopher R. "After Ten Years of the Medicare End-Stage Renal Disease Program." *American Journal of Kidney Disease* 3: 1–2, 1983.

———. "Treatment of End-stage Renal Disease by Dialysis." *Transplantation Proceedings* 17: 1497–1499, February 1985.

Blagg, Christopher R., and Scribner, R. H. "Long-term Dialysis: Current Problems and Future Prospects." *American Journal of Medicine* 68: 633–635, 1980.

Brahams, Diana. "End-Stage Renal Failure: The Doctor's Duty and the Patient's Right." *Lancet* 1: 386–387, 1984.

Calabresi, Guido, and Bobbitt, Philip. *Tragic Choices.* New York: Norton, 1978.

Caplan, Arthur L. "Kidneys, Ethics, and Politics: Policy Lessons of the ESRD Experience." *Journal of Health Politics, Policy and Law* 6: 488–503, Fall 1981.

———. "Organ Transplants: The Costs of Success." *Hastings Center Report* 13: 23–32, December 1983.

Casey, T. A., and Mayer, D. J. *Corneal Grafting: Principles and Practice.* Philadelphia: W. B. Saunders, 1984.

Chalmers, T. C. "Randomization and Coronary Artery Surgery." *Annals of Thoracic Surgery* 14: 323–327, 1982.

Christopherson, Lois K. "Cardiac Transplantation: Preparation for Dying or for Living." *Health and Social Work* 1: 58–72, 1976.

———. "Heart Transplants." *Hastings Center Report* 12: 18–21, February 1982.

———. "Quality of Life: Organ Transplantation and Artificial Organs." *International Journal of Technology Assessment in Health Care* 2: 553–562, 1986.

Consensus Conference. "Liver Transplantation." *Journal of the American Medical Association* 250: 2961–2964, 1983.

Cooper, Michael H., and Culyer, A. *The Price of Blood.* London: Institute of Economic Affairs, 1968.

Coster, D. J.; Alfrich, S. J.; Wedding, T. R.; Williams, K. A. "Corneal Transplantation: Collection, Assessment, Storage, and Distribution of Corneas for Grafting." *Transplantation Proceedings* 19: 2851–2854, 1987.

Douglas, James F. "Renal Failure and the Law." *Lancet* 1: 1319–1321, 1985.

Drake, Alvin W.; Finkelstein, S. N.; Sapolsky, H. M. *The American Blood Supply.* Cambridge, MA: MIT Press, 1982.

Eckman, Mark H.; Sonnenberg, Frank A.; Jacoby, Itzhak; Pauker, Stephen G. "HLA-Matched Donor Registries for Bone Marrow Transplants: A Decision Analysis." *International Journal of Technology Assessment in Health Care* 2: 507–532, 1986.

Evans, Roger W.; Manninen, D. L.; Maier, A; Garrison, L. P., Jr.; Hart, L. G. "The Quality of Life of Kidney and Heart Transplant Recipients." *Transplantation Proceedings* 17: 1579–1582, February 1985.

Evans, Roger W.; Manninen, D. L.; Overcast, T. D.; Garrison, L. P., Jr.; et al. *The National Heart Transplantation Study: Final Report.* Seattle, WA: Battelle Human Affairs Research Centers, 1984.

Flechner, S. M.; Novick, A. C.; Braun, W. E.; Popowniak, K. L.; Steinmuller, D. "Functional Capacity and Rehabilitation of Recipients with a Functioning Renal Allograft for Ten Years or More." *Transplantation* 35: 572–576, 1983.

Fox, Renee C. "A Sociological Perspective on Organ Transplantation and Hemodialysis." *Annals of the New York Academy of Science* 1969: 406–428, 1969.

Fox, Renee C., and Swazey, Judith P. *The Courage to Fail: A Social View of Organ Transplants and Dialysis,* 2d ed. Chicago: University of Chicago Press, 1978.

Gilks, W. R.; Gore, S. M.; Bradley, B. A. "Analyzing Transplant Survival Data." *Transplantation* 42: 46–49, 1986.

Gutman, R. A.; Stead, W. W.; Robinson, R. R. "Physical Activity and Employment Status of Patients on Maintenance Dialysis." *New England Journal of Medicine* 304: 309–313, 1981.

Halper, Thomas. "Life and Death in a Welfare State: End-stage Renal Disease in the United Kingdom." *Milbank Memorial Quarterly, Health and Society* 63: 52–93, Winter 1985.

Höckerstedt, Krister, and Kankaanpää, Jari, "Liver Transplantation in Europe—Present Status." *International Journal of Technology Assessment in Health Care* 2: 451–464, 1986.

Jennett, Bryan. "Implants, Transplants and Artificial Organs: Technical Feasibility versus Social Desirability." *International Journal of Technology Assessment in Health Care* 2: 365–368, 1986.

Kahan, B. D.; Flechner, S. M.; Lorber, M. I.; Golden, D.; Conley, S.; Van Buren, C. T. "Complications of Cyclosporine-Prednisone Immunosuppression in 402 Renal Allograft Recipients Exclusively Followed at a Single Center for from One to Five Years." *Transplantation* 43: 197–204, 1987.

Katz, Jay, and Capron, Alexander M. *Catastrophic Disease: Who Decides What? A Psychological and Legal Analysis of the Problems Posed by Hemodialysis and Organ Transplantation.* New York: Russell Sage Foundation, 1975.

Kolata, Gina B. "Dialysis After Nearly a Decade." *Science* 208: 473–476, 1980.

Korcok, Milan. "The Business of Hearts." *Canadian Medical Association Journal* 132: 676, 680–687, 1985.

Krakauer, H.; Grauman, J. S.; McMullan, M. R.; Creede, C. "The Recent U.S. Experience in the Treatment of End-stage Renal Disease by Dialysis and Transplantation." *New England Journal of Medicine* 308: 1558–1561, 1983.

Landgraf, R. "General Considerations in Pancreatic Transplantation." *Transplantation Proceedings* 18: Suppl 3: 50–51, 1986.

McKengney, F. Patrick, and Lange, Paul. "The Decision To No Longer Live on Hemodialysis." *American Journal of Psychiatry* 128: 264–274, 1971.

McNeil, B. J., and Cravalho, E. G., eds. *Critical Issues in Medical Technology.* Boston, MA: Auburn House Publishing, 1982.

Macoviak, J. A.; Oyer, P. E.; Stinson, E. B.; Jamieson, S. W.; Baldwin, J. C.; Shumway, N. E. "Four-year Experience with Cyclosporine for Heart and Heart-lung Transplantation." *Transplantation Proceedings* 17: Supplement 2: 97–101, 1985.

Macpherson, Stuart G. "Kidney Transplantation in the United Kingdom." *International Journal of Technology Assessment in Health Care* 2: 497–506, 1986.

McVie, J. G.; Dalesio, Otilia; Smith, I. E., eds. *Autologous Bone Marrow Transplantation and Solid Tumors.* New York: Raven Press, 1984.

Massachusetts Task Force on Organ Transplantation. *Report.* (Boston: Massachusetts Department of Public Health, October 1984).

Monaco, A. P. "Problems in Transplantation: Ethics, Education, and Expansion." *Transplantation* 43: 1–4, 1987.

Neu, S. N., and Kjellstrand, C. M. "Stopping Long Term Dialysis: An Empirical Study of Withdrawal of Life-Supporting Treatment." *New England Journal of Medicine* 314: 14–20, 1986.

O'Grady, John G., and Williams, Roger. "An Appraisal of Liver Transplantation in Great Britain." *International Journal of Technology Assessment in Health Care* 2: 465–470, 1986.

Overcast, Thomas D.; Merrikin, Karen J.; Evans, Roger W. "Malpractice Issues in Heart Transplantation." *American Journal of Law and Medicine* 10: 363–395, Winter 1985.

Penn, Israel. "Cancers Following Cyclosporine Therapy." *Transplantation* 43: 32–35, 1987.

Petty, Charles S., and Heck, Ellen. "Life From Death—The Ultimate Goal of Transplantation." *New York Law School Review* 27: 1207–1220, 1982.

"Proceedings of an International Conference on the Pharmacology of Cyclosporine." *Transplantation Proceedings* 18: Suppl 5: 1–272, 1986.

"Proceedings of the Eleventh International Congress of the Transplantation Society." *Transplantation Proceedings* 19: 1–2786, 1987.

Prottas, Jeffrey; Segal, Mark; Sapolsky, Harvey. "Cross-National Differences in Dialysis Rates." *Health Care Financing Review* 4: 91–103, 1983.

Ramsey, Paul. *The Patient as Person*. New Haven: Yale University Press, 1970.

Reiser, Stanley J.; Dyck, Arthur J.; Curran, William J., eds. *Ethics in Medicine: Historical Perspectives and Contemporary Concerns*. Cambridge, MA: MIT Press, 1977.

"Renal Failure and Transplantation in Blacks." *Transplantation Proceedings* 19: Suppl 2: 1–120, 1987.

Rettig, Richard A. "Critical Issues in the Assessment of End-Stage Renal Disease." In *Critical Issues in Medical Technology*, Barbara J. McNeil and Ernest G. Cravalho, eds. Boston: Auburn House Publishing Company, 1982, pp. 273–287.

Sale, George E., and Shulman, Howard M., eds. *The Pathology of Bone Marrow Transplantation*. New York: Masson Pub., 1984.

Sanders, David J., and Dukeminier, Jesse, Jr. "Medical Advance and Legal Lag: Hemodialysis and Kidney Transplantation." *UCLA Law Review* 15: 357–419, February 1968.

Saudek, Christopher D. "Developing and Assessing an Implantable Infusion Pump: Interactions of University, Industry, and Government." *International Journal of Technology Assessment in Health Care* 2: 471–482, 1986.

Schersten, Tore; Brynger, Hans; Karlberg, Ingvar; Jonsson, Egon. "Cost-Effectiveness Analysis of Organ Transplantation." *International Journal of Technology Assessment in Health Care* 2: 545–552, 1986.

Simmons, Robert G.; Anderson, C.; and Kamstra, L. "Comparison of Quality of Life of Patients on Continuous Ambulatory Peritoneal Dialysis, Hemodialysis, and After Transplantation." *American Journal of Kidney Diseases* 4: 253–255, 1984.

Simmons, Robert G.; Klein, S. D.; Simmons, R. L. *Gift of Life: The Social and Psychological Impact of Organ Transplantation*. New York: Wiley and Sons, 1977.

Steinbrook, Robert L. "Kidneys for Transplantation." *Journal of Health Politics, Policy and Law* 6: 504–519, Fall 1981.

Stone, William J., and Rabin, Pauline L., eds. *End-Stage Renal Disease*. New York: Academic Press, 1983.

Task Force on Organ Transplantation. *Organ Transplantation: Issues and Recommendations*. Washington, D.C.: Government Printing Office, 1986.

Task Force on Organ Transplantation. *Report to the Secretary and the Congress on Immunosuppressive Therapies*. Washington, D.C.: Government Printing Office, 1985.

Tendler, Moshe D. "Transplantation Surgery—Rabbinic Comment." *Mount Sinai Journal of Medicine* 51: 54–57, 1984.

Tyden, G., and Groth, C. G. "Pancreatic Transplantation." *International Journal of Technology Assessment in Health Care* 2: 483–496, 1986.

Veatch, Robert M. *A Theory of Medical Ethics*. New York: Basic Books, 1981.

Weiner, Roy S.; Hackel, Emanuel; Schiffer, C. A., eds. *Bone Marrow Transplantation*. Arlington, VA: American Association of Blood Banks, 1983.

Williams, G. M.; Ferree, D.; Bollinger, R. R.; LeFor, W. M. "Reasons Why Kidneys Removed for Transplantation are Not Transplanted in the United States." *Transplantation* 38: 691–694, 1985.

Organ Procurement

AMA Council on Scientific Affairs. "Xenografts: Review of the Literature and Current Status." *Journal of the American Medical Association* 254: 3353–3357, 1985.

Andrews, Lori B. "My Body, My Property." *Hastings Center Report* 16: 28–38, 1986.

Annas, George J. "Life, Liberty, and the Pursuit of Organ Sales." *Hastings Center Report* 14: 22–23, February 1984.

Arrow, Kenneth. "Gifts and Exchanges." *Philosophy and Public Affairs* 1: 343–362, 1972.

Bialasiewicz, A. A. "Screening for Potentially Pathogenic Agents in Cornea Donors." *American Journal of Ophthalmology* 103: 104–105, 1987.

Brams, Marvin. "Transplantable Human Organs: Should Their Sale Be Authorized by State Statutes?" *American Journal of Law and Medicine* 3: 183–195, Summer 1977.

Buchanan, Allen. "Our Treatment of Incompetents." In *Health Care Ethics: An Introduction.* Donald VanDeVeer and Tom Regan, eds. Philadelphia: Temple University Press, 1987, pp. 215–238.

Caplan, Arthur L. "Ethical and Policy Issues in the Procurement of Cadaver Organs for Transplantation." *New England Journal of Medicine* 311: 981–983, 1984.

————. "Requests, Gifts, and Obligations: The Ethics of Organ Procurement." *Transplantation Proceedings* 18: 49–56, 1986.

Chapman, Fern. "The Life-and-Death Question of an Organ Market." *Fortune,* 108–112, June 11, 1984.

Cook, William. "Incompetent Donors: Was the First Step or the Last Taken in Strunk v. Strunk?" *California Law Review* 58: 754–774, 1970.

Council on Scientific Affairs, American Medical Association. "Organ Donor Recruitment." *Journal of the American Medical Association* 246: 2157–2158, 1981.

DeChesser, A. P. "Organ Donation: The Supply/Demand Discrepancy." *Heart and Lung* 15: 547–551, 1986.

Deodhar, E. D. "Review of Xenografts in Organ Transplantation." *Transplantation Proceedings* 18: Suppl 2: 83–87, 1986.

Dukeminier, Jesse. "Supplying Organs for Transplantation." *Michigan Law Review* 68: 811–885, 1968.

Emery, R. W.; Cork, R. C.; Levinson, M. M.; et al. "The Cardiac Donor: A Six Year Experience." *Annals of Thoracic Surgery* 41: 356–362, 1986.

Evans, Roger W.; Manninen, D. L.; Garrison, L. P.; Maier, A. M. "Donor Availability as the Primary Determinant of the Future of Heart Transplantation." *Journal of the American Medical Association* 255: 1892–1898, 1986.

Fellner, C. H., and Schwartz, S. H. "Altruism in Disrepute: Medical vs. Public Attitudes Towards the Living Organ Donor." *New England Journal of Medicine* 284: 582–612, 1971.

Fletcher, John C.; Robertson, John A.; Harrison, Michael R. "Primates and Anencephalics as Sources for Pediatric Organ Transplants." *Fetal Therapy* 1: 150–164, 1986.

Gunby, P. "Media-abetted Liver Transplants Raise Questions of 'Equity and Decency.'" *Journal of the American Medical Association* 249: 1973–1974, 1980–1982, 1983.

Iglehart, John K., "The Politics of Transplantation." *New England Journal of Medicine* 310: 864–868, 1984.

Lenehan, G. P. "The Gift of Life: Organ Donation and the Emergency Nurse." *Journal of Emergency Nursing* 12: 189–191, 1986.

Levey, A. S.; Hou, S.; Bush, H. L. "Kidney Transplantation from Unrelated Donors: Time to Reclaim a Discarded Opportunity." *New England Journal of Medicine* 314: 914–916, 1986.

Levine, Carole. "Why Blacks Need More Kidneys but Donate Fewer." *Hastings Center Report* 15: 3, 1985.

Mahowald, Mary B.; Silver, Jerry; Ratcheson, Robert A. "The Ethical Options in Fetal Transplants." *Hastings Center Report* 17: 9–15, 1987.

Manninen, D. L., and Evans, R. W. "Public Attitudes and Behavior Regarding Organ Donation." *Journal of the American Medical Association* 253: 3111–3115, 1985.

Matas, Arthur J.; Arras, John; Muyskens, James; Tellis, Vivian; Veith, Frank. "A Proposal for Cadaver Organ Procurement: Routine Removal with Right of Informed Refusal." *Journal of Health Politics, Policy and Law* 10: 231–244, 1985.

May, William F. "Religious Justifications for Donating Body Parts." *Hastings Center Report* 15: 38–42, 1985.

Meryman, H. T. "Tissue and Organ Banking: An Inevitability." *Progress in Clinical and Biological Research* 224: 337–343, 1986.

Miller, M. "A Proposed Solution to the Present Organ Donation Crisis Based on a Hard Look at the Past." *Circulation* 75: 20–28, 1987.

Murray, Thomas. "Gifts of the Body and the Needs of Strangers." *Hastings Center Report* 17: 30–38, 1987.

Muyskens, J. "An Alternative Policy for Obtaining Cadaver Organs for Transplantation." *Philosophy and Public Affairs* 8: 88–99, 1978.

Overcast, Thomas D.; Evans, Roger W.; Bowen, L. E.; Hoe, M. M.; Livak, C. L. "Problems in the Identification of Potential Organ Donors: Misconceptions and Fallacies Associated with Donor Cards." *Journal of the American Medical Association* 251: 1559–1562, 1984.

Perry, Clifton. "Human Organs and the Open Market." *Ethics* 91: 63–71, October 1980.

Peters, David A. "Marketing Organs for Transplantation." *Dialysis and Transplantation* 13: 40, 42, 1984.

———. "Protecting Autonomy in Organ Procurement Procedures: Some Overlooked Issues." *Milbank Memorial Quarterly* 64: 241–270, 1986.

Prottas, Jeffrey M. "Encouraging Altruism: Public Attitudes and the Marketing of Organ Donation." *Milbank Memorial Fund Quarterly, Health and Society* 61: 278–306, Spring 1983.

———. "Obtaining Replacements: The Organizational Framework of Organ Procurement." *Journal of Health Politics, Policy and Law* 8: 235–250, Summer 1983.

———. "Organ Procurement in Europe and the United States." *Milbank Memorial Fund Quarterly* 63: 94–126, Winter 1985.

Robertson, John A. "Organ Donations by Incompetents and the Substituted Judgment Doctrine." *Columbia Law Review* 76: 48–78, 1976.

Ryon, B. "Voice Technology: A New Tool in Healthcare." *Hospital Topics* 64: 33–35, 1986.

Sadler, Alfred M., and Sadler, Blair L. "A Community of Givers, Not Takers." *Hastings Center Report* 14: 6–9, 1984.

Sadler, H.; Davison, L.; Carroll, C.; Kountz, S. "The Living, Genetically Unrelated, Kidney Donor." *Seminars in Psychiatry* 3: 86–101, 1971.

Schwartz, Howard S. "Bioethical and Legal Considerations in Increasing the Supply of Transplantable Organs: From UAGA to 'Baby Fae.'" *American Journal of Law and Medicine* 10: 397–437, 1985.

Schwindt, Richard, and Vinig, Aidan R. "Proposal for a Future Delivery Market for Transplant Organs." *Journal of Health Politics, Policy and Law* 11: 483–500, 1986.

Scott, Russell. *The Body as Property.* New York: Viking Press, 1981.

Sharpe, G. "Commerce in Tissue and Organs." *Transplantation Proceedings* 17: Suppl 4: 33–39, 1985.

Simmons, R. L.; Thompson, E. J.; Kyellstrand, C. M. "Parent-to-Child and Child-to-Parent Kidney Transplants: Experience with 101 Transplants at One Center." *Lancet* 1: 321–324, 1976.

Skelley, Luke. "Practical Issues in Obtaining Organs for Transplantation." *Law, Medicine and Health Care* 13: 35–37, 1985.

Starzl, Thomas E. "Will Live Organ Donations No Longer Be Justified?" *Hastings Center Report* 15: 5, April 1985.

Steinbrook, Robert L. "Unrelated Volunteers as Bone Marrow Donors: Altruism and Organ Donation." *Hastings Center Report* 10: 11–14, February 1980.

Toledo-Pereyra, Luis H., ed. *Basic Concepts of Organ Procurement, Perfusion, and Preservation for Transplantation.* New York: Academic Press, 1982.

Veatch, Robert M. "The Ethics of Xenografts." *Transplantation Proceedings* 18: Suppl 2: 93–97, 1986.

Winkel, F. W. "Public Communication on Donorcards: A Comparison of Persuasive Styles." *Social Science and Medicine* 19: 957–963, 1984.

Youngner, Stuart, et al. "Psychosocial and Ethical Implications of Organ Retrieval." *New England Journal of Medicine* 313: 321–324, August 1985.

Recipient Selection

Abram, Harry S., and Wadlington, Walter. "Selection of Patients for Artificial and Transplanted Organs." *Annals of Internal Medicine* 69: 615–620, 1968.

Alexander, Shana. "They Decide Who Lives, Who Dies." *Life* 53: 102–104, 1962.

Annas, George. "The Prostitute, the Playboy, and the Poet: Rationing Schemes for Organ Transplantation." *American Journal of Public Health* 75: 187–189, 1985.

Basson, M. D. "Choosing Among Candidates For Scarce Medical Resources." *Journal of Medicine and Philosophy* 4: 313–333, 1979.

Brodehl, J.; Offner, G.; Pichlmayr, R.; Ringe, R. "Kidney Transplantation in Infants and Young Children." *Transplantation Proceedings* 18: Suppl 3: 8–11, 1986.

Broome, John. "Selecting People Randomly." *Ethics* 95: 38–55, 1984.

Burdelski, M.; Schmidt, K.; Hoyer, P. F.; Galaske, R.; Brodehl, J.; Pichlmayr, R. "Indications for Liver Transplantation in Pediatric Patients." *Transplantation Proceedings* 18: Suppl 3: 89–91, 1986.

Calabresi, Guido, and Bobbitt, Philip. *Tragic Choices.* New York: W. W. Norton and Co., 1978.

Caplan, Arthur. "Equity in the Selection of Recipients for Cardiac Transplantation." *Circulation* 75: 10–19, 1987.

Childress, James. "Ensuring Care, Respect, and Fairness for the Elderly." *Hastings Center Report* 14: 27–31, 1984.

―――. "Rationing of Medical Treatment." *The Encyclopedia of Bioethics*, Warren T. Reich, ed. New York: The Free Press, 1978, pp. 1414–1419.

―――. "Who Shall Live When Not All Can Live?" *Soundings* 43: 339–362, 1970.

Cohen, Carl. "On the Quality of Life: Some Philosophical Reflections." *Circulation* 66:29–33, 1982.

Conrad, Constance C., and Fotion, Nicholas G. "First-Come, First-Served: Analysis of an Allocation Principle." *Pharos* 48: 15–17, 1985.

Copeland, Jack, et al. "Selection of Patients for Cardiac Transplantation." *Circulation* 75: 2–9, 1987.

Higginbotham, L. "Due Process in the Allocation of Scarce Lifesaving Medical Resources." *Yale Law Journal* 84: 1734–1739, 1975.

Kanoti, G. A. "Ethical Considerations in Solid Organ Pediatric Transplants." *Transplantation Proceedings* 18: Suppl 2: 43–46, 1986.

Katz, Al. "Process Design for Selection of Hemodialysis and Organ Transplant Recipients." *Buffalo Law Review* 22: 373–418, 1973.

Levine, Robert J. "Total Artificial Heart Implantation―Eligibility Criteria." *Journal of the American Medical Association* 252: 1458–1459, 1984.

Merrikin, Karen J., and Overcast, Thomas D. "Patient Selection for Heart Transplantation: When Is a Discriminating Choice Discriminatory?" *Journal of Health Politics, Policy and Law* 10: 7–32, 1985.

Moore, G. L. "Who Should be Dialyzed?" *American Journal of Psychiatry* 127: 1208–1209, 1971.

Moskop, John C. "Organ Transplantation in Children: Ethical Issues." *Journal of Pediatrics* 110: 175–180, 1987.

Pozza, G.; Secchi, A.; Bonisolli, L. "Prognostically Poor Signs in Type I Diabetes Mellitus, and How to Identify High-Risk Patients." *Transplantation Proceedings* 18: Suppl 3: 52–53, 1986.

Primo, G.; Wellens, F.; Leclers, J. L.; De Smet, J. M. "Current Indications and Experience with Heart-Lung Transplantation." *Transplantation Proceedings* 18: Suppl 3: 41–42, 1986.

Rescher, Nicholas. "The Allocation of Exotic Medical Lifesaving Therapy." *Ethics* 79: 173–186, 1969.

Sands, P.; Livingston, G.; Wright, R. G. "Psychological Assessment of Candidates for a Hemodialysis Program." *Annals of Internal Medicine* 64: 602–610, 1966.

Shatin, Leo. "Medical Care and the Social Worth of a Man." *American Journal of Orthopsychiatry* 36: 96–101, 1966.

Vaux, Kenneth, ed. *Who Shall Live?* Philadelphia: Fortress Press, 1970.

Wardener, H. E. de. "Some Ethical and Economic Problems Associated with Intermittent Hemodialysis." In *Ethics in Medical Progress*, G.E.W. Wolstenholme and M. O'Connor, eds. Boston: Little, Brown, 1966, pp. 104–125.

Costs, Funding, and Diffusion of Technology

Aaron, H. J., and Schwartz, W. B. *The Painful Prescription: Rationing Hospital Care.* Washington, D.C.: The Brookings Institution, 1984.

Ackerman, Bruce. *Social Justice in the Liberal State.* New Haven: Yale University Press, 1980.

Agich, George, and Begeley, Charles, eds. *What Price Health?* Dordrecht, Holland: Reidel Publishing Co., 1986.

Altman, Stuart H., and Wallack, Stanley S. *Medical Technology: The Culprit Behind Health Care Costs?* Washington, D.C.: Government Printing Office, 1979.

Angell, Marcia. "Cost Containment and the Physician." *Journal of the American Medical Association* 254: 1203–1207, 1985.

Annas, George. "Regulating the Introduction of Heart and Liver Transplantation." *American Journal of Public Health* 75: 93–95, 1985.

Aroesty, Jerome, and Rettig, Richard A. *The Cost Effects of Improved Kidney Transplantation.* Santa Monica, CA: The Rand Corporation, 1984.

Arras, John D. "Health Care Vouchers for the Poor." *Hastings Center Report* 11: 29–39, 1981.

Banta, H. D., ed. *Resources for Health: Technology Assessment for Policy Making.* New York: Praeger, 1982.

Barry, Brian M. *The Liberal Theory of Justice.* Oxford: Clarendon Press, 1973.

Blendon, R. J., and Altman, D. E. "Public Attitudes About Health-Care Costs: A Lesson in National Schizophrenia." *New England Journal of Medicine* 311: 613–616, 1984.

Blumenstein, James F. "Constitutional Perspectives on Governmental Decisions Affecting Human Life and Health." *Law and Contemporary Moral Problems* 40: 230–305, 1976.

Brook, Robert, and Lohr, Kathleen. "Will We Need to Ration Effective Health Care?" *Issues in Science and Technology* 68–77, 1986.

Buchanan, Allen E. *Ethics, Efficiency, and the Market.* Totowa, N.J.: Rowman and Allenheld, 1985.

_____ . "The Right to a Decent Minimum in Health Care." *Philosophy and Public Affairs* 13: 55–78, 1984.

Bunker, J. P.; Fowles, J.; Schaffarzick, R. "Evaluation of Medical Technology Strategies: Effects of Coverage and Reimbursement." *New England Journal of Medicine* 306: 620–624, 687–692, 1982.

Callahan, Daniel. "How Much Is Enough? A National Perspective." *Alabama Journal of Medical Sciences* 17: 76–80, 1980.

Caplan, Arthur L. "If There's a Will, Is There a Way?" *Law, Medicine and Health Care* 13: 32–34, 1985.

Casscells, Ward. "A Clinician's View of the Massachusetts Task Force on Organ Transplantation." *Law, Medicine and Health Care* 13: 27–28, 1985.

_____ . "Heart Transplantation: Recent Policy Developments." *New England Journal of Medicine* 315: 1365–1368, 1986.

Council of the Transplantation Society. "Commercialisation in Transplantation: The Problem and Some Guidelines for Practice." *Lancet* 2: 715–716, 1985.

Daniels, Norman. *Just Health Care.* New York: Cambridge University Press, 1985.

————. "Why Saying No to Patients in the United States Is So Hard." *New England Journal of Medicine* 314: 1381–1383, 1986.

Dworkin, Ronald. *Taking Rights Seriously.* Cambridge, MA: Harvard University Press, 1977.

Evans, Roger W. "Coverage and Reimbursement for Heart Transplantation." *International Journal of Technology Assessment in Health Care* 2: 425–449, 1986.

————. "Economic and Social Costs of Heart Transplantation." *Heart Transplantation* 1: 243–251, 1983.

————. "The Economics of Heart Transplantation." *Circulation* 75: 63–76, 1987.

————. "Health Care Technology and the Inevitability of Resource Allocation and Rationing Decisions," Part I and Part II. *Journal of the American Medical Association* 249: 2047–2053, 2208–2219, April 1983.

————. "Heart Transplants and Priorities." *The Lancet* 1: 852–853, 1984.

————. "The Socioeconomics of Organ Transplantation." *Transplantation Proceedings* 17: 129–136, 1985.

Farley, Pamela. "Who Are the Underinsured?" *Milbank Memorial Fund Quarterly* 63: 476–503, 1985.

Foote, Susan B. "Coexistence, Conflict, and Cooperation: Public Policies Toward Medical Devices." *Journal of Health Politics, Policy and Law* 11: 501–524, 1986.

Freishat, H. W. "Technology Versus Regulation: Which is the Lower Cost Alternative?" In *Critical Issues in Medical Technology,* B. J. McNeil and E. G. Cravalho, eds. Boston: Auburn House, 1982.

Fried, Charles. *Right and Wrong.* Cambridge, MA: Harvard University Press, 1978.

Gibbard, Allan. "The Prospective Pareto Principle and Equity of Access to Health Care." *Milbank Memorial Fund Quarterly* 60: 399–428, 1982.

Gillon, Raanan. "Justice and Allocation of Medical Resources." *British Medical Journal* 291: 266–268, 1985.

Havighurst, Clark C. "The Ethics of Cost Control in Medical Care." *Soundings* 60: 22–39, 1977.

————. "Regulation of Health Facilities and Services by 'Certificate of Need.'" *Virginia Law Review* 59: 1143–1194, 1973.

Havighurst, Clark C.; Blumstein, James F.; Bovbjerg, Randall. "Strategies in Underwriting the Costs of Catastrophic Disease." *Law and Contemporary Problems* 40: 122–195, 1976.

Hayek, Friedrich. *Legislation and Liberty: The Mirage of Social Justice.* Chicago: University of Chicago Press, 1977.

Hodgson, T. A., and Meiners, M. R. "Cost-of-illness Methodology: A Guide to Current Practices." *Milbank Memorial Fund Quarterly* 60: 429–462, 1982.

Iglehart, John K. "Another Chance for Technology Assessment." *New England Journal of Medicine* 309: 509–512, 1983.

————. "Funding the End-Stage Renal Disease Program. *New England Journal of Medicine* 306: 492–496, 1982.

————. "Transplantation: The Problem of Limited Resources." *New England Journal of Medicine* 309: 123–128, July 1983.

Jackson, D. L. "Letter to the Editor: Ohio's Plan for Organ Transplantation." *New England Journal of Medicine* 312: 995–996, 1986.

Jennett, J. *High Technology Medicine, Benefits and Burdens,* 2d ed. Oxford: Oxford University Press, 1986.

Johnson, Dana E. "Life, Death, and the Dollar Sign: Medical Ethics and Cost Containment." *Journal of the American Medical Association* 252: 223–224, 1984.

Jonsen, Albert R. "Bentham in a Box: Technology Assessment and Health Care Allocation." *Law, Medicine, and Health Care* 14: 172–174, September 1986.

————. "Organ Transplants and the Principle of Fairness." *Law, Medicine and Health Care* 13: 37–39, 44, 1985.

Kissick, William L. "Organ Transplantation and the Art of the Possible." *Law, Medicine and Health Care* 13: 34–35, 1985.

Knox, R. A. "Heart Transplants: To Pay or Not to Pay." *Science* 209: 570–581, 1980.

Korper, Samuel; Vang, Johannes; Weissman, Norman. "Status of Insurance Coverage for Organ Transplants in the United States: A Review of Recent Surveys." *International Journal of Technology Assessment in Health Care* 2: 563–570, 1986.

Lomasky, Loren E. "Medical Progress and National Health Care." *Philosophy and Public Affairs* 10: 65–88, 1981.

Lowrie, E. G., and Hampers, C. L. "The Success of Medicare's End-Stage Renal Disease Program: The Case for Profits and the Private Marketplace." *New England Journal of Medicine* 305: 434–438, 1981.

Machan, Tiber R., and Johnson, M. Bruce. *Rights and Regulation: Ethical, Political, and Economic Issues.* Cambridge, MA: Ballinger Publishing Company, 1983.

McCarthy, Charles R. "Regulating Aspects of the Distinction Between Research and Medical Practice." *IRB: A Review of Human Subjects Research* 6: 7–8, 1984.

Mechanic, David. "Cost Containment and the Quality of Medical Care: Rationing Strategies in an Era of Constrained Resources." *Milbank Memorial Quarterly, Health and Society* 63: 453–475, 1985.

Menzel, Paul T. *Medical Costs, Moral Choices: A Philosophy of Health Care Economics in America.* New Haven: Yale University Press, 1983.

Miller, F. H., and Miller, G.A.H. "The Painful Prescription: A Procrustean Prospective?" *New England Journal of Medicine* 314: 1381–1384, 1986.

Moskop, John C. "The Moral Limits to Federal Funding for Kidney Disease." *Hastings Center Report* 17: 11–15, 1987.

Nozick, Robert. *Anarchy, State and Utopia.* New York: Basic Books. 1974.

President's Commission for the Study of Ethical Problems in Medicine and Biomedical and Behavioral Research. *Securing Access to Health Care.* Washington, D.C.: Government Printing Office, 1983.

Rawls, John. *A Theory of Justice.* Cambridge, MA: Harvard University Press, 1971.

Reiss, John B.; Burckhardt, John; Hellinger, Fred. "Costs and Regulation of New Medical Technologies: Heart Transplants as a Case Study." In *Critical Issues in Medical Technology.* Barbara J. McNeil and Ernest G. Cravalho, eds. Boston: Auburn House Publishing Company, 1982, pp. 399–417.

Rettig, Richard A. "The Policy Debate on Patient Care Financing for Victims of End-Stage Renal Disease." *Law and Contemporary Problems* 40: 196–230, 1976.

_____. "The Politics of Health Cost Containment: End-Stage Renal Disease." *Bulletin of the New York Academy of Medicine* 56: 115–138, January-February 1980.

_____. *Valuing Lives: The Policy Debate on Patient Care Financing for Victims of End-stage Renal Disease.* Santa Monica, CA: The Rand Corporation, March 1976.

Rettig, Richard A., and Harman, Alvin J. *The Development of Medical Technology: A Policy Perspective.* Santa Monica, CA: The Rand Corporation, 1979.

Rettig, Richard A., and Marks, Ellen. *The Federal Government and Social Planning for End-Stage Renal Disease: Past, Present, and Future.* Santa Monica, CA: The Rand Corporation, 1983.

Roberts, S. D.; Maxwell, D. R.; Gross, T. L. "Cost-effective Care of End-stage Renal Disease: A Billion Dollar Question." *Annals of Internal Medicine* 92: 243–248, 1980.

Robertson, John. "Supply and Distribution of Hearts for Transplantation: Legal, Ethical and Policy Issues." *Circulation* 75: 77–87, 1987.

Ruby, Gloria; Banta, H. David; Burns, Anne K. "Medicare Coverage, Medicare Costs, and Medical Technology." *Journal of Health Politics, Policy and Law* 10: 141–155, 1985.

Shelp, Earl, ed. *Justice and Health Care.* Boston: D. Reidel, 1981.

Spece, Roy. "Is It Federal Policy to Force Inappropriate Treatment on Defective Neonates and to Reimburse Physicians for Unnecessary Aortocoronary Bypass Surgeries But to Refuse Needed Heart Transplantation to Disabled Patients?" *Public Law Forum* 4: 21–39, 1984.

Sterba, James. *The Demands of Justice.* South Bend, IN: Notre Dame University Press, 1980.

Thurow, Lester. "Medicine Versus Economics." *New England Journal of Medicine* 313: 611–614, 1985.

Transplantation Society. "Commercialisation in Transplantation: The Problems and Some Guidelines." *Lancet* 2: 715–716, 1985.

Veatch, Robert M., and Branson, Roy, eds. *Ethics and Health Policy*. Cambridge, MA: Ballinger Publishing Co., 1976.

Wilensky, Gail G. "Viable Strategies for Dealing With the Uninsured." *Health Affairs* 33–46, 1987.

Experimentation with Human and Animal Subjects

American Medical Association Council on Scientific Affairs. "Xenografts: Review of the Literature and Current Statutes." *Journal of the American Medical Association* 254: 3353–3357, 1985.

Annas, George J. "Baby Fae: The 'Anything Goes' School of Human Experimentation." *Hastings Center Report* 15: 15–17, February 1985.

Barber, Bernard; Lally, John; Makarushka, Julia L.; Sullivan, Daniel. *Research on Human Subjects: Problems of Control in Medical Experimentation*. New York: Russell Sage Foundation, 1973.

Barclay, W. R. "Consensus Development Conferences." *Journal of the American Medical Association* 240: 378–379.

Beardsley, Tim. "U.S. Laboratory Animals: N.I.H. Watchdog Committees." *Nature* 315: 267, 1985.

Brieger, Gert H. "Human Experimentation: History." In *Encyclopedia of Bioethics*, Warren T. Reich, ed. New York: The Free Press, 1978, pp. 684–692.

Calabresi, Guido. "Reflections on Medical Experimentation in Man." *Daedalus* 98: 387–405, 1969.

Cantrell, Crispin. "A Physician's Liability for Experimental Procedures." *Medicine and Law* 3: 339–344, 1984.

Caplan, Arthur L. "Ethical Issues Raised by Research Involving Xenografts." *Journal of the American Medical Association* 254: 3339–3343, 1985.

Capron, Alexander M. "Human Experimentation: Basic Issues." In *Encyclopedia of Bioethics*, Warren T. Reich, ed. New York: The Free Press, 1978, pp. 692–699.

———. "When Well-Meaning Science Goes Too Far." *Hastings Center Report* 15: 8–9, February 1985.

Childress, James F. *Who Should Decide? Paternalism in Health Care*. New York: Oxford University Press, 1983.

Cohen, Carl. "The Case for the Use of Animals in Biomedical Research." *New England Journal of Medicine* 315: 865–870, 1986.

Curran, William J. "Governmental Regulation of the Use of Human Subjects in Medical Research: The Approach of Two Federal Agencies." *Daedalus* 98: 542–594, 1969.

"Declaration of Helsinki: Recommendations Guiding Medical Doctors in Biomedical Research Involving Human Subjects." *New England Journal of Medicine* 271: 473, 1964.

Dodds, W. Jean, and Orlans, F. Barbara, eds. *Scientific Perspectives on Animal Welfare*. New York: Academic Press, 1982.

Eudey, Ardith A. "Ethical Concerns in Primate Use and Husbandry." *International Journal for the Study of Animal Problems* 2: 96–102, 1981.

Flannery, Ellen J. "Should It Be Easier or Harder to Use Unapproved Drugs and Devices?" *Hastings Center Report* 16: 17–23, 1986.

Fox, Michael W. *Returning to Eden: Animal Rights and Human Responsibility*. New York: Viking Press, 1980.

Frankel, Mark S. "Human Experimentation: Social and Professional Control." In *Encyclopedia of Bioethics*, Warren T. Reich, ed. New York: The Free Press, 1978, pp. 702–710.

French, Richard D. "Animal Experimentation: Historical Aspects." In *Encyclopedia of Bioethics*, Warren T. Reich, ed. New York: The Free Press, 1978, pp. 75–78.

Freund, Paul A., ed. *Experimentation with Human Subjects*. New York: George Braziller, 1970.

Fried, Charles. *Experimentation: Personal Integrity and Social Policy.* New York: American Elsevier, 1974.

_____ . "Human Experimentation: Philosophical Aspects." In *Encyclopedia of Bioethics*, Warren T. Reich, ed. New York: The Free Press, 1978, pp. 699–702.

Goldman, Jerry, and Katz, Martin. "Inconsistency and Institutional Review Boards." *Journal of the American Medical Association* 248: 197–202, 1982.

Gore, Albert, Jr. "The Need for a New Partnership." *Hastings Center Report* 25: 13, February 1985.

Gray, Bradford H. *Human Subjects in Medical Experimentation.* New York: John Wiley and Sons, 1975.

Greenwald, Robert A.; Ryan, Mary Kay; Mulvihill, James E. *Human Subjects Research: A Handbook for Institutional Review Boards.* New York: Plenum Press, 1982.

Hoff, Christina. "Immoral and Moral Uses of Animals." *New England Journal of Medicine* 302: 115–118, 1980.

Hutzler, J. C. "When Is a Research Procedure Ready for Clinical Application?" *Transplantation Proceedings* 18: Suppl 2: 78–79, 1986.

Ingelfinger, Franz J. "Ethics of Human Experimentation Defined by a National Commission." *New England Journal of Medicine* 296: 44–45, 1977.

Iglehart, John K. "The Use of Animals in Research." *New England Journal of Medicine* 313: 395–400, 1985.

Jako, G. J. "Insurance Industry and Biomedical Research." *New England Journal of Medicine* 310: 1674, 1984.

Jonas, Hans. "Philosophical Reflections on Experimenting with Human Subjects." *Daedalus* 98: 219–247, 1969.

Kahn, C. R. "A Proposed New Role for the Insurance Industry in Biomedical Research Funding." *New England Journal of Medicine* 310: 257–258, 1984.

Katz, Jay. *Experimentation With Human Beings.* New York: Russell Sage Foundation, 1972.

_____ . *The Silent World of Doctor and Patient.* New York: The Free Press, 1984.

Kurlansky, P. A.; Sadeghi, A. M.; Michler, R. E.; Smith, C. R.; Marboe, C. C.; Thomas, W. G.; Coppey, L. J.; Reemtsma, K.; Rose, E. A. "Prolonged Cardiac Exnograft Survival: A Favorable Comparison with Allografts in Primates." *Current Surgery* 45: 413–415, 1986.

Levine, Robert J. *Ethics and Regulation of Clinical Research.* Baltimore: Urban and Schwarzenberg, 1981.

Levy, Charlotte L. *The Human Body and the Law: Legal and Ethical Considerations in Human Experimentation,* 2d ed. New York: Oceana Publications, 1983.

McCormick, Richard A., "Was There Any Real Hope for Baby Fae?" *Hastings Center Report* 15: 12–13, February 1985.

McKinlay, J. B. "From 'Promising Report' to 'Standard Procedure': Seven Stages in the Career of a Medical Innovation." *Milbank Memorial Fund Quarterly* 59: 374–411, 1981.

Macklin, Ruth, and Sherwin, Susan. "Experimenting on Human Subjects: Philosophical Perspectives." *Case Western Reserve Law Review* 25: 434–471, 1975.

Mendelsohn, Everett; Swazey, Judith P.; Taviss, Irene, eds. *Human Aspects of Biomedical Innovation.* Cambridge, MA: Harvard University Press, 1971.

Miller, Harlan B., and Williams, William H., eds. *Ethics and Animals.* Clifton, N.J.: Humana Press, 1983.

Moss, Thomas H. "The Modern Politics of Laboratory Animal Use." *Science, Technology, and Human Values* 9: 51–56, 1984.

National Commission for the Protection of Human Subjects of Biomedical and Behavioral Research. *The Belmont Report: Ethical Guidelines for the Protection of Human Subjects of Research.* Washington, D.C.: Government Printing Office, 1978.

_____ . *Research Involving Children: Report and Recommendations, and Appendix.* Washington, D.C.: Government Printing Office, 1977.

National Commission for the Protection of Human Subjects of National Institutes of Health. *Issues in Research with Human Subjects.* Washington, D.C.: Government Printing Office, 1980.

Overcast, Thomas D., and Sales, Bruce D. "Regulation of Animal Experimentation." *Journal of the American Medical Association* 254: 1944–1949, 1985.

Paton, William. *Man and Mouse: Animals in Medical Research*. New York: Oxford University Press, 1984.

Perry, S., and Kalverer, J. T., Jr. "The NIH Consensus Development Program and the Assessment of Health-Care Technologies: The First Two Years." *New England Journal of Medicine* 303: 169–172, 1980.

President's Commission for the Study of Ethical Problems in Medicine and Biomedical and Behavioral Research. *Implementing Human Research Regulations: The Adequacy and Uniformity of Federal Rules and of Their Implementation*. Washington, D.C.: Government Printing Office, 1983.

———. *Protecting Human Subjects: The Adequacy and Uniformity of Federal Rules and of Their Implementation*. Washington, D.C.: Government Printing Office, 1981.

"Protection of Human Subjects." *Code of Federal Regulations*, Title 45, Part 46: 98–117, 1984.

Ramsey, Paul. "The Enforcement of Morals: Nontherapeutic Research on Children." *Hastings Center Report* 6(4): 21–30, 1976.

Reemtsma, Keith. "Clinical Urgency and Media Scrutiny." *Hastings Center Report* 15: 10–11, 1985.

Regan, Tom. *The Case for Animal Rights*. Berkeley: University of California Press, 1983.

———. "The Other Victim." *Hastings Center Report* 15: 9–10, 1985.

Regan, Tom, and Singer, Peter, eds. *Animal Rights and Human Obligations*. Englewood Cliffs, N.J.: Prentice-Hall, 1976.

Rennie, D. "Consensus Statements." *New England Journal of Medicine* 304: 665–666, 1981.

Rolllin, Bernard E. *Animal Rights and Human Morality*. Buffalo, N.Y.: Prometheus Books, 1981.

Rosner, Fred. "Is Animal Experimentation Being Threatened by Aminal Rights Groups?" *Journal of the American Medical Association* 254: 1942–1943, 1985.

Rowan, Andrew. *Of Mice, Models, and Men: A Critical Evaluation of Animal Research*. Albany, N.Y.: State University of New York Press, 1984.

Ryder, Richard. *Victims of Society*. London: National Anti-Vivisection Society, 1983.

Sechzer, Jeri A., ed. "The Role of Animals in Biomedical Research." *Annals of the New York Academy of Sciences* 406: 1–229, 1983.

Sheldon, Richard. "The IRB's Responsibility to Itself." *Hastings Center Report* 15: 11–12, February 1985.

Singer, Peter. *Animal Liberation: A New Ethics for our Treatment of Animals*. New York: Random House, 1975.

Sperlinger, David, ed. *Animals in Research: New Perspectives in Animal Experimentation*. New York: John Wiley, 1981.

Veatch, Robert M. "Protecting Human Subjects: The Federal Government Steps Back." *Hastings Center Report* 11: 9–11, 1981.

Wigodsky, Herman S. "New Regulations, New Responsibilities for Institutions." *Hastings Center Report* 11: 12–14, 1981.

The Artificial Heart

Annas, George J. "Consent to the Artificial Heart: The Lion and the Crocodiles." *Hastings Center Report* 13: 20–22, April 1983.

———. "No Cheers for Temporary Artificial Hearts." *Hastings Center Report* 15: 27–28, 1985.

———. "The Phoenix Heart: What We Have to Lose." *Hastings Center Report* 15: 15–16, 1985.

Artificial Heart Assessment Panel, National Heart and Lung Institute, "The Totally Implantable Artificial Heart: Economic, Ethical, Legal, Medical, Psychiatric and Social Implications." In *Ethics and Health Policy*, Robert M. Veatch and Roy Branson, eds. Cambridge, MA: Ballinger, 1976, 219–246.

Berenson, Claudia K., and Grosser, Bernard I. "Total Artificial Heart Implantation." *Archives of General Psychiatry* 41: 910–916, 1984.

Bernstein, Barton J. "The Misguided Quest for the Artificial Heart." *Technology Review* 87: 12–19, 1984.

———. "The Pursuit of the Artificial Heart." *Medical Heritage* 2: 80–100, 1986.

Caplan, Arthur L. "The Artificial Heart." *Hastings Center Report* 12: 22–24, 1982.

Cole, Helene. "Another Artificial Heart Receives FDA Approval for Clinical Trials." *Journal of the American Medical Association* 253: 2617–2621, 1985.

Cooley, D. A. "Clinical Trials of Two-Staged Cardiac Transplantation Using an Orthotopic Mechanical Heart." *Transplantation Proceedings* 16: 882–885, 1984.

Cooley, D. A.; Liotta, D.; Hallman, G. L.; Bloodwell, R. D.; Leachman, R. D.; Milan, J. D. "Orthotopic Cardiac Prothesis for Two-Staged Cardiac Replacement." *American Journal of Cardiology* 24: 723–730, 1969.

Cortesini, R. "Perspectives on Heart Substitution." *Transplantation Proceedings* 16: 877–879, 1984.

DeVries, W. C.; Anderson, J. L.; Joyce, L. D.; Anderson, F. L.; Hammond, E. H.; Jarvik, R. H.; Kolff, W. J. "Clinical Use of the Total Artificial Heart." *New England Journal of Medicine* 310: 273–278, 1984.

Galletti, P. M. "Replacement of the Heart with a Mechanical Device: The Case of Dr. Barney Clark." *New England Journal of Medicine* 310: 312–314, 1984.

Glaser, R. J. "The Artificial Heart—Show Business or Science?" *The Pharos* 48: 38, 1985.

Green, Harold. "An NIH Panel's Early Warnings." *Hastings Center Report* 14: 13–15, 1984.

Jacobs, G.; Harasaki, R.; Kiraly, R.; Golding, L.; Nose, Y. "Approaches to the Artificial Heart." *Transplantation Proceedings* 16: 893–897. 1984.

Jarvik, R. K. "The Total Artificial Heart." *Scientific American* 249: 74–80, 1981.

Jonsen, Albert R. "The Artificial Heart's Threat to Others." *Hastings Center Report* 16: 9–11, 1986.

Kolff, W. J. "Artificial Heart Substitution: The Total or Auxiliary Artificial Heart." *Transplantation Proceedings* 16: 898–907, 1984.

———. "Artificial Organs—Forty Years and Beyond." *Transactions of the American Society of Artificial Internal Organs* 29: 6–21, 1983.

———. "For the Clinical Application of the Artificial Heart." *Heart Transplantation* 1: 159–160, 1982.

Lubeck, Deborah P. "The Artificial Heart: Costs, Risks, and Benefits—An Update." *International Journal of Technology Assessment in Health Care* 2: 369–386, 1986.

Lubeck, Deborah P., and Bunker, J. P. *The Implications of Cost-Effective Analysis of Medical Technology. Background Paper No. 2: Case Studies of Medical Technology: Case Study 9, The Artificial Heart: Costs, Risks, and Benefits.* Washington, D.C.: Government Printing Office, 1982.

Maxwell, James H.; Blumenthal, David; Sapolsky, Harvey M. "Obstacles to Developing and Using Technology: The Case of the Artificial Heart." *International Journal of Technology Assessment in Health Care* 2: 411–424, 1986.

Murray, K. D., and Olsen, D. B. "The Utah Artificial Heart: Success in the Laboratory and Its Application to Man." *Journal of Contemporary Law* 1: 4–28, 1984.

National Heart, Lung and Blood Institute, Working Group on Mechanical Circulatory Support. *Artificial Heart and Assist Devices: Directions, Needs, Costs, Societal and Ethical Issues.* Bethesda, MD: NIH Publication No. 85-2723, 1985.

Norman, J. C. "Mechanical Ventricular Assistance: A Review." *Artificial Organs* 5: 103–117, 1981.

Pae, W. E., Jr., and Pierce, W. S. "Temporary Left Ventricular Assistance in Acute Myocardial Infarction and Cardiogenic Shock: Rationale and Criterion for Utilization." *Chest* 79: 692, 1981.

Pennock, J. L.; Pierce, W. S.; Wisman, C. B.; Bull, A. P.; Waldhausen, J. A. "Survival and Complications Following Ventricular Assist Pumping for Cardiogenic Shock." *Annals of Surgery* 198: 469–478, 1983.

Pierce, W. S. "Artificial Hearts and Blood Pumps in the Treatment of Profound Heart Failure." *Circulation* 68: 883–888, 1983.

Pierce, W. S.; Pan, G.V.S.; Myers, J. L.; Pae, W. E., Jr.; Bull, A. P.; Waldhausen, J. A. "Ventricular Assist Pumping in Patients with Cardiogenic Shock after Cardiac Operations." *New England Journal of Medicine* 305: 1606–1610, 1982.

Preston, Thomas A. "The Artificial Heart Controversy: Research, Rationing, and Regulation." *Medical World News* February 11, 1985, 37.

————. "Ethical Issues in the Implantation of the Total Artificial Heart." *New England Journal of Medicine* 311: 61–62, 1984.

————. "Who Benefits from the Artificial Heart?" *Hastings Center Report* 15: 5–7, 1985.

Rachels, James. "Barney Clark's Key." *Hastings Center Report* 13: 17–19, 1983.

Relman, Arnold. "Artificial Hearts—Permanent and Temporary." *New England Journal of Medicine* 314: 644–645, 1986.

————. "Privatizing Artificial Heart Research." *Connecticut Medicine* 49: 135, 1985.

Rosenzweig, D. Y. "Insurance Industry and Biomedical Research." *New England Journal of Medicine* 310: 1674–1675, 1984.

Sammons, J. H. "AMA's Technology Assessment." *Science* 219: 1375–1377, 1983.

Shaw, Margery W., ed. *After Barney Clark: Reflections on the Utah Artificial Heart Program.* Austin: University of Texas Press, 1983.

Strauss, Michael J. "The Political History of the Artificial Heart." *New England Journal of Medicine* 310: 332–336, 1984.

Swazey, Judith P.; Watkins, Judith C.; Fox, Renee C. "Assessing the Artificial Heart: The Clinical Moratorium Revisited." *International Journal of Technology Assessment in Health Care* 2: 387–410, 1986.

Watson, J. T. "The Present and Future of Cardiac Assist Devices." *Artificial Organs* 9: 138–143, 1985.

Wheelright, Jeff, and Haupt, Donna E. "Bill's Heart: The Troubling Story Behind a Historic Experiment." *Life* 8: 33–42, 1985.

Woolley, F. R. "Ethical Issues in the Implantation of the Total Artificial Heart." *New England Journal of Medicine* 310: 292–296, 1984.

Yared, S. F.; Johnson, G. S.; DeVries, W. C. "Results of Artificial Heart Implantation in Man." *Transplantation Proceedings* 18: 69–74, June 1986.

Informed Consent

Alfidi, Ralph J. "Informed Consent: A Study of Patient Reaction." *Journal of the American Medical Association* 216: 1325–1329, 1971.

Annas, George J. "Radical Faith: The Right Stuff?" *Nursing Law and Ethics* 1: 3, 7, 1980.

Annas, George J.; Glantz, Leonard H.; Katz, Barbara F., eds. *Informed Consent to Human Experimentation.* Cambridge, MA: Ballinger Publishing Co., 1977.

Battin, Margaret P. "Non-Patient Decision-making in Medicine: The Eclipse of Altruism." *Journal of Medicine and Philosophy* 10: 19–44, 1985.

Capron, Alexander M. "Informed Consent in Catastrophic Disease Research and Treatment." *University of Pennsylvania Law Review* 123: 340–438, 1974.

Cassell, Eric J. "Informed Consent in the Therapeutic Relationship: Clinical Aspects." In *Encyclopedia of Bioethics*, Warren T. Reich, ed. New York: The Free Press, 1978, pp. 767–770.

Curran, William J. "Governmental Regulation of the Use of Human Subjects in Medical Research: The Approach of Two Federal Agencies." *Daedalus* 98: 402–405, 1969.

————. "A Problem of Consent: Kidney Transplants in Minors." *New York University Law Review* 34: 891–922, 1959.

Demy, N. J. "Informed Opinion on Informed Consent." *Journal of the American Medical Association* 217: 696–697, 1971.

Diamond, G. A.; Campion, M.; Mussoline, J. F.; D'Amico, R. A. "Obtaining Consent for Eye Donation." *American Journal of Ophthamology* 103: 198–203, 1987.

Drane, James. "The Many Faces of Competency." *Hastings Center Report* 15: 17–21, 1985.

Dunstan, G. R., and Seller, Mary J., eds. *Consent in Medicine: Convergence and Divergence in Tradition.* London: King Edward's Hospital Fund, 1983.

Epstein, L. C., and Lasagna, L. "Obtaining Informed Consent: Form and Substance." *Archives of Internal Medicine* 123: 682–688, 1969.

Faden, Ruth R., and Beauchamp, Tom L. *A History and Theory of Informed Consent.* New York: Oxford University Press, 1986.

Fellner, C. H. "Selection of Living Kidney Donors and the Problem of Informed Consent." *Seminars in Psychiatry* 3: 79–85, 1971.

Fellner, C. H., and Marshall, J. R. "Kidney Donors—The Myth of Informed Consent." *American Journal of Psychiatry* 126: 1245–1251, 1970.

Fisher, Sue, and Todd, Alexandra D., eds. *The Social Organization of Doctor-Patient Communication.* Washington, D.C.: Center for Applied Linguistics, 1983.

Fletcher, John C. "The Evolution of the Ethics of Informed Consent." In *Research Ethics*, Kare Berg and K. E. Teanoy, eds. New York: Alan R. Liss, 1983.

_____ . "The Realities of Patient Consent to Medical Research." *Hastings Center Studies* 1: 39–49, 1973.

Fletcher, John C.; Dommel, F. William; Cowell, Daniel D. "Consent to Research with Impaired Human Subjects." *IRB* 7: 1–6, 1985.

Fost, Norman. "Consent as a Barrier to Research." *New England Journal of Medicine* 300: 1272–1273, 1979.

Freedman, Benjamin. "A Moral Theory of Informed Consent." *Hastings Center Report* 5: 32–39, 1975.

Gaylin, Willard, and Macklin, Ruth, eds. *Who Speaks for the Child? The Problem of Proxy Consent.* New York: Plenum Press, 1982.

Gray, Bradford H. "Informed Consent in Human Research: Social Aspects." In *Encyclopedia of Bioethics*, Warren T. Reich, ed. New York: The Free Press, 1978, pp. 751–754.

Hagman, D. G. "The Medical Patient's Right to Know: Report on a Medical-Legal-Ethical, Empirical Study." *U.C.L.A. Law Review* 17: 758–816, 1970.

Holder, Angela R. "Informed Consent: Its Evolution." *Journal of the American Medical Association* 214: 1181–1182, 1970.

_____ . "Informed Consent—Limitations." *Journal of the American Medical Association* 214: 1611–1612, 1970.

_____ . "Informed Consent—The Obligation." *Journal of the American Medical Association* 214: 1383–1384, 1970.

Ingelfinger, F. J. "Informed (But Uneducated) Consent." *New England Journal of Medicine* 287: 465–466, 1972.

Katz, Jay. "Informed Consent: A Fairy Tale?" *University of Pittsburgh Law Review* 39: 137–174, 1977.

_____ . "Informed Consent in the Therapeutic Relationship: Legal and Ethical Aspects." In *Encyclopedia of Bioethics*, Warren T. Reich, ed. New York: The Free Press, 1978, pp. 770–778.

Knoll, Elizabeth, and Lundberg, George D. "Informed Consent in Baby Fae." *Journal of the American Medical Association* 254: 3358–3360, 1985.

Lebacqz, Karen, and Levine, Robert J. "Informed Consent in Human Research: Ethical and Legal Aspects." In *Encyclopedia of Bioethics*, Warren T. Reich, ed. New York: The Free Press, 1978, pp. 754–761.

Ludlam, James E. *Informed Consent.* Chicago: American Hospital Association, 1978.

McCormick, Richard A. "Proxy Consent in the Experimental Situation." *Perspectives in Biology and Medicine* 18: 2–20, 1974.

Macklin, Ruth. "Dilemmas of Informed Consent for Surgery." *Bulletin of the American College of Surgeons* 67: 6–9, 1982.

Makarushka, Julia L. "The Requirement for Informed Consent in Research on Human Subjects: The Problem of the Uncontrolled Consequences of Health-related Research." *Clinical Research* 24: 64–67, 1976.

Meisel, Alan. "The 'Exceptions' to the Informed Consent Doctrine: Striking a Balance Between Competing Values in Medical Decisionmaking." *Wisconsin Law Review* 1979: 413–488, 1979.

Meisel, Alan, and Roth, L. H. "What We Do and Do Not Know About Informed Consent." *Journal of the American Medical Association* 246: 2473–2478, 1981.

Meisel, Alan; Roth, Loren; Lidz, Charles. "Toward an Informed Discussion of Informed Consent: A Review of the Empirical Studies." *American Journal of Psychiatry* 134: 285–289, 1977.

Melton, Gary B.; Koocher, Gerald P.; Saks, Michael J., eds. *Children's Competence to Consent.* New York: Plenum Press, 1983.

Miller, Leslie J. "Informed Consent: I, II, III, IV." *Journal of the American Medical Association* 244: 2100–2103, 2347–2350, 2556–2558, 2661–2662, 1980.

Mills, Don H. "Whither Informed Consent?" *Journal of the American Medical Association* 229: 305–310, 1974.

President's Commission for the Study of Ethical Problems in Medicine and Biomedical and Behavioral Research. *Making Health Care Decisions: The Ethical and Legal Implications of Informed Consent in the Patient-Practitioner Relationship.* Washington, D.C.: Government Printing Office, 1982.

Schultz, Marjorie M. "From Informed Consent to Patient Choice: A New Protected Interest." *Yale Law Journal* 95: 219–299, 1985.

Simonaitis, Joseph E. "More About Informed Consent." *Journal of the American Medical Association* 225: 95–96, 1973.

––––––. "Recent Decisions on Informed Consent." *Journal of the American Medical Association* 221: 441–442, 1970.

Taub, Harvey A. "Comprehension of Informed Consent for Research: Issues and Directions for Future Study." *IRB: A Review of Human Subjects Research* 6: 7–10, 1986.

Waitzkin, H., and Soeckle, J. D. "The Communication of Information About Illness: Clinical, Sociological, and Methodological Considerations." *Advances in Psychosomatic Medicine* 8: 180–215, 1972.

Death

Abram, Morris B. "The Need for Uniform Law on the Determination of Death." *New York Law School Review* 27: 1187–1205, 1982.

Ad Hoc Committee of the Harvard Medical School to Examine the Definition of Brain Death. "A Definition of Irreversible Coma." *Journal of the American Medical Association* 205: 337–340, 1968.

Agich, George J., and Jones, Royce P. "The Logical Status of Brain Death Criteria." *Journal of Medicine and Philosphy* 10: 387–395, 1985.

Annas, George J. "Defining Death: There Ought to Be a Law." *Hastings Center Report* 13: 20–21, 1983.

Beauchamp, Tom L., and Perlin, Seymour, eds. *Ethical Issues in Death and Dying.* Englewood Cliffs, N.J.: Prentice–Hall, 1978.

Bellioti, R. "Do Dead Human Beings Have Rights?" *Personalist* 60: 201–210, 1979.

Bernat, James L. "The Definition, Criterion, and Statute of Death." *Seminars in Neurology* 4: 45–51, 1984.

Bernat, James L.; Culver, Charles M.; Gert, Bernard. "Defining Death in Theory and Practice." *Hastings Center Report* 12: 5–9, February 1982.

––––––. "On the Definition and Criterion of Death." *Annals of Internal Medicine* 94: 389–394, 1981.

Capron, Alexander M. "Anencephalic Donors: Separate the Dead From the Dying." *Hastings Center Report* 17: 5–9, February 1987.

––––––. "Legal and Ethical Problems in Decisions for Death." *Law, Medicine, and Health Care* 14: 141–144, 1986.

––––––. "Legal Aspects of Pronouncing Death." In *Encyclopedia of Bioethics,* Warren T. Reich, ed. New York: The Free Press, 1978, pp. 296–301.

Capron, Alexander M., and Kass, Leon. "A Statutory Definition of the Standards for Determining Human Death: An Appraisal and a Proposal." *University of Pennsylvania Law Review* 121: 87–118, 1972.

Christopherson, Lois K., and Gonda, T. A. "Patterns of Grief: End Stage Renal Failure and Kidney Transplantation." *Journal of Thanatology* 3: 49–57, 1975.

Feinberg, Joel. "The Mistreatment of Dead Bodies." *Hastings Center Report* 15: 31–37, 1985.

Gatch, Milton McC. "Death: Post-Biblical Christian Thought." In *Encyclopedia of Bioethics*, Warren T. Reich, ed. New York: The Free Press, 1978, pp. 249–253.

Green, Michael B., and Wikler, Daniel. "Brain Death and Personal Identity." *Philosophy and Public Affairs* 9: 389–394, 1980.

Gutmann, James. "Death: Western Philosophical Thought." In *Encyclopedia of Bioethics*, Warren T. Reich, ed. New York: The Free Press, 1978, pp. 235–243.

High, Dallas M. "Death: Philosophical and Theological Foundations." In *Encyclopedia of Bioethics*, Warren T. Reich, ed. New York: The Free Press, 1978, pp. 301–307.

Hovde, Christian A. "Cadavers: General Ethical Concerns." In *Encyclopedia of Bioethics*, Warren T. Reich, ed. New York: The Free Press, 1978, pp. 139–143.

Kabakow, Bernard. "Definition of Death and Dying." *Mount Sinai Journal of Medicine* 51: 69–72, 1984.

Kalish, Richard A. "Death: Attitudes Toward." In *Encyclopedia of Bioethics*, Warren T. Reich, ed. New York: The Free Press, 1978, pp. 286–291.

Kass, Leon R. "Thinking About the Body." *Hastings Center Report* 15: 20–30, 1985.

Korein, Julius. "The Diagnosis of Brain Death." *Seminars in Neurology* 4: 52–72, 1984.

Institute of Society, Ethics and the Life Sciences, Task Force on Death and Dying. "Refinements in Criteria for the Determination of Death." *Journal of the American Medical Association* 221: 48–53, 1972.

Landy, David. "Death: Anthropological Perspective." In *Encyclopedia of Bioethics*, Warren T. Reich, ed. New York: The Free Press, 1978, pp. 221–229.

Maguire, Daniel. *Death by Choice.* Garden City, N.Y.: Doubleday, 1973.

May, William F. "Attitudes Toward the Newly Dead." *Hastings Center Studies* 1: 3–13, 1973.

Molinari, Gaetano F. "Criteria for Death." In *Encyclopedia of Bioethics*, Warren T. Reich, ed. New York: The Free Press, 1978, pp. 292–296.

Morison, Robert S. "Death: Process or Event?" *Science* 173: 694–698, 1971.

Parsons, Talcott. "Death in the Western World." In *Encyclopedia of Bioethics*, Warren T. Reich, ed. New York: The Free Press, 1978, pp. 255–260.

President's Commission for the Study of Ethical Problems in Medicine and Biomedical and Behavioral Research. *Defining Death: Medical, Legal and Ethical Issues in the Determination of Death.* Washington, D.C.: Government Printing Office, July 1981.

Reynolds, Frank E. "Death: Eastern Thought." In *Encyclopedia of Bioethics*, Warren T. Reich, ed. New York: The Free Press, 1978, pp. 229–235.

Rosenberg, Jay F. *Thinking Clearly About Death.* Englewood Cliffs, N.J.: Prentice-Hall, 1983.

Schiffer, R. B. "The Concept of Death: Tradition and Alternative." *Journal of Medicine and Philosophy* 3: 24–37, 1978.

Siegel, Seymour. "Death: Post-Biblical Jewish Tradition." In *Encyclopedia of Bioethics*, Warren T. Reich, ed. New York: The Free Press, 1978, pp. 246–249.

Stuart, F.; Zeith, F.; Crangord, R. "Brain Death Laws and Patterns of Consent to Remove Organs for Transplantation From Cadavers in the United States and Twenty-Eight Other Countries." *Transplantation* 31: 238–244, 1981.

Suckiel, Ellen K. "Death and Benefit in the Permanently Unconscious Patient: A Justification of Euthanasia." *Journal of Medicine and Philosphy* 3: 38–52, 1978.

VanTill, H.A.H. "Diagnosis of Death in Comatose Patients Under Resuscitation Treatment: A Critical Review of the Harvard Report." *American Journal of Law and Medicine* 2: 1–40, 1976.

Veatch, Robert M. *Death, Dying, and the Biological Revolution.* New Haven: Yale University Press, 1976.

—————. "The Whole-Brain Oriented Concept of Death: An Out-moded Philosophical Formulation." *Journal of Thanatology* 3: 13–30, 1975.

Wurzburger, Walter S. "Cadavers: Jewish Perspectives." In *Encyclopedia of Bioethics*, Warren T. Reich, ed. New York: The Free Press, 1978, pp. 144–150.

Youngner, S. J.; Allen, Martha; Bartlett, E. T.; Cascorbi, H. F.; Hau, Toni; Jackson, D. L.; Mahowald, M. B.; Martin, B. J. "Psychosocial and Ethical Implications of Organ Retrieval." *New England Journal of Medicine* 313: 321–323, 1986.